D1879832

EMERGING PATTERN OF RURAL WOMEN LEADERSHIP IN INDIA

EMERGING PATTERN OF RURAL WOMEN LEADERSHIP IN INDIA

A. Celine Rani

PUBLICATIONS

KALPAZ PUBLICATIONS
DELHI - 110052

EMERGING PATTERN OF RURAL WOMEN LEADERSHIP IN INDIA
[*Women Studies*]

Rs. 675

ISBN: 81-7835-036-X

©A. Celine Rani

All rights reserved. No part of this book may be reproduced in any manner without written permission.

Published in 2002 in India by
Kalpaz Publications
C-30, Satyawati Nagar
Delhi-110052
e-mail: kalpaz@hotmail.com

Laser Typeset at: Alphabet, Delhi
Printed at: Mehra Offset Press, New Delhi

Dedicated to the memory of

L. Amaladass, A. Alice Mary

and

S.S. Savarimuthu, S. Yagammal

Contents

Preface 9

Acknowledgements 11

Abbreviations 13

List of Tables 15

List of Figures 19

1. **Introduction** 21
Statement of the Problem •Review of Literature •A Framework for Analysis •Approaches to Identify the Patterns of Rural Leadership •Positional Approach •Reputational Approach •Decisional Approach •Integrated Approach •Methodology

2. **The Setting** 61
Section 1: Process of Emergence of Women in World and Indian Politics •Section II: Historical Background of PRIs •Post-Independence Development •Constitutional Status •Panchayat Raj Institutions in Tamil Nadu •Section III

3. **Socio-Economic Status of Women Leaders** 85
Testing of Hypothesis •Summary

4. **Political Background of Women Leaders** 113
Testing of Hypothesis •Summary

5. Identification of Power Bases and Categorisation of Women Leaders 131

6. Findings, Conclusions and Suggestions 179
Major Findings •Identification of Power Bases and Categorisation of Women Leaders •Conclusion •Suggestions for Further Research •Recommendations

Glossary 193

Interview Schedule 195
PART - I : Personal Profile 195
PART - II : Positional Profile 200
Part - III : Reputational Profile 201
Part - IV : Decision-Making Profile 202

Appendices 203

Appendix - I 203

Appendix - II 207

Bibliography 213

Index 227

Preface

Sociological history of almost every nation unfailingly and uniformly disseminates a disheartening fact that inhumane and unjust treatment had been meted out to the womenfolk, besides deliberate infringement of their very basic rights. This gender inequality that has been in vogue since the inception of humanity itself is found to have transcended territorial boundaries cutting across caste and creed. This sad state of affairs continues unperturbed inspite of the upsurge of occasional social reformers who strained their nerve to eliminate the lop-sided status of women and to liberate them from the social bondage and in spite of the efforts of the rulers of the nations to obliterate the social stigma of women slavery.

It is the concept of democracy and socialism that has been finally the inspiring force and effective tool in brining out the egalitarian society wherein sex-based imbalances are curbed and empowerment of women is made possible in legal terms. India, the largest democratic state in the world, finds itself in tact and in the fore-front, in battling the combat to liberate women socially and politically as well, The 73rd Constitutional Amendment Act which is a mile-stone in the history of Indian Parliament, is, no doubt, a panacea for the empowerment of rural women in respect of the governance of rural local bodies. As India lives in villages, statutory political empowerment of rural women is certain to enhance the status of womenfolks as a whole.

The crucial stipulation of the 73rd Constitutional Amendment Act has compelled each of the State Governments in India to conduct elections for Panchayati Raj Institutions by providing one-third reservations of seats for women at all levels and in all positions. In Tamil Nadu, the local body elections were held promptly on 9th & 12th of October 1996. This raised the eyebrows of many together with some suspicious and pertinent questions. Did the rural women come forward to contest the elections of their own accord? Did the social customs and religious tenets not impede their participation in the election? Who stood behind their political entry? How did the rural electorate relish the women aspiring for the mantle of the rural governance? Did the prevalent illiteracy and political ignorance of rural women subside the tempo and spirit of the elections? What were the factors that influenced the emergence of rural women leadership? What are the factors responsible for the emergence of the rustic women folk to the power centre at the grassroots and what is the pattern of their emergence are the major areas analysed in this study.

GANDHIGRAM, **A. CELINE RANI**
August, 2002

Acknowledgements

I am profoundly indebted to Dr. G. Palanithurai, my Research Supervisor, for his valuable guidance and inspiring encouragement for the completion of this thesis.

I am whole-heartedly grateful to Dr. S. Baskaran, Professor and Head, Department of Political Science, Annamalai University, Annamalai Nagar, for his constant motivation, critical comments and useful suggestions on my thesis at various stages.

I am also deeply grateful to Dr. B.S. Bhargava, Senior Fellow, Institute of Social Sciences, Bangalore, for providing me with his valuable suggestions and unending support to the research work.

I express my sense of gratitude to Dr. B.S. Nagarajan, former Director, Department of Adult and Continuing Education and Extension, Gandhigram Rural Institute Gandhigram, for his encouragement right from the stage when the idea of this thesis was conceived.

My gratitude is due to Dr. C. Ramanujam, Assistant Chief, Population Research Centre, Institute of Rural Health and Family Welfare Trust, Gandhigram and Mr. J. Joseph Durai Selvam , for their help in the statistical analysis of the study.

My sincere thanks are due to the concerned authorities in the Dindigul Collectorate and in the Panchayat Union offices of Dindigul District for providing me with necessary secondary data related to the thesis.

I acknowledge my deep sense of gratitude to the respondents of the study and the local informants for their spontaneous and uninhibited co-operation in providing the primary data which form the core of the research work.

I express my gratitude to Dr. M.A. Jeyaraju, Dr. K. Somasundaram and the staff of the Computer Centre and other administrative authorities of Gandhigram Rural Institute, for their co-operation.

Finally, I wish to convey my thanks to the staff of the Department of Political Science and Development Administration, Gandhigram Rural Institute and to Mr. P. Maruthai Pandian, for their co-operation.

I take this opportunity to thank my family members who have always been beacon light for me since the dawn of my higher academic pursuits. I am particularly thankful to M/s Kalpaz Publications for readily accepting to publish this book and for the quick processing of its publication.

Gandhigram **A. CELINE RANI**
August, 2002

Abbreviations

AIADMK	All-India Anna Dravida Munnetra Kazhagam
BJP	Bharatiya Janata Party
BC	Backward Community
Congress (I)	Congress (Indira)
CPI	Communist Party of India
CPI (M)	Communist Party of India (Marxist)
DK	Dravidar Kazhagam
DMK	Dravida Munnetra Kazhagam
FC	Forward Community
GO	Government Order
IRDP	Integrated Rural Development Programme
ITI	Industrial Training Institute
MBC	Most Backward Community
MDMK	Marumalarchi Dravida Munnetra Kazhagam
MGR	M.G. Ramachandran
MLA	Member of Legislative Assembly
MP	Member of Parliament
PMK	Pattali Makkal Katchi
PRI	Panchayati Raj Institution
SC/ST	Scheduled Caste/Scheduled Tribe
TLC	Total Literacy Campaign
TMC	Tamil Manila Congress
UC	Union Chairman
VAO	Village Administrative Officer
VPP	Village Panchayat President

List of Tables

2.1	Right to Franchise Given to Women	62
2.2	Representation of Women in Lok Sabha, India	65
2.3	Details of Reservation of Seats and Offices of Panchayati Raj Institutions in Tamil Nadu	77
2.4	Administrative Set-up of Dindigul District	80
2.5	Population of Dindigul District (Census 1991)	81
2.6	Area, Sex Ratio and Density of Population in Dindigul District-1991	81
2.7	Educational Institutions in Dindigul District	81
2.8	Literacy Profile	82
3.1	Distribution of Respondents by Age	86
3.2	Distribution of Respondents by Caste	88
3.3	Distribution of Respondents by Religion	90
3.4	Distribution of Respondents by Education	91
3.5	Distribution of Family Heads Respondents by Education	92
3.6	Distribution of Respondents by Occupation	94
3.7	Distribution of Respondents by Occupation of Family Heads	95
3.8	Annual Income of Respondents' Families	97
3.9	Land Holdings of Respondents	98
3.10	Total Asset Value of Respondents	100
3.11	Marital Status of Respondents	101
3.12	Distribution of Respondents by Family Size	102
3.13	Distribution of Respondents by Type of Family	103
3.14	Distribution of Respondents byPlace of Residence	104
3.15	Distribution of Respondents by Type of House	105
3.16	Distribution of Respondents by Possession of Modern Facilities	106

3.17 Leadership vis-a-vis Socio-Economic Status 107
4.1 Age of Attaining Political Awareness by Respondents 114
4.2 Age of Entering Politics by the Respondents 115
4.3 Sources of Inspiration for Political Interest of Respondents 116
4.4 Party Affiliation of Family Heads of Respondents 118
4.5 Positions Held by Respondents in Political Parties 118
4.6 Positions in Political Parties Held by Family Heads of Respondents 119
4.7 Nature of Participation in Political Activities of Family Heads of Respondents 121
4.8 Stimulants For Political Participation of the Respondents 123
4.9 Political Ambitions of Respondents 124
4.10 Leadership vis-a-vis Political Background 135
5.1 Positions Held by Respondents 135
5.2 Positions Held by Family Heads of Respondents 140
5.3 Votes Polled vis-a-vis Positional Scores 141
5.4 Social Correlates of Reputation of Respondents' Families 145
5.5 Economic Correlates of Reputation of Respondents' Families 146
5.6 Political Correlates of Reputation of Respondents' Families 147
5.7 Community Service Correlates of Reputation of Respondents' Families 148
5.8 Votes Polled vis-a-vis Reputational Scores 151
5.9 Decision on Candidature of Respondents 153
5.10 Prior Participation in Socio-Political Activities by Respondents 154
5.11 Prior Participation in Socio-Political Activities by Family Heads of Respondents 155
5.12 Number of Socio-Political Activities Family Heads of Respondents Participated in 156
5.13 Modes of Settling Socio-Political Issues by Respondents 157
5.14 Modes of Settling Issues by Family Heads of Respondents 157

5.15 Election Promises of Respondents 158
5.16 Strategies Adopted by Respondents during Electioneering 159
5.17 Votes Polled visa-vis Decisional Scores 160
5.18 Votes Polled vis-a-vis Combined Scores on Position and Reputation 162
5.19 Votes Polled vis-a-vis Combined Scores on Reputation and Decision-Making 163
5.20 Votes Polled vis-a-vis Combined Scores on Decision-Making and Position 164
5.21 Votes Polled vis-a-vis Combined Scores on Position, Reputation and Decision-Making 165
5.22 Leadership vis-a-vis Position and Integration of Position with other Bases of Power 167
5.23 Leadership vis-a-vis Reputation and Integration of Reputation with other Bases of Power 167
5.24 Leadership vis-a-vis Decision-Making and Integration of Decision-Making with other Bases of Power 168
5.25 Distribution of Respondents by their Power Bases 169
5.26 Leadership Pattern of Respondents 170
5.27 Distribution of Respondents with Single Base of Power 173

List of Figures

1.1	Nature of Panchayats Based on Reservation	46
1.2	Communities of Respondents	47
1.3	Percentage of Votes Polled by the Respondents	47
2.1	Women's Representation in Parliament of Different Countries	63
2.2	Map of Dindigul District	79
3.1	Age of Respondents: A Comparative Analysis	87
3.2	Communities of Respondents: A Comparative Analysis	89
3.3	Religion of Respondents: A Comparative Analysis	90
3.4	Educational Level of Respondents: A Comparative Analysis	91
3.5	Education of Family Heads of Respondents: A Comparative Analysis	93
3.6	Occupation of Respondents: A Comparative Analysis	95
3.7	Occupation of Family Heads of Respondents: A Comparative Analysis	96
3.8	Annual Income of Respondents: A Comparative Analysis	97
3.9	Land Holdings of Respondents: A Comparative Analysis	99
3.10	Asset Value of Respondents: A Comparative Analysis	100
3.11	Socio-Economic Status Scores of Respondents	107
4.1	Nature of Political Participation of Family Heads: A Comparative Analysis	122
4.2	Political Ambitions of Respondents: A Comparative Analysis	125
4.3	Political Background Scores of Respondents: A Comparative Analysis	127
5.1	Positional Scores of Respondents : A Comparative Analysis	142

5.2 Correlates of Ascribed Reputation of Respondents: A Comparative Analysis 149
5.3 Reputational Scores of Respondents: A Comparative Analysis 151
5.4 Decisional Scores of Respondents: A Comparative Analysis 160
5.5 Combined Scores on Position and Reputation of Respondents 162
5.6 Combined Scores on Reputation and Decision-Making of Respondents 163
5.7 Combined Scores on Decision-Making and Position of Respondents 165
5.8 Combined Scores on Position, Reputation and Decision-Making of Respondents 166
5.9 Venn Diagramatic Representation of Pattern of Rural Women Leadership 171
5.10 A Simple Framework of the Analysis of Leadership Pattern 172

One

Introduction

Statement of the Problem

The present study makes an attempt to investigate the emerging pattern of rural women leadership in Panchayati Raj Institutions in Tamil Nadu.

Leadership plays an important role in shaping the socio-economic and political structure of any society.[1] Emergence and development of leadership is the result of social interaction among the members of the community. Establishment of leadership pattern is fully determined by the individual's power and influence over the society.[2] In any developing society, where the process of modernisation of political structure is going on at a rapid pace, the study of the emerging pattern of leadership is of crucial importance. The leadership pattern appears to be changing from the traditional-oriented system to the modern institutional system.[3]

In rural India, traditionally, leadership positions were secured by persons belonging to higher castes with better economic conditions.[4] The Zamindars, village headmen and the village priests acquired their leadership as hereditary right. All the community issues pertaining to social action, resolution of all types of issues and rural development activities were under the control of the traditional institutions.

The tradition of the Indian rural society is that man is superior to woman. Keeping in line with this tradition, the leadership in villages seemed to be male dominated.[5] After the dawn of Independence, with the introduction of Village Panchayats, Land Reforms, the Co-operative Movement and the Community Development Programme, a new type of leadership has emerged gradually in rural India, replacing the traditional leadership. Replacement of the tradition-oriented power group by a progress-oriented power group may indicate a process of far-reaching changes in the community. The establishment of the Indian Republic in 1950 brought to women the promise of adult franchise, equality of opportunity and equal rights on par with men in all spheres of life.

As women represent an important sector of human resource affecting national development and also form half of the population,[6] women's participation in grassroots democracy has widely been recognised. To provide enhanced representation to rural women in Panchayati Raj Institutions (PRIs), specific provisions have been incorporated in the Constitution of India through the Seventy-third Constitution (Amendment) Act 1992. The significant provision of the new Panchayati Raj Act is the reservation of one-third of the seats for women in all positions in local bodies.

Against this backdrop, the present study aims at examining the emerging pattern of rural women leadership in PRIs with reference to the Village Panchayats in Dindigul District in the State of Tamil Nadu. The main questions addressed in this study are: (1) has the socio-economic status of rural women helped in the process of their emergence as leaders?; (2) has the political background of rural women leaders and their families enabled them to so emerge?; (3) can the positions held by the rural women and their family heads in various socio-political organisations influence their emergence?; (4) can the reputation of rural women and their families promote the process of achieving leadership?; (5) can the participation of rural women and their family heads in the decision-making process on the local community issues enable rural women to secure leadership?; and, (6) will the syntheses of different bases of power facilitate the emergence of rural women leadership?

To find answers to the questions posited above, the present study makes an in-depth analysis of the emerging pattern of rural women leadership in the Village Panchayats of Dindigul District in the State of Tamil Nadu in India.

Review of Literature

More than four decades have gone by since the inception of PRIs in India and their significance has been felt in all aspects of rural governance. It has been observed that three electoral phases of PRIs have passed since Independence.[7] The first phase was "traditional" in nature, and was infected by the caste factor. The second phase, known as "transitional", lasted from 1965 to the late 1970s and was marked by the entrance of youth into elections. The third phase was known as "democratic" and political parties directly entered the scene therein.

In the next phase, the "constitutionalisation" of PRIs has opened new avenues for rural women to empower themselves through the provision of reservation of seats in authoritative bodies. The resultant political empowerment of rural women in the PRIs could enable numerous rural women to improve their socio-economic conditions, participatory capacities and leadership potentialities. Therefore the study focuses on the emerging pattern of women leadership in rural areas.

A number of field studies of leadership have been undertaken by several scholars through different perspectives. Among the pioneering studies of village leadership, those by Oscar Lewis[8] and H.S.Dhillon are valuable and noteworthy.[9] These studies have dealt with the varied roles of caste and kinship factions in the decision-making process in rural India. But these two studies do not adequately cover the dynamism and mobility pattern of the leaders. Yogendra Singh provides useful insights in this regard: while examining the nature of the power structure in six villages of Uttar Pradesh, he has discussed the patterns of traditional and emerging leadership.[10] R.L. Park and A.I.Tinker have extensively analysed the changes brought about in the leadership positions in the rural areas by the community development programme through the PRIs.[11] B.N. Singh, in his study of Etawah District (U.P.), identified the emerging pattern of youth leadership positions. To him, the transformation was the result of land reforms, education and democratization. This new leadership, he found, was adequately interested in community development projects and was keen to ensure that these be developed as people's programmes with government participation. The sources of recruitment of the new leadership were also wider, not confined to traditionally - entrenched landlords, village chiefs and a few caste Hindu families.[12] E. Wood is of the opinion that aristocratic leadership was supplied by the upper echelon of the caste structure, namely Brahmins and Rajputs. However, he has conceded that paternalistic and lineage-based leadership has been vanishing.[13] J.T. Hitchcock,[14] H.Orenstein,[15] and Alan Beals[16] point out that the traditional institutions such as kinship, caste, wealth and the like continue to be influential, though the degree of their influence varies from area to area.

The sociologists M.N. Srinivas[17] and S.C. Dube[18] have made specific contributions to the study of leadership both in terms of concepts and methods. Srinivas regards the concept of dominant caste as crucial for the study of leadership. He observes that the dominant caste is functional for the maintenance of village community and also works as a referral point for the lower castes to improve their position, both social and economic. On the other hand, Dube feels that the concept of dominant caste is not of much help, since only a handful of individuals or families in a caste hold the prestige of status symbols, financial resources and position of influence within and outside the caste group which gets further weakened in the wake of village factionalism.

There are studies on leadership pattern following the personal and social background characteristics of the emerging leaders. The studies[19] of Baijnath Singh, Briraj Chauhan, Indira Singh, Ranganath, Pradipto Ray, Lalit Sen and P. Roy and Harijindar Singh are significant in this direction. The main findings of these studies conclude that ascriptive factors play a prominent role in the process of emergence of leadership though some leaders are found to emerge from the weaker sections and lower castes.

Some of the studies by scholars [20] like Iqbal Narayan, V.M. Sirsikar, L.P. Vidyarthi, F.M. Abraham, D.C. Miglani and G. Narayana Reddy relate to the politics of the elite in Indian villages. The conclusions drawn from these studies explain the modalities of the political role played by the rural elite in Indian polity, economy and society. The significant common finding of these studies refers to the fact that the rural elite and leaders are a group of persons within the social framework, but with a qualitative difference between them and the rest of the society.

There are studies in the same category which portray the characteristics of leadership with reference to rural groups and factions. More specifically the works [21] of A.P. Barnabas, Oscar Lewis, Beals, Orenstein, Kamal Krishan and L.K. Sen, K. Chakrabarathi and S.K. Bhattacharya, M.L. Sharma, A.R. Desai, N.K. Sukla, K.L. Sharma, D.P. Miller, S.K. Chauhan and Sushila Mehta reveal that the base of Indian rural power structure is caste and that rural factions are determined by variables like land, family, kinship and personal feuds. These studies also conclude that the rural leaders mostly emerge from high castes, upper classes and rich families.

The studies on emerging leadership in rural India resulted from a seminar held at Ranchi University in 1962.[22] All the papers of the seminar dealt with the leadership pattern in U.P., Bihar, Rajasthan and Punjab and they are important in this regard. The studies by scholars [23] like Awtar Singh, S.N. Mishra, S.R. Mehta, K.D. Gangrade, D.S. Chawdry, Harginder Sigh and Paramatma Saran on emerging leadership pattern in rural India reflect that the traditional leadership has been gradually replaced by the institutional one with the change in the socio-political and economic conditions of the villages. The authors of these studies have employed different approaches for identification of leadership. It is now appropriate to review some important studies closely relevant to the present study in order to identify the gap.

Floyd Hunter[24] (1953), in his study of **"Community Power Structure - A Study of Decision Makers"**, attempts to locate leadership through reputational approach with the application of a two-step procedure in Atlanta city. Hunter concluded that a high proportion of "top leaders" identified by him inherited ascribed bases of power. These top leaders were "men of independent decisions". The top leaders had an "under structure" of powerful leaders with considerable social stature and influence, who implemented the decisions and policies of the top leaders. Hunter was the pioneer to use the reputational approach in identifying the community power structure.

C. Wright Mills [25]**(1956),** in his work entitled **"The Power Elite"**, endeavours to classify the elite in New York through the positional approach. In his study, those who occupied the greatest number of the most important offices in manufacturing firms, banks, the military, political organisations, voluntary agencies and religious groups were considered to be the key decision-makers in the community. Each potential leader was assigned a total score representing the sum of the scores for all the offices he held. Based on the total scores the elite were classified as "top leaders", "middle level leaders" and the "mass". The author also found that the "top elites" were bound by internal discipline and community of interests. The "middle level leaders" took active part in group pressures, bureaucratic lobbying and congressional manoeuvring. The "mass" were active in various political activities. This research work is helpful to identify the power holders and to classify leaders on the basis of the positions held by them.

Robert A. Dahl [26] **(1961)** has attempted to answer the question "Who governs?" through his work **"Who Governs? Democracy and Power in American City"**. He used the decision-making approach in the above work. Dahl categorised the leaders of New Haven into three categories as social, economic and political notables and further compared the influence of these notables among themselves in decision-making in New Haven. This study, furnishes guidelines for undertaking similar studies in India.

In his work **"Men at the Top", Robert Presthus**[27] **(1964)** has employed both the decisional and the reputational approaches to identify: (1) the nature of leadership in two cities of New York as to whether it is monolithic or pluralistic, and (2) to compare the validity of the two approaches. The author concluded that the monolithic and pluralistic elite were found to exist in the two cities of New York. The reputational method tended to identify the men with command of resources who had potential power, but did not openly exercise it in specific decisions. The decisional method focused on behaviour and identified persons who played an active role even though they did not occupy a position which could get them a place on the reputational list. The author found that the reputational and decisional methods were complementary to each other in identifying the leaders.

L.C. Freeman et al.[28] **(1970)** studied power structure in Syracuse by utilising all the three approaches through their work entitled **"Locating Leaders in Local Communities: A Comparison of Some Alternative Approaches"**. The findings of the study reveal that the three approaches and their syntheses did not agree fully in determining the leaders. The reputational and the positional methods seemed to be in substantial agreement in locating leaders. Most of the reputed leaders were also the heads of the largest organisations, but, they were not always active participants in decision-making. The study also concluded that there were probably three types of community leaders: institutional leaders, effectors and the activists. This study can be used as a model in comparative studies of community power structure.

Floyd Hunter[29](1980) attempts to reexamine the community power structure in Atlanta City through his work entitled **"Community Power Succession: Atlanta's Policy Makers Revisited"**, using the reputational approach. The major findings of this study can be summed up as follows: (1) a high proportion of the very top leaders had ascriptive and achieved status in the same ratio as bases of power; and, (2) role changes had occurred in black power structure, but such changes had not perceptibly shifted the industrial and technological hold on power by the larger Atlanta power structure.

The above - mentioned and reviewed studies are essential and imperative for this study as they provide theoretical and methodological guidance. In the Indian context, a variety of studies have been conducted on leadership, which examine mere substantial aspects of the subject.

K. Ranga Rao[30] (1968), in his study **"Rural Leadership and Conflict: Study of Andhra Village"**, investigates the rural leadership in terms of formal (positional) and informal (hereditary or reputational) or traditional (reputational) and modern (positional) institutions. The study concludes that the traditional leadership is losing its hold gradually though it has some control over sources of power in Andhra Pradesh in the context of the changing composition of leadership.

T.K. Oomen[31](1969) deals with identification of leadership in terms of formal, informal and modern leadership traits in his work **"Myth and Reality in India's Communitarian Villages"**. Though the author has not specifically used the positional approach, he has utilised it in combination with other methods of identification of leaders in villages. The author concludes that the real leadership operating in the organisations is traditional in nature while the ideal leader in the village is conceived in terms of ethical qualities.

T.K. Oomen[32]**(1970)**, in his another study entitled **"Rural Community Power Structure in India"**, has initially made attempts at adopting the positional, the reputational and the decisional approaches at the village level. He has actually used the institutional approach comprising both the positional and the reputational approaches and studied community power structure in three Rajasthan villages. His study shows that neither the village Patels (titles given to important and influential men in prestigious positions) nor the leading descendants of Jagirdars (landlords) or lineage heads of various castes - all of whom lead the power groups in villages - are on the executive committee of the Village Panchayats. It does not mean that they are not important in the power context of the village. Actually, they constitute an important "power reservoir" running the whole show from behind the scene.

S.R. Mehta[33]**(1972)**, in his work **"Emerging Pattern of Rural Leadership"**, attempts to identify the leadership pattern in the changed social structure of three villages of Ropar District of Punjab. He has used the positional and the reputational approaches supplemented by socio-metric technique with participant observation to study the pattern of interaction between leaders and also their outlook, which forms the central part of the study. He concludes that the leadership pattern is diffused rather than specific and it will depend on the nature of the social structure of the community. The author has taken the concepts as well as the methodological tools from similar studies.

Avatar Singh[34]**(1973), in his study "Leadership Patterns and Village Structure"**, attempts to delineate leadership patterns related to six Indian villages based on two operational measures, namely position and action participation and on four theoretical dimensions of leadership, which are degree of organisation, scope and extent of action participation, recognition, and, cohesiveness. The author says that the leaders are not determined by their own pronouncements but by what they do and that the leadership behaviour is confirmed by the extent of recognition by community members. In this work, the author has adopted only the position and the action participation (decision-making) approaches, but not the reputational approach to study the leadership pattern.

K.D. Gangrade[35] **(1974)** attempts to identify the major sources of power for rural leaders in his study **"Emerging Patterns of Leadership"**. This study focuses its attention on the analysis of the leadership in the context of the interaction between the traditional institutions and modern structures of power. The author has used decision-making process in self-help projects and in panchayat elections to locate leadership. The study has concluded that there are mainly two sources of power for leadership in the rural society: (1) traditional sources by virtue of case and kinship; and, (2) positional sources through positions held in various organisations of rural developmental activities. In exceptional cases, personal qualities constitute the sources of power.

P.C. Deb and B.K. Agarwal[36] **(1974),** in their work **"Rural Leadership in Green Revolution",** attempt to locate the leadership pattern in two villages of Ludhiyana District. With different levels of agricultural development and in the context of socio-economic characteristics, participatory role in developmental activities has been found to influence the leadership in this study. The reputational approach has been used to identify the leadership in the villages. In this study, leaders have been identified as community leaders, traditional leaders, non-traditional leaders and specialised leaders. The level of the leaders' influence over community affairs has also been analysed.

S.K. Lall [37] **(1974),** in his study **"Urban Elite",** simultaneously employs all the three approaches of position, reputation and issue participation to identify the urban elite. He also attempts to examine the efficacy of the three approaches when they are used individually and when they are used in combination. He concludes that the three approaches have helped in bringing out subtleties of the power structure which could have remained concealed if only one of the approaches had been used. Each approach has proved a check on the other.

Iqbal Narain, K.C. Pande and Mohan Lal Sharma[38]**(1976),** in their work **" The Rural Elite in an Indian State: A Case Study of Rajasthan",** have made an attempt to identify the rural elite in the context of rural power structure and the linkages of these rural elite with the higher political leadership. The reputational and the positional approaches have been used in their study. The main findings of the study reveal that the rural elite, predominantly socio-economic elite, have affiliation with different political parties. Unlike Dahl's, this study presents a situation wherein a good deal of socio-economic inequality exists between the rural elite and the common masses.

Harzinder Singh[39] **(1976)** adopts the decision-making approach in his study entitled **"Authority and Influence in Two Sikh Villages",** to identify the nature of the rural leadership. He has found that there were three kinds of influentials in each community: top polymorphic influentials, who were active in all issues; other polymorphic influentials, who were active in more than one issue, but not in all issues; and, monomorphic influentials, who were active only in one issue.

S.N. Mishra[40]**(1977)** has dealt with the community leadership pattern in the village of Darauli of District Siwan (Bihar) in his study **"Patterns of Emerging Leadership in Rural India".** He has adopted the positional and the decisional methods. He has found that associational leadership has been gradually emerging sidelining kinship-based leadership and ascriptive leadership is giving way to the young and action - oriented leadership with diffused structure.

Paramatma Saran[41] **(1978)** has undertaken a study of **"Rural Leadership in the Context of India's Modernization",** with reference to sixteen villages of Bihar. The author has employed a combination of the positional, the reputational and the decisional approaches to identify the leadership patterns in terms of conflict between tradition and modernity in rural India. He has found the positional and the reputational methods to be more meaningful and reliable. The basic determinants of leadership are, according to his findings, caste, wealth, education, joint family and religion. He concludes that the attitudes and values of leaders are influenced by the economic, social and political conditions of the society. He has also concluded that there was a continuity between tradition and modernity.

Desingu Setty[42] **(1982)** attempts to classify the leaders of two Valaya Communities of Tamil Nadu in his study entitled **"A Study of Leadership in Two Valaya Communities of Tamil Nadu".** The author has utilised a combination of the positional, the reputational and the decisional approaches for the purpose of studying the leadership position in a tribal community. Adopting the combined approach, the author has classified the leaders into primary, secondary and tertiary leaders, based on the functional position, the expertise enjoyed by the leaders and the importance accorded to them by the people in diverse activities.

M.M. Sinha[43]**(1983)** has undertaken a study of **"Modernization and Community Power: A Comparative Study of Two Indian Villages"(Kanti and Rajanganj).** This study sets out to answer the following questions: (1) what kinds of individuals and collectivities have access to power and through what sources?; (2) to what degree leadership is concentrated?; and, (3) what means or instruments are used to exert pressure on power relationships?. The analysis of the study was carried out using the reputational and the decisional methods. These methods were adopted for not only identifying different types of leaders but also for comparison. The author concludes that the economic leaders tend to dominate both the political and the social aspects of village life in Kanti, whereas, in Rajanganj, a distinction between economic and political leaders is discernible. Community leadership in Rajanganj is more dispersed than in Kanti. Unlike in Kanti, the mode of governance in Rajanganj is competitive, fragmenting the traditional power structure. This study is significant in the sense that the reputational and the decisional approaches are employed in the study for comparison of leadership in the villages.

V.R. Dutta[44] **(1986),** in his work on **"Decision-Making in Urban Governments and Politics",** endeavours to identify the key decision - makers in the Varanasi Municipal Corporation. The investigation has been done based on the corporators' socio-economic status, political background, political ambition, sources of induction into politics, participation in civic problems and contact with the citizens of the city.

All the three approaches have been simultaneously used to identify the different types of leaders. Municipal councillors identified simultaneously on the basis of the three approaches may be termed as key leaders. The author concludes that a little more than half of the key actors came from high socio-economic groups and the other half belonged to middle and low socio-economic brackets. This trend shows that the civic community of Varanasi appears to have a pluralist model of power structure. This study may be taken as a model for similar research studies in rural areas.

G. Narayana Reddy[45] **(1986),** in his work "**Rural Elite and Community Work",** attempts to examine the power structure, the relationship between community characteristics and the nature of power distribution and the consequences of variations in the power structure on management of community issues in two villages of Karnataka. The leaders of the two villages have been identified through a combined approach comprising of the positional, the reputational and the decisional methods. The findings of the study regarding the nature of leadership indicate that the majority of the leaders in both the villages were polymorphic, who were influentials in more than one issue or all the issues, while a very small number of leaders were found to be monomorphic, who were influentials only in one issue. The author has also identified the leaders as primary, secondary and tertiary, based on their attributes of position, reputation and decision - making. This study is a valuable addition to the existing literature on categorisation of leaders based on their attributes of position, reputation and issue participation.

A.T. Kitur[46]**(1992),** in his work **"Emerging Pattern of Leadership: A Study of PRIs in Dharwad District"**, attempts to analyse the emergence of rural leadership on the basis of their socio-economic background. This study concludes that the panchayat leadership was younger in age, involved itself in the process of rural development and modernisation and hailed from the locally dominant caste. The weaker sections of the society were not able to penetrate into the panchayat power structure except in the case of their reserved seats. The panchayat leadership was composed of literate groups even with graduates in some Mandal Panchayats and Zilla Parishads. Landlords and moneyed people only were able to contest the election and they monopolised the panchayat powers.

D.C. Miglani[47] **(1993)** deals with the emerging trends of leadership in his research work **"Politics and Rural Power Structure"**. The substantial part of the study relates to the identification of individuals and collectivities controlling the rural power structure in Hariyana and how and why they happen to control the rural power structure in Hariyana. The author has made use of the positional and the reputational approaches to identify the elite of the village of Amupur. The findings reveal that the power structure was heavily in favour of the locally "dominant social group", taking ritual status, control of land and numerical strength as the three attributes of dominance. The study has concluded that three groups with a reasonably high social status had established their dominance in the Village Panchayat. Though the conclusions cannot be generalised, they could be valid to a considerable extent for similar villages.

K. Subha[48]**(1994),** in her study of **"Women in Local Governance",** has made an attempt to explore the working of the Bangalore Municipal Corporation since its inception in 1949 and to evaluate the role of women councillors in policy - making and administration, and, the extent to which it has met the requirements of women. This study has also attempted to highlight the potentialities and the attributes of women who were at the helm of affairs in this urban body. She has also made some practical suggestions for the development of women at the grassroots and their effective participation in political mobilisation.

George Mathew[49]**(1995),** in his article **"Will Reservation Ensure Participation?",** has highlighted the experience of women in Karnataka, as revealed in the study **"The Women Representatives of Karnataka Panchayati Raj Institutions between 1987-1990",** conducted by Institute of Social Sciences, Bangalore. The study revealed that the majority of the elected women members of Zilla Parishad in Karnataka had no experience of active politics; usually a male member of the family had been instrumental in persuading the women to contest; in many cases, the women continued to devote all their time for household chores as usual, while the men in their families were involved in discharging their political responsibilities on their behalf; and, the elected women were very often the relatives of political leaders, young in age, low in educational status with their occupation being agriculture, household work and social work. He has also pointed out the fact that the total number of elected women was about 43 percent, 10 per cent more than the mandatory one third reservation for women.

Subash C. Arora and R.K. Prabhakar[50]**(1996)**, in their microscopic study **"A Profile of Women Contestants - A Study of Rohtak Municipal Council Elections"**, analyses the socio - economic background of the women contestants to the Municipal Council of Rohtak. The major findings of the study are: (1) a large number of women came forward to contest for the seats reserved for them; (2) the SC contestants by and large had a poor economic background and low educational standards compared to the other contestants; (3) a vast majority of the contestants, both from the general and the SC categories were married and had three or more children; (4) young and middle aged contestants dominated the election scene; and, (5) the majority of the contestants were housewives belonging to middle class families, engaged in either business or government service or both. The conclusions of the study point out the quality and the nature of women leadership emerging in urban local bodies.

Snehalata Panda[51] **(1996)** attempts to explore the emerging pattern of women's leadership profile in Chatrapur Block of Ganjam District of Orissa, in her study **"Emerging Pattern of Leadership Among Rural Women in Orissa".** She undertook the study following the amendment to Orissa Gram Panchayat Act 1991, in tune with the Constitutional Amendment providing reservation for women in PRIs. The study has reached the following conclusions: (1) traditional social structure and cultural milieu had little influence on the perception of the rural people in choosing women as panchayat representatives;(2) personal merit contributed significantly to the choice of women representatives; (3) age, relative freedom from family responsibilities and communication skills were major determinants of their selection; (4) they had traits of leadership and the capability to arrive at a decision, choosing from among several alternatives; (5) guidance from their male colleagues, family members and the villagers helped them in developing their participatory skills; and, (6) Their non-party background, responsibilities which they shared as change-agents and, above all, the class from which they came, indicated positive directions of change in rural leadership.

Dilip K. Ghosh[52]**(1997),** in his study of **"Grassroot Women Leaders: Who are They? A Study in West Bengal District",** tries to identify the class of rural women who were able to emerge as rural leaders by virtue of the Seventy-third Constitution Amendment and their own characteristics. The author chose Birbhum District as his study area and the women members of all Gram Panchayats were selected for the study. The study concludes that rural women participated in grassroots politics in large numbers irrespective of caste, creed and religion; mostly women of younger age group, with lower status of education compared to their male counterparts, came to the forum of PRIs; a large number of women leaders came from agricultural families, while the majority of them were housewives.

K. Jeyalakshmi [53]**(1997),** in her case study entitled **"Empowerment of Women in Panchayats - Experiences of Andhra Pradesh",** sets out to analyse the role of women as decision-makers in the local institutions and to identify their priorities in bringing about development in Jamasthan Palli - an all - women panchayat. The study concludes that reservation ensured opportunities for all social groups to participate in the governance of panchayats, thereby promoting grassroots level leadership.

Snehalata Panda[54]**(1997),** in her study **"Political Empowerment of Women: A Case Study of Orissa",** attempts to explore the rural socio-political situation and the performance of women representatives in PRIs in Orissa with the mandatory one-third reservation for women provided by the New Panchayati Raj Act 1994. The author concludes that women entered politics due to the mandatory provision of one-third reservation; most of the women were non - political and entered politics due to persuasion by their family members or pressure from the village community or pressure from a political party; and, some entered politics due to personal interest. The study indicates that there is a positive change in the socio-political dynamics of the rural society.

Manu Basker[55] **(1997),** in his work **"Women Panchayat Members in Kerala — A Profile",** attempts to sketch a picture of the socio- economic background and political motivation of women who became panchayat members in the Village Panchayats of Thiruvananthapuram District.

The study has observed that the political leadership of women in grassroots democracy in Kerala has been influenced by caste and community representation in tune with the body politic of the State. The study has also found that variables like age, occupation and income determine entry into politics and that the influence of political parties is strong during elections, while it plays an insignificant role in motivating women into politics.

P. Jeyabal and K. Dravidamani[56] **(1997),** in their study entitled **"Women Panchayat Presidents",** attempt to analyse the socio-economic conditions of the women Village Panchayat presidents in Lalgudi Panchyat Union, to find out their level of awareness of the New Panchayati Raj system and to assess their planning and execution of their panchayat activities. The study concludes that the majority of the women panchayat presidents were from a young age group (21-35), backward communities, and Hindu religion. All the respondents were married, had limited experience in political and social service activities, and, were educated up to Higher Secondary level. The study also reveal that the majority of the women presidents were persuaded and guided by their husbands and their relatives to contest their election and that they had low awareness of the Panchayati Raj system.

V.B. Athreya and K.S. Rajeswari[57] **(1998),** in their study **"Women Participation in Panchayati Raj: A Case Study from Tamil Nadu",** attempt to explore the socio-economic and political background of women panchayat leaders, their problems and perspectives and the support they receive from various quarters in the process of contesting for and functioning in panchayats at different levels. The study has found that political background and family support were important factors for women to enter the political arena and socio-economanic characteristics like age, education and income influenced the leadership of women.

The above empirical studies present different perspectives on the pattern of emerging rural leadership in different regions of independent India. Though all the inferences are not uniform, they all have a leaning towards a pattern of changing trend from traditional leadership to modern leadership.

There are numerous[58] research studies, books, articles and monographs on women and politics, women and reservation, political empowerment of women, women's leadership in PRIs, women and rural development, the role of women in PRIs, women's participation in the Panchayati Raj system, and, women in local governance. In the case of literature on the emerging pattern of rural women leadership in Tamil Nadu, there are only few research studies. These studies too have been conducted from the perspective of socio-economic and political status of women and their family members. But no study of the emerging pattern of rural women leadership has so far been made from the perspective of the power bases of position, reputation and decision-making besides the socio-economic and political background of rural women. Thus there is a gap in the existing literature on the emerging pattern of rural women leadership in PRIs. The present study, "Emerging Pattern of Rural Women Leadership in Tamil Nadu with Special Reference to Dindigul District," is a modest attempt to fill the gap.

A Framework for Analysis

There has been so much empirical research in the field of leadership and group dynamics in the past five or six decades. The leadership of the Village Panchayats has been researched more extensively than that of the two higher tiers, namely Panchayat Samiti (middle tier) and Zilla Parishad (top tier), which have come into being since the late fifties.[59] Leadership is the outcome of the complex integration of individuals and social functions closely related to formal and informal group life[60]. To have a clear understanding of this research problem, it will be helpful to investigate the problem against the backdrop of a theory.

M.G. Ross and C.E. Henry[61] have presented three theories of leadership: (1) trait or "Great Man" theory, (2) leadership as a function of the group, and, (3) leadership as a function of the situation[62] in which the group is placed. The three types of leadership have to be taken into consideration for a clear understanding of the concept of leadership. A group is the combination of various individual members and, hence, individual personality traits cause variations in the contribution made by each member of the group.[63] In order to exhibit one's leadership quality one has to expose some qualities which are significantly different from those of the other members of the group. Leadership regarded as an activity of influencing people to co-operate towards some goal is found desirable.[64] Leadership is also understood as a relation between an individual and a group established around some common interest and behaviour as directed or determined by the leader.[65] The modern trend is to view the concept of leadership based on the functional aspect. Leadership is thus a function of a group. The dimensions of leadership are leadership behaviour, leadership action and integration between leaders and non-leaders.[66] Interpersonal leadership is largely determined by the structure of the group rather than by the personality of the individual.[67]

The leadership concept in the changing group system may be viewed on traditional — modern dimensions. Max Weber considers traditionalism as one of the bases of authority, the others being charisma and law.[68] The theories of leadership are not mutually exclusive and they have their own shortcomings. In this sense no theory has been fully formulated so far to cater to the need of the present study. However, a syntheses of all the available theories may be useful for this study.

The following approaches, which may help in tracing the emerging pattern of rural women leadership, are ramifications of the theoretical discussions presented above.

Approaches to Identify the Patterns of Rural Leadership

A number of studies have been undertaken in India and abroad on leadership patterns of communities. Most of these studies have employed either the positional approach, the reputational approach, the decisional approach, or, a synthesis of these three approaches to locate the community leaders.[69] Used exclusively, none of the approach provides consistent and reliable results. However, recent comparative studies on community leadership through these three approaches seem to provide some consensus regarding the methodological problem.[70] In the following pages, the three approaches and their syntheses are examined in order to identify the pattern of leadership emerging through them.

Positional Approach

The positional approach is the oldest and simplest method employed to identify community leadership. The positional approach presumes that those who occupy key positions in the formal, social, economic, political and voluntary organisations of the community are the leaders. Mills[71] called these key positions "the strategic command posts". There have been three major criticisms of the positional approach. Critics like Hunter[72], Dhal[73] and Polsby[74] have questioned the validity of the assumption itself. They asserted that formal position is not necessarily correlated with actual power.

Mills's concept of group cohesiveness holds that those in positions possess a large quantum of resources, thereby enjoying commanding power. Pluralists like Dhal, N.W. Polsby and R.E. Wolfinger have objected to this view on the ground that different positions in society entail different kinds of resources, causing a need for negotiated compromise.

Mills's concept of community of interest is also criticised based on the fact that widely dispersed resources in the community may lead to rivalry and consequent neglect of common interest.[75]

Nevertheless, C.M. Bonjean and D.M. Olsen[76] have reported that the positional approach is the simplest, the quickest and the most reliable method for identification of leaders in small communities where resources of power are mostly centralised.

Reputational Approach

The reputational approach originated from the theoretical formulations of Weber and H.D. Lasswell. This approach is found to be the most widely adopted approach in identifying community leaders. Hunter[77] employed the reputational approach for the first time to investigate the community power structure in Atlanta city. This approach is based on the assumption that those having a "reputation for power" are indeed leaders. Scholars[78] like R.C. Angell, Earnest A.T. Barth and B. Abulaban, D.C. Miller, R.D. Schulz and L.U. Bloomberg and O.E. Klapp and L.V. Paggett in Western countries, and, Dhillon, Lewis and S.K. Lall in India are some of the scholars who have applied this approach for identifying leaders. However, it does not measure the leadership itself but rather the reputation for leadership.[79]

The reputational approach elicits from informants (knowledgeable persons, experts, sample of community members) a list of the most powerful and influential leaders in the community. This is done by directing one question or a series of questions to informants. The final list of leaders usually consists of those who have received the greatest number of mentions.[80]

The merits of this approach are its "transportability and its economy of operation"[81] However, it is not free from criticism. According to R.Wolfinger, "this technique makes the erroneous assumption that appearance and reality are equivalent".[82] It is also claimed that it is not certain whether the leaders identified by this approach have influence in some specified areas or enjoy general influence.

Decisional Approach

The decisional approach is otherwise known as "event analysis" or "issue participation approach". Political scientists like Dhal[83] and his associates at Yale University have mostly made use of this approach. The assumption behind this approach presupposes that "active participation in decision-making process implies influence and exercise of actual power".[84]

This approach is more effective for exploring important aspects of community decision-making. It facilitates conceptualization and measuring power more empirically, yielding fairly reliable results. This approach is also subject to criticism on three major grounds. The bias of the investigator selecting the issues can have critical effect on the empirical findings. Regarding the feasibility of the study, this approach consumes more time in establishing rapport and confidence in the community and in ascertaining the decision-making process. "The decision-making approach ignores those actors who may be able to keep latent issues from emerging into open controversy".[85] The submerging of important issues in a community is called the phenomenon of "non-decision-making". When such a situation exists it will be a non-event which is not observable [86].

To sum up, every approach of identifying and measuring leadership has its own advantages and disadvantages. None is ideal. Without common sense and judgement, all can produce ludicrous results; used skillfully, however, each is likely to be useful.[87]

Integrated Approach

An integrated approach will be of much use in understanding the leadership patterns in rural villages in a fuller perspective. In the light of the controversies and criticism with regard to each of the three approaches taken individually, it becomes imperative to test the validity of the approaches through comparative analysis. Each approach may turn up its own leaders and those who are determined by two or more of the methods may constitute some other types of leaders. Freeman *et al.* have studied the power structure in Syracuse by applying all the three approaches and have also compared the findings made through each of the approaches.

After the review of the theoretical framework for locating community leaders, the researcher intends to apply the approaches of position, reputation and decision-making individually and in an integrated form to identify the pattern of rural women leadership that has emerged through the election for the Village Panchayat Presidents in Dindigul District in October 1996.

The modification the researcher intends to make in the proposed framework is that, while the community leaders are identified through their respective resources of power in the original theory, the power bases of the rural women who have emerged as leaders are to be identified in the present study. From a functional perspective, this is a converse process.

Methodology

Objectives

To investigate the various factors contributing to the emergence of rural women as leaders and to identify the pattern of emergence of rural women leadership, the following objectives have been deduced from the theory for this study :

1. To find out the age group that facilitates the emergence of rural women leadership.
2. To identify the influence of caste in the emergence of rural women leadership.

3. To investigate the relevance of education in promoting the emergence of rural women leadership.
4. To study the impact of money power in fostering rural women leadership.
5. To find out the relationship between the political background and the emergence of rural women leadership.
6. To analyse the contributory role of positional status towards the emergence of rural women leadership.
7. To measure the influence of family reputation on the emergence of rural women leadership.
8. To trace the link between the decision-making capacity and the emergence of rural women leadership.
9. To probe the interdependence of the various bases of power of rural women leadership.

Hypotheses

On the basis of the issues raised and the objectives mentioned, a battery of six hypotheses have been formulated for empirical testing:

1. The socio-economic status is a significant factor in determining rural women leadership.
2. The higher the political background of the family, the greater will be the emergence of rural women leadership.
3. The positions of the rural women and their family heads as bases of power have their own impact on the emergence of rural women as leaders.
4. The higher the reputation of the family, the greater will be the prospects for the rural women to emerge as leaders.
5. Decision-making of the rural women and their family heads plays a significant role in the process of the emergence of rural women as leaders.
6. The different types of syntheses of position, reputation and decision-making as bases of power significantly enhance the emergence of rural women leadership.

These hypotheses have to be empirically tested through the data collected from 206 rural women leaders in Dindigul District. The major findings of the analysis are to be discussed in detail in the order of the issues dealt with.

Operational Definition

The key concepts used in the study are operationally defined hereunder.

Panchayat Village

Panchayat Village means any local area comprising a revenue village or any portion of a revenue village or contiguous portions of two or more revenue villages with a population estimated at not less than 500.

Village Panchayat

Village Panchayat is the administrative body of a Panchayat Village as envisaged in section 6 of the Tamil Nadu Panchayat Act 1994.

Panchayat Union

Panchayat Union means any local area consisting of a certain number of Village Panchayats and forming a development block for the purposes of the National Extension Service Scheme or Community Development Programme. In the present study, Panchayat Union means any of the fourteen Panchayat Unions of Dindigul District.

Rural Women

Rural Women in the present study refer to those women living in 107 panchayat villages spread over in the 14 Panchayat Unions of Dindigul District.

Rural Women Leaders

It refers to the rural women who polled first and second largest number of votes in the election held in October 1996 for the office of chairpersons in the 107 Village Panchayats of Dindigul District reserved for women.

Villagers

Villagers are people living in panchayat villages.

Power Bases

The positions held in socio-political organisations, the reputation and the decision-making capabilities with regard to the socio-political issues of the rural women leaders and their family heads constitute the power bases in the present study.

Socio-Economic Status

Socio-economic status is the relative ranking of the rural women leaders and their family heads based on the social prestige and financial conditions determined by the socio-economic variables analysed in this study.

Political Background

The political background is the relative ranking of the rural women leaders and their family heads in politics, which is determined by the political background variables under consideration in the present study.

Electioneering Work

Electioneering work refers to the election campaigning activities of a person for the victory of a political party's candidates in the general elections or for personal victory in party elections or in general elections.

Party Protest Activities

They refer to direct actions like road blockade, bandh, demonstrations, fast, and picketing organised for general causes.

Family Head

Family head is either father or brother in the case of spinsters and destitute, husband in the case of married women, son in the case of widows, or any male or female member managing the family.

Local Informants

Local informants are those persons in the villages who are considered knowledgeable and reliable for providing data regarding the rural women leaders and their families.

Place of Residence

It refers to the location of the dwelling houses of the rural women leaders which may be either within or outside the concerned Village Panchayat limits.

Caste Leaders

In the present study caste leaders include the hereditary or elected leaders of village caste groups with titles such as **Oor Gounder, Oor Naicker, Pannadi, Nattanmai, Periyathanam and Maniyam** and also leaders of caste groups at District or State levels.

Religious Leaders

Religious leaders refer to temple priests (Poosaries and Gurukkals), leaders (Gurusamies) for groups of Lord Ayyappan devotees, Melmaruvathur Athiparasakthi devotees, Pathayathra pilgrims of Lord Murugan and Annai Vellankanni.

Mahalir Mantrams

Mahalir mantrams are women welfare organisations registered under the Societies Act 1975 functioning in villages under the patronage of Voluntary Organisations and Social Welfare Departments.

Self-Help Groups

Self-help groups are women welfare organisations in the villages of Dindigul District rendering mutual financial assistance out of the fund raised by themselves.

Rasigar Mantrams

They refer to the clubs of fans of cinema actors and actresses in Dindigul District.

Situational Leaders

Situational leaders are those persons who have emerged as leaders not on the basis of their positional, reputational and decision-making background, but due to peculiar situations arising out of some other manifest or latent factors prevailing at the time of the Village Panchayat elections.

Universe of the Study

Under the Tamil Nadu Panchayat Act 1994, elections were held on the 9th and 12th of October 1996 for 306 Village Panchayats spread over the 14 Panchayat Unions (middle tier) of Dindigul District. Of the 306 Village Panchayats, 83 Village Panchayats were reserved for general women and 24 Village Panchayats were reserved for SC/ST women, accounting for a total of 107 Village Panchayats.

In the present study, the elected women Village Panchayat Presidents and their immediate rivals in these 107 Village Panchayats constituted the universe.

The Break-up of the Universe is given below

Unopposed and elected women Village Panchayat Presidents	6
Contested and elected women Village Panchayat Presidents	101
Immediate rivals of the contested and elected women Village Panchayat Presidents	101
Total	208

Of the 101 immediate rivals, two could not be interviewed because of the obscurity of their residences in the hilly regions. All the remaining 206 members were contacted as respondents of the present study by adopting census survey.

Fig. 1.1: Nature of Panchayats Based on Reservation.

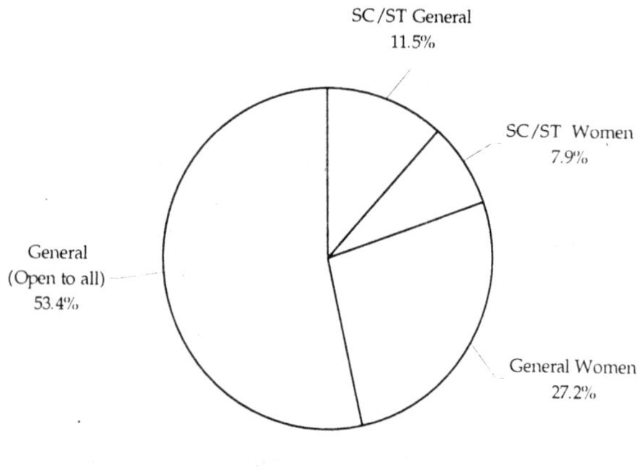

Fig. 1.2: Community of Respondents.

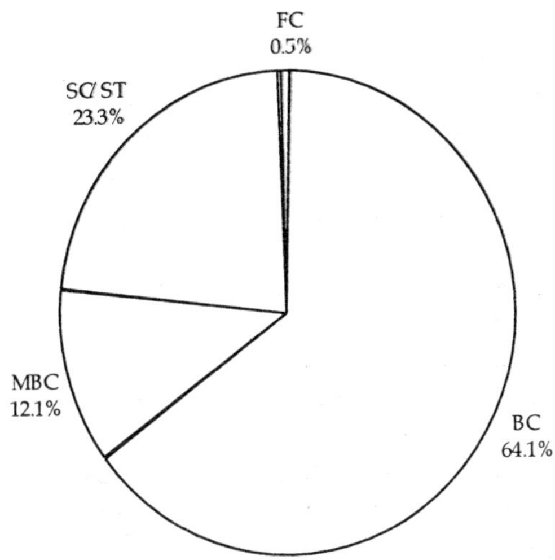

Fig. 1.3: Percentage of Votes Polled by the Respondents.

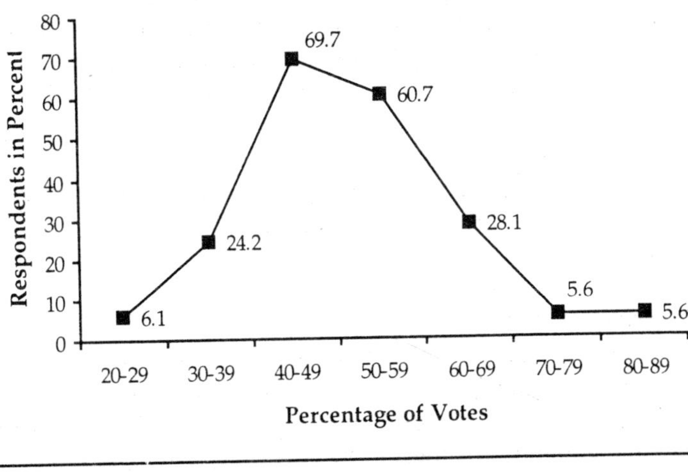

Tools Used

This study was conducted as an empirical research using census survey method. An empirical study of this type requires procedures that will reduce bias and increase reliability. Keeping this in mind, an interview schedule was prepared.

The interview schedule is divided into three parts. The first part consists of items relating to the socio-economic background of the respondents such as age, caste, religion, education, occupation, annual income, land holdings, assets etc. of the respondents and their family heads. The second part contains specific questions intended to elicit information about the political background of the respondents such as the political affiliation of their family heads, sources of political inspiration and nature of political participation. The third part is the most important as it includes questions on all aspects of position, reputation and decision-making and, as a matter of fact, the analysis of the data collected in this part constitutes the substantive part of this study. After a pilot study, the interview schedule was modified and restructured for the final study.

Method of Data Collection

The interview schedule was administered to the respondents through informal interviews and discussions to elicit information relating to the socio-economic, political, positional, reputational and decision-making profiles of the respondents and their family heads. The collected data was confirmed by holding informal interviews with responsible and knowledgeable local informants like VAOs, school teachers, temple priests and caste leaders.

Variables of the Study

In order to gather the data required for testing the hypotheses, the important and relevant variables involved in this study were identified as below:

Independent Variables

Social variables, economic variables, political background variables, positional variables, reputational variables and decision-making variables of respondents and their family heads constitute the independent variables of this study.

Social Variables

Social variables include age, caste, religion, marital status, education, occupation, size of family, type of family, place of residence, type of house of the respondents and education and occupation of their family heads.

Economic Variables

Economic variables include annual income, total asset value of house property, land holdings, modern household appliances, machinery and firm investments of the respondents and their families.

Political Background Variables

They refer to the age of attainment of political awareness, age of entering politics, sources of inspiration for political interest, positions in political parties, stimulants for political participation and political ambitions of respondents and political affiliations, positions in political parties and nature of political participation of their family heads.

Positional Profile Variables

Positional profile variables relate to the positions held by the respondents and their family heads in socio-political and community service organisations such as Mahalir Mantrams, Self-Help Groups, governmental organisations, political parties, trade unions, Village Panchayats, Co-operative Societies, voluntary organisations, social service organisations, caste organisations and Rasigar Mantrams.

Reputational Profile Variables

Reputational profile variables include the correlates of both ascribed and achieved reputation of the respondents.

Correlates of Ascribed Reputation

The correlates of ascribed reputation denote

(a) Social correlates,
(b) Economic correlates,
(c) Political correlates, and
(d) Community service correlates of reputation

(a) **Social Correlates**

Periyathanam family, hereditary caste leader, family with first respect, temple trustee, village priest, Gurrukkal or Poosary, highly educated family and professional position.

(b) **Economic Correlates**

Pannaiyar family, wealthy family, factory/mill/stone crusher owner, family with car and telephone.

(c) **Political Correlates**

Family member or relative of Ex-Village Panchayat President/Union Chairman/MLA/MP, contact with high profile leaders and freedom fighter's family.

(d) **Community Service Correlates**

Social service, donations to all castes and creeds, annadhanam, interest-free financial assistance, free medical services with indigenous medicines and settling domestic disputes.

Correlates of Achieved Reputation

Correlates of achieved reputation refer to the reverence secured by means of one's own personal traits like hospitality, honesty, helping tendency, sociability, tolerance, courage for articulation, intelligence, self-confidence and fighting spirit for good causes.

Decisional Profile Variables

Decisional profile variables are sources of inducement for final decision of respondents to contest the election, participation in socio-political activities prior to the elections, modes of settling issues, election promises and the strategies adopted during electioneering. The socio-political activities relate to basic amenities, developmental schemes and social problems.

Dependent Variable

Dependent variable refers to the leadership of the respondents measured in terms of votes polled by them in the Village Panchayat election.

Data Base

The main source of primary data was the field survey based on the interview schedule and discussion with the respondents and the verification of the same with responsible and knowledgeable persons in the respective villages.

The secondary sources of data were the government census, reports, documents and legislations of the government, books on the present research topic and on related aspects of the current study. Secondary sources also included articles in research journals, magazines, dailies and other published documents.

Method and Tools of Data Analysis

The collected data are tabulated and the analysis is presented in three sections. The first section deals with the socio-economic profile of the respondents. The socio-economic variables are tabulated in a composite manner with the help of a linear unweighted sum of the scores given to each category within each of the variables. This indicates the overall socio-economic status of each leader.

The second section analyses the political background of the respondents. The political background of each of the respondents is measured as is done in the case of the socio-economic status.

The third section deals with the analysis of the data collected about the position, the reputation and the decision-making of the respondents. The positional, the reputational and the decisional status of the respondents is identified following the procedures adopted in the previous two sections. The outcome of the analysis of the three sections is used to test the hypotheses of the study.

For the analysis of the data, simple tabular analysis, measures of central tendency, Chi Square test of significance, Pearson's correlation coefficient and Multi-variate regression analysis are used.

The Chi square test is used to identify the level of association between leadership and the independent variables.

Pearson's correlation coefficient is used to ascertain whether the association between the dependent and the independent variables is positive or negative.

Measures of central tendency are used to obtain an overall

idea about the implications of the independent and the dependent variables.

Multi-variate regression analysis is used to find out the level of influence of extraneous variables over the dependent variable, namely the leadership.

The means of positional, reputational and decisional scores of respondents are taken as cut-off points for identifying the positional, the reputational and the decisional leaders.

Preparation of Indices

There is no standardised formal and statistically validated index to measure the socio-economic status, political background, positional, reputational and decision-making profiles of rural people of different social settings. Different scholars have adopted their own indices specially prepared to suit their area of study. To quote a few, the Omaris index of socio-economic status includes the following items: area of residence, monthly income, occupational status, type of housing, condition of house, house ownership or rental status, level of living and formal social participation.[88] Udaipareek and Trivedi's socio-economic scale (rural) consists of nine items namely caste, occupation, education, social participation of the heads of the family, their land, house, farm powers, material possessions and the general nature of the family.[89] V.R. Dutta prepared his own indices to measure the socio-economic status, the positional, the reputational and the decision-making profiles[90] of Municipal corporators.

Following the above scholars, the researcher of the present study prepared her own indices for the analysis of the data.

The percentage of votes polled by the respondents are calculated by taking into account the sum of votes polled by an elected respondent and her immediate rival as the total number of votes of the respective Village Panchayat. On this basis the respondents are grouped as elected and defeated, the elected respondents falling under the group of 50-100 percentage of votes and the defeated respondents falling under the group of 0-49 percentage of votes.

For the purpose of testing the hypotheses, the defeated and the elected respondents were grouped into low, medium and high groups on the basis of the composite score of each independent variable.

Scheme of Scoring

The composite score of each independent variable was obtained by the linear sum of unweighted scores assigned to each category within each component of the variable.

In order to assess the personal reputation of the respondent, ten correlates of personal reputation (traits) namely hospitality, honesty, helping tendency, sociability, accessibility, tolerance, courage for articulation, intelligence, self-confidence and fighting spirit were taken into consideration. If a respondent possessed at least five of the ten correlates of personal reputation, she was deemed to have acquired personal reputation and a score of 10 was given to her.

Under this scheme of scoring, each respondent may get scores ranging from 0-40 for socio-economic status, 0-35 for political background, 0-42 for positional profile, 0-30 for reputational profile and 0-50 for decision-making profile.

Using this scheme of scoring, the indices for assessing the socio-economic status, political background, positional, reputational and decision-making profiles were prepared as shown in Appendix II.

Plan of the Study

This study has been divided into six chapters.

The introductory chapter presents the statement of the problem, review of literature, theoretical framework, objectives, hypotheses, methodology and sources of the study.

Chapter two presents a brief historical background of the process of emergence of women in Indian politics, a brief historical background of the evolution of the Panchayati Raj system in India and the profile of the Dindigul District.

Chapter three presents the socio-economic status of the respondents and its analysis.

The political background of the respondents and their family members is analysed in the fourth chapter.

The main theme of chapter five is to identify the power bases for the emergence of the respondents as rural women leaders and to categorise them based on their power bases.

The sixth chapter presents the major findings, conclusions and suggestions.

References

1. Udai Pareek and S.K. Reddy, "Studies in Indian Rural Leadership-A review", **Studies on Rural Leadership** (ed.) Udai Pareek, Delhi: Behavioural Science Centre, 1966, pp. 101-112. Also see Leela Dube, "Studies on Leadership in Village India", **Emerging Patterns of Rural Leadership in South Asia,** Hyderabad: National Institute of Community Development,1965, pp.107-134.
2. Charles P. Loomis, **Social Systems; Essays on the Persistence and Change,** New Jersey: Princeton, 1963.
3. Ferdinand Tonnies, **Community and Society,** Translated from German and edited by Charles Loomis, New York: Harper and Row, 1963.
4. Iqbal Narain, **The Rural Elite in an Indian State — A Case Study of Rajasthan,** New Delhi: Monohar Book Depot., 1976, p. 72.
5. D.C. Miglani, **Politics and Rural Power Structure,** New Delhi: Deep and Deep Publications, 1993, p. 199; G.D. Bhatt, **Emerging Leadership Pattern in Rural India — An Empirical Study,** New Delhi: M D Publications Pvt. Ltd., 1994, p. 131.
6. B.S. Bhargava, and K. Subha, "Women in Panchayati Raj: Some Reflections on Karnataka's Experience", **Kurukshetra,** Vol. XLII, No. 9, June, 1994, p. 42.
7. S.N.Mishra, "Dynamics and Dimensions of Panchayati Raj Elections", **The Indian Journal of Public Administration**, Vol. XXXVII, No. 3, July-September, 1991, pp. 335-348.
8. Oscar Lewis., "Village Life in Northern India", in **Village India** (ed.), M. Marriot, Chicago: The University of Chicago Press, 1955, pp. 145-70.
9. H.S. Dhillon, **Leadership and Groups in a South Indian Village,** New Delhi: Planning Commission, 1955.
10. Y. Singh, "Changing Power Structure of Village Community: A Case Study of six main Villages in Eastern U.P", in A.R. Desai, (ed.), **Rural Sociology in India,** Bombay: Popular Prakashan, 1969, pp. 711-23.
11. R.L. Park and A.I. Tinker, (eds), **Leadership and Political Institution in India,** New Jersey: Princeton, 1959.
12. B.N.Singh, "Leadership Patterns in two North Indian Villages", **Studies in Rural Leadership**, (ed.), Udai Pareek, *Op. cit*.
13. E. Wood, " Patterns of Influences in Rural India", in R.L. Park and A. I. Tinker, (eds.) *Ibid*., pp. 372-90.
14. J.T. Hitchcock, "Leadership in North Indian Village", in R.L. Park and A.I. Tinker, (eds.), Ibid., pp. 395-414.
15. H. Orienstein, "A Bombay Village", in R.L. Park and A.I. Tinker, (eds.), Ibid., pp. 414-26.

16. Alan Beals, "Leadership in a Mysore Village", in R.L. Park and A.I. Tinker, (eds.), *Ibid*., pp. 426-37.
17. M.N. Srinivas, "The Dominant Caste in Rampura", in **American Anthropologist**, Vol. 61, No. 1, February, 1969, pp. 1-16.
18. S.C. Dube, " Caste Dominance in Factionalism", **Contribution to Indian Sociology, New Series,** No. 11, Deccember, 1968, p. 81.
19. B.N. Singh, " Impact of Community Development Programme on Rural Leadership", in R.L. Park and A.I. Tinker, (eds.), Op.cit.; Briraj Chawhan, "Leadership in Rajasthan Village", in L.P. Vidyarthi, (ed.), **Leadership in India, Bombay:** Asia Publishing House, 1967; Indira Singh, "Leadership in a Sikh Village," in L.P. Vidyarthi, (ed.), Ibid.; Ranganath, "Changing Pattern of Rural Leadership in Uttar Pradesh", in L.P. Vidyarthi, (ed.), Ibid.; Pradipto Ray", The Characteristics of Emergent Leaders", in L.P. Vidyarthi, (ed.), Ibid.; Lalit K. Sen and P. Roy, **Awareness of Community Development in Village India,** Hyderabad: National Institute of Community Development, 1967; Harijinder Singh, **Village Leadership: A Case Study of Village Mohali in Punjab,** New Delhi: Sterling Publishers,1969.
20. Iqbal Narain, et al., **The Rural Elite in an Indian State: A Case Study of Rajasthan,** *Op. cit*.; V .M. Sirsikar, **The Rural Elite in Developing Society: A Study in Political Sociology,** New Delhi: Orient Long Mans Limited, 1970; L.P. Vidyarthi, (ed.), **Leadership in India,** *Op. cit*.; A.Carter, **Elite in Rural India : Political Stratification and Alliances in Western Maharashtra,** New Delhi: Vikas Publishing House, 1974; F.M. Abraham, **Dynamics of Leadership in Village India,** Allahabad: Indian International Publication, 1974; D.C. Miglani, **Politics and Rural Power Structure,** *Op. cit*.; G. Narayana Reddy, **Rural Elite and Community Work-A Socio-Political Perspective,** Allahabad: Chugh Publications, 1986.
21. A.P. Barnaba, "Characteristics of Lay Leader in Extension Work", **Journal of the M.S. University of Baroda,** 1968; Oscar Lewis, **Village Life in Northern India,** Illinois: University of Illinois Press, 1958; A.R. Beals, Leadership in Mysore Village", in R.L. Park and A.I. Tinker,(eds.), *Op. cit*.; H . Orenstein, "Leadership and Caste in Bombay Village", R.L. Park and A.I. Tinker (eds.), Ibid.; Krishna Kamal, "Leadership in Panchayat Elections of Uttar Pradesh", in L.P. Vidyarthi, (ed.), *Op. cit*.; L.K. Sen, **Opinion Leadership in India,** Hydrabad: National Institute of Community Development, 1969; Krishna Chakra Bharathi and S.K. Bhattacharya, **Leadership Factions and Panchayati Raj: A Case Study of West-Bengal,** New Delhi: Rawat Publications, 1993 ; M.L. Sharma, **Dynamics of Rural Power Structure — A Study of Rajasthan,** Jaipur:National Publishing House, 1984; A.R. Desai, (ed.), **Rural Sociology in India,** *Op. cit*.; N.K. Shukla, **Social Structure of an Indian Village,** New Delhi: Cosmo Publications, 1976; D.C. Miller, **From Hierarchy to Stratification-Changing Patterns of Social Inequality in a North Indian Village,** Delhi: Oxford University Press, 1975; S.K. Chawhan, **Caste, Status and Power-Social Stratification in Assam,** New Delhi: Classical Publishing Co. 1980; Sushila Mehta, **Social Conflicts in a Village Community,** New Delhi: S. Chand and Co. Pvt. Ltd., 1971.

22. L.P. Vidyarthi, (ed.), *Op. cit.*
23. Avtar Singh, **Leadership Pattern and Village Structure: A Case Study of Six Indian Villages,** New Delhi: Sterling Publishers Pvt. Ltd., 1973 ; S.N. Mishra, **Patterns of Emerging Leadership in Rural India,** Patna: Associated Book Agency, 1977; S.R. Mehta, **Emerging Pattern of Rural Leadership,** New Delhi: Wiley Eastern Pvt. Ltd., 1972 ; K.D. Gangrade, **Emerging Patterns of Leadership,** Delhi: Rachna Publications, 1974 ; D.S. Chawdry, **Emerging Leadership in an Indian State, A Case Study of Rajasthan,** Rohtak: Manthan Publications, 1981 ; Harijinder Singh, **Village Leadership: A Case Study of Village Mohali in Punjab,** *Op. cit.*; Paramatma Saran, **Rural Leadership in the Context of India's Modernisation,** New Delhi: Vikas Publishing House, 1978.
24. Floyd Hunter, **Community Power Structure — A Study of Decision Makers,** Chapel Hill: University of North Carolina Press, 1953.
25. C. W. Mills, **The Power Elite,** New York: Oxford University Press, 1956.
26. Robert A. Dahl, **Who Governs?: Democracy and Power in an American City,** New Haven: Yale University Press, 1961.
27. Robert Presthus, **Men at the Top,** New York: Oxford University Press, 1964.
28. Linton C. Freeman, et al, "Locating Leaders in Local Communities: A Comparison of some Alternative Approaches", in M. Aiken and P.E. Mott, (eds.), **The Structure of Community Power,** New York: Random House, 1970.
29. Floyd Hunter, **Community Power Succession: Atlanta's Policy Makers Revisited,** Chapel Hill : University of North Carolina Press, 1980.
30. K. Ranga Rao, "Rural Leadership and Conflict Study of Andhra Village", **Economic and Political Weekly,** Vol. III, No. 17, April 27, 1968.
31. T.K. Oomen, "Myth and Reality in Indias Communitarian Villages", in A.R. Desai (ed.), **Rural Sociology in India,** *Op. cit.*, pp. 653-674.
32. T.K. Oomen, " Rural Community Power Structure in India", **Social Forces,** Vol. 49, No.2, December, 1970, pp. 226-39.
33. S.R. Mehta, **Emerging Pattern of Rural Leadership,** *Op. cit.*
34. Avtar Singh, **Leadership Pattern and Village Structure,** *Op. cit.*
35. K.D. Gangrade, **Emerging Patterns of Leadership,** *Op. cit.*
36. P.C. Deb and B.K. Agarwal, **Rural Leadership in Green Revolution,** Delhi: Researchco Publications, 1974.
37. S.K. Lall, **The Urban Elite,** Delhi: Thompson Press (India) Ltd., 1974.
38. Iqbal Narain, K.C. Pandae and Mohan Lal Sharma, **The Rural Elite in an Indian State: A Case Study of Rajasthan,** *Op. cit.*
39. Harizinder Singh, **Authority and Influence in Two Sikh Villages,** New Delhi: Sterling Publishers Pvt. Ltd., 1976.
40. S.N. Mishra, **Pattern of Emerging Leadership in Rural India,**Patna: Associated Book Agency, 1977.
41. Paramatma Saran, **Rural Leadership in the Context of India's Modernization,** New Delhi: Vikas Publishing House, 1978.
42. Desingu Setty., " A Study of Leadership in Two Valaya Communities in Tamil Nadu", **Indian Journal of Social Work,** Vol. XLII, No. 4, January, 1982, pp. 403-417.

43. Murali M. Sinha, **Modernisation and Community Power: A Comparative Study of Indian Villages,** New Delhi: Vikas Publishing House Pvt. Ltd., 1983.
44. Vijay Rajan Dutta, **Decision Making in Urban Government and Politics,** Allahabad: Chugh Publications, 1986
45. G. Narayana Reddy, **Rural Elite and Community Work,** *Op. cit.*
46. A.T. Kitur, " Emerging Pattern of Leadership: A Study of PRIs in Dharward District", **ISDA Journal,** Vol. 2, April,1992, pp. 163-179.
47. D.C. Miglani, **Politics and Rural Power Structure,** *Op. cit.*
48. K. Subha, **Women in Local Governance,** Jaipur: RBSA Publishers, 1994.
49. George Mathew, "Will Reservation Ensure Participation?", **Social Welfare,** Vol. 42, No. 5-6, August-September, 1995, pp. 32-35,37.
50. Subash C. Arora and R.K. Prabakhar, " A Profile of Women Contestants — a Study of Rohtak Municipal Council Elections", **Nagar Lok,** Vol. XXVIII, No. 1, January-March, 1996, pp. 64-77.
51. Snehalata Panda, "Emerging Pattern of Leadership among Rural Women in Orissa," **Journal of Rural Development,** Vol. 15, No. 4, October-December, 1996, pp. 721-27.
52. Dilip. K. Ghosh, "Grassroots Women Leaders: Who are they? A Study in West Bengal District", **Journal of Rural Development,** Vol. 16, No. 2, April-June,1997, pp. 291-311.
53. K. Jeyalakshmi, " Empowerment of Women in Panchayats Experience of Andhra Pradesh-Case Study", **Journal of Rural Development,** Vol. 16, No.2 April-June 1997, pp. 369-378.
54. Snehalata Panda, Political Emperment of Women -A Case Study of Orissa, **Journal of Rural Development,** Vol. 16, No. 4, October-December,1997, pp. 663-672.
55. Manu Baskar, "Women Panchayat Members in Kerala. A Profile", **Economic and Political Weekly,** Vol. XXXII, No. 17, April, 1997, pp. 13-20.
56. P. Jeyapal and Dravidamani, "Women Panchayat Presidents", **Social Welfare,** Vol. 44, No. 1, April, 1997, pp. 29-33.
57. V.B. Atherya and K.S. Rajeswari, Womens' Participation in Panchayati Raj: A Case Study From Tamil Nadu, **Research Report,** Chennai: M.S. Swaminathan Foundation,1998.
58. B.S. Bhargava and K.C, Vidya, "Position of Women in Political Institutions— With Special Reference to Panchayati Raj System in Karnataka", **Journal of Rural Development,** Vol. 11, No. 5, September, 1992, pp. 601-28; Divya Pandal, "Women's Participation in Policy and Decision-Making Process: A Grassroots Experience", in Ranjana Kumari, (ed.), **Women in Decision-Making,** New Delhi: Vikas Publishing House, 1992, pp. 55-68 ; Ashok Kumar, "Women's Participation in Local Bodies", in Ashok Kumar, (ed.), **Women in Contemporary Indian Society,**Vol. 2. New Delhi: Anmol Publishers, 1992, pp. 18-32; Susheela Kaushik, "Organising Women for Panchayat Raj", **Search News,** Volume VIII, Land 2, January-June , 1993, pp. 17-26; G. Palanithurai, "Empowerment of Women - A Novel Exercise", **Kurukshetra,** Vol. XLII, No. 9, June 1994, pp. 50-53, 66; Mohinder Singh, "Political Equality for Women", **Social Welfare,** Vol. 41, No. 10, January,

1995, pp. 13-15; Neera Agnimithra, "Women in Panchayats: Empowerment or Illusion", **Gandhi Marg,** Vol. 17, No. 4, January-March, 1996, pp. 441-445; Shamim Aleema, "Political Participation and Share of Women in Political Power", in Aleema Shamim (ed.), **Women's Development Problems and Prospects,** New Delhi: APH Publishing Corp.,1996, pp. 67-77; O.P. Bohra, "Women in Decentralised Democracy", **Indian Journal of Rural Development,** Vol. 16, No. 4, October-December, 1997, pp. 673-83, Hyderabad: NIRD, K.C. Vidya, **Political Empowerment of Women at the Grass roots,** New Delhi: Kanishka Publishers, 1997; Sukla Deb Kanango, "Panchayati Raj and Emerging Women Leadership: An Overview", **Social Action,** Vol. 46, No. 1, January-March, 1996, pp. 76-91; G. Palanithurai, " Women Participation in Local Governance: a Case Analysis of Tamil Nadu" Paper presented in the National Seminar on **Women in Local Governance: Exploring New Frontiers** organised by Institute of Social Studies Trust, Bangalore, from 3rd to 5th February,1999.

59. N.R. Inamdar, " Panchayati Raj Leadership: Emerging Dimensions", **Journal of Rural Development,** Vol. 10, No. 5, September-October, 1991, pp. 561-73, Hyderabad: NIRD.
60. R.C. Clark, **A Review of Leadership Studies, Selected Readings and References,** in 4H Club Work, p. 85.
61. Murray G. Ross and Charless E. Hendry, **New Understanding of Leadership: A Survey and Application of Research,** New York: Association Press, 1957.
62. Cecil A. Gibb, "Leadership", in **Handbook of Social Psychology,** (Ed.), Gardner Lindzey, New York: Addison Wesley Publishing Company, Vol-II, 1954, p. 901.
63. *Ibid.*, p. 889.
64. Ordway Tead, **The Art of Leadership,** New York: McGraw Hill Book Co., 1963.
65. Richard Schmidt, "Leadership", **Encyclopaedia of Social Sciences,** (ed.),R.A. Edwin Seligman, Vol. IX-X, New York: The Macmillan Company and Free Press, 1972, pp. 91-113; S.C. Dube, "A Framework for the Study of Rural Leadership in Transitional Societies", in **Emerging Paterns of Rural Leadership in Southern Asia,** Hyderabad: National Institute of Community Development, 1965. pp. 24.
66. Murray G. Ross and Charles E. Hendry, *Op. cit.* p. 22.
67. David Krech and Richard S. Crutchfield, **Theory and Problem of Social Psychology,** New York: Mcgraw Hill Book Co, 1948, p. 401.
68. Max Weber, " Types of Authority", **Essays in Sociology,** (ed.), H.H. Gerth and C.W. Mills, Oxford: University Press, 1946.
69. An excellant review of these approaches is found in Charles M. Bonjean and David M. Olsen, " Community Leadership : Directions of Research", **Administrative Science Quarterly** Vol. 9. No. 3, December, 1964, pp. 278-300.
70. G. Narayana Reddy, **Rural Elite and Community Work,** *op. cit.*, p.16.
71. C.W. Mills, **The Power Elite,** New York: Galexy, 1959, p. 4.
72. Floyd Hunter, *Op. cit.*

73. Robart A. Dhal, *op. cit.*
74. N.W. Polsby, " How to Study Community Power: The Pluralist Alternative," **Journal of Politics,** Vol. 22, August, 1960, pp. 474-484.
75. C.W. Mills cited in D. Ricci, **Community Power and Democratic Theory,** New York: Random House, 1971, p. 120.
76. C.M. Bonjean and D.M. Olsen, "Community Leadership: Directions of Research", in M. Aiken an P.E. Mott, (ed.) **The Structure of Community Power,** New York: Random House, 1970, p. 204.
77. Floyd Hunter, *Op. cit.*
78. Robert Cooley Angell, "The Moral Integration of American Elites", **American Journal of Sociology,** Vol. 61, No. 1, July, 1957, Part II.; Robert E. Agger, "Power Attributions in the Local Community", **Social Forces,** Vol. 34, 1956, pp. 322-31.; Earnest A.T. Barth and Bahu Abu-Laban, "Power Structure and the Negro Sub-Community", **American Sociological Review,** Vol. 24, 1959, pp. 69-76; Delbert C. Miller, Decision-Making Cliques in Community Power Structure," **American Journal of Sociology,** Vol. 64, No. 3, November, 1958, pp. 299-310; Robert D. Schulze and L.U. Bloomberg, "The Determination of Local Power Elites", **American Journal of Sociology,** Vol. 63, No. 3, November, 1957, P. 296 quoted in Robert Presthus, **Man at the Top,** New York Oxford University Press 1964, p. 58; Orrin E. Klapp and L. Vincent Padgett, " Power Structure and Decision Making in a Maxican Border City," **American Journal of Sociology,** Vol. 65, No. 4, January, 1960, pp. 400-406; H.S. Dhillon, *Op. cit.*; Oscar Lewis, *Op. cit.*; S.K. Lall, *Op. cit.*
79. H.J. Ehrilich, "The Reputational Approach to the Study of Community Power", **American Sociological Review,** Vol. 26, December, 1961, p. 926.
80. P.E.Mott and M. Aiken, **The Structure of Community Power,** New York: Random House, 1970, p. 194.
81. Lawrence. J.R. Herson, " In the Foot Steps of Community", **American Political Science Review,** Vol. 55, No. 4, December, 1961, pp. 818-19, 821.
82. Raymond Wolfinger, "Reputation and Reality in the Study of Community Power", **American Sociological Review,** Vol. 20, October, 1960, pp. 636-44.
83. Robert A. Dahl, *Op. cit.*
84. M. Aiken and P.E. Mott (eds.), *Op. cit*, p. 197.
85. *Ibid.*, p. 207.
86. *Ibid.*, p. 317. cited in G.Narayana Reddy, *Op. cit.*, p. 24.
87. Robert A. Dahl, *Op. cit*, quoted in D.C. Miglani, *Op. cit.*, p. 165.
88. P.T. Omari, "Factors Associated with the Urban Adjustment of Rural Southern Immigrants", **Social Forces,** Vol. 35, No. 1, October, 1956, pp. 47-53.
89. Udai Pareek and C. Trivedi, **Mannual of the Socio-Economic Status Scale (Rural),** Delhi: Manasayan, 1954.
90. V.R. Dutta, *Op. cit.*, pp. 77-80.

Two

The Setting

This chapter is organised in three sections. In the first section, an attempt has been made to examine the process of emergence of women in world and Indian politics.

The second section is devoted to tracing the evolution of the Panchayati Raj system in India and the historical background of Local Self Government in Tamil Nadu.

The third section presents the profile of the study area, namely the Dindigul District in the State of Tamil Nadu.

SECTION 1

Process of Emergence of Women in World and Indian Politics

In most of the countries of the world, only a slow glacial pace of change is perceived in the emergence of women in politics. This is so because dominant social customs and norms all over laid down that women's role was domestic and not political.[1] In 1993, there were only six women heads of government worldwide. Worldwide, only one elected politician in nine is a woman. Over 100 countries in the world have no women in parliament at all. The highest number of women in the US Congress at any one time was during the 1961-62 session. Only six out of 185 member countries of the UN have each a woman permanent representative.

Women represent only 22 per cent of the total diplomatic personnel in UN missions. There is better parliamentary representation in developing nations (12 per cent), than in industrialised nations (9 per cent). Bahrain, Kuwait and the United Arab Emirates continue to deny women the right to vote or stand for election. In Eastern Europe, women's participation in parliament dropped sharply (from 22 per cent in 1987 to 6.5 per cent in 1993), largely as a result of the collapse of socialist governments and the elimination of quotas for women in parliament.[2] Theoreticians and protagonists of democracy can not perceive how a system could be democratic if half of mankind, i.e., women, are not given equal rights with men.

Indian women were not provided with the fundamental rights of education, property, franchise and other political freedoms till the early part of the British regime in India.

Industrialisation, westernisation and, above all, education have been the causes for transformation in many spheres of human life, one such eminent change being in the concept of women's role in politics. As a result of this change, women began to assert their rights and started realising that they have inherent abilities on par with men and that, except for some biological differences, they are in no way inferior to their male counterparts.

TABLE 2.1
RIGHT TO FRANCHISE GIVEN TO WOMEN

Sl. No.	*Country*	*Franchise Right*	
		Partial	*Full*
1.	New Zealand	-	1893
2.	Finland	-	1906
3.	Norway	-	1913
4.	Denmark	-	1915
5.	Sweden	1863	1919
6.	U.S.A	1970	1920
7.	U.K	1918	1928
8.	India	1919-35	1949
9.	Japan	-	1945
10.	France	1944	1946
11.	Greece	-	1952
12.	Pakistan	-	1956
13.	Morocco	1945	1962
14.	Switzerland	-	1971

Source: Indira Mahindra, **Rebellious Home Makers**, Bombay: S.N.D.T. Womens' University, 1980, p. 175.

Fig. 2.1: Women's Representation in Parliament of Different Countries.

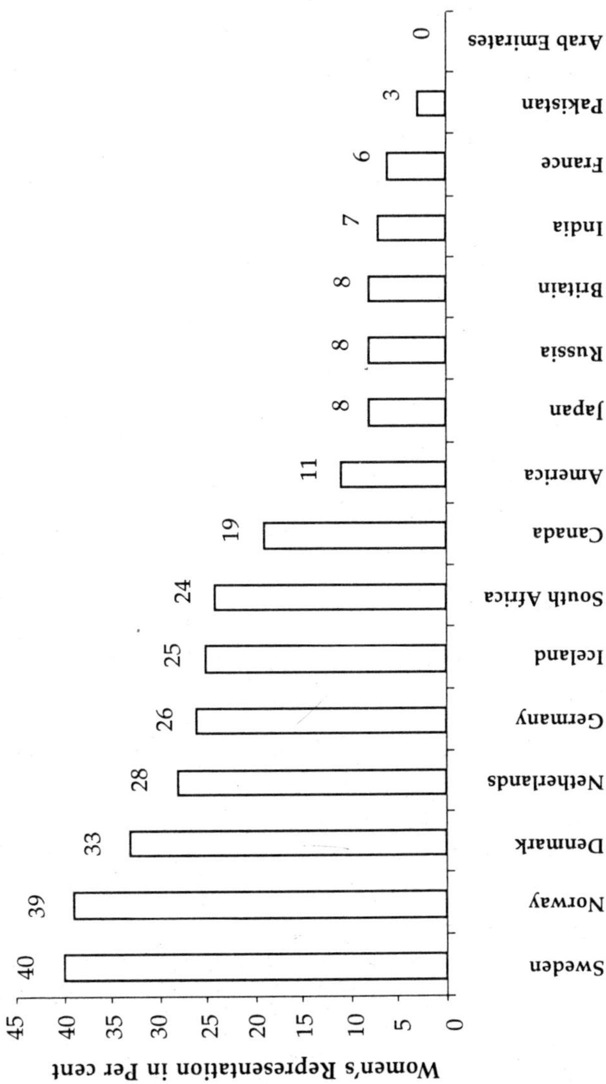

Social reformers like Raja Ram Mohan Roy and Swami Dayananda Saraswathi rose to the occasion and fought for the liberation of oppressed and suppressed women in India. The Brahma Samaj was formed in Bengal and the Arya Samaj in Punjab by Swami Dayananda Saraswathi in 1873. Though the Arya Samaj was very active in the promotion of women's education, Swami Dyananda Saraswathi was very clear about women's role: "The woman should do the domestic duties in obedience to her husband. The work outside should belong to the province of the man's duties".[3]

In the beginning of the 20th century, the Saradha Act gave an impetus to women's movements fighting for their rights. G.K. Gokalae worked hard to impress on the Indian women that only education could get rid of their social and political deprivations. Sarojini Naidu, along with other women from progressive politicized families, actively mobilised support for women's education and then for their franchise.

In the early twentieth century, many women's organisations sprang up. They include the Women India Association (WIA, 1917), the National Council of Women of India (NCWI, 1925), and the All-India Women's Conference (AIWC, 1926).[4] The basic concern of these women's organisations was to seek legislative enactment for upliftment of women and gender equality in many fields of human activity, besides demanding adult suffrage. A lead in this regard was given by Annie Besant who urged women to join the Home Rule League. As a result of the efforts of leading women leaders like Margaret Cousins, Joshi and Herabai Tata besides Anni Besant and Sarojini Naidu, voting rights for women were provided first by the Madras Legislature in 1920. After securing the right to vote, the next item on the agenda was to obtain the right to sit in the Legislative Council in order to promote the cause of political equality between men and women.

In 1925, Mahatma Gandhi stated "As long as the women of India do not take part in the public life there can be no salvation for the country".[5] After the first world war, a large number of women joined India's freedom struggle. Mahatma Gandhi made women an integral part of all struggles which were launched during the freedom movement against British colonialism.[6]

TABLE 2.2
REPRESENTATION OF WOMEN IN LOK SABHA, INDIA

Year	*Total Seats*	*Total Women Members*	*Percentage*
1952-57	499	24	4.4
1957-62	500	27	5.4
1962-67	503	34	6.7
1967-71	523	31	5.9
1971-76	521	22	4.2
1977-80	544	19	3.4
1980-84	544	28	5.1
1985-90	544	44	8.1
1990-91	529	28	5.3
1991-96	509	36	7.1
1996	537 (Declared)	34	6.3

Source: Chief Election Commision Office. 1996 Election results.

In 1926, Dr. Muthulakshmi Reddy became the first woman to be nominated to the Madras Legislative Council. In the 1932 elections to the Provincial Assemblies many women contested and only a few of them got elected. The first Indian woman to get a berth in any Indian Cabinet was Vijayalakshmi Pandit in Uttar Pradesh. Following this, several prominent leaders like Padmaja Naidu, Raj Kumari, Begum Hamid Ali, Amrit Kaur and Sucheta Kripalani registered their significant presence in Indian politics.

The Constitution of India promises equal rights to women. There would not be any discrimination on the basis of sex for political positions. However, it is found that the constitutional rights as such have not been availed adequately by Indian women to participate in the political process of the country. The patriarchal culture has the effect of diluting freedom and equality in the political sphere. Indeed, the existing social and economic pattern of society has marginalised women with the result that there are only a few women in public life.

The Balwantrai Mehta Committee (1957) widely recognised women's participation in grassroots democracy and hence recommended co-option of two women members to the PRIs.[7] The Ashok Mehta Committee (1978) on Panchayati Raj Institutions (PRI's) laid special emphasis on the need to reorganise and strengthen women's constructive decision-making and managerial roles and pointed out in its report the role and relevance of women representatives in decision-making on development projects and their involvement as an integral part of the total development of the village. Therefore, it recommended two women members through a method of co-option by election to the PRIs. The Ashok Mehta Committee also recommended that a committee with all the women members of the Mandal Panchayats represented on it should be formed so that decisions are made by women themselves on priorities and choices involved in welfare and development programmes meant for women and children.[8]

The National Plan of Action for Women (1976)[9] recommended to the Government of India to take some legislative, administrative and other measures to improve the status of Indian women in general. The Committee on the Status of Women in India influenced the preparation of the National Plan of Action.

Despite a woman Prime Minister, a few women Chief Ministers or Governors and some other women holding important political offices, the level of political participation of women has been very low in India. Even after fifty years of Independence and succeeding legislation for political empowerment of women, the women of India have not shown progress in the political process on the expected lines.

Adequate representation for women at different levels of political institutions thus became essential and this could be ensured only through reservation. Hence the Seventy-third Constitution (Amendment) Act 1992. The Seventy-third Amendment of the Constitution mandated one-third reservation of seats for women in all local level elected bodies. As a result, women in rural areas participated in the local body elections of October 1996 and made their entry in the rural power structure.

Rural Women in Tamil Nadu

Rural women in Tamil Nadu constitute nearly 66 per cent of the female population of Tamil Nadu. Living in villages, the rural women have less facilities for education, employment and for occupying political offices. Social customs and conventions seem to suppress rural women more than their urban counterparts.

Rural Women and Education

Education is an essential resource for fostering one's socio-economic development and political empowerment. Unfortunately, the literacy rate of women in general and rural women in particular has not increased considerably in Tamil Nadu. Only a small percentage of rural women in Tamil Nadu receive higher education and very few get opportunities for professional courses.

Rural Women and Employment

Women's employment paves the way for women's integration in the process of national development. Rural women in Tamil Nadu spend most of their time on household chores. A study, "The Women of Rural Asia", by Whyte Robert Orr and Pauline Whyte, while pointing out the minimum and maximum contribution of men and women to domestic work, reveals the fact that women devote 17 hours a day to work related to cooking, fuel collection, washing utensils, child care, sweeping and such other activities.[10] Most of the rural women of Dindigul District seem to engage themselves in agriculture and activities like dairying, animal husbandry, sericulture, handlooms, and handicrafts. A few of them are involved in building construction activities also. As pointed out in the "Report of the National Commission on Self-employed Women and Women in the Unorganised Sector", women of the unorganised sector do not get the focus of attention of the planners and the implementers.[11]

The role of rural women in Dindigul District in agricultural operations such as sowing, weeding, transplanting and harvesting is substantial. In the Panchayat Union areas of Nilakottai, Authur, Reddiyarchathram and Dindigul, flower cultivation is one of the major income generation activities. Further, flower cultivation has the potential of generating employment for rural women in collecting the flowers from the plants and threading them into garlands at home. Selling the flowers as street vendors is one of the jobs meant for rural women. Tanneries, cotton mills and other factories in Dindigul and Vedasanthur Panchayat Union areas provide employment to rural women as industrial labourers. Vending vegetables, garlic, fruits and betel form part of women's employment in Dindigul District.

In the Palani and the Sirumalai hills, the coffee-estates generate employment opportunities for women and the cultivation of potatoes, vegetables and fruits in Kodaikannal Panchayat Union area provides agricultural employment to women.

For the educated women, the teaching profession in schools, colleges, universities and jobs such as school noon-meals organisers, health assistants, and Balwadi teachers seem to be the major source of employment.

Women Heading Families

The phenomenon of women heading families is very rare in a patriarchal society. Women may head households under the circumstances of migration of the male head of the family to another place, widowhood, separation or destitution or divorce. In the case of handicapped male heads of families and of the men's unwillingness to work and contribute to the families, women take the responsibility of heading the families.[12] The rural women of Dindigul District also head families in such circumstances.

Women's Leadership

The political participation of rural women in Dindigul District was low prior to the PRIs election of October 1996. The one - third reservation of seats at all levels of PRIs has enabled the women to emerge as rural woman leaders. The efficacy of their leadership is yet to be assessed. Fatima Beebi, a rural woman leader in a village of Andhra Pradesh, has been acclaimed as one of the best rural women leaders by the UNO.[13] It is hoped that Fatima Beebi will be a torch-bearer to all rural women leaders in India.

Dindigul District, to its credit, has a very popular and dynamic rural woman leader, namely Mrs. A.S. Ponnammal. Mrs. Ponnammal hails not only from a tiny rural village, called Alaganpatti, but also from a *Harijan* community. Though educated only upto school level, she has achieved the credit of being the senior most member of the Tamil Nadu Legislative Assembly by virtue of her position as MLA. ever since the Independence of India with only a short break of a very few years. The dynamic leader Mrs. Ponnammal, who possesses all the requisites of leadership, is at present the MLA. of Nilakottai Constituency of Dindigul District and also the chairperson of the Nilakottai Panchayat Union.

SECTION II

Historical Background of PRIs

The village has always remained the most important unit of Indian social and economic life. It has naturally constituted the primary territorial unit of administration since very ancient times.[14]

Manu distinguishes three kinds of settlements-Village (Gram), Town (Pura) and City (Nagara). But even according to him, the village was a fundamental unit of administration.[15]

The importance of villages in Indian administration is attributable to the fact that the vast majority of the Indian population even now, 74.33 per cent according to the 1991 census, live in 5.6 lakh villages.[16]

Origin of Village Administration

From the earliest Vedic age the village administration was carried on under the village headman who was called the Gramini. He used to be the leader of the village. Generally, he was a nominee of the king. "The Graminini's post may have been sometimes hereditary and sometimes nominated or elective". [17]

In olden days every village was a republic. The village was governed by the Panchayat or Village Council.[18] The expression "Panchayat" is now understood all over India as an association of villagers selected for the purpose of village administration including the administration of justice. Why the number "five" (Panch) is stressed, cannot be stated with certainty. According to Prihaspathi, two, three or five persons shall be appointed to look after the welfare of the association (the village) and an association of five persons for this purpose may, perhaps have given rise to the expression "Panchayat".[19] The Greek Ambassador Megasthenes who visited the court of Chandragupta in 303 BC, describes village communities as rural units and little independent republics, aptly said to be self-contained and self-governed.[20]

During the Tamil Samgam period in Tamil Nadu (3rd century BC - 4th century AD), the residents of "Ur" (Village) met and transacted local government affairs through the Village Assembly called "Ur Mantram" or "Avai". The Sangam system of local government survived the Kalabhra Interregnum (3rd century - 6th century AD) and was revived during the Pallava-Pandya period (6th-9th century AD). The local government developed into a closely knit and integrated system during the golden age of the Cholas (9th - 13th century AD). Such a vibrant local government, however, declined, if not completely disappeared, under the Muslim and the Vijayanagar rule (14th- 17th century AD).[21]

Local Government in British India

When the British set foot in India they were solely interested in trading. So setting up Village Panchayats was not on their agenda. The British rulers were satisfied with the creation of local bodies of nominated members in the major towns. In 1688, the first Municipal Corporation was established in Madras with a Mayor and 12 Aldermen including several Portuguese and Indians. This body was empowered to levy taxes for building a guild hall and schools. Gradually, the sphere of activities of this corporation and similar bodies set up in other major towns and their taxation powers widened.

Lord Mayo's Resolution (1870)

In 1870, the Viceroy, Lord Mayo, passed a resolution for decentralisation of power to bring about administrative efficiency in meeting the demands of the people and also out of fiscal compulsion.

The Bengal Chowkidari Act (1870)

This Act marked the beginning of the revival of the traditional village panchayat system. The Act empowered district magistrates to set up Panchayats of nominated members in the villages to levy and collect taxes to pay for the chowkidars or watchmen engaged by them.

Ripon's Resolution (1882)

The resolution recommended that the smallest administrative unit the sub-division, taluka or the tahsils—should ordinarily be placed under a local board, two-thirds of whose membership was to be composed of elected representatives. Above the local boards, the Provincial Governments might create District Boards, with powers of co-ordination or control. The term of the members was to be for two years and compulsory retirement by rotation was to be provided for.

Royal Commission on Decentralisation (1909)

The Commission, after reviewing the working of the local and the District Boards in the various Provinces of the country, came to the conclusion that due chiefly to their unrepresentative character and inadequate powers, these bodies had not been a success.

The Commission recommended the creation of an electorate consisting of the members of the Village Panchayats, the provision for an elected majority on all boards and a due representation to minorities through nomination. They also recommended the formation of Village Panchayats and reconstitution of the local boards where they had been abolished so that the local-government might be built up from the bottom.

Montague-Chelmsford Report (1918)

The report put local self-government under the domain of Indian ministers in the Provinces. To make local self-government both fully representative and responsible, the report suggested that there should be complete popular control in local bodies.

Government of India Resolution (1918)

It accepted the principle of substantial elected majorities on all the boards. The elective principle was to be reinforced by the democratisation of the local electorate. The representation of minorities was to be secured by retaining the practice of nomination rather than by introducing some system of communal or proportional representation.

Post-Independence Development

Balwantrai Mehta Committee (1957)

The Committee felt that development cannot progress without responsibility and power being given to the community. It was with this objective that the committee recommended the early establishment of statutory elected local bodies and devolution to them of the necessary resources, power and authority. Therefore, in order to encourage people's participation and to overcome the defects of the Community Development Programme, PRIs came into being in almost all the States. These became the basic institutional apparatus through which socio-economic transformation of rural India was to be achieved. The committee was particular that women should find representation in the rural political institutions. Hence, it recommended the co-option of two women members to PRIs.

Ashok Mehta Committee (1977)

The Committee recommended the reorganisation of the Panchayati Raj bodies into two main tiers. It felt that the three tiers in vogue could continue for some more time, but, in the long run, only two tiers should take the responsibilities of local and regional development.

The Committee recommended that the Block should not be the first point of decentralisation. It should only have an executive committee of the Zilla Parishad to implement the development programmes formulated and approved by the Zilla Parishad. However, it added that, in some States where the Block is regarded as a decentralised unit closer to the people, it could continue as a transitional measure. In view of the fact that the then existing Village Panchayats were financially as well as leadership-wise weak, the Committee recommended the constitution of Mandal Panchayats.

The Committee also suggested that each Mandal Panchayat should be based around a service centre which would be a big village, a small town or central village accessible almost equally from all the other villages forming the Mandal Panchayat. The Committee further assessed that the inability of the PRIs to come up to expectation lay in their weak financial resources.

G.V.K. Rao Committee (1985)

At the initiative of the Planning Commission, this committee was appointed and it recommended a bold scheme of democratic decentralisation in which the district level body was to be of pivotal importance.

L.M. Singvi Committee (1986)

This Committee, formed at the instance of the Ministry of Rural Development, recommended the re-establishment of the nearly forgotten Gram Sabha, comprising all the inhabitants of a village, and called the embodiment of direct democracy.

The Committee wanted to vest PRIs with constitutional status and it also suggested the formation of Nyaya Panchayats for a cluster of villages.

Sarkaria Commission (1988)

This Committee did not favour the ideas of the L.M. Singvi Committee to confer constitutional status on the PRIs, but advocated that the power of enacting any law on Panchayats should vest exclusively with the States.

Constitutional Status

Sixty-fourth Constitution Amendment Bill (1989)

This Bill sought to make it obligatory for all the States to establish a three-tier system of panchayats at the village, intermediate and district levels. However, the States having a population of less than 20 lakh would not be obliged to establish panchayats at the intermediate level. The term of the panchayats was to be for five years and, in case of dissolution, they were to be reconstituted within six months.

Another significant provision stipulated that the Election Commission was to be responsible for the superintendence, direction and control of preparation of electoral rolls and the conduct of elections to the panchayats.

It also stipulated that all the seats in panchayats at all levels be filled up by direct elections. However, the State Legislature could provide for representation in the panchayats without voting rights of members of the Legislative Assembly.

As nearly as 30 per cent of the total number of seats to be filled by direct election in every Panchayat was to be reserved for women and allotted by rotation to different constituencies in a panchayat.

Seventy-second Amendment Bill (1991)

The Bill provided for the Constitution of the Gram Sabha. Gram Sabha means a body consisting of persons registered in the electoral rolls relating to a panchayat village. The Gram Sabha may exercise such powers as the Legislature of a State may provide it with. The Bill also provides that not less than one-third of the total number of seats to be filled by direct election in every panchayat shall be reserved for women and not less than one-third of the total number of offices of chairpersons in the panchayat at each level shall be reserved for women.

The term of the panchayats is for five years with a provision for reconstitution within six months if dissolved sooner. The Governor of a State shall as soon as, may be within one year, from the commencement of the Act, and thereafter at the expiration of every fifth year, constitute a Finance Commission.

The Act leaves it to the jurisdiction of the State Legislature to provide for the composition of the Commission, the qualifications and other details. In matters of elections, audit of accounts, imposition of taxes etc., the State Legislature has been empowered to make provisions.

The Lok Sabha passed the Bill on 22nd December 1992, while the Rajya Sabha passed it the following day. After the ratification by more than half of the State Assemblies, the President gave his assent on 20th April 1993. The Act was brought into force by a government notification on 24th April 1993 as the Seventy-third Constitution (Amendment) Act 1992.

Panchayat Raj Institutions in Tamil Nadu[22]

The structural pattern of Panchayati Raj adopted in Tamil Nadu and the functional arrangement-constitutional, financial, administrative etc. have undergone several transformations from time to time. Factors leading to the adoption of a particular pattern of Panchayati Raj in Tamil Nadu are traceable more to local conditions than to central directions.

Madras Municipal Corporation, 1688

Tamil Nadu has the unique distinction of having the earliest formed Municipal Corporation in the country. In 1688, a Municipality was established at Madras with a Mayor and twelve Aldermen, including several Portuguese and Indians.

Rural Local Government in the Madras Presidency (1864-1870)

Much attention was paid in the Madras Presidency to the revival and development of rural local bodies. In 1864, Lord Robert, the Madras Governor, replaced the exploiting local chieftains with a new class of district collectors. Distinguished collectors like Lionelplace, Col. Alexander Read, John Hodgsen and Sir Thomas Munro penetrated into the "impregnable mysteries" of the villages and found by experience that it was possible and advantageous to work through the indigenous institutions, reforming and adapting them to suit their ends. In particular, Thomas Munro, an ardent admirer of the Village Panchayat system, attempted to revive the system by a series of his Resolutions.

The Madras Local Boards Act 1884

With Ripon's Resolution on Local Self-Government, a network of local bodies came into existence. The Madras Local Boards Act V of 1884 provided for a three tier self-government system consisting of District Boards, Taluk Boards and Union Boards. The Madras Local Boards Act of 1920 gave an independent status to each class of local boards and eliminated the ex-officio official elements. The Madras Village Panchayats Act of 1920 was passed with the object of providing for the "administration of village by the villagers themselves, thereby developing the system of self-government in the rural areas". By 1920, the foundation for a three-tier system of local government was well laid with the Village Panchayat as the basic unit.

Madras Village Panchayats Act 1950

Inaugurating the Conference of Provincial Ministers on Local Self-government in 1948, the then Prime Minister Jawaharlal Nehru observed that "Local Self-Government is and must be the basis of any true system of democracy".

Article 40 of the Indian Constitution, which came into force in 1950, directs the States to "take steps to organise Village Panchayats to endow them to function as units of Self-government". The Madras Village Panchayats Act of 1950 was enacted in pursuance of this objective. Adult suffrage was introduced by the Madras Village Panchayat Act 1950. Seats were reserved for SC/ST and panchayats were given judicial powers. District Boards were formed. However, only a very little breakthrough was made between 1947 and 1957 when the Report of the Balwantrai Mehta Committee was published. The Balwantrai Mehta Committee (1957) suggested the integration of the Community Development Programme and the National Extension Service Scheme with a popularly elected democratic decentralised body scheme. This paved the way for the formation of a new three-tier Panchayati Raj — Panchayat at village level, Panchayat Union at the block level and Zilla Parishad at the district level.

While District Boards were abolished in 1957, District Development Councils were set up in all the districts by the District Development Council Act of 1958. The District Development Council's role was basically advisory in nature, with respect to both the local bodies and the government.

The Tamil Nadu Panchayat Act 1958-based on a White Paper of 1957-introduced a number of changes. All Panchayat Presidents were made members of the corresponding Panchayat Union Councils. This provided an organic link between the two tiers. The Inspector of Panchayats was given the power to co-opt at least one woman member to any panchayat body wherever there was none.

In 1981, an amendment was introduced which enabled the Inspector to nominate a woman member to every Village Panchayat. Fifteen per cent of the posts of Panchayat Presidents were also to be filled by women.

In 1989, an amendment was introduced to reserve thirty per cent of the total seats at the level of the Village Panchayat for women. In 1991, by another amendment it was stated that if women were not elected to these seats, women could be co-opted to ensure 30% representation in the Village Panchayats. Depending on the number of Village Panchayats in a Panchayat Union, a maximum of five seats were to be filled by women in the Panchayat Union Council. In addition, the Collector could nominate a maximum of two women to the Panchayat Union Council.

Local Body Elections in Tamil Nadu

After Independence, elections were held only four times to the local bodies in Tamil Nadu as per the Madras Panchayats Act 1958. The first elections were held in 1960 followed by the second in 1965 and the third in 1970. The next Panchayat elections were due in 1975. But they were not conducted under some pretexts. After an interval of 16 years, the Fourth Panchayat Elections in Tamil Nadu were held in 1986. Again the elections that were due in 1991 were put off due to various reasons. After the enactment of the Seventy-third Constitution (Amendment) Act 1992, the Village Panchayat elections in Tamil Nadu were conducted in October 1996 as per the Tamil Nadu Panchayat Act 1994.

Table 2.3 furnishes the details pertaining to the number of Village Panchayats, Panchayat Unions and District Panchayats together with the seats reserved for women (including SC/ST women) at all levels of the three-tier system in Tamil Nadu.

TABLE 2.3
DETAILS OF RESERVATION OF SEATS AND OFFICES OF PANCHAYATI RAJ INSTITUTIONS IN TAMIL NADU

No. of Offices	*Village Panchayats*	*Panchayat Unions*	*District Panchayats*	*Total*
1. Chairperson	12584	384	28	12996
2. Wards	40734	6499	648	47881
3. Membership in wards	97014	6499	648	104161
4. Reservation for SC in the office of chairperson	2951	88	6	3045
5. Reservation for ST in the office of chairperson	84	3	-	87
6. Reservation for women in the office of Chairperson	4244	98	8	4350
7. Reservation for SC in the office of ward member	23243	1532	156	24931
8. Reservation for ST in the office of ward member	857	55	7	919
9. Reservation for women in the office of ward member	32331	2351	182	34864

Source: State Election Commission, Chennai.

SECTION III

Profile of Dindigul District [23]

Dindigul District, comprising three revenue divisions, namely Dindigul, Palani and Kodaikanal and six taluks, namely Dindigul, Natham, Nilakottai, Kodaikanal, Palani and Vedasandur was established by bifurcating Madurai District through G.O. Ms. No. 640 (Revenue) dated 22nd April 1985. The new Dindigul District was inaugurated on 15.9.1985 with Dindigul as its Head quarters. The district is spread over an area of 6,480.18 square kilometres.

Dindigul was not conspicuous during the Pandya-Chola domination of Madurai. It assumed historical importance only with the advent of the Nayaks to Madurai. The strategic location of Dindigul between Madurai and Coimbatore was responsible for the contest between the Nawabs of the Carnatic, the Mysoreans and the British, which ultimately ended with its capture by the British.

Thadicombu, 10 km. north of Dindigul, was the first place to come under the rule of the British in Madurai District. It was ceded to the British by the King of Mysore in 1792. Mr. Alexander Macleod assumed charge as the first Collector of Dindigul and administered 18 palayams with Thadicombu as Headquarters. For a period of time Thadicombu was the Taluk Headquarters. But, with the passage of time, Dindigul became popular and was made the Taluk Headquarters

Dindigul Municipality

The Dindigul Municipality is one of the oldest Municipalities in Tamil Nadu. It was constituted on 1st November 1866. In the beginning, the Municipal Council consisted of the District Magistrate, the Local Magistrate and the Forest Range Officers as councillors. In addition to these, five ex-officio councillors were appointed. None of the Councillors was elected by the people.

After the Madras Local Boards Act of 1884, the number of Councillors in the Dindigul Municipality was increased to twelve. Their term of office was for three years. Three-fourths of the Councillors were elected by the municipal tax payers. The Chairman was the executive head of the Municipality. He was elected by the Councillors and appointed with the permission of the government. The District Collector was entrusted with the

Fig. 2.2

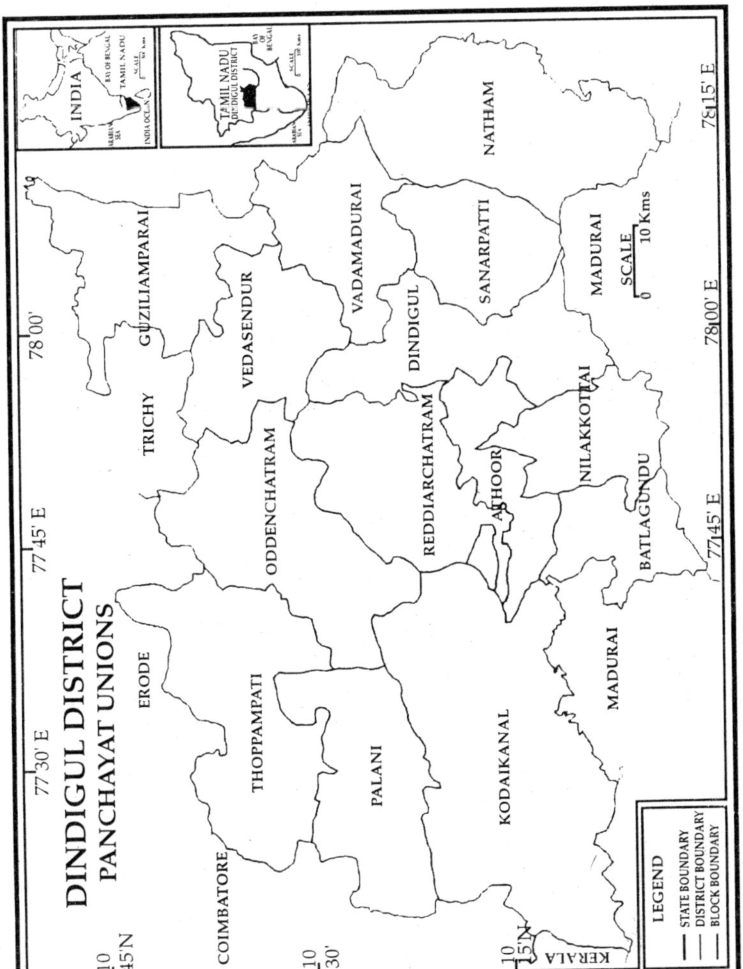
DINDIGUL DISTRICT
PANCHAYAT UNIONS
INDIA
TAMIL NADU
DINDIGUL DISTRICT
NATHAM
VADAMADURAI
SANARPATTI
GUZILIAMPARAI
VEDASENDUR
DINDIGUL
MADURAI
SCALE
0 10 Kms
TRICHY
ODDENCHATRAM
REDDIARCHATRAM
NILAKKOTTAI
ATHOOR
BATLAGUNDU
ERODE
THOPPAMPATI
PALANI
KODAIKANAL
MADURAI
COIMBATORE
KERALA
LEGEND
STATE BOUNDARY
DISTRICT BOUNDARY
BLOCK BOUNDARY
77 30' E
77 45' E
78 00'
78 00' E
78 15' E
77 45' E
10 45'N
10 30'
10 15'N

powers of supervision and control over the activities of the council. Mr. Gabriel Stokes was the first elected Chairman of the Dindigul Municipality. He was elected on 1st March 1885.

Dindigul Municipality During Freedom Struggle and After

The Dindigul Municipal Council passed a resolution on 21st December 1921 supporting the Non-cooperation Movement launched by Mahatma Gandhi. During the Civil Disobedience Movement, Dindigul Municipality unanimously passed a resolution in support of the Dandi March and the Vedaranyam March.

When the Quit India Movement was launched by Mahatma Gandhi in 1942, the Dindigul Municipal Council passed a resolution in support of the movement and, in consequence, the British Government ordered the suspension of the Dindigul Municipal Council for six months.

After Independence, Dindigul emerged as an important town in Tamil Nadu. It was classified as a city on 13th June 1951. Dindigul Municipality celebrated its centenary in 1966. In 1977 Dindigul Municipality was declared a first grade Municipality.

Statistical Profile of Dindigul District

The data pertaining to administrative set up, population, educational institutions and literacy rate in Dindigul District are furnished hereunder:

TABLE 2.4
ADMINISTRATIVE SET-UP

Sl.	*Units of Administration*	*Number*
1.	Revenue Divisions	3
2.	Development Divisions	2
3.	Taluks	6
4.	Municipalities	3
5.	Town Panchayats	24
6.	District Panchayat	1
7.	Panchayat Unions	14
8.	Village Panchayats	306
9.	Villages	358
10.	Hamlets	2607

Source: S.V. Irudiyaswami, **Know Your District - Dindigul Anna District,** Kodaikkanal : Alluvalar Manamakil Mantram, 1966, p. 9.

Note: Dindigul District was for some time called Dindigul Anna District.

TABLE 2.5
POPULATION OF DINDIGUL DISTRICT (CENSUS 1991)

Particulars	*Male*	*Female*	*Total*
Population	890783	869818	1760601
Rural	699122	684458	1383580
Urban	191661	185360	377021
Literate	546720	344354	891074
Electorate	661849	660175	1322054

Source: Statistical Hand Book of Tamil Nadu 1991, Statistical Section, Collector's Office, Dindigul.

TABLE 2.6
AREA, SEX RATIO AND DENSITY OF POPULATION IN DINDIGUL DISTRICT - 1991

Particulars	*All India*	*Tamil Nadu*	*Dindigul District*
Area in Sq km	3287263	130058	6480.18
Sex Ratio	929	974	976
Density per Sq km	257	429	271

Source: Tamil Nadu—An Economic Appraisal 1994-95, Government of Tamil Nadu, Madras.

TABLE 2.7
EDUCATIONAL INSTITUTIONS IN DINDIGUL DISTRICT

Sl.	*Category of Institutions*	*Number*
1.	Universities	2
2.	Arts Colleges	6
3.	Engineering Colleges	2
4.	Polytechnics	4
5.	Industrial Training Institutes (ITI)	3
6.	Higher Secondary Schools (Govt.)	15
7.	Higher Secondary Schools (Private)	21
8.	High Schools (Govt.)	40
9.	High Schools (Private)	15
10.	Middle Schools	172
11.	Primary Schools	1088

Source: Statistical Hand Book of Tamil Nadu, 1991 and Statistical Section, Collector's Office, Dindigul.

TABLE 2.8
LITERACY PROFILE

Sl.	Particulars	Dindigul Dt*	Tamil Nadu**	All-India**
1.	Male Literate	56.68	67.2	64.1
2.	Female Literate	43.94	42.8	39.3
3.	Urban Literate	77.3	78.0	73.0
4.	Rural Literate	52.01	54.6	44.7

Source:* Annual Credit Plan Document for Dindigul Anna District (1994-95). Tamil Nadu—An Economic Appraisal 1994-95, Government of Tamil Nadu, Madras.

**1. Centre for Monitoring Indian Economy, Basic Statistics Relating to the Indian Economy: September 1993, Mumbai, October 1993.

2. Centre for Monitoring Indian Economy: India's Social Sectors, February 1996, Mumbai, March 1996.

Agriculture and Land Use

The total geographical area of Dindigul District is 508016 ha. and net cultivable area is 274707 ha. Out of the net area sown, as low as 9% is sown more than once. Dry farming is predominant in the district and the important wet land tract is located in the Shanmuganathi and Kodaganar basin. Paddy is the principal crop (37%) followed by oil seeds (23%), and, fruits and vegetables (24%).

The Sirumalai and the Virupatchi Hills are known for a special variety of plantains. Fruits like orange, lime, mango and grapes are specialities in Dindigul, Nilakottai and Palani Taluks. Cole crops, potato and temperate fruits grow chiefly in Kodaikanal Hills. The lower plains of Kodaikanal Hills yield coffee and cardamom.

Irrigation

About 29% of the net area sown is irrigated. Wells form the chief source of irrigation followed by tanks. There are 78429 wells to provide irrigation to 59923 ha. Palar-Porandalar, Kodaganar and Manjalar schemes are important irrigation schemes. Canals irrigate 12310 ha. Tank irrigation covers 13234 ha.

Industries

Next to farming, a sizable section of the population in Dindigul District depends on industries. Dindigul is an important industrial centre. A number of spinning mills are located in Vedasandur and Vadamadurai Panchyat Unions, Besides a few paper mills, tobacco and cigar, metal, dyes and iron industries are also found in this district.

Dindigul District has thriving cottage handloom and other industries at Chinnalapatti, which is located 11 km from Dindigul Town. Chinnalapatti art silk sarees and *sungudi* (cotton) sarees are famous throughout India. More than 1000 families are engaged in these industries. In addition, khadi industry (spinning, weaving and dyeing) is promoted by Gandhigram in a big way.

References

1. M. Robin (ed.), **Sisterhood is Powerful**, New York: Random House, 1970.; and Callestine Nare, **Women Power: The Movement for Women's Liberation,** New York: Tower Publications, cited in Kiran Saxena, "Empowerment of Women: The Indian Context", **The Indian Journal of Political Science,** Vol. 55, No. 4, October - December 1994, p. 391.
2. Amarjit Kaur, "Aspirations, Concerns and Perceptions", in **Convention of Women Employees,** Salem: Canara Bank Employees' Union State Committee Tamil Nadu, 23 November, 1996, p. 26.
3. Swami Dayananda Saraswathi, **Sathyartha Prakash** (Light of truth), trans Shri. Durga Prasad, New Delhi: Jan Gyan Prakashan, 1970, p. 105.
4. Maitrayee Choudhri, **Women's Movement: Reform or Revival,** Delhi: Radiant, 1993, pp. 137-163.
5. Shashi S. Narayana, "Gender Equality through Reservation in Decision-Making Bodies", **Social Action**, Vol. 45., No. 2, April-June, 1998, p. 147.
6. Pratima Asalana, **Women's Movement in India**, Delhi: Vikas Publishers, 1994, cited in Keeran Saxena, *Op. cit.*, pp. 391-400.
7. Government of India, Committee on Plan Projects, Report of the Team for the Study of Community Projects and National Extension Service,Vol.1, 1957, pp. 45-52.
8. R.S.Rajput, and D.R. Maghe, **Panchayati Raj in India:Democracy at Grassroots**, New Delhi: Deep and Deep Publications, 1984, p. 236.
9. Government of India, National Perspective Plan for Women 1988-2000 A.D., Ministry of Human Resource Development, of Women and Child Welfare, **Report of the Core Group**, New Delhi: Akashdeep Printers,1988, p. 4; Government of India, Committee on Plan Projects, *Op. cit.*, p. 47.
10. Robert Orr Whyte and Pauline whyte, **The Women of Rural Asia,** Colorado, USA: West View Press, 1982, p. 137, cited in P. Manikayamba, **Women in Panchayati Raj Structures,** New Delhi: Gian Publishing House, 1989, p. 19.

11. Shramshakti: **Report of the National Commission on Self-Employed Women and Women in the Informai Sector,** June, 1988, in Handbook of Policy and Related Documents on Women in India, New Delhi: National Institute Public Co-operation and Child Development, 1988, p. 97.
12. Government of India Ministry of Human Resource Development, *Op. cit.*, p. 7.
13. UN Awards Women Sarpanch "**Indian Express,** September, 29, 1998, p. 9; S. Gopinath Reddy, Prestigious UNDP award for A.P. Women", **Indian Express,** October, 2, 1998, W. Chandrakanth, "A Becon Light for the Poor," **The Hindu,** Sunday, October, 25, 1998, p. 24.
14. Venkatarangaiah and Pattabhiram, **Local Government in India: Select Readings,** NewDelhi: Allied Publishers,1969; Rajeswar Dayal, **Panchayati Raj in India,** Delhi: Metropolitan, 1970; S.K. Dey, **Panchayati Raj: A Synthesis,** Bombay: Asia Publishing House, 1961; H.D. Lakshmi Narayan, **Democracy in Rural India: Problems and Process,** New Delhi: National,1980; B. S.Bhargava, "Panchayati Raj: Power to the People" **Kurukshetra,** Vol. XXXVI, No. 3, December, 1987.
15. A.K. Majumdar, and Bhanwar Singh, (eds.), **Historical And Conceptual Development of Panchayati Raj,** New Delhi: Radha Publications, 1997, p. 37.
16. Center of Monitaring Indian Economy Basic Statistics Relation, **The Indian Economy,** Vol. 1, All India, 1990. Registrar General of India 1991, **Final Population Total Paper - 2** of 1992.
17. A.K. Majumdar, and Banwar Singh, *Op. cit.*, p. 39.
18. *Ibid.*, p. 41.
19. **Report of the Study Team on Nyaya Panchayats,** New Delhi: Government of India, 1962, p. 6.
20. A.K. Majumdar and Banwar Singh, *Op. cit.*, p. 42.
21. G. Venkatesan, **Local Self Government in India,** Madurai : Indira Pathipagam, 1982, p. 7.
22. S. Saraswathi, **The Madras Panchayat System: A Historical Survey,** Vol.1, Delhi: Impex India, 1973; A.K. Majumdar and Banwar Singh, (ed.) *Op. cit.*; G. Palanithurai, (ed.) Caste Politics and Society in Tamil Nadu, Delhi: Kanishka Publishers, 1994; B.S. Bhargava, and V. Venkatakrishnan, Panchayati Raj in Tamil Nadu, in G. Palanithurai (ed.), *Ibid.* pp. 199-233; M.Arulselvam, **Tamil Nadu Panchayats And Municipal Laws,** Vol.1 Madras: Malathi Publications, 1994; Committee on Plan Projects, **Report of the Team for the Study of Comunity Projects and National Extension Service,** loc. cit.; M. Venkatarangaiya and M. Pattabhiraman, *Op. cit.*
23. **Annual Credit Plan Document for Dindigul Anna District,** (1994-95), Dindigul: Canara Bank; S.V. Irudayaswami, **Know Your District-Dindigul Anna District,** Kodaikanal: Aluvalar Manamakil Mandram, 1966; Village Immersion Programme — India A World Bank Programme, **Profile of Dindigul District Booklet III**, Gandhigram: Gandhigram Rural Institute, 1998.

Three

Socio-Economic Status of Women Leaders

A leader is a person, whose guidance and direction are supposed to be accepted by the rest of the people in the community. Leadership signifies a blend of personal traits of the leaders and the social setting in which they are placed. A leader is basically a human being and is related to other human beings through different sets of relationships.[1] Sociologists[2] have described social mobility to be highly dependent on the social circumstances of the individual. The social background of the leaders not only manifests the ascriptive status and, style of life but also the capacity of the leaders to attain and sustain power. In ascription-oriented societies, such as India, the socio-economic status of an individual is relevant in determining the nature and pattern of leadership.

In this context, this chapter is devoted to the analysis of the socio-economic background of rural women leaders, specifically to find out whether the socio-economic correlates like age, caste, religion, education, occupation, income, land holdings and assets have any significant role in determining the emergence of rural women as leaders in the Village Panchayats of Dindigul District.

Age

Age is one of the determining factors in the emergence of leadership, particularly that of village leadership.[3] Age not only relates to the physical and mental make-up of an individual but also serves as an index of the individual's experience, awareness and wisdom in general. Traditionally, age is considered an important factor in respect of one's status and prestige, particularly in rural societies; it was once the privilege of the older people to occupy the various key positions in the villages.[4] Age is quite significant to a leader for whom both experience and maturity are essential in role performance.[5] All the same, it is also true that, in the context of multi-dimensional problems in the development process and strange inequalities and disparities, it is only the young and energetic leadership, which can deliver the goods. Though the rural leadership still continues to be dominated by the aged, empirical studies indicate that the installation of young leaders is on the increase in Panchayats.[6]

Table 3.1 shows that 43.2 per cent of both the elected and the defeated respondents belong to the age group of 31-40 years, 36.4 per cent are in the age group of 21-30 years, 15.1 per cent are from the age group of 41-50 years and only 5.3 per cent come under the age group of 51-60 years. The analysis of the data indicates that 79.6 per cent of the respondents belong to the age group of 21-40 years.

TABLE 3.1
DISTRIBUTION OF RESPONDENTS BY AGE

Sl. No.	*Age Group (in years)*	*Respondents*					
		No. Elected		*Defeated*		*Total*	
		No.	*%*	*No.*	*%*	*No.*	*%*
1.	21-30	43	40.2	32	32.3	75	36.4
2.	31-40	43	40.2	46	46.5	89	43.2
3.	41-50	15	14.0	16	16.2	31	15.1
4.	51-60	6	5.6	5	5.1	11	5.3
	Total	107	100.0	99	100.0	206	100.0

Source: Computed.
Mean age of the women leaders : 34.4 years.

This finding is also supported by the study of George Mathew,[7] which indicated the emergence of younger women as leaders in Village Panchayats. This finding has been further substantiated by the study of V.B. Athereya and K.S. Rajeswari,[8] which found that the provision of reservation for women in local bodies has led to 83.0 per cent young women (21-40 years) emerging as leaders.

Three reasons can be attributed to the phenomenon of many young women emerging as leaders. The first reason, may be the reduction in the age limit of voters from 21 to 18 years possibly resulting in the phenomenon of "youth choosing the youth".

Fig. 3.1: Age of Respondents : A Comparative Analysis

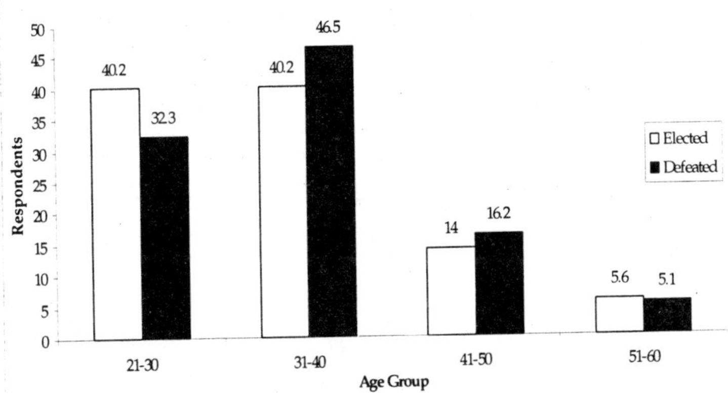

The second reason may be the fact that the aged rural women are more orthodox and prestige-conscious than their younger counterparts and will not easily bow down before persons inferior to them in social status for the sake of getting votes.

The third reason may be the fact that the aged rural women do not possess physical and psychological strength to compete with young rural women in hectic election activities.

Thus the new political culture pushing back the old belief that higher age signifies maturity and knack of solving ticklish problems has brought young rural women to the forefront in the emergence of leadership.

Caste

The Indian social system is dominated by castes and their specific status.[9] Caste prescribes one's status and a person knows from birth his position in the social ranking system. In traditional rural societies, leadership has been a monopoly of the high caste Hindus and the big landlords.[10] It is therefore necessary to understand whether the leadership institutionalised in high caste groups has been modified by the new political order and factors like the introduction of statutory Panchayats, the provision for one-third reservation of seats for women and the provision for party-free and direct elections to the Village Panchayats.

TABLE 3.2
DISTRIBUTION OF RESPONDENTS BY CASTE

Sl. No.	Caste	Respondents					
		Elected		Defeated		Total	
		No.	%	No.	%	No.	%
1.	FC	-	-	1	1.0	1	0.5
2.	BC	68	63.5	62	62.6	130	63.1
3.	MBC	14	13.1	11	11.1	25	12.1
4.	SC/ST	25	23.4	25	25.3	50	24.3
	Total	107	100.0	99	100.0	206	100.0

Source: Computed.

Table 3.2 indicates that 63.1 per cent of the respondents belong to Backward Communities, 24.3 per cent hail from SC/ST Communities, 12.1 per cent are from Most Backward Communities and only 0.5 per cent are from Forward Community.

It is evident that the present rural power structure is dominated by the Backward Community people. It is observed from the data that only one respondent belongs to the Forward Community (Brahmin Caste) and she too was defeated, while one SC woman has emerged as elected leader from a Village Panchayat reserved for women in the general category.

The analysis reveals that 63.1 per cent of the respondents who have emerged as rural women leaders in Dindigul District are from backward communities with numerical dominance.[11] This finding reinforces the observations of Anil Bhatt[12] that the leadership is moving to the numerically dominant groups and castes from the monopoly of high caste Hindus and big landlords. This finding is also corroborated by the conclusion of M.N. Srinivas[13] that usually the leaders of the locally dominant castes form the bulk of the leadership in panchayats. The studies undertaken by different scholars have reached the same conclusion in this regard.[14]

Fig. 3.2: Communities of Respondents : A Comparative Analysis.

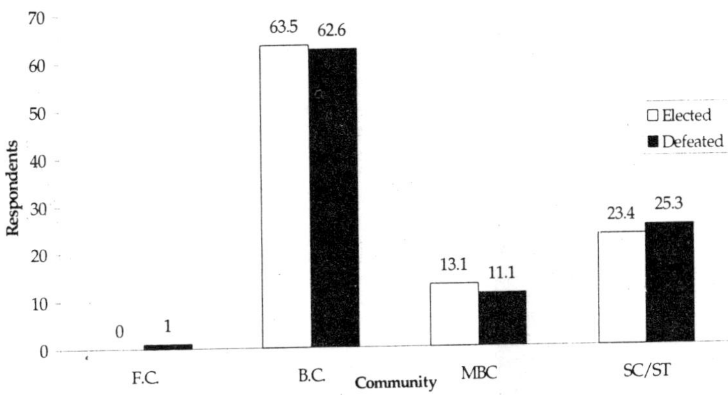

Religion

Like caste, religion has its share in the emergence of rural leadership. Most of the village panchayats under study have a predominant Hindu population. Only very few Panchayats have a sizable population of other religions, namely Christianity and Islam.

Table 3.3 shows that 89.3 per cent of the respondents profess the Hindu faith, while 9.2 per cent are Christians and 1.5 per cent are Muslims. The Christian and Muslim respondents have emerged as leaders only in villages dominated by Christians and Muslims. This finding is substantiated by the observation of Chandra Pal Singh[15] and B.N. Ghosh[16] that Muslims take leadership roles wherever they are of sizable proportion in the village. It is, therefore, apparent that religion and caste play the same role in that their numerical dominance determines the leadership.

TABLE 3.3
DISTRIBUTION OF RESPONDENTS BY RELIGION

Sl. No.	Religion	Respondents					
		Elected		Defeated		Total	
		No.	%	No.	%	No.	%
1.	Hindu	95	88.8	89	89.9	184	89.3
2.	Muslim	3	2.8	-	-	3	1.5
3.	Christian	9	8.4	10	10.1	19	9.2
	Total	107	100.0	99	100.0	206	100.0

Source: Computed.

Fig. 3.3: Religion of Respondents : A Comparative Analysis.

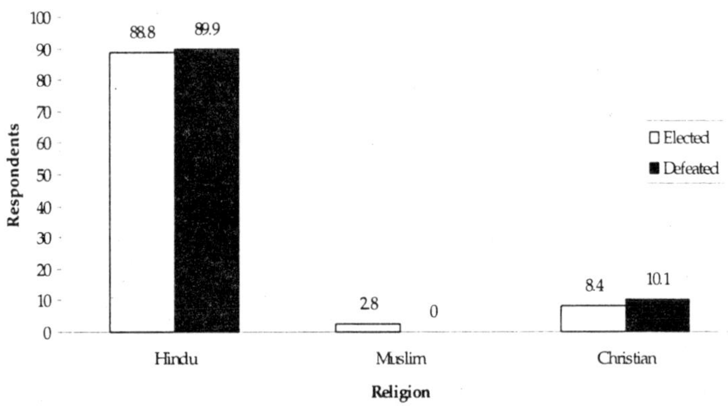

Education

In any developing society education plays a key role in the sharing of power and the shaping of the leadership pattern. Traditionally literacy and leadership were not associated with each other.[17] Education fosters all-round development in man - body, mind and soul. It is the fundamental basis for effective socio-political participation.[18] It is only education that can synthesise and crystallise values based on social justice and egalitarianism in a pluralistic society like India.[19] It is an important instrument of political socialisation and seeking active participation of the people.[20] Against this backdrop it becomes imperative to analyse the level of education achieved by the respondents and the heads of their families.

TABLE 3.4
DISTRIBUTION OF RESPONDENTS BY EDUCATION

Sl. No.	*Educational Level*	*Respondents*					
		Elected		*Defeated*		*Total*	
		No.	*%*	*No.*	*%*	*No.*	*%*
1.	Illiterate	2	1.9	-	-	2	0.9
2.	Primary	16	15.0	22	22.2	38	18.4
3.	Secondary	60	56.1	59	59.7	119	57.8
4.	Higher Secondary	13	12.1	10	10.1	23	11.2
5.	Diploma	4	3.7	4	4.0	8	3.9
6.	College	12	11.2	4	4.0	16	7.8
	Total	107	100.0	99	100.0	206	100.0

Source: Computed.

Fig. 3.4 : Educational Level of Respondents : A Comparative Analysis.

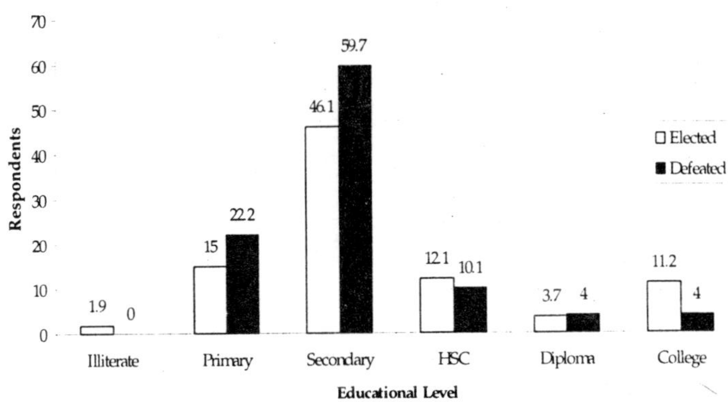

Table 3.4 classifies the respondents according to their levels of education. Out of the 206 respondents, 57.8 per cent are found to have studied up to the secondary level, 18.4 per cent up to the

primary level, 11.2 per cent up to the diploma level, and, 7.8 per cent have studied up to college level, while 0.9 per cent are illiterate.

It is apparent that 99.1 per cent of the respondents are literate and 80.7 per cent have studied beyond the primary level of education. This finding is supported by the observations of V.B. Athereya[21] and B.N. Ghosh.[22] With this educational background, the rural leaders have to implement the developmental schemes of village panchayats and redress the grievances of local people through proper decision-making.

Education of Family Heads of Respondents

One's education lays foundation for the progress of one's generation as a whole. If the head of a family is educated, naturally his/her family members get enough opportunities to develop themselves educationally and hence in all respects. In this context, the educational level achieved by the family heads of the respondents may have an impact on the pattern of the emergence of rural women leadership. Therefore, it is worthwhile to analyse the educational background of family heads of the respondents.

It is evident from Table 3.5 that 38.8 per cent of the family heads of the respondents are educated up to the secondary level of education, 24.8 per cent up to the higher secondary level, 22.3 per cent up to the college level, 6.8 per cent up to the diploma level, and, 5.3 per cent up to the primary level, while 2.0 per cent are illiterate.

TABLE 3.5
DISTRIBUTION OF RESPONDENTS BY EDUCATION OF FAMILY HEADS

Sl. No.	*Level of Education*	*Respondents*					
		Elected		*Defeated*		*Total*	
		No.	*%*	*No.*	*%*	*No.*	*%*
1.	Illiterate	1	0.9	3	3.0	4	2.0
2.	Primary	5	4.7	6	6.1	11	5.3
3.	Secondary	38	35.5	42	42.4	80	38.8
4.	Higher Secondary	27	25.2	24	24.2	51	24.8
5.	Diploma	5	4.7	9	9.1	14	6.8
6.	College	31	29.0	15	15.2	46	22.3
	Total	107	100.0	99	100.0	206	100.0

Source: Computed.

Fig. 3.5: Education of Family Heads of Respondents : A Comparative Analysis.

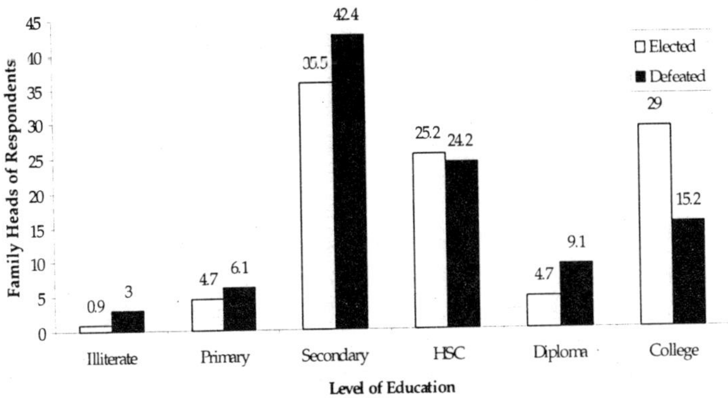

Since 92.7 per cent of the heads of families under the present study have studied up to the secondary level and beyond, they may be able to direct and guide their rural women in the right track of leadership.

Occupation

Occupation is another factor influencing the rural power structure. People spend most of their lifetime on their bread - winning task. Besides being a source of income, the occupation of a person determines the style of life and the class status of that person.[23] The competence, skill and knowledge required for the occupation are considered prestigious sources of leadership. One's occupation significantly influences one's socio-political values and ideology.[24] Occupation is not only important in the distribution of status and prestige, but also a good measure of socio-economic mobility.[25]

As agriculture is the predominant occupation in villages, naturally agriculturists are in large number among the rural leaders. Nevertheless, the presence of business people, traders, retired government employees and even agricultural coolies in villages also contributes to the emergence of rural leadership. Generally the rural womenfolk do not involve directly in the occupations mentioned above, but they assist their male counterparts in an indirect way, mainly remaining as housewives. The housewives may can afford to utilise their leisure time to serve the Village Panchayats.

Table 3.6 reveals that 68.5 per cent of the respondents are housewives as against 15.5 per cent of agriculturists, 8.3 per cent are government servants retired from service, and 7.7 per cent are agricultural coolies.

In Indian society, only men are traditionally expected to be the bread-winners of the family through their occupations and the women are supposed to look after the domestic chores, helping now and then their husbands in their respective occupations. In the context of a rural society, this is more true, and this fact is substantiated by the finding of Dilip K.Gosh,[26] that the majority of the respondents remain only housewives.

TABLE 3.6
DISTRIBUTION OF RESPONDENTS BY OCCUPATION

Sl. No.	*Occupation*	*Respondents*					
		Elected		*Defeated*		*Total*	
		No.	*%*	*No.*	*%*	*No.*	*%*
1.	Agricultural Coolie	2	1.9	14	14.1	16	7.7
2.	Agriculture	17	15.9	15	15.2	32	15.5
3.	Retired Government Servant	15	14.0	2	2.0	17	8.3
4.	Housewife	73	68.2	68	68.7	141	68.5
	Total	107	100.0	99	100.0	206	100.0

Source: Computed.

The housewives are familiar with and directly affected by problems like scarcity of drinking water, dearth of educational, sanitation, child welfare and streetlight facilities and the like. So the respondents, 68.5 per cent of whom are housewives, can focus all their attention on identifying local grievances and getting them redressed using their office as Village Panchayat chiefs.

Fig. 3.6: Occupation of Respondents : A Comparative Analysis.

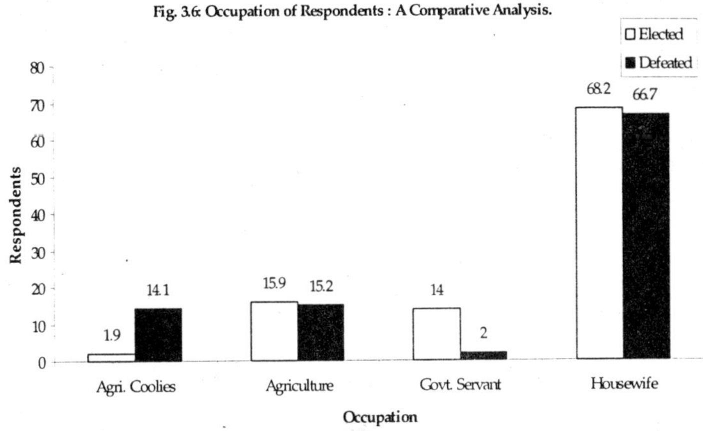

Occupation of Family Heads of Respondents

The reservation provision in the new Panchayati Raj Act has opened new avenues for the emergence of rural women as leaders. However, the new women entrants to panchayat leadership are only novices requiring the guidance and encouragement of their family heads. In this context, the occupations of the family heads have a key role in shaping the leadership pattern of rural women.

TABLE 3.7
DISTRIBUTION OF RESPONDENTS BY OCCUPATION OF FAMILY HEADS

Sl. No.	Occupation	Respondents					
		Elected		Defeated		Total	
		No.	%	No.	%	No.	%
1.	Agricultural Coolie	6	5.7	18	18.2	24	11.7
2.	Agriculture	35	32.7	13	13.1	48	23.3
3.	Business	18	16.8	31	31.3	49	23.4
4.	Government Servant	24	22.4	18	18.2	42	20.3
5.	Agriculture and Business	24	22.4	17	17.2	41	19.9
6.	Govt. service and agriculture	-	-	2	2.0	2	1.0
	Total	107	100.0	99	100.0	206	100.0

Source: Computed.

Table 3.7 reveals that 55.9 per cent of the family heads of the respondents are agriculturists, or agriculturists-cum-businessmen, agricultural coolies or government servants engaged in agricultural operations as well, 44.1 per cent are either purely businessmen or government servants. It is therefore evident that the majority of the rural women leaders have emerged from agricultural families, which is also substantiated by the findings of Dilip K. Gosh[27] and George Mathew.[28]

Fig. 3.7: Occupation of Family Heads of Respondents : A Comparative Analysis.

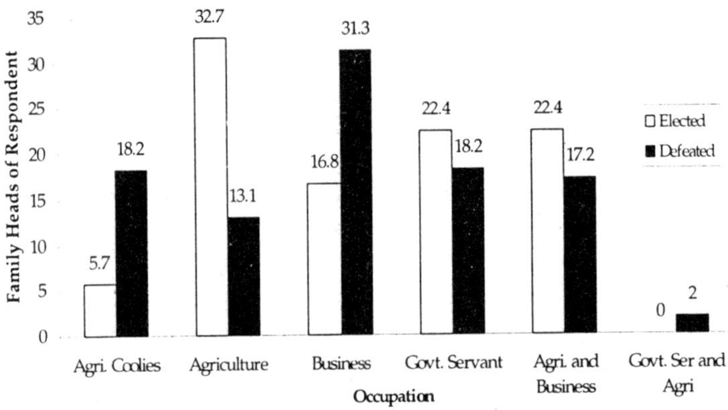

Annual Income

Annual income, yet another important determinant of village leadership, has a bearing on the pattern of emerging rural women leadership. The economic status of a rural woman is one of the sources of her social status. As a matter of fact, in the rural scenario, it is the rich who contest and emerge as leaders in local elections. Contesting the election itself is a costly affair which poor people cannot afford to do. Economically privileged have good opportunities to emerge as leaders besides influential persons who are respected, followed and obeyed by villagers because of their wealth, family, caste and other reasons.[29]

It is a hard task to gather correct data regarding the economic status of persons in villages. The data in Table 3.8 were collected from the respondents and they were later counter-checked with the responsible local informants.

Table 3.8 categorises the respondents into six groups on the basis of the annual income of their families. The Table indicates that 59.2 per cent of the respondents have an annual income of Rs. 61,000/- and above.

TABLE 3.8
ANNUAL INCOME OF RESPONDENTS' FAMILIES

Sl. No.	*Income Group (in '000)*	*Respondents*					
		Elected		*Defeated*		*Total*	
		No.	*%*	*No.*	*%*	*No.*	*%*
1.	Up to 20	5	4.6	15	15.2	20	9.7
2.	21-40	12	11.2	19	19.2	31	15.1
3.	41-60	16	15.0	17	17.2	33	16.5
4.	61-80	31	29.0	26	26.2	57	27.7
5.	81-100	16	15.0	10	10.1	26	12.6
6.	Above 100	27	25.2	12	12.1	39	18.9
	Total	107	100.0	99	100.0	206	100.0

Source: Computed.

Fig. 3.8: Annual Income of Respondents : A Comparative Analysis.

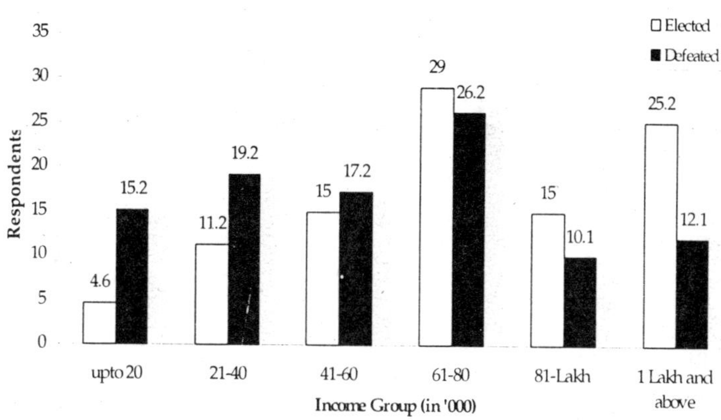

It is observed that 9.7 per cent of the respondents belong to the annual income group of Rs. 20,000/- and below. An annual income of Rs. 61,000/- and above is considered high for any village family. On the basis of this estimation, 59.2 per cent of the respondents can be said to have emerged from sound economic strata of the rural communities.

Land Holdings

Land is the most important possession, the principal recognised wealth and it is also closely linked with power over man.[30] Land ownership is a crucial factor in establishing dominance. M.N. Srinivas has pointed out that three conditions normally facilitate the dominance of a caste - considerable stretches of cultivable land, numerical strength of the family and a high place in the local hierarchy.[31] Possession of land determines the socio-economic status of an individual and subsequently on the emergence of leadership. Land holdings is thus a basis of power structure and leadership in rural India.[32] Louis Dumont holds that territory, power and social dominance result from the possession of land.[33] The respondents of the present study are rural women living in the villages of Dindigul District. They depend upon land holding not only for their economic development, but also for their social status. Accordingly, this section is devoted to the analysis of the land holdings of the respondents.

TABLE 3.9
LAND HOLDINGS OF RESPONDENTS

Sl. No.	*Type of Land Holdings*	*Respondents*					
		Elected		*Defeated*		*Total*	
		No.	*%*	*No.*	*%*	*No.*	*%*
1.	River Irrigated	3	2.8	3	3.0	6	2.9
2.	Well Irrigated	43	40.2	39	39.4	82	39.8
3.	Dry	4	3.7	14	14.2	18	8.7
4.	River and well Irrigated	5	4.7	4	4.0	9	4.4
5.	Well Irrigated and dry	34	31.8	20	20.2	54	26.2
6.	River Irrigated and dry	2	1.9	4	4.0	6	2.9
7.	All the three Categories	1	0.9	-	-	1	0.5
8.	Landless	15	14.0	15	15.2	30	14.6
	Total	107	100.0	99	100.0	206	100.0

Source: Computed.

Fig. 3.9: Land Holding of Respondents : A Comparative Analysis.

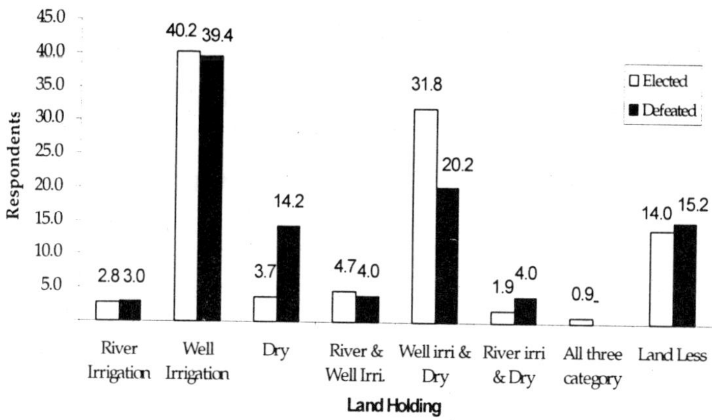

According to Table 3.9, 85.4 per cent of the respondents are in possession of land holdings of different categories as against 14.6 per cent of the respondents who are landless. The landless respondents may either be coolies or retired government servants or business people. The respondents with irrigated land holdings (76.7 per cent) enjoy better economic and social status and that has enabled them to emerge as leaders.

This finding is reinforced by the conclusion of D.C. Miglani[34] that the rural power structure is dominated by the agriculturists and landowners.

Assets

Assets include both movable and immovable properties. The immovable properties include land holdings, house buildings, house sites, industrial firms etc. The movable properties include four-wheelers, two-wheelers, modern household appliances, livestock etc. In the case of business people, the investment is taken into account for assessing the value of their assets. Land and house properties are symbols of prestige. One's total economic status is assessed on the basis of the overall value of all the assets. Besides social status, economic status is also significant to leadership because it determines the capacity to achieve as well as sustain power. Empirical studies have concluded that the leadership of the poorer and weaker sections is generally less effective.[35]

In this context, an analysis of the total value of all the assets of the respondents becomes relevant.

Table 3.10 shows that 62.6 per cent of the respondents have emerged from the asset group of Rs.6 lakh and above, which may be regarded as high asset value, while 37.4% of the respondents have emerged from the asset group of Rs.5 lakh and below:

TABLE 3.10
TOTAL ASSET VALUE OF RESPONDENTS

Sl. No.	*Asset Value (in Lakhs)*	*Respondents*					
		Elected		*Defeated*		*Total*	
		No.	*%*	*No.*	*%*	*No.*	*%*
1.	0 - 5	32	29.9	45	45.5	77	37.4
2.	6 - 10	22	20.6	20	20.2	42	20.4
3.	11 - 15	11	10.3	10	10.1	21	10.2
4.	16 - 20	15	14.0	12	12.1	27	13.1
5.	21 - 25	6	5.6	2	2.0	8	3.9
6.	26 -	21	19.6	10	10.1	31	15.0
	Total	107	100.0	99	100.0	206	100.0

Source: Computed.

Fig. 3.10: Asset Value of Respondents : A Comparative Analysis.

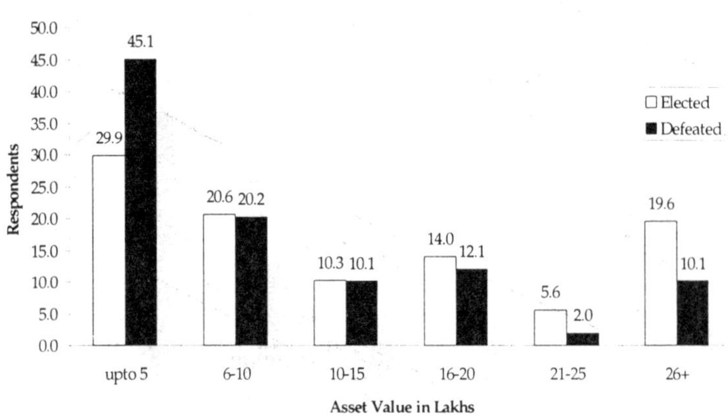

This finding is supported by the observation of N. Sivanna[36] that economically well-off sections of the society have a definite hold on the affairs of the local level administration.

Marital Status

Marriage is one of the social institutions cutting across religion, caste and culture and it is looked upon as a necessary and holy sacrament. Marriage is also an important status-giving device.[37] The institution of marriage enlarges the social boundary of an individual. It is a source of personal gratification as well as an extension of social relations and responsibilities.[38] In the process of achieving leadership, marital status helps a leader in identifying his political roles and in enlarging his support-base. Of course unmarried persons can devote more attention to the cause chosen by them. However, in Indian society widows are still viewed as inauspicious. Against this backdrop, the analysis of the marital status of the respondents is pertinent in relation to their emergence as leaders.

TABLE 3.11
MARITAL STATUS OF RESPONDENTS

Sl. No.	*Marital Status*	*Respondents*					
		Elected		*Defeated*		*Total*	
		No.	*%*	*No.*	*%*	*No.*	*%*
1.	Spinster	4	3.7	3	3.0	7	3.4
2.	Married and living with husband	100	93.5	91	92.0	191	92.7
3.	Widowed	3	2.8	4	4.0	7	3.4
4.	Deserted	-	-	1	1.0	1	0.5
	Total	107	100.0	99	100.0	206	100.0

Source: Computed.

It is apparent from Table 3.11 that 96.6 per cent of the respondents are married, 0.5 per cent are deserted and 3.4 per cent are widows, while 3.4 per cent are spinsters.

The finding drawn from the analysis is that only very few unmarried respondents are found involved in the process of the emergence of rural women leadership.

The emergence of 3.4 per cent widows as leaders in the Village Panchayats shows that villagers are becoming modernised to the extent of giving widows a chance to enter public life. This finding is supported by the observations of Ujwala S. Hiremath[39] in her study "Women in Grassroots Politics".

Family Size

Families can be classified into three groups according to their size: (1) ideal family (2+1), (2) small family (2+2) and (3) large family (2+3and above). All the three groups have their advantages and disadvantages in respect of the emergence of rural women as leaders.

TABLE 3.12
DISTRIBUTION OF RESPONDENTS BY FAMILY SIZE

Sl. No.	*Family Size*	*Respondents*					
		Elected		*Defeated*		*Total*	
		No.	*%*	*No.*	*%*	*No.*	*%*
1.	Ideal Family (2+1)	7	6.5	12	12.1	19	9.2
2.	Small Family (2+2)	43	40.2	55	55.6	98	47.6
3.	Large Family (2+3 and above)	57	53.3	32	32.3	89	43.2
	Total	107	100.0	99	100.0	206	100.0

Source: Computed.

Table 3.12 shows that 56.8 per cent of the respondents belong to either ideal or small families and 43.2 per cent to large families. It is further found that 9.2 per cent of the respondents are from ideal families and 9.08 per cent have a family of four members (2+2) and above.

Type of Family

The significance of the type of family as an influencing factor of leadership has been stressed in many studies. A member of a large family is assured of the support of the other members of the family. Joint family adds to the social prestige of the family and a member of a large family gets enough spare time for public activities. The inherited social position and the reputation of the joint family play an effective role in determining the leadership pattern. Besides, the behaviour and the achievement of the living members also determine the leadership of the other members.[40]

The type of family has a bearing on the perception of an individual in visualising social problems. In a joint family system, hierarchy is maintained. The influence of the elders on the decision-making process of the youth is unavoidable.[41] In the case of nuclear families, there will be only mutual influence of the spouses in the thought process. It is therefore very important to examine the type of family of the respondents and the consequent impact on the emergence of leadership.

TABLE 3.13
DISTRIBUTION OF RESPONDENTS BY TYPE OF FAMILY

Sl. No.	*Type of Family*	*Respondents*					
		Elected		*Defeated*		*Total*	
		No.	%	*No.*	%	*No.*	%
1.	Nuclear Family	67	62.6	69	69.7	136	66.0
2.	Joint Family	40	37.4	30	30.3	70	34.0
	Total	107	100.0	99	100.0	206	100.0

Source: Computed.

From the data in Table 3.13, it is obvious that 66.0 per cent of the respondents are from nuclear families. This observation is substantiated by the finding of C.P. Singh[42] that most of the rural leaders come from nuclear families. This fact may be attributed to the change in the social system in respect of family life.

Residence

In Indian polity, the "sons of the soil" concept is very much realised and applied in almost all the spheres where elections are held. This concept assumes importance based on the belief that only local leaders have easy accessibility, thorough understanding of the needs and issues of the people and natural self-interest in the development of their own electoral areas.

The residence of the contestants for the office of the Village Panchayat Presidents may be within or outside the respective Panchayat limits. Besides being daughters of the soil, the respondents with local residences may have more chances of achieving leadership than those having residences outside the Panchayat limits.

TABLE 3.14
DISTRIBUTION OF RESPONDENTS BY PLACE OF RESIDENCE

Sl. No.	*Place of Residence*	*Respondents*					
		Elected		*Defeated*		*Total*	
		No.	*%*	*No.*	*%*	*No.*	*%*
1.	Within the Panchayat	103	96.3	89	89.9	192	93.2
2.	Outside the Panchayat	4	3.7	10	10.1	6	6.8
	Total	107	100.0	99	100.0	206	100.0

Source: Computed.

Table 3.14 shows that 93.2 per cent of the respondents live within their Panchayat limits. This fact justifies the positive impact of local residence on the emergence of leadership. This finding is also supported by the observation of A.P. Barnabas[43] that length of residence and caste in the village are two important determinants of leadership.

Type of House

House not only signifies shelter and security against natural calamities, but also promotes the psychological gratification and social status of the dweller.[44] For the rural people, the type of house is a symbol of status. The leaders living in their traditional and palatial residences are more respected and hence an analysis of the type of the house of the leaders becomes relevant.

TABLE 3.15
DISTRIBUTION OF RESPONDENTS BY TYPE OF HOUSE

Sl. No.	*Type of House*	*Respondents*					
		Elected		*Defeated*		*Total*	
		No.	*%*	*No.*	*%*	*No.*	*%*
1.	Colony House	3	2.8	6	6.1	9	4.4
2.	Thatched House	2	1.9	8	8.1	10	4.8
3.	Tiled House	42	39.2	43	43.4	85	41.3
4.	Terraced House	60	56.1	42	42.4	102	49.5
	Total	107	100.0	99	100.0	206	100.0

Source: Computed.

Table 3.15 reveals that 90.8 per cent of the respondents live in terraced or tiled houses compared to 9.2 per cent living in thatched houses or in colony houses. The type of house is related to the economic conditions of the dwellers. It also tells upon the social status of the residents. In this sense, respondents living in terraced or tiled houses are found to have more opportunities to emerge as leaders.

Modern Facilities

Modern facilities include household appliances and transport and communication equipment possessed by the respondents. The possession of modern facilities reflects not only the prosperity but also the status of a person.

Table 3.16 indicates the standard of living of the respondents in terms of the modern equipment and appliances possessed by them. As many as 80.6 per cent of the respondents possess either colour TV or Black and White TV; while 71.4 per cent possess mixies; 70.4 per cent have grinders; 25.2 per cent possess refrigerators; 13.6 per cent have washing-machines; 71.8 per cent possess motorbikes; 24.3 per cent own telephones; and, 11.2 per cent possess cars.

TABLE 3.16
DISTRIBUTION OF RESPONDENTS BY POSSESSION OF MODERN FACILITIES

Sl. No.	*Modern Facilities*	*Respondents*					
		Elected		*Defeated*		*Total*	
		No.	*%*	*No.*	*%*	*No.*	*%*
1.	Colour TV	45	42.1	36	36.4	81	39.3
2.	Black and White TV	42	39.2	43	43.4	85	41.3
3.	Mixie	84	78.5	63	63.0	147	71.4
4.	Grinder	79	73.8	66	66.7	145	70.4
5.	Refrigerator	30	56.1	22	22.2	52	25.2
6.	Washing Machine	21	19.6	7	7.0	28	13.6
7.	Motorbike	84	78.5	64	64.6	148	71.8
8.	Car	18	16.8	5	5.1	23	11.2
9.	Telephone	25	23.4	25	25.3	50	24.3

Source: Computed.
Elected N =107; Defeated N = 99; Total N = 206.

From the above findings, it is concluded that the respondents of the current study are availing themselves the facility of Televisions more than of the other facilities. Thus, the majority of the respondents have a broader base for political socialisation, which, in turn, may facilitate their political participation. The possession of these modern facilities also gives a status to the respondents and hence facilitates the emergence of their leadership.

Leadership vis-a-vis Socio-Economic Status

The emergence of rural women leadership cannot be measured on the basis of a single influencing factor. The collective impact of multiple socio-economic factors like age, caste, education, occupation, annual-income, land holdings, assets, marital status, type of family, size of family, type of house, place of residence and possession of modern facilities is vital in determining the emergence of leadership and hence it deserves an in-depth analysis.

The respondents of the study are classified into three categories according to their socio-economic status as low (status), medium (status) and high (status).[45]

Testing of Hypothesis

Hypothesis 1: "The socio-economic status is a significant factor in determining rural women leadership".

In statistical terms, the hypothesis means that there is a significant relation between socio-economic status scores and the votes polled by the respondents in the Village Panchayat elections.

TABLE 3.17
LEADERSHIP VIS-A-VIS SOCIO-ECONOMIC STATUS

Votes Polled	*Socio-Economic Scores*			
	Low	*Medium*	*High*	*Total*
Defeated (0-49)	32 (32.3)	54 (54.6)	13 (13.1)	99 (48.1)
Elected (50-100)	16 (15.0)	66 (61.7)	25 (23.3)	107 (51.9)
Total	48 (23.3)	120 (58.3)	38 (18.4)	206 (100)

Source: Computed.
Note: Figures in the parentheses show percentages.

Fig. 3.11: Socio-Economic Status Scores of Respondents : A Comparative Analysis.

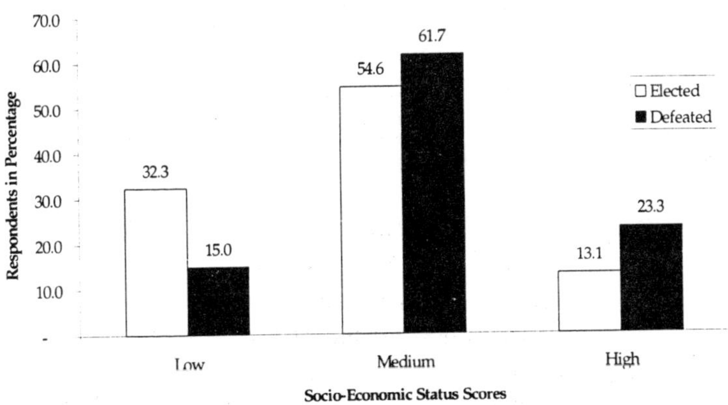

Table 3.17 shows that 85 per cent of the elected respondents belong to medium or high socio-economic status groups as against

67.7 per cent of the defeated respondents belonging to the medium and high status groups. It is also observed that 15.0 per cent of the elected respondents belong to the low socio-economic status group compared to 32.3 per cent of the defeated respondents coming under the same group.

The statistical analysis brings out the fact that the votes polled and the socio-economic status scores secured by the respondents are significantly associated with each other.

$$(\chi^2 = 10.03 \text{ ; D.F.} = 2; P < 0.01)$$

This inference leads to the conclusion that the hypothesis 1, namely "The socio-economic status is a significant factor in determining rural women leadership", is affirmatively validated.

Summary

The present chapter has analysed the emergence of rural women leadership in relation to the Village Panchayats by taking into account the multiple determinants characterising the Village Panchayat power structure. The age, caste, religion, education, marital status, type of family, size of family and place of residence have been analysed as social correlates of leadership. Emergence of rural women leadership has also been analysed in the light of the economic correlates such as occupation of respondents, occupation of family heads, annual income and total assets which include the money value of land holdings, house properties, household appliances, livestock, machinery and other implements. The collective impact of socio-economic determinants on the emergence of rural women leadership has also been statistically tested.

The main findings drawn from the analysis may be enumerated as hereunder:

1. Regarding the age of the respondents, 79.6 per cent belong to the younger age group (21-40 years) with the average age being 34.4 years. This is a clear pointer to the emergence of young rural women as leaders in the Village Panchayats of Dindigul District.
2. Regarding the community, 63.1 per cent of the respondents belong to the Backward Communities with numerical dominance. This establishes the conclusion that numerical dominance of different castes determines the emergence of leadership in Village Panchayats.

3. Regarding the religion, 89.3 per cent of the respondents are Hindus and the rest are either Christians or Muslims. As the dominant caste determines the emergence of rural leadership, so does the dominant religion.
4. Regarding education, 99.1 per cent of the respondents are literate, with 7.8 per cent having studied up to college level.
5. The heads of the families of the respondents also have more or the same levels of education as the respondents. However, 22.3 per cent of them have studied up to college level.
6. Regarding marital status, 96.6 per cent of the respondents are married, 0.5 per cent are deserted, 3.4 per cent are widowed and 3.4 per cent are spinsters.
7. Regarding residence, 93.2 per cent of the respondents reside within their Panchayat limits. Regarding type of houses, 49.5 per cent of the respondents are found to live in terraced houses. It is also found that 66.0 per cent of the respondents belong to nuclear families and 56.8 per cent to small families.
8. As for the occupation, 68.5 per cent of the respondents are housewives assisting the heads of their families and 7.7 per cent are agricultural coolies.
9. Regarding annual income, 59.2 per cent of the respondents belong to the annual income group of Rs. 61,000/- and above. These respondents may be said to have emerged from the sound economic strata of rural communities.
10. In respect of land holdings, 85.4 per cent of the respondents have land holdings. While 76.7 per cent of the respondents have lands with irrigation facilities, 8.7 per cent have only dry lands.
11. Concerning assets, 62.6 per cent of the respondents belong to the asset group of Rs. 6 lakh and above. Wealth of Rs.6 lakh and above is considerably high in rating in the context of the Indian rural economy and hence the inference that wealth has its contributory role in the emergence of leadership.
12. In respect of modern facilities, the families of 80.6 per cent of the respondents possess TV, while 24.3 per cent have telephones and 11.2 per cent own cars.
13. The statistical analysis of the socio-economic status of the respondents as contributing to the emergence of leadership has affirmatively established that the socio-economic status

is a significant factor in determining rural women leadership. However, the mere presence of socio-economic status alone will not ensure the emergence of leadership. The emergence of leadership will be achieved only when it is initiated with political background. Hence the following chapter is devoted to the study of the political background of the rural women leaders.

References

1. Trueman, et.al., "United Senator and the Class Structure", in H. Eulau, S.J. Eldesrweld and M. Janowitz, (ed.), **Political Behaviour—A Reader in Theory and Research.,** Delhi: Amerind Publishers Pvt. Ltd., 1972, p. 184.
2. S.M. Lipset, and R. Bandix, **Social Mobility in Industrial Society,** Berkeley and Loss Angels: University of California Press, 1959, pp. 63-64; C.A. Anderson, "Skeptical Note on the Relation of Vertical Mobility to Education", **American Journal of Sociology,** Vol. LXVI, No. 5, March, 1961, pp. 560-70; R. Stalcup, **Educational Sociology,** U.S.A: Mersill and Co., 1967, pp. 7-17; M.N. Srinivas, **India's Villages,** Bombay: Asia Publishing House, 1960, p. 2.
3. H.C. Srivastava, **Dysfunctional Para-politics and Elite Action in India,** Varanasi: Bhartiya Vidhya Prakashan, 1967, p. 27; S.N. Mishra, **Pattern of Emerging Leadership in Rural India, Patna:** Associated Book Agency, 1977, p. 110.
4. B.S. Bhargava, **Grass Roots Leadership: A Study of Leadership in PRIs,** New Delhi: Ashish Publishing House, 1979, p. 31 ; S.R. Mehta, **Emerging Pattern of Rural Leadership,** New Delhi: Wiley Eastern Private Limited, 1972, p. 80.
5. B.S. Bhargava, **Emerging Leadership in Panchayati Raj System: A Study in a District of Rajasthan,** Bangalore: Institute of Socio Economic Change, 1977, p. 107; Dhan Singh Yadhave, **Grass-Roots Leadership-Jackhod and Deoroda-in Surajgarh Block, District Jhun Jhuna of Rajasthan,** M.A Dissertation Unpublished, Pilani: Department of Social Studies, B.L.T.S, 1973; N.R. Inamdar, **Functioning of Village Panchayats,** Bombay: Popular Prakashan, 1970; N. Patnaik and H.D. Laxminarayan, **"Functional Politics in Village India",** Man in India, Vol. 49, No. 2, August-September, 1969, p. 177.
6. D.R. Singh, **Rural Leadership Among Scheduled Castes,** Allahabad: Chugh Publications, 1985, p. 30.
7. George Mathew, "Will Reservation Ensure Participation?", **Social Welfare,** Vol. 42, No. 5-6. August-September, 1995, pp. 32-35, 37.
8. V. B. Athereya, K. S. Rajeswari, **Women's Participation in Panchayati Raj: A Case Study from Tamil Nadu,** Sponsored by the National Commission for Women Co-ordinated by the Center For Development Studies and Action, Chennai: M.S. Swaminathan Research Foundation, 1998, p. 13.

9. Talcott Parsons, **The Social System,** New York: The Free Press of Glencoe, 1964.
10. M.N. Srinivas, "The Dominant Caste in Rampura", **American Anthropologist,** Vol. 61, No. 1, 1959, p. 61; F.G. Bailey, **Caste and the Economic Frontier,** Bombay: Oxford University Press, 1958, p. 191; D.N. Majumdar, and *et al.*, "Inter-caste Tensions", in A.R. Desai, **Rural Sociology in India,** (ed.), Bombay: Popular Prakashan, 1969, p. 399; Andre Beteille, **Caste: Old and New,** Bombay: Asia Publishing House, 1969, pp. 208-211.
11. Opinionated Statement given by the respondents at the time of data collection and counter checked with local informants.
12. Anil Bhatt, "Dominant Caste and Political Process", in **Dimensions of Social Change,** (eds.), M.N. Srinivas *et al.*, New Delhi: Allied Publishers, 1977. pp 297-319.
13. M.N. Srinivas, **Caste in Modern India and other Essays.** Bombay: Asia Publishing House, 1962. M.N. Srinivas defines "Dominant Caste" thus "A Caste may be said to be dominant when it preponderates numerically over the other castes, and when it also wields preponderant economic and political power. A large and powerful caste group can be more easily dominant if its position in the local caste hierarchy not too low". "The Dominant Caste in Rampura", **American Anthropologist,** Vol. 61, 1959, p. 1.
14. Andre Beteille, **Cast, Class and Power,** Bombay : Oxford University Press, 1969; D.R. Singh, **Rural Leadership Among Scheduled Caste,** *Op. cit.* p. 29.
15. Chandra Pal Singh, **Dimensions of Rural Leadership,**New Delhi:Anmol Publications, 1991, p. 51.
16. B.N. Ghsh, **Rural Leadership and Development,** New Delhi: Mohit Publications, 1996, p. 72.
17. Rajeswar Dayal, **Panchayati Raj in India,** New Delhi : Metropolitan Book Company Pvt. Ltd, 1970, p. 247.
18. Mumtaz Ali Khan, **Scheduled Castes and Their Status in India,** New Delhi: Uppal Publishing House, 1980, p. 46.
19. S.K. Goyal, The Study of Scheduled Caste Students of College Eastern U.P", **Research Project** Sponsored by Indian Council of Social science Research, New Delhi 1973-74, p. 9.
20. Khan, Mumtaz Ali, Loc. cit.
21. V.B. Athereya, and K.S. Rajeswari, *Op. cit.*, p. 14.
22. B.N. Ghosh, *Op. cit.*, p. 74.
23. R.M. MacIver, and C.H. Page, **Society: An Introductory Analysis,** London:Macmillan, 1967, p. 390.
24. Murphy and Moris, "Occupational Status Subjective Social Class Identification and Political Affiliation", **American Sociological Review,** Vol. 26, May, 1961, p. 383.
25. S.K. Goyal, *Op. cit.*, p. 116.
26. Dilip K. Gosh, "Grassroots Women Leaders; Who are they? A Study in West Bengal District", **Journal of Rural Development**, Vol. 16, No. 2, April-June, 1997, pp. 291-311, Hydrabad: NIRD.
27. Dilip K. Gosh, *Ibid.*, p. 305.

28. George Mathew, *Op. cit.*, p. 34.
29. H.S. Dhillon, **Leadership and Group in South Indian Village,** P.E.O., New Delhi: Planning Commission, 1955, p. 115.
30. Louis Dumont, **Homo Hierarchicus,** Bangalore: Vikas Publication, 1966, p. 126.
31. M.N. Srinivas, **Social Change in Modern India,** Berkely: University of California Press, 1966, pp. 12-13.
32. D.R. Singh, *Op. cit.*, p. 39.
33. Louis Dumont, *Op. cit.*, p. 153.
34. D.C. Miglani, **Politics and Rural Power Structure,** New Delhi: Deep and Deep Publications, 1993, p. 181.
35. S.R. Mehta , **Emerging Pattern of Leadership in Rural India,** Patna: Associated Book Agency, 1977; K.D. Gangrade, **Emerging Patterns of Leadership-Comparative Study of Leadership and Social Structure,** Delhi: Rachana Publications. p. 244; S.N. Mishra, **Pattern of Emerging Leadership in Rural India,** Patna: Associated Book Agency, 1977; D.R. Singh, *Op. cit.*, p. 49-50.
36. N.Sivanna, **Panchayati Raj Reforms and Rural Development,** Allahabad: Chugh Publications, 1990, p. 93.
37. H.S. James, "Marriage as Status Achieving Device", **Sociology and Social Research,** 29 September-October, 1944, p. 132.
38. K.M. Kapadia, **Marriage and Family in India,** London: Oxford University Press, 1966, p. 104.
39. Ujwala S. Hiremath, "Women in Grassroots Politics", **Social Welfare,** Vol. 44, No. 2, May, 1997, p. 12.
40. M.E. Opler and R.D. Singh, "Economic Political and Social Change in North Central India", **Human Organisation,** Vol. II, No. 2, Summer 1952.
41. Palanithurai,G., **Peoples Perception of Politics: An Indian Perspective,** Delhi: Kanishka Publications, 1995, p. 21.
42. Chandra Paul Singh, *Op. cit.*, p. 54.
43. A.P. Barnabas, "Who are the Village Leader?",**Kurukshetra** Vol.6, No. 5, 1958, pp. 385-389.
44. V. Hole, "Social Effects of Planned Housing", **The Town Planning Review,** Vol. 25, No. 2, July, 1959, p. 163-73.
45. The grouping of the elected and the defeated leaders into different S.E.S. groups is made on the basis of the composite scores assigned to the influencing factors of leadership. In order to obtain the composite socio-economic score, the seven determinants of leadership namely caste, education, occupation, Heads education and occupation, annual income and total assets are taken into consideration. The composite scores are obtained with the help of a linear unweighted sum of the ranks given to each category within each of the variables.

Four

Political Background of Women Leaders

The leaders in the village are the change agents of the society. Their understanding and perception of the political system will enhance the functioning of the rural polity.[1]

The political involvement of the citizens is a *sine-quo-non* for every political system and it is the principal means by which consent is granted or withdrawn in a democracy making the rulers accountable to the ruled.[2] Political participation is the extent to which individuals are involved at various levels in the political system.[3] An individual's social environment comprises diverse elements that will prevail on the nature and extent of that individual's political participation. The most important among these diverse elements are sex, age, education, occupation, income, residence, mobility, religion, race and group influence.[4] The success of democracy depends upon the levels of political awareness and political participation by the members in the society and polity.

The socio-economic variables produce only "distal" effect and as such do not automatically assure a person power and influence in proportion to his base values such as respect, status and wealth.[5] Factors like pattern of party affiliation, media of political socialisation, political links, length of active political life, etc. go a long way in determining influence and resource potential of political actors.[6] To achieve political leadership, the base values of the political actors need to be manipulated along with political participation characterised by factors like age of political awareness, age of entering politics, sources of political inspiration, pattern of party affiliation, political positions and political ambitions. This chapter, therefore, proposes to analyse the political background of the respondents based on the aforesaid political factors.

Age of Attainment of Political Awareness

Awareness means having knowledge or being conscious about something. Hence the term "Political Awareness" implies the knowledge possessed by a person with regard to political institutions, political parties, political leaders, elections and election procedures, political system, and the various activities of the government. The political awareness is a prerequisite for a person's effective political participation. The efficacy of leadership depends upon the level of political awareness of the leaders. Political awareness once attained may stimulate political interest and hence motivate the political entry of the individual. In this context, it becomes pertinent to look into the age at which the respondents attained their political awareness.

TABLE 4.1
AGE OF ATTAINING POLITICAL AWARENESS BY RESPONDENTS

Sl. No.	*Age Group*	*Respondents*					
		Elected		*Defeated*		*Total*	
		No.	*%*	*No.*	*%*	*No.*	*%*
1.	16-20	42	39.3	24	24.2	66	32.0
2.	21-25	41	38.3	48	48.5	89	43.2
3.	26-30	24	22.4	27	27.3	51	24.8
	Total	107	100.0	99	100.0	206	100.0

Source: Computed.

The data in Table 4.1 reveal that 43.2 per cent of the respondents became aware of politics at the age of 21-25 years, 24.8 per cent became aware of politics at the age of 26-30 years, and, 32.0 per cent have attained political awareness during their teenage period (16-20 years).

The inference drawn from the analysis is that political awareness has been acquired by 75.2 per cent of the respondents even while they were below 25 years of age. This is an encouraging trend presaging for their future effective political participation.

Age of Entering Politics

The age of entering politics is a key variable which helps to study the trend of politicisation among persons of different age groups.[7] The distribution in Table 4.2 relates to the different age groups in which the respondents entered politics.

Table 4.2
Age of Entering Politics by the Respondents

Sl. No.	*Age Group*	*Respondents*					
		Elected		*Defeated*		*Total*	
		No.	*%*	*No.*	*%*	*No.*	*%*
1.	21-30	46	43.0	33	33.3	79	38.3
2.	31-40	43	40.2	49	49.5	92	44.7
3.	41-50	14	13.1	12	12.1	29	12.6
4.	51-60	4	3.7	5	5.1	9	4.4
	Total	107	100.0	99	100.0	206	100.0

Source: Computed.

The data in Table 4.2 indicate that 83.0 per cent of the respondents entered politics when they were less than 40 years of age as against 4.4 per cent who entered politics at the age of 51 years and above. A study by Manu Basker[8] has found that 63.0 per cent of the women began to participate in political activities when they were between 26 and 40 years of age. The respondents, being rural women, did not have many opportunities for participating in active politics. The hitherto politically inactive respondents entered politics through Village Panchayat elections under the one-third reservation provision. However, the majority (83.0 per cent) of them entered politics in the age group of 21-40 years.

Sources of Inspiration for Political Interest

The culture of a social group does not die with the extinction of the existing members of the group. Indeed, one of the salient features of culture is its intergenerational continuity. It is a continuum, on the strength and willingness on the part of the new members of the group. The willingness, however, is not a matter of rational choice on the part of the individuals, but it is a matter of learned behaviour.[9]

Political interest is the first and foremost psychological component of political participation. It not only reflects the commitment and attachment of the political actor to the state and polity, but also expresses their will to participate in and understand the complexities of the state and polity. Such political interest does not arise by itself normally, but it is inculcated in persons through extraneous sources.

The political actors assume their roles on the motivation and inspiration of some one behind them. The role played by them mainly depends upon the nature and source of their political inspiration. Accordingly, a search for the different sources of inspiration for the political interest of the respondents is pertinent.

TABLE 4.3
SOURCES OF INSPIRATION FOR POLITICAL INTEREST OF RESPONDENTS

Sl. No.	*Source*	*Respondents*					
		Elected		*Defeated*		*Total*	
		No.	*%*	*No.*	*%*	*No.*	*%*
1.	Family	20	18.8	20	20.2	40	19.4
2.	Mass media	4	3.7	13	13.0	17	8.3
3.	Political party	4	3.7	5	5.1	9	4.4
4.	Family and Mass media	50	46.7	42	42.4	92	44.7
5.	Family and Political Parties	3	2.8	5	5.1	8	3.9
6.	Political party and Mass media	-	-	5	5.1	5	2.4
7.	All the three Sources	26	24.3	9	9.0	35	16.9
	Total	107	100.0	99	100.0	206	100.0

Source: Computed.

Table 4.3 shows that family and Mass Media have jointly been the source of inspiration for political interest in respect of 44.7 per cent of the respondents whereas the family alone has played this role in respect of 19.4 per cent of respondents. It is also found that the family, Mass Media and the political parties have cumulatively been the promoters of political interest for 16.9 per cent of the respondents. The comparative analysis of different sources responsible for imbibing political interest reveals that the family and Mass Media have played a key role. It is concluded that political parties as sources of inspiration for the respondents are less effective. This may be due to the gender factor of the respondents.

Party Affiliation

Women in Indian polity evince less interest in affiliating themselves to any political party because of their preoccupation with domestic functions. Yet, a few may have interest for public activities under the influence of their politicalised family heads. Political affiliation and consequent subscription to certain ideologies definitely have much to do with the involvement and efficacy of political leaders. Hence the political affiliations of the respondents have to be studied in the light of the political affiliations of the male heads of their families.

The data in Table 4.4 reveal that the family heads of 76.7 per cent of the respondents have affiliation with political parties. It is observed that family heads of 27.2 per cent of the respondents are affiliated to the DMK, 21.8 per cent to the AIADMK, 13.6 per cent to the TMC party and 9.7 per cent to the Congress(I) party. It is also found that the family heads of 1.5 per cent of the respondents owe allegiance to the CPI, 0.9 per cent to the MDMK, and, 0.5 per cent each to the BJP, the CPI(M), the PMK and the DK.

It is, therefore, apparent that the largest number (42.8 per cent) of the family heads of the respondents are affiliated to the DMK or its allies (TMC, CPI and CPI(M)) at the time of the Village Panchayat elections held in October 1996.

TABLE 4.4
PARTY AFFILIATION OF FAMILY HEADS OF RESPONDENTS

Sl. No.	*Political Party*	*Respondents*					
		Elected		*Defeated*		*Total*	
		No.	*%*	*No.*	*%*	*No.*	*%*
1.	DMK	42	39.3	14	14.1	56	27.2
2.	AIADMK	12	11.2	33	33.3	45	21.8
3.	TMC	15	14.0	13	13.1	28	13.6
4.	CONG(I)	8	7.5	12	12.1	20	9.7
5.	CPI	-	-	3	3.0	3	1.5
6.	CPI(M)	1	0.9	-	-	1	0.5
7.	MDMK	1	0.9	1	1.0	2	0.9
8.	BJP	1	0.9	-	-	1	0.5
9.	PMK	1	0.9	-	-	1	0.5
10.	DK	-	-	1	1.0	1	0.5
11.	No-party Affiliation	26	24.3	22	22.2	48	23.3
	Total	107	100.0	99	100.0	206	100.0

Source: Computed.

Positions in Political Parties

A person's membership of or sympathy for a political party is an important indicator to understand the pattern of the person's political career.[10]

TABLE 4.5
POSITIONS HELD BY RESPONDENTS IN POLITICAL PARTIES

Sl. No.	*Position*	*Respondents*					
		Elected		*Defeated*		*Total*	
		No.	*%*	*No.*	*%*	*No.*	*%*
1.	Office-bearers	2	1.9	2	2.0	4	1.9
2.	Member	22	20.5	20	20.2	42	20.4
3.	No Position	83	77.6	77	77.8	160	77.7
	Total	107	100.0	99	100.0	206	100.0

Source: Computed.

The data in Table 4.5 indicate that only 1.9 per cent of the respondents are office-bearers of political parties, followed by 20.4 per cent holding only membership in political parties, and, 77.7 per cent are not even members of any political party.

It is apparent that an almost equal number of the defeated respondents (20.2 per cent) and the elected respondents (20.5 per cent) hold membership in political parties. As for positions as office-bearers in political parties, the respondents lag very far behind, perhaps in view of the existing Indian rural social setting and gender differentiation.

If political leaders come forward with an attitudinal change to enroll women as members and office-bearers as well in their political parties by making special reservation, the situation may change favourably.

Positions in Political Parties Held by the Family Heads

Indian women are still confined mostly to domestic functions and the heads of the families are, almost in all cases, only males. The heads of the families, as males, have more opportunities than the women to associate themselves with political parties. The political involvement of the family heads plays a major role in the emergence of leadership of the respondents.

TABLE 4.6
POSITIONS IN POLITICAL PARTIES HELD BY FAMILY HEADS OF RESPONDENTS

Sl. No.	*Position*	*Respondents*					
		Elected		*Defeated*		*Total*	
		No.	*%*	*No.*	*%*	*No.*	*%*
1.	Office-bearer	27	25.2	20	20.2	47	22.8
2.	Member	54	50.5	57	57.6	111	53.9
3.	No Position	26	24.3	22	22.2	48	23.3
	Total	107	100.0	99	100.0	206	100.0

Source: Computed.

It is evident from Table 4.6 that 22.8 per cent of the family heads of the respondents are office-bearers in their respective political parties at village or district levels. It is further found that 23.3 per cent of the family heads are simply non-political as against 76.7 per cent being political either as members or office-bearers in some political party or other. The findings of Table 4.6 support the general perception that men participate more actively in politics than women.

In general, the emergence of leadership in any political system is made easier by the political affiliation and subsequent political activities of the individuals concerned. However 77.7 per cent (see Table 4.5) of the respondents are found to have achieved their emergence as rural women leaders despite their non-political status. This phenomenon may be attributed to the reservation provision adopted in the Village Panchayat elections held in October 1996 on non-party basis.

Participation in Political Activities

Political participation is a complex phenomenon. It denotes a series of voluntary political activities[11] which have a bearing on the political process. "Political process" refers to the activities of people in various groups as they struggle for and use power to achieve personal or group purposes.[12] Lester Milbrath[13] puts these voluntary political activities under the following three categories: "Gladiatorial activities", "Transitional activities" and "Spectator activities." Gladiatorial activities include holding party offices, fighting the elections as party candidates, raising party funds, attending party meetings and joining the party campaigns. Transitional activities include attending party meetings as party supporters or sympathisers or just as neutrals, but attentive listeners, making contributions to party funds and coming in contact with public officials or party personnel. Spectator activities refer to voting, influencing others to vote, making and joining political discussions, exposing oneself to political stimuli and wearing a button or showing a sticker representing one's party.

Political participation is classified into two types-active and passive political participation. The more active forms of involvement include formal enrollment in a political party, canvassing and registering voters, speech-making, working in campaigns and competing for public and party offices.[14] An analysis of the nature of involvement in political activities by the heads of families of the respondents is relevant in the context of the emergence of respondents' leadership.

TABLE 4.7
NATURE OF PARTICIPATION IN POLITICAL ACTIVITIES OF FAMILY HEADS OF RESPONDENTS

Sl. No.	Political Activities	Respondents								
		Elected			Defeated			Total		
		In-active	Active	V. Active	In-active	Active	V. Active	In-active	Active	V. Active
1.	Voting in General Elections	-	-	107 (100)	-	22 (22.2)	77 (77.7)	-	22 (10.7)	184 (89.3)
2.	Attending Party Co-nferences and Meetings	2 (1.8)	69 (64.5)	36 (33.7)	12 (12.1)	72 (72.7)	15 (15.2)	14 (6.8)	141 (68.4)	51 (24.8)
3.	Participating in Party Protest Activities	24 (22.4)	74 (69.2)	9 (8.4)	42 (42.4)	50 (50.5)	7 (7.1)	66 (32.0)	124 (60.2)	16 (7.8)
4.	Electioneering work	19 (17.8)	67 (62.6)	21 (19.6)	26 (26.3)	60 (60.6)	13 (13.1)	45 (21.8)	127 (61.7)	34 (16.5)
5.	Raising Funds	62 (57.9)	25 (23.4)	20 (18.7)	60 (60.6)	16 (16.2)	23 (23.2)	122 (59.2)	41 (19.9)	43 (20.9)
	Total	107 (20.0)	235 (43.9)	193 (36.1)	140 (28.3)	220 (44.4)	135 (27.3)	247 (24.0)	455 (44.2)	328 (31.8)

Source: Computed.

Table 4.7 shows that 44.2 per cent of the family heads of the respondents are active in all five political activities under consideration as against 24 per cent being politically inert and 31.8 per cent being very active.

Fig. 4.1: Nature of Political Participation of Family Heads : A Comparative Analysis.

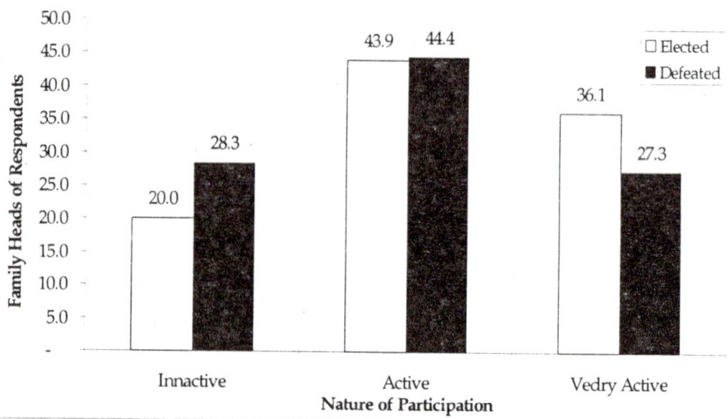

A comparative analysis of the nature of participation of the family heads reveals that the family heads of the elected respondents are politically more active than the family heads of the defeated respondents. The findings of Table 4.7 leads to the conclusion that the active political participation of the family heads tells upon the emergence of leadership of the respondents.

Stimulants for Political Participation

Political equality is one of the cardinal principles of democracy as it provides for equal opportunity to all citizens of the country to play their role in the nation's decision-making process. The right to contest in elections is one of the fundamental rights enshrined in India's Constitution. Women, because of gender disparity, experience discrimination by the society in terms of denial of equal access to the power structure.[15] The decision of women to participate in political activities in general and to contest the elections in particular is very much influenced by the perception of their families.[16] This is more so in the case of women in rural Indian polity. Nevertheless, the Seventy-third Amendment of the Constitution and the corresponding changes in the Panchayati Raj legislation providing one-third mandatory reservation for women has paved the way for greater political participation of rural women.

Despite the facilitating provision of reservation, rural women have to be motivated and encouraged towards political participation by the members of the society.

In this context, it becomes worthwhile to analyse the stimulants responsible for the political participation of the respondents.

TABLE 4.8
STIMULANTS FOR POLITICAL PARTICIPATION OF THE RESPONDENTS

Sl. No.	*Stimulants*	*Respondents*					
		Elected		*Defeated*		*Total*	
		No.	*%*	*No.*	*%*	*No.*	*%*
1.	Family Members	19	17.8	59	59.6	78	37.8
2.	Personal Interest	33	30.8	15	15.2	48	23.3
3.	Request of the Villagers	48	44.9	23	23.2	71	34.5
4.	Political Parties	7	6.5	2	2.0	9	4.4
	Total	107	100.0	99	100.0	206	100.0

Source: Computed.

The data in Table 4.8 shows that 37.8 percent of the respondents have been prompted by their family members towards political participation, 34.5 per cent have participated in politics at the request of the general public in their respective villages, and, 23.3 per cent involved themselves in politics of their own accord. It is also found that only 4.4 per cent of the respondents participated in politics stimulated by political parties. Similar findings are found in the study of Snehalata Panda,[17] which concluded that women entered politics due to the persuasion of their family members or pressure from village community or pressure from the political parties or due to personal interest.

The finding that 23.3 per cent of the respondents have participated in politics due to their personal interest is an indicator for prospective emergence of rural women leadership in Dindigul District.

Political Ambition

Political Scientists like Herald Lasswell[18] and Joseph Schlesinger[19] are very enthusiastic in analysing the political ambitions of political actors in their studies. They have also attempted to study the political consequences of the ambitions possessed by political actors. Joseph Schlesinger categorised political ambitions as: (a) Discrete ambition, (b) Static ambition, and, (c) Progressive ambition. Discrete ambition signifies the intention of a leader to occupy a particular position for a stipulated period only; Static ambition implies the desire of a leader to hold an office for a long term; and, Progressive ambition refers to the aspiration of the leader to acquire higher position than the one he is occupying currently.

There is always the possibility for political actors to shift their ambitions from one to another during their political career.

Whatever may be the type of political ambition of individuals, it is certain to tell upon their emergence as leaders. Against this backdrop, it is pertinent to study the political ambitions of the respondents.

TABLE 4.9
POLITICAL AMBITIONS OF RESPONDENTS

Sl. No.	*Type of Political Ambition*	*Respondents*					
		Elected		*Defeated*		*Total*	
		No.	*%*	*No.*	*%*	*No.*	*%*
1.	Discrete Ambition	6	5.6	22	22.2	28	13.6
2.	Static Ambition	61	57.0	61	61.6	122	59.2
3.	Progressive Ambition	40	37.4	16	16.2	56	27.2
	Total	107	100.0	99	100.0	206	100.0

Source: Computed.

The data in Table 4.9 indicate that 59.2 per cent of respondents hold static political ambitions. The reason expressed by the respondents at the time of data collection for possessing static ambition was that they wanted to serve the people in their own Village Panchayats for a long time.

It is also observed that 13.6 per cent of the respondents have discrete political ambitions. When questioned as to the reasons for the discrete ambition, the respondents replied that they contested the current election only to oblige relatives and the general public in their villages and that they may not contest next time because of their age, health and other family problems.

Fig. 4.2: Political Ambition of Respondents : A Comparative Analysis.

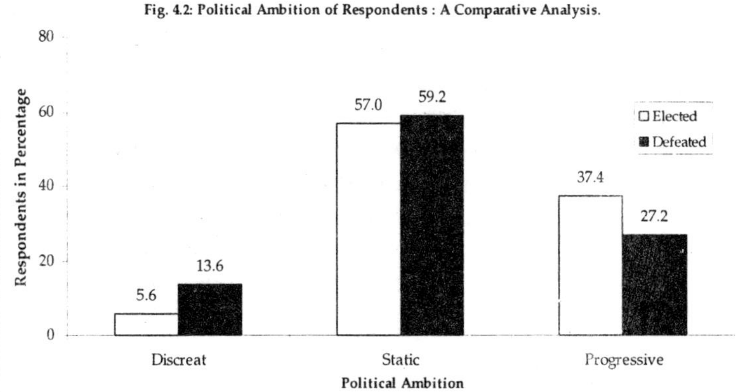

Table 4.9 also shows that 27.2 per cent of the respondents hold progressive political ambitions. The reason for their progressive political ambition was that they were aspiring to move to higher political positions. The respondents of this category are highly educated or retired Government employees or they hail from politically-oriented families. These respondents want to make use of their present position as a stepping stone to acquire experience and popularity for fulfilment of their progressive political ambition.

Political Background

In the light of the various discussions and analyses in the preceding section of this chapter, it is found that the political background of the respondents is weak. As the heads of the families are males and the deciding authorities with more exposure to the outside world, they have more political involvement compared to their womenfolk. Therefore, the analysis of the emergence of the leadership of the respondents has to be carried out taking into account the political background of their family heads.

It is, therefore, decided to analyse the integrated impact of multiple political variables, namely age of political awareness, age of entering politics, sources of inspiration for political interest, positions held in political parties, stimulant for political participation and political ambitions of the respondents together with the party affiliations, positions held in political parties, nature of involvement in political activities of the family heads on the emergence of leadership.

The elected and defeated respondents are categorised on the basis of their political background scores as low, medium and high groups.[20]

Testing of Hypothesis

Hypothesis 2: "The higher the political background of the family, the greater will be the emergence of rural women leadership."

The content of this hypothesis in statistical terms is that there is significant relation between the votes polled and the scores secured for political background by the respondents.

TABLE 4.10
LEADERSHIP VIS-A-VIS POLITICAL BACKGROUND

Votes Polled	*Political Background Scores*			
	Low	*Medium*	*High*	*Total*
Defeated (0-49)	22 (22.2)	61 (61.6)	16 (16.2)	99 (48.1)
Elected (50-100)	12 (11.2)	57 (53.3)	38 (35.5)	107 (51.9)
Total	34 (16.5)	118 (57.3)	54 (26.2)	206 (100.0)

Source: Computed. Note: Figures in parentheses are percentages

Table 4.10 reveals that 88.8 per cent of the elected respondents belong to medium and high political background groups as against 77.8 per cent of the defeated respondents and that 11.2 per cent of the elected respondents belong to the low political background group compared to 22.2 per cent of the defeated ones.

The statistical analysis shows that there is significant association between the votes polled and the political background scores secured by the respondents.

$$(\chi^2 = 11.75; D.F.=2; P<.01)$$

Therefore the statistical analysis leads to the conclusion that hypothesis 2, namely **"The higher the political background of the family, the greater will be the emergence of rural women leadership"** is validated affirmatively.

Fig. 4.3: Political Background Scores of Respondents : A Comparative Analysis.

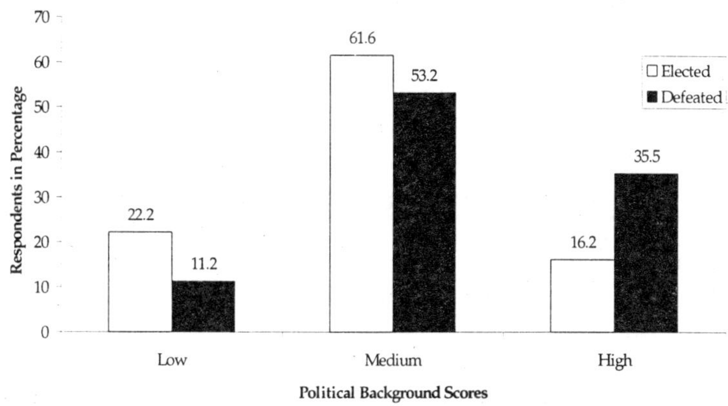

Summary

The main findings drawn from the analysis of the data pertaining to the political background of the respondents may be summarised as hereunder:

1. Regarding the age of attainment of political awareness, 75.2 per cent of the respondents acquired it even while they were below 25 years of age.
2. As to the age of entry into politics, 83.0 per cent of the respondents entered politics even before the age of 40 years.
3. As regards the sources of inspiration for political interest, family and mass media have been the motivating sources for the political interest of 44.7 per cent of the respondents. The political parties have been sources of political inspiration, for only 4.4 per cent of the respondents.
4. With regard to political affiliation, 76.7 per cent of the family heads of the respondents are affiliated to political parties like, the DMK, the AIADMK, the TMC, the CONGRESS (I), the CPI, the CPI(M), the BJP, the MDMK, the PMK and the DK. The affiliation to the DMK party by the family heads of the respondents is numerically larger

(27.2 per cent) compared to the affiliation to the other political parties.

5. Regarding the positions held in political parties, 1.9 per cent of the respondents are office-bearers in their political parties at village or district levels as against 22.8 per cent of their family heads.
6. Regarding the nature of political participation, 76.0 per cent of the family heads of the respondents are either active or very active in political participation as against 24.0 per cent being politically inert.
7. As for the stimulants for political participation, 72.3 per cent of the respondents have been motivated either by their family members or by the general public of their villages and only 4.4 per cent have been stimulated by political parties. However, 23.3 per cent of the respondents have involved themselves in politics out of their own interest.
8. Concerning political ambition, 59.2 per cent of the respondents have static ambitions followed by 27.2 per cent with progressive ambition and 13.6 per cent with discrete ambition.
9. There is a significant relationship between the emergence of the respondents as leaders and the political background of their families.

In the present and preceding chapters, the socio-economic status and political background of the respondents have been discussed as correlates for the emergence of rural women leadership. But the substantive part of the study is to identify the power bases through which the respondents have emerged as leaders and to categorise the pattern of rural women leadership that has emerged in the Village Panchayats of Dindigul District. This forms the subject matter of discussion in the next chapter.

References

1. C.E Merriam, and H.F Cornell, **American Party System,** New York: The Mac-Millan Co., 1949, p. 464.
2. Amal Kumar Mukhopadhyaya, **Political Sociology: An Introductory Analysis,** Calcutta: K.P. Bagchi and Company, 1980, p. 120.

3. Michal Rush and Philip Althoff, **An Introduction to Political Sociology,** London: Thomas Nelson and Sons Ltd, 1971, p. 75.
4. Amalkumar Mukhopadhyaya. *Op. cit.*, p. 126.
5. Iqbal Narain, K.C. Pande, and Mohan Lal, **Rural Elite and Elections in an Indian State — A Study of Panchayati Raj Leadership in the Context of Rajasthan Electoral Politics,** Jaipur: National Publishing House, 1976, p. 51.
6. Giovanni Sartori has forcefully made in this regard a point by way of plea to restore the autonomous character and identity of political science. See his article "From the Sociology of Politics to Political Sociology", in S.M. Lipset (ed,) **Politics and the Social Sciences,** New Delhi: Wiley Eastern, Private Ltd., 1972, pp. 66-17.
7. V.R. Dutta, **Decision-Making in Urban Government and Politics,** Allahabad: Chugh Publications, 1986, p. 39.
8. Manu Basker, "Women Panchayat Members in Kerala—A Profile", **Economic and Political Weekly,** Vol. XXXII, No. 17, April, 1997.
9. Amal Kumar Mukhopadhyay, *Op. cit.*, p. 103.
10. V.R. Dutta, *Op. cit.*, p. 10.
11. J.L. Woodward and E. Roper, "Political Activity of American Citizen", in H. Eulau, S.J. Eldersweld & M. Janowitz (eds), **Political Behaviour: Reader in Theory and Research,** New Delhi: American Publishing Co. Pvt. Ltd., 1972, p. 133.
12. Bertram, M.Grass., "Political Process", in the **Encyclopedia of Social Sciences,** Vol. 11 and 12, New York: MacMillan Company and the Free Press, 1972, p. 265.
13. Lester Milbrath., **Political Participation,** Chicago: Rand McNally, 1965.
14. Herbert McCluskey., "Political Participation", in David.L.Sills(ed.), **International Encyclopaedia of Social Sciences,** Vol. 11 and 12, New York: Macmillan and The Free Press, 1972, pp. 252-53.
15. Ranjana Kumari, **Women in Politics and Political Process—Introduction,** New Delhi: Friedrich Ebert Stifftung (FES), 1992. p.1.
16. Sukla Deb Kanango, "Panchayati Raj and Emerging Women Leadership", **Social Action,** Vol. 46, January-March, 1996, p. 84; Snehalat Panda, "Political Empowerment of Women—A Case Study of Orissa, **Journal of Rural Development,** Vol. 16, No. 4, October-December, 1997, pp. 663-72.
17. Snehalata Panda, "Political Empowerment of Women — A Case Study of Orissa", **Journal of Rural Development,** Vol. 16, No.4, October-December, 1997, pp 663-72.
18. Harold Lasswell, **Psycopathology in Politics,** New York: Viking, 1960, cited in V.R. Dutta, *Op. cit.* p. 49.
19. Joseph A. Schlesinger, **Ambition and Politics: Political Careers in the United States,** Chicago, Rand Mc Nally, 1966, cited in V.R. Dutta, loc. cit.
20. The Categorising of the elected and defeated rural women leaders into three group is effected on the basis of the composite scores obtained by them for their political background with the help of a linear unweighted sum of the ranks given to each category within each of the variables.

Five

Identification of Power Bases and Categorisation of Women Leaders

The substantive issue of the study is the identification of the pattern of rural women leadership in Dindigul District of Tamil Nadu. The elected women and their immediate rivals in the elections for the office of Village Panchayat president are presumed to have emerged as rural women leaders. For finding the pattern of their leadership, an appropriate methodology has to be employed.

A large number of studies have been undertaken on the subject of identification of community leaders in India and abroad. These studies have adopted one or another of the following three approaches to identify the community leaders: (i) Positional Approach, (ii) Reputational Approach and (iii) Decisional Approach.[1] Despite their wide application by researchers both in and outside India, they suffer from inadequacies and shortcomings. Vehement criticisms and counter-arguments against the acceptability of these approaches have revealed the actual weaknesses of the approaches. Consequently scholars have shifted their methodology to a combined approach for the identification of leaders in the community, at least in similar studies in the Western countries. Scholars like L.C. Freeman et al., R. Presthus, W.Jr. Bloomberg and M. Sunshine have used all the three methods while L.V. Blankenship, I. Belknap and J.H. Steinle and D.C. Miller have used two of the three approaches.[2] In fact, "until more comparative studies are done, conclusions of this kind are virtually guesses."[3]

With the underlying assumption that the elected rural women Village Panchyat Presidents and their immediate rivals in the elections to the Village Panchayats in Dindigul District are identified as leaders in this study, the core task of this chapter is to categorise them under different patterns. The approaches mentioned above and their syntheses are employed in this study not for the identification of the leaders, but for the identification of the power bases through which their leadership has emerged. The identified power bases will help to assess the pattern of the rural women leadership that has emerged.

The application of different approaches by the scholars in identifying the community leaders has facilitated the location of different types of leaders.[4] A synthesis of the three approaches may give rise to yet other types of leaders. But the agreement and disagreement between these combinations and the validity and reliability of the findings can only be ascertained through a comparative analysis. Freeman et al., have utilised a synthesis of the three approaches and compared the findings of each of the approaches[5] to identify different types of leaders in the community.

In the following pages, the positional approach, the reputational approach, and the decisional approach (issue participation approach or event-analysis), a combination of any two of them and a synthesis of all the three are examined in order to categorise the rural women who have emerged as leaders of the Village Panchayats in Dindigul District.

Positional Approach

The oldest and the simplest method of identifying community leadership is through the positional approach. Till 1953, it was very popular in application. The pivotal assumption of this approach is that "those holding positions of authority actually make key decisions, while those who do not occupy such positions do not make decisions".[6] Different criteria have been followed by different scholars in identifying the key positions. Following K. Marx, R. Lynds and C.W. Mills assumed that those who were at the apex of the economic concerns were better situated to decide and thus economic dominants were regarded as the positional elite.[7] S.A. Stouffer, on the other hand, selected top civic and political status as the bases for this approach. R.O. Schulze and Bloomberg chose economic dominance and such other objective criteria to determine the positional elite. Jennings chose government officials, civil staff personnel and economic dominants as the positional elite.[8] C.M. Bonjean and D.M. Olsen have found that the positional approach for leader identification is the quickest, the most efficient and the most reliable method in small communities where the resources are concentrated.[9] T.K. Oomen,[10] K. Ranga Rao,[11] and Yogendra Singh[12] are some of the Indian scholars who have discussed leadership in villages in terms of formal or modern(positional) and informal or traditional (reputational) leadership concepts. These authors have not specifically utilised the positional approach, but they have made use of it in combination with other techniques of leader-identification in villages. Anyhow, no scholar has undertaken a detailed comparative study of the power structure in Indian villages using all the three approaches.[13] In villages and at grassroots level, the scope for using the positional approach to identify the leaders is meagre and many political scientists are sceptical whether it will elicit agreeable outcomes. However, since this study is poised to take up a comparative analysis of the results of all the three approaches, the utility of the positional approach for the emergence of rural women leadership may be examined in the villages of Dindigul District.

The preliminary study of the respondents revealed that the majority of them do not hold key posts at the apex of social, political, economic and voluntary organisations. This is mainly due to the fact that the respondents are women by gender and they are new entrants to politics in the wake of the one-third mandatory reservation provision for women in the local body power structure. In this context, the positions held by the family heads of the respondents are considered relevant, as they are likely to influence the emergence of rural women leadership. Therefore, an enquiry has been made in respect of positions held by respondents and their family heads in various formal and informal organisations separately.

Positions of Respondents

The positional approach has been, so far, utilised for urbanised communities in the cities of Western Countries. The scholars who utilised the positional approach for identifing the elite have been of the opinion that it could not be availed of for identification of leaders in villages wherein the formal and informal organisations of power and authority are comparatively very few.

Contrary to this notion, the positional approach is being brought into play in this study for the identification of the leadership pattern in the villages of Dindigul District based on the assumption that the fifty years of Independence of India have brought about political consciousness and avowed political transformation in Indian villages close to the heels of such transformation in urbanised community structures. The prevalence of informal and formal socio-political organisations like Mahalir Mantrams, Self-help Groups, Governmental Organisations, Political Parties, Trade Unions, Village Panchayats, Co-operative Societies and Voluntary Organisations in the villages of India constitutes the basis for women to wield power through different positions in them.

Village Panchayats and Co-operative Societies are statutory organisations, while Trade Unions and Political Parties are organisations empowered with political rights. Governmental Organisations include the Education Department, the Arivoli Iyakkam (TLC), Defence Service Wings, Health and Revenue Departments and the like. The positions as teachers and Project Co-ordinators of Arivoli Iyakkam provide ample avenues to participate in the process of decision-making in villages. The retired teachers use their former positions and the status acquired therefrom in the course of their emergence as rural leaders. Mahalir Mantrams are developmental organisations initiated and patronised by the government whereas Voluntary Organisations are Non-governmental Service Organisations.

The respondents or their family heads might have held positions as elected or co-opted members in Village Panchayats or even the position of the President. These positions act as support bases for the development of the popularity and the influence of the position-holder.

The position of President or that of a Director of a Co-operative Credit Society empowers the incumbent to offer financial assistance to the members. To obtain fertilizers, licences and permits, the villagers have to approach the positional leaders of Co-operative Societies. Thus the positional leaders have become very important persons in the dispension of developmental benefits, thereby enlarging their sphere of influence.

The major political parties have established their respective village units together with the provision for women's wings almost in all the villages. Similarly the Trade Unions of factories and mills in and around the villages provide berths to the position-holders to earn popularity and influence over the working class.

Self-help Groups of women existing in the majority of the villages of Dindigul District have been constituted basically for their mutual monetary betterment. The positions of office-bearers in such financial groups naturally enable the influence of the position-holders and their families to spread among the villagers in respect of financial transactions.

Against this backdrop, an analysis of the positions held by the respondents in the aforesaid organisations becomes imperative for ascertaining whether the position has been a power base for the emergence of the respondents as leaders.

TABLE 5.1
POSITIONS HELD BY RESPONDENTS

Sl. No.	*Socio-Political Organisations*	*Respondents*					
		Elected		*Defeated*		*Total*	
		M	*OB*	*M*	*OB*	*M*	*OB*
1.	Mahalir Mantram	37 (34.6)	31 (29.0)	45 (45.5)	19 (19.2)	82 (39.8)	50 (24.3)
2.	Self-help Group	34 (31.8)	38 (35.5)	40 (40.4)	20 (20.2)	74 (35.9)	58 (28.2)
3.	Governmental Organisation	10 (9.3)	4 (3.7)	-	1 (1.0)	10 (4.9)	5 (2.4)
4.	Political Party	22 (20.5)	2 (1.9)	20 (20.2)	2 (2.0)	42 (20.4)	4 (1.9)
5.	Trade Union	6 (5.6)	- -	4 (4.0)	- -	10 (4.9)	- -
6.	Village Panchayat	1 (0.9)	- -	1 (1.0)	- -	2 (1.0)	- -
7.	Co-operative Society	9 (8.4)	2 (1.9)	12 (12.1)	4 (4.0)	21 (10.2)	6 (2.9)
8.	Voluntary Organisation	8 (7.5)	- -	11 (11.1)	- -	19 (9.2)	- -

Source: Computed.
Note: Figures in parentheses are percentages.
Total N = 206; Elected N = 107; Defeated N = 99; M - Member; OB - Office-bearer

The data in Table 5.1 indicate the positions held by the elected and the defeated respondents in different organisations wherein positions have been classified into two types as members and office-bearers of the organisations. The tabular analysis brings out that 39.8 per cent of the respondents have membership in Mahalir Mantrams, that 35.9 per cent are members in Self-help Groups, and that 20.4 per cent are members in Political Parties. In Voluntary Organisations and Co-operative Societies, membership is held by 9.2 per cent and 10.2 per cent of the respondents respectively. Only 4.9 per cent of the respondents are identified each as members in Trade Unions or former personnel in governmental service. A meagre one per cent of the respondents were co-opted women members in previous Village Panchayats.

As office-bearers in the different organisations, the score of the respondents is very poor: 28.2 per cent of the respondents hold positions as office-bearers in Self-help Groups as against 24.3 per cent being office-bearers in Mahalir Mantrams. In Political Parties, Co-operative Societies and Government Service Organisations, a low percentage of 1.9 per cent, 2.9 per cent and 2.4 per cent respectively of the respondents are office-bearers, while none are office-bearers in Trade Unions, Village Panchayats and Voluntary Organisations.

The overall observation of the data in the Table leads to the conclusion that 2.4 per cent of the respondents are office-bearers and 8.4 per cent are members in socio-political organisations other than those meant for women only. However 37.9 per cent of the respondents are found to be members and 26.3 per cent office-bearers in organisations meant for women only.

Similar findings have been observed by Manu Basker[14] in his study of Women Panchayat Members in Kerala.

Positions of Family Heads

In general, the emergence of leadership depends upon not only the individuals concerned, but also the influence of their family heads. This is more so in the case of rural women. In this context, it is pertinant to analyse the nature of the positions held by the heads of the families of the respondents.

In the study of the positions held by the family heads of the respondents, the Caste Organisations, Religious Organisations, Governmental Organisations, Political Parties, Village Panchayats, Rasigar Mantrams, Co-operative Societies, and, Social Service Organisations, Voluntary Organisations are considered for analysis.

In Indian villages, almost all the castes have their own Caste Panchayats (Caste Councils), which are informal organisations. These organisations are constituted by the heads of leading lineages and caste people in the village. The Caste Organisations are the "courts" at the village level, devoid of legal legitimacy. However, they are empowered with moral and social legitimacy. These Caste Panchayats wield power mainly with regard to the social and the cultural aspects of life. In principle, these Panchayats are meant for the welfare and upliftment of the members of the respective castes. They maintain customary law and order. Defiance of the customary rules and regulations will be severely dealt with by these Panchayats. Even excommunication may be imposed on the defaulters in the community.[15] At times, the Caste Associations or Panchayats may be dysfunctional because of internal squabbles. On the whole, however, the village Caste Panchayats are still functional and their members and office-bearers are still powerful in decision-making on the majority of the community's affairs.[16]

As for the numerical strength of castes, the Gounders dominate over the Vanniars, the Pillais, the Mukkulathors and the other castes in Dindigul District. The apex position-holders in **Gounder** Caste Organisations are designated as **"Oor Gounders", or "Pannadis". " Oor Naicker"** is the designation of their counter parts in **Naicker** cast organisation, It is **"Nattanmais"** or **"Periathanams"** in Vanniar, Pillai and Mukkulothor and other Caste Organisations in Dindigul District. These chief persons are endowed with enormous social powers over their community people. The caste people without membership in their Caste Organisations have to suffer a lot in their social life besides their loss of share in the decision-making process in matters pertaining to community and village affairs.

Despite the traditional caste outfits, village units of State-wide Caste associations like Kongu Vellala Gounder Sangam, Devendrakula Vellalar Sangam, Vanniar Sangam, Mukkulathor Sangam, Thevar Peravai, Nadar Maha Jana Sangam and the like have been installed in many of the villages of Dindigul District. The membership in these village units is found to be limited in contrast to the membership in traditional Village Caste Councils wherein the membership comes by virtue of one's birth in the respective castes.

In general, the traditional village Caste organisations and the branches of State-wide Caste organisations are like-minded in their objectives and co-operative in their functions. Hence the position-holders in the State-wide Caste organisations also wield power in the process of decision-making within their community power structure.

Religious organisations usually cut across caste barriers and they are constituted only to promote the spiritual and religious life of the people. Within a religion, there are different sub-organisations like associations of **Ayyappan devotees, Melmaruvathur Aathiparasakthi devotees** and **Padhayathra pilgrims of Lord Palani Muguran** and **Annai Velankanni.** Religious organisations are not as powerful as caste organisations in the villages of Dindigul District. Nevertheless, the membership and the positions as office-bearers in religious organisations help one to widen the boundaries of influence and to assume important roles in the process of decision-making on village religious affairs. On the basis of numerical strength, Hindus overwhelmingly dominate over Christians and Muslims in the villages of Dindigul District. In Nilakottai, Authoor, Dindigul and Sanarpatti Unions of Dindigul District, there are a few villages with Christians forming the majority and Hindus the minority and Natham Union has one village with Muslims forming the majority and Hindus the minority. Religious Organisations in such villages are found to play a role in the emergence of leaders. Therefore, the members and office-bearers of religious organisations are bound to have authority in their respective areas of power structure.

Generally, every village in Tamil Nadu is found to have at least two or three Rasigar Mantrams (Fans Clubs). In most of the villages, it is not the name-boards of the village, but the name-boards of Rasigar Mantrams which cordially welcome every new entrant to the village. The Rasigar Mantrams constituted with the sole objective of extolling the name and fame of cine actors and actresses at times render social services like Annadhanam (free meals to the poor) and Blood Donations. Certain Rasigar Mantrams, at the behest of their leaders, resort to political campaigns and struggles against social evils.

In Tamil Nadu, the leaders of the Dravidian Movement introduced the strategy of using film as a medium for political communication and they succeeded in their effort through the late Sri M.G. Ramachandran,[17] a former Chief Minister of Tamil Nadu. The cine-artists, on their part, take all efforts for establishing Rasigar Mantrams in their names to propagate their ideals and mobilise popular support for their survival in the cine and the political fields. Next to the M.G.R Rasigar Mantram, Rajinikanth Rasigar Mantram has flourished through the length and breath of Tamil Nadu in such a proportion that "it has played an important role in defeating Selvi J. Jeyalalitha, a former Chief Minister of Tamil Nadu and electing the DMK-TMC combine in the eleventh general elections."[18] Youngsters, both literate and illiterate, have started seeking political power through the Rasigar Mantrams. The positions as members and office-bearers in Rasigar Mantrams have their definite impact on the emergence of rural leadership.

At this juncture, it becomes worthwhile to survey the positions held by the family heads of the respondents in organisations considered responsible for their emergence as leaders.

Through the data of Table 5.2, it is understood that 53.9 per cent of the family heads of the respondents are merely members in political parties, 37.4 per cent are members in Caste organisations, 28.6 per cent are members in Social Service Organisations, and, 21.4 per cent are members in Rasigar Mantrams, while less than 20 per cent are members in all the other organisations under consideration.

The Table also shows that 33.0 per cent of the family heads of the respondents hold positions at the apex of Caste organisations as office-bearers and 22.8 per cent each are found office-bearers in Political Parties and in previous Village Panchayats. Less than 20 per cent are seen to hold positions as office-bearers in all the other organisations.

Political Organisations, Caste Organisations and Village Panchayats are ranked first (76.7 per cent), second (70.4 per cent) and third (36.9 per cent) respectively in respect of positions (either as member or office-bearer) held by the family heads of the respondents. Nearly 30 per cent of the respondents belong to families holding positions as members or office-bearers in Rasigar Mantrams and Social Service Organisations.

TABLE 5.2
POSITIONS HELD BY FAMILY HEADS OF RESPONDENTS

Sl. No.	Organisations	Family Heads					
		Elected		Defeated		Total	
		M	OB	M	OB	M	OB
1.	Caste Organisation	39 (36.4)	42 (39.3)	38 (38.4)	26 (26.3)	77 (37.4)	68 (33.0)
2.	Religious Organisation	7 (6.5)	19 (17.8)	16 (16.2)	10 (10.1)	23 (11.2)	29 (14.1)
3.	Governmental Organisation	19 (17.8)	1 (0.9)	18 (18.2)	1 (1.0)	37 (18.0)	2 (1.0)
4.	Political Party	54 (50.5)	27 (25.2)	57 (57.6)	20 (20.2)	111 (53.9)	47 (22.8)
5.	Trade Union	13 (12.1)	- -	5 (5.1)	- -	18 (8.7)	- -
6.	Village Panchayat	27 (25.2)	34 (31.8)	2 (2.0)	13 (13.1)	29 (14.1)	47 (22.8)
7.	Co-operative Society	5 (4.7)	9 (8.4)	1 (1.0)	5 (5.1)	6 (2.9)	14 (6.8)
8.	Voluntary Social Service Organisation	34 (31.8)	- -	25 (25.3)	1 (1.0)	59 (28.6)	1 (1.0)
9.	Rasigar Mantram	17 (15.9)	14 (13.0)	27 (27.3)	2 (2.0)	44 (21.4)	16 (7.8)

Source: Computed.
Note: Figures in parentheses are percentages.

An overall review shows that 12.1 per cent of the family heads of the respondents are office-bearers and 21.8 per cent are members in politicaly-oriented, caste-based village organisations, in previous Village Panchayats or in other organisations under consideration.

The conclusion drawn from the above findings is that the majority of the respondents come from families that are politically-oriented or caste- leadership-oriented.

Leadership vis-a-vis Position

The basic assumption behind the positional approach is that people who hold important positions in formal as well as informal organisations are leaders in a village. In order to examine the level of influence of positions as bases of power on the emergence of leadership, the multiple positions held by the respondents and their family heads in different organisations under consideration are analysed statistically.[19]

Testing of Hypothesis

Hypothesis 3: "The positions of the rural women and their family heads as bases of power have their own impact on the emergence of rural women as leaders".

The statistical version of this hypothesis implies that there is a positive relationship between the votes polled and the positional scores secured by the respondents.

TABLE 5.3
VOTES POLLED VIS-A-VIS POSITIONAL SCORES

Votes Polled	*Level of Positional Profile Scores*			
	Low	*Medium*	*High*	*Total*
Defeated (0-49)	44 (44.4)	46 (46.5)	9 (9.1)	99 (48.1)
Elected (50-100)	31 (29.0)	57 (53.3)	19 (17.8)	107 (51.9)
Total	75 (36.4)	103 (50.0)	28 (13.6)	206 (100)

Source: Computed. Note: Figures in parentheses are percentages.
Mean Positional Score: 9.20

Table 5.3 reveals that 71.1 per cent of the elected respondents and 55.6 per cent of the defeated respondents come under high and medium levels of positional scores whereas 44.4 per cent of the defeated respondents and 29.0 per cent of the elected respondents fall under low level of positional scores.The statistical analysis concludes that there is a positive relationship between the votes polled and the positional scores secured by the respondents.

$$(\chi^2 = 6.70 \ ; \ D.F.= 2 \ ; \ P< .005)$$

Hence the affirmative validation of the third hypothesis of the study, namely " **The positions of the rural women and their family heads as bases of power have their own impact on the emergence of rural women as leaders".**

Fig. 5.1: Positional Scores of Respondents : A Comparative Analysis.

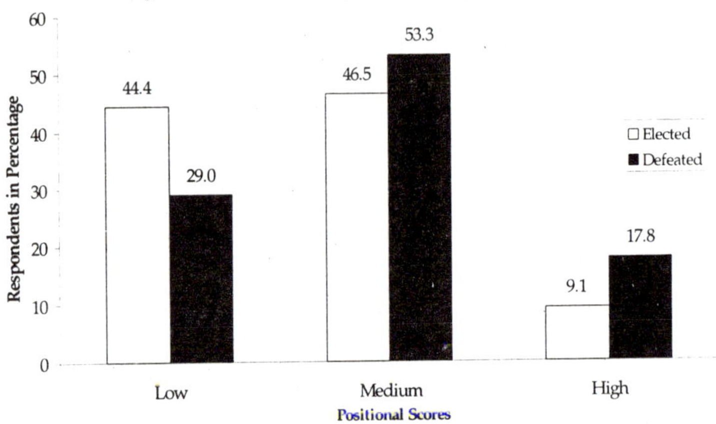

Reputational Approach

People acquire reputation by virtue of their social status, which mostly depends on caste, land holdings, wealth, public positions and combinations of a few or all of these. In the Indian rural scenario, age also contributes to reputation because wisdom and knowledge necessary for solving disputes are correlated with age.[20] However, the young men who are active in public affairs along with their academic credentials or new skills are not to be ignored. Besides, a person may be weighed in the light of his/her personality traits and activities as good, bad, efficient, inefficient, courageous, cowardly, cunning etc., all of which may alter the reputation of a person in a community.[21]

Techniques Adopted

Generally, in the reputational approach, the respondents (experts or knowledgeable persons or randomly-selected members from cross sections of the society) are asked to name the most powerful and influential leaders in the community for the purpose of locating the leaders. The final selection of leaders is made based on the number of mentions with the help of an appropriate cut-off point. This may be called one-step procedure.

There is another method of this approach, called two-step procedure, to locate leaders in the community. In this method, lists of leaders of all categories are compiled and a panel of judges or experts is asked to choose the leaders from among the names in the lists. Reputational leaders are recognised on the basis of the number of choices made by the panel of judges. This method was used by Hunter in his study in 1953. But the technique of analysis in the present study is the other way about.

In the present study, all those women who have been elected as Village Panchayat Presidents and their immediate rivals in the Village Panchayat elections of Dindigul District are presumed to have emerged as rural women leaders. To identify the level of influence of reputation over the emergence of rural women leadership, relevant data concerned with the reputation were collected from the respondents and the collected data were later confirmed with the responsible and knowledgeable local informants like VAOs, temple priests, school teachers and caste leaders.

The inherited social position and the reputation of a family play an important role in determining its leadership position. Besides, the behaviour and the achievement of the living members also determine the status of the family and leadership of its members.[22]

The reputation flowing from one's familial lineage is termed ascribed reputation, while the reputation secured by virtue of one's personal traits and social interaction is called achieved reputation. Both these reputations have their role in determining the emergence of leadership. Those persons who have emerged as leaders by means of reputation are called reputational leaders. The correlates of both ascribed and achieved reputations possessed by the respondents are to be examined for declaring them reputational leaders.

Correlates of ascribed Reputation

The determinants of ascribed reputation are classified into four groups as: (i) Social Correlates, (ii) Economic Correlates, (iii) Political Correlates, and, (iv) Community Service Correlates for the sake of simple percentage tabular analysis.

All the determinants of ascribed reputation are analysed in the light of the data collected for the purpose of identifying the role played by ascribed reputation in the process of the emergence of rural women leadership.

Social Correlates

Reputation is socially correlated with one's status and prestigious positions. In villages,the caste chiefs called Periyathanams wield considerable social power and respect in the midst of their community people. The caste chiefs generally come from the same familial lineage, or else they are elected by the community people based on the exigency of situations.

It is still seen that there are certain notables in villages who are honoured with "First Respect" at the time of village festivals. The honour of first respect is due to them because of the past or present glory of their families or their own noble deeds.

Temple trustees usually hail from pious and honest families. There are both elected and hereditary trustees in the villages of Dindigul District. These trustees are privileged to get respect from the devotees and religious-minded people of the villages. Similarly, village priests performing poojas (adoration rituals) and other religious activities in the temples of the villages are also reputed for their positions. Illiteracy is a social stigma in Indian villages. If the members of the rural families are highly educated and hold professional positions as doctors, engineers and lawyers, they are viewed with respect.

It is therefore pertinent to analyse the social correlates of reputation which contribute to the emergence of rural women leadership.

TABLE 5.4
SOCIAL CORRELATES OF REPUTATION OF RESPONDENTS' FAMILIES

Sl. No.	*Social Correlate*	*Respondents*					
		Elected		*Defeated*		*Total*	
		No.	*%*	*No.*	*%*	*No.*	*%*
1.	Periyathanam Family	48	44.9	40	40.4	88	42.7
2.	Hereditary Caste Leader	43	40.2	31	31.3	74	35.9
3.	First Respect Family	22	20.5	6	6.1	28	13.6
4.	Temple Trustee	21	19.6	12	12.1	33	16.0
5.	Village Priests (Poosary, Gurukkal)	16	15.0	8	8.1	24	11.8
6.	Highly Educated Family	43	40.2	25	25.3	68	33.0
7.	Professional Position	18	16.8	7	7.1	25	12.1

Source: Computed.
Total N = 206; Elected N = 107; Defeated N = 99.

The data in Table 5.4 show that 42.7 per cent of the respondents hail from Periyathanam families compared to 35.9 per cent coming from the families of hereditary caste leaders and 33.0 per cent belonging to highly educated families. It is also seen that less than 17.0 per cent of the respondents are associated with the other social correlates of reputation.

The inference drawn from the above findings is that caste leadership forms the basis of reputation for the majority (42.7 per cent) of the respondents.

Economic Correlates

In the villages of Tamil Nadu, rich landlords called Pannaiyars not only have economic status but also social status. Pannaiyars are considered to be the patrons of those who work under them.

Wealthy families in villages may be of rich landlords or of other sources of wealth. Telephone and car are the symbols of prestige for the wealthy people in villages. Wealth accumulates to a person through different means such as agricultural operations, business, trade, contracts etc. If the wealth of a person is beneficial to the community in some form or other, the wealthy person is deemed to possess reputation. Wealthy people owning factories and mills, are likely to command respect from the workers and the families dependent on them for their livelihood and prosperity. Therefore, the economic correlates of the reputation of the respondents deserve an in-depth study with regard to their emergence as leaders.

TABLE 5.5
ECONOMIC CORRELATES OF REPUTATION OF RESPONDENTS' FAMILIES

Sl. No.	*Economic Correlate*	*Respondents*					
		Elected		*Defeated*		*Total*	
		No.	*%*	*No.*	*%*	*No.*	*%*
1.	Pannaiyar Family	22	20.6	12	12.1	34	16.5
2.	Wealthy Family	60	56.1	47	47.5	107	59.1
3.	Factory/Mill/ Stone Crusher Owner	4	3.3	4	4.0	8	3.9
4.	Family with Car and Telephone	18	16.8	5	5.1	23	11.2

Source: Computed.
Total N = 206; Elected N= 107 ; Defeated N = 99

Table 5.5 indicates that 59.1 per cent of the respondents come from wealthy families as against 16.5 per cent from families of big landlords, while 11.2 per cent hail from families who own car and telephone.

The conclusion drawn from the above findings is that the majority of the respondents are from wealthy families and hence wealth as a correlate of reputation has considerable impact on the emergence of the respondents as leaders.

Political Correlates

The families from which people rise to political offices like Panchayat President, Union Chairman, MLA and MP are held in high esteem by the villagers and consequently any member of such a family is treated with high reputational status by the neighbours and the public. Apart from these people, there are others having close contact with high profile political or non-political leaders. Such people also are found to draw reputation from others.

Patriotism is a significant and essential attribute for every citizen of the country. People with love for their mother-land ought to have great respect for the freedom fighters and their families.

In this context, the political correlates enhancing the reputation of the respondents need to be analysed in respect of the emergence of their leadership.

TABLE 5.6
POLITICAL CORRELATES OF REPUTATION OF RESPONDENTS' FAMILIES

Sl. No.	*Political Correlate*	*Respondents*					
		Elected		*Defeated*		*Total*	
		No.	*%*	*No.*	*%*	*No.*	*%*
1.	Relative/Family member of Ex V.P.P/Union Chairman/ MLA/MP	89	83.2	74	74.7	163	79.1
2.	Contact with high profile leaders	81	75.7	73	73.7	154	74.8
3.	Freedom fighter's family	10	9.4	4	4.0	14	6.8

Source: Computed.
Total N = 206 ; Elected N = 107 ; Defeated N = 99

It is evident from Table 5.6 that 79.1 per cent of the respondents are people whose family members or relatives are former members or office-bearers of Village Panchayats/Panchayat

Union or MLAs/MPs, that 74.8 per cent are from families having contact with high profile leaders, and, that 6.8 per cent belong to families of freedom fighters.

The above findings lead to the conclusion that politically related families have contributed more to the emergence of the leadership of the respondents than the families of freedom fighters.

Community Service Correlates

People unselfishly rendering social services, free medical services (indigenous), Annadhanam (free meals to the poor) and financial assistance, contributing donations for common causes and settling domestic disputes enjoy the goodwill of others. Therefore, the families rendering community services have to be identified for the study of the emergence of the respondents as leaders.

TABLE 5.7

COMMUNITY SERVICE CORRELATES OF REPUTATION OF RESPONDENTS' FAMILIES

Sl. No.	*Community Service Correlate*	*Respondents*					
		Elected		*Defeated*		*Total*	
		No.	*%*	*No.*	*%*	*No.*	*%*
1.	Social Services	41	38.3	23	23.2	64	31.1
2.	Donations to all castes and creeds	90	84.1	82	82.8	172	83.5
3.	Annadhanam	49	45.8	21	21.2	70	34.0
4.	Intrest-free financial assistance	20	18.7	5	5.1	25	12.1
5.	Free medical services (Indigenous medicine)	11	10.3	9	9.1	20	9.7
6.	Settling domestic disputes	87	81.3	65	65.7	152	73.8

Source: Computed.

Total No = 206; Elected N = 107; Defeated 99.

Table 5.7 shows that 83.5 per cent of the respondents come from families which give donations to all people irrespective of their caste and creed as and when requested for common causes; that 73.8 per cent belong to families which come forward to settle disputes between the members of families and between neighbours; that 34 per cent are from families which have the practice of offering Annadhanam to the people in the villages; and, that 31.1 per cent are from families which render social services, such as helping to get old age pension, ration card, and admission to schools and colleges, hospitalising the sick people and releasing people from police custody etc.

The conclusion drawn from the findings of Table 5.7 is that generous donations and peace-making among members of families and among villagers are two important community service correlates contributing to the reputation of the respondents.

An overall analysis of the four groups of correlates of reputation reveals the fact that the political correlates of reputation (53.6 per cent) dominate over the community service correlates of reputation (40.7 per cent) followed by the social (23.6 per cent) and the economic correlates (22.7 per cent) in the process of the emergence of the respondents as leaders.

The comparative analysis shows that the reputation of the families of the elected respondents is more than that of the families of the defeated respondents.

Fig. 5.2: Correlates of Ascribed Reputation of Respondents : A Comparative Analysis.

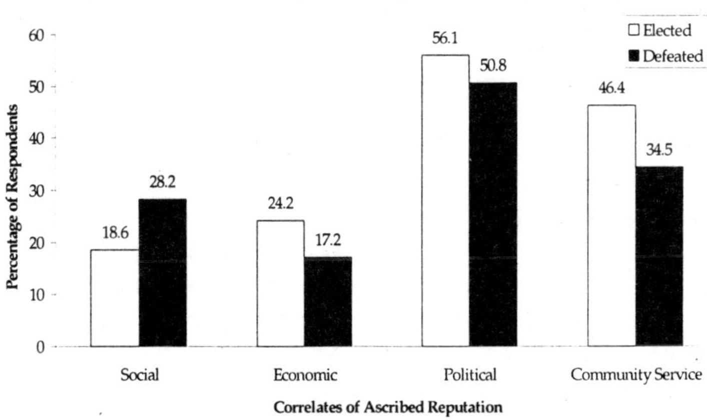

Correlates of Achieved Reputation

Achieved reputation or personal reputation refers to the reverence secured by means of one's own personal traits like hospitality, honesty, helping tendency, sociability, accessibility, tolerance, courage for atriculation, intelligence, self-confidence and fighting spirit. These personal traits constitute the correlates of personal reputation for the present study.

A respondent is deemed to have achieved reputation if she possesses at least any five of the aforesaid ten correlates of personal reputation. When the respondents were asked to mention the factors responsible for their emergence as leaders, a few of the respondents replied that they emerged as leaders because of their personal reputation in addition to the influence of their family reputation.

Such responses were further verified in consultation with the knowledgeable and responsible local informants like VAOs, temple priests, school teachers and caste leaders.

In the present study, 11.2 per cent of the respondents have been identified as persons with personal reputation. It is encouraging to learn that at least 11.2 per cent of the respondents were able to acquire personal reputation.

Leadership vis-a-vis Reputation

The underlying assumption in the reputational approach is that those who possess reputation for power emerge as leaders. With a view to identifying the level of influence of reputation as a base of power on the emergence of leadership, the reputation of the respondents, both ascribed and achieved, are analysed statistically.

Testing of Hypothesis

Hypothesis 4: "The higher the reputation of the family, the greater will be the prospects for the rural women to emerge as leaders".

The implication of this hypothesis in the statistical sense is that the votes polled by the respondents have positive relationship with the reputational scores of the respondents.

TABLE 5.8
VOTES POLLED VIS-A-VIS REPUTATIONAL SCORES

Votes Polled	*Levels of Reputational Scores*			
	Low	*Medium*	*High*	*Total*
Defeated (0-49)	85 (85.9)	9 (9.1)	5 (5.1)	99 (48.1)
Elected (50-100)	71 (66.3)	19 (19.2)	17 (17.8)	107 (51.9)
Total	156 (75.7)	28 (13.6)	22 (10.7)	206 (100)

Source: Computed.
Note: Figures in parentheses are percentages.
Mean Reputational Score: 7.88

Fig. 5.3: Reputational Scores of Respondents : A Comparative Analysis.

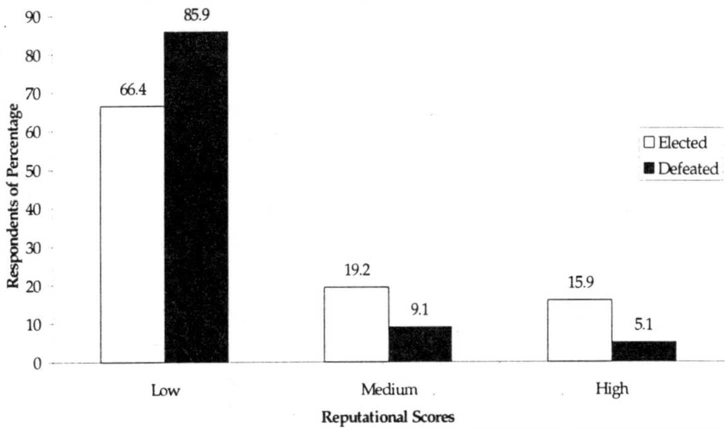

Table 5.8 indicates that 33.6 per cent of the elected respondents and 14.2 per cent of the defeated respondents come under high or medium levels of reputational scores, while 85.9 per cent of the defeated respondents and 66.3 per cent of the elected respondents fall under low level of reputational scores.

The statistical analysis of the votes polled and the reputational scores secured by the respondents brings out the fact that there is a direct and positive relationship between them.

$$(\chi^2 = 11.08; \text{D.F.} = 2; P<0.01)$$

Therefore, the fourth hypothesis of the study, namely **"The higher the reputation of the family, the greater will be the prospects for the rural women to emerge as leaders"** is affirmatively validated.

Decisional Approach

The decisional approach enunciated by Dahl and his associates[23] is also well-known as the "Event Analysis' or the "Issue Participation Approach." This approach lays emphasis on the assumption that those who actually participate in the decision-making process are the leaders as they have demonstrated their influence in real-life situation.

In order to empirically analyse the emergence of rural women leadership through this approach, certain specific determinants are conceptualised and their contributory role in the emergence of leadership is examined.

Political decision-making in villages is varied and is multidimensional. One's entry into politics itself requires deep contemplation and wise decision-making. The initial decision of one to enter the political power structure may be made on the volition of the individual concerned or by the influence of external motivating forces.

In the present study, the respondents were asked who decided their candidature for the Village Panchayat Election held in October 1996. The data collected in this respect are displayed in Table 5.9.

Table 5.9 reveals that 51.5 per cent of the respondents have contested the Panchayat elections in order to abide by the decision of their family members as against 33.0 per cent having been fielded by the general public of the village and 13.1 per cent having decided their candidature by themselves.

The significant inference drawn from the analysis is that political parties have an insignificant role in deciding the candidature in the Village Panchayat elections.

TABLE 5.9
DECISION ON CANDIDATURE OF RESPONDENTS

Sl. No.	*Deciding Source*	*Respondents*					
		Elected		*Defeated*		*Total*	
		No.	*%*	*No.*	*%*	*No.*	*%*
1.	Respondents themselves	16	15.0	11	11.1	27	13.1
2.	General Public of the village	48	44.9	20	20.2	68	33.0
3.	Family Members	42	39.2	64	64.6	106	51.5
4.	Political Parties	1	0.9	4	4.0	5	2.4
	Total	107	100.0	99	100.0	206	100.0

Source: Computed.

Prior Socio-Political Activities

Decision-making needs to be carried out judiciously at various stages of community welfare activities. The leadership of a person can be measured in terms of his/her efficiency exhibited in the process of decision-making. Abnormal rural life situations arising out of natural calamities, explosion of communal riots and other untoward incidents warrant timely and effective decisions by the leaders.

Most Indian villages suffer due to the dearth of basic amenities. These basic issues provide avenues for the leaders to establish the validity of their leadership by means of proper decision-making and implementation. According to R.M. Stogdill,[25] "Leadership is not a matter of passive status, or of the mere possession of some combination of traits. It appears rather to be a working relationship among members of a group in which the leader acquires status through active participation and demonstration of his capacity for carrying co-operative tasks through to completion."

Decision-making or issue participation by a person demands comparatively long period for judgement. Hence the leadership of a person through the decisional approach has to be assessed over a considerable period of time in terms of his/her performance on chosen socio-political issues. Therefore, the present section proposes to analyse the level of involvement of the respondents in socio-political activities prior to the Village Panchayat elections held in October 1996.

The analysis in this section starts with a study of the factors responsible for the entry of the respondents into the rural political structure. Then it turns to assess the level of influence the respondents acquired through their socio-political activities pertaining to the realisation of basic amenities, developmental schemes and alleviation of social problems affecting the villagers.

Basic amenities considered for the present study include potable water, streetlights, approach roads, hospitals, schools, transports, sanitation, grave-yards and other facilities.

The developmental schemes in villages considered for this study include desilting of existing tanks, construction of percolation ponds and check dams, installation of ration shops, building community halls and houses for Harijans, renovation of temples and schools, organising maternity centres, co-operative credit and milk societies, self-employment schemes, Balwadis, IRDP loan schemes and the like.

The social problems of the villages taken up for the present study include issues like family disputes, caste and religious conflicts, group clashes, inter-village enmity, untouchability and the like.

TABLE 5.10

PRIOR PARTICIPATION IN SOCIO-POLITICAL ACTIVITIES BY RESPONDENTS

Sl. No.	*Prior Socio-Political Activities*	*Respondents*					
		Elected		*Defeated*		*Total*	
		No.	*%*	*No.*	*%*	*No.*	*%*
1.	Basic Amenities	18	16.8	9	9.0	27	13.1
2.	Developmental Schemes	4	3.7	-	-	4	1.9
3.	Social Problems	3	2.8	-	-	3	1.5
4.	Nil Participation	82	76.7	90	90.9	172	83.5

Source: Computed.

Table 5.10 indicates that 83.5 per cent of the respondents have not played any role in any of the aforesaid socio-political activities, while only 16.5 per cent of respondents have taken part in different socio-political activities. It is apparent that the elected respondents outshine their rival respondents in their decisional role in the socio-political activities.

Prior Socio-political Activities of Family Heads

In general, rural women, because of their gender difference, are not as exposed to community issues as their male counterparts and hence their poor performance on the decisional role in socio-political activities. In this context, it is, therefore, necessary for the present study to analyse the issue participation level of the family heads of the respondents.

TABLE 5.11
PRIOR PARTICIPATION IN SOCIO-POLITICAL ACTIVITIES BY FAMILY HEADS OF RESPONDENTS

Sl. No.	*Socio-Political Activities*	*Respondents*					
		Elected		*Defeated*		*Total*	
		No.	*%*	*No.*	*%*	*No.*	*%*
1.	Basic Amenities	90	84.1	87	87.9	177	85.9
2.	Developmental Schemes	27	25.2	9	9.1	36	17.5
3.	Social Problems	35	32.7	26	26.2	61	29.6
4.	Nil Participation	17	15.9	12	12.1	29	14.1

Source: Computed.

The data distribution of Table 5.11 shows that 85.9 per cent of the family heads of the respondents participated in the decision-making process for securing basic amenities and that 29.6 per cent played a decisional role in social problems and 17.5 per cent in Developmental Schemes. It is also seen that the family heads of elected respondents outnumber the family heads of defeated respondents in participating in prior socio-political activities.

The conclusion drawn from the above findings leads to the fact that basic amenities largely attract the attention of leaders for issue participation.

TABLE 5.12
NUMBER OF SOCIO-POLITICAL ACTIVITIES FAMILY HEADS OF RESPONDENTS PARTICIPATED IN

Sl. No.	*Number of Activities*	*Respondents*					
		Elected		*Defeated*		*Total*	
		No.	%	*No.*	%	*No.*	%
1.	One Activity	28	26.2	52	52.5	80	38.8
2.	Two/Three Activities	62	57.9	35	35.4	97	47.1
3.	No Activity	17	15.9	12	12.1	29	14.1

Source: Computed.

The data in Table 5.12 show that 47.1 per cent of the respondents' family had participated in settling more than one socio-political issue, while 38.8 per cent engaged themselves in settling only one issue and the remaining 14.1 per cent did not participatie in any of the socio-political issues under consideration.

From the above findings, it is concluded that 47.1 per cent of the family heads of the respondents are polymorphic, while 38.8 per cent are monomorphic in respect of settling socio-political issues.

Settling of Issues

Modes of settling issues related to socio-political activities assume as much importance as decision-making itself. Once the decisions are made, it is only the nature of the modes which determine the successful settling of the issues. In the present study, the following modes of settling issues are considered for analysis:

1. Articulation through letters.
2. Signature campaign.
3. Direct contact with authorities.
4. Direct actions like demonstration, fast and road blockade.
5. Picketing and undergoing imprisonment.

Table 5.13 shows that 5.8 per cent of the respondents employed all the five methods of settling issues during their issue participation.

It is observed that 16.5 per cent of the respondents used one to five modes of settling socio-political issues in their villages prior to their emergence as leaders.

TABLE 5.13
MODES OF SETTLING SOCIO-POLITICAL ISSUES BY RESPONDENTS

Sl. No.	*Number of Modes*	*Respondents*					
		Elected		*Defeated*		*Total*	
		No.	*%*	*No.*	*%*	*No.*	*%*
1.	One Mode	2	1.9	5	5.0	7	3.4
2.	Two Modes	3	2.8	-	-	3	1.5
3.	Three Modes	7	6.5	-	-	7	3.4
4.	Four Modes	4	3.7	1	1.0	5	2.4
5.	Five Modes	9	8.4	3	3.0	12	5.8
6.	None	82	76.7	90	90.9	172	83.5

Source: Computed.

TABLE 5.14
MODES OF SETTLING ISSUES BY FAMILY HEADS OF RESPONDENTS

Sl. No.	*Number of Modes*	*Respondents*					
		Elected		*Defeated*		*Total*	
		No.	*%*	*No.*	*%*	*No.*	*%*
1.	One Mode	14	13.1	24	24.2	38	18.4
2.	Two Modes	11	10.3	10	10.1	21	10.2
3.	Three Modes	29	27.1	23	23.2	52	25.2
4.	Four Modes	12	11.2	15	15.2	27	13.1
5.	Five Modes	24	22.4	15	15.2	39	18.9

Source: Computed.

From the data in Table 5.14, it is understood that 25.2 per cent of the family heads of the respondents have used any three modes of settling village issues, that 18.9 per cent adopted all the five modes, and, that 38.8 per cent employed one or two or four modes of settling issues.

It is noted that 67.4 per cent of the respondents' family heads adopted more than one mode in settling issues in socio-political activities.

Promises Made

Apart from the usual issues, the leaders have to enlarge their decisional capabilities at the time of their elections to political offices. An election manifesto is a set of promises to be fulfilled by the contestants in the event of victory. Decision-making has its role in the declaration of the election manifesto and, in this context, it becomes pertinent to analyse the promises made by the respondents during their electioneering.

TABLE 5.15
ELECTION PROMISES OF RESPONDENTS

Sl. No.	*Promises*	*Respondents*					
		Elected		*Defeated*		*Total*	
		No.	*%*	*No.*	*%*	*No.*	*%*
1.	Basic Amenities	104	97.2	95	96.0	199	96.6
2.	Welfare Schemes	91	85.0	78	78.8	169	82.0
3.	Communal Harmony	54	50.5	26	26.3	80	38.8

Source: Computed.

It is obvious from the data in Table 5.15 that 96.6 per cent of the respondents have promised to provide basic amenities in the event of their victory, that 82.0 per cent assured welfare schemes, and, that 38.8 per cent promised to bring about communal harmony in the villages.

From the above findings, it is inferred that provision of basic amenities is the core issue in villages. A similar finding has been reported by Ujwala Hiremath, who states that women had a manifesto of development items for the village — electricity, roads, toilets, schools, water facility, transport facilities, old age pension — in Panchayati Raj elections.

Election Strategies

Strategies for consolidation of support bases are vital at the time of electioneering and hence foolproof decision-making on election strategies has to be ensured so as to optimise the prospects of emerging as leaders.

It is apparent from Table 5.16 that 58.7 per cent of the respondents have regarded ensuring the support of the influential people as the best strategy for election, while 36.9 per cent depended on the support of political parties followed by 30.1 per cent pinning hopes on caste support and 11.2 per cent depending on their own personal popularity.

The findings drawn from the above Table suggest that emerging as leaders requires the support of influential persons, political parties and caste people in that order.

TABLE 5.16
STRATEGIES ADOPTED BY RESPONDENTS DURING ELECTIONEERING

Sl. No.	*Strategies*	*Respondents*					
		Elected		*Defeated*		*Total*	
		No.	*%*	*No.*	*%*	*No.*	*%*
1.	Political Party Support	41	38.3	31	31.3	76	36.9
2.	Caste Support	33	30.8	31	31.3	62	30.1
3.	Influential People's Support	84	78.5	37	37.4	121	58.7
4.	Personal Popularity	18	16.8	5	5.1	23	11.2

Source: Computed.

Leadership vis-a-vis Decision-Making

The decision-making approach rests on the assumption that those who actually participate in the decision-making process are the leaders as they have already demonstrated their influence in actual-life situations. In the light of this assumption, an attempt has been made to ascertain the level of influence of the decision-making of the respondents and their family heads on the emergence of respondents as leaders.

Testing of Hypothesis

Hypothesis 5: "Decision-making of the rural women and their family heads plays a significant role in the process of the emergence of rural women as leaders".

This hypothesis, in its statistical terms, means that the votes polled and the decision-making scores secured by the respondents have a positive association.

TABLE 5.17
VOTES POLLED VIS-A-VIS DECISIONAL SCORES

Sl. No.	Votes Polled	Levels of Decisional Scores			
		Low	Medium	High	Total
1.	Defeated (0-49)	50 (50.5)	42 (42.4)	7 (7.1)	99 (48.1)
2.	Elected (50-100)	21 (19.6)	63 (58.9)	23 (21.5)	107 (51.9)
	Total	71 (34.5)	105 (51.0)	30 (14.5)	206 (100)

Source: Computed.
Note: Figures in parentheses are percentages.
Mean Score of Decision-making = 15.68

Table 5.17 shows that 80.4 per cent of the elected respondents come under either the medium or the high group of decisional scores as against 49.5 per cent of the defeated respondents, while 50.5 per cent of the defeated and 19.6 per cent of the elected respondents fall under the low group of decisional scores.

Fig. 5.4: Decisional Scores of Respondents : A Comparative Analysis.

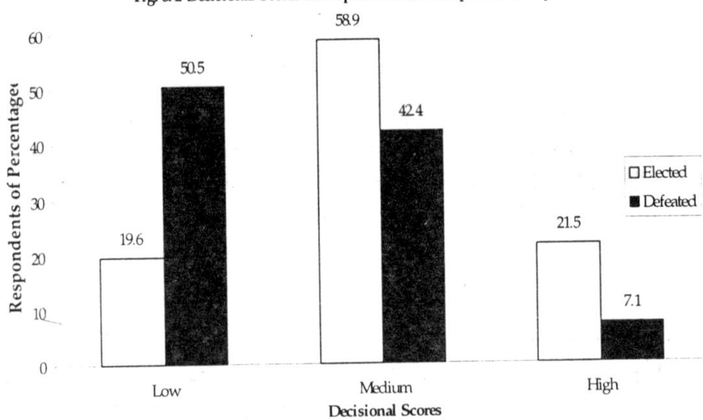

The statistical analysis of the votes and the decisional scores of the respondents brings out the fact that there is a significant association between the variants.

$(\chi^2 = 24.30; \text{D.F.} = 2; P<0.01)$

Hence, the fifth hypothesis of the study, namely **"Decision-making of the rural women and their family heads plays a significant role in the process of the emergence of rural women as leaders"** is validated empirically.

Integrated Approach to the Identification of Power Bases

An empirical study based on the integrated application of the Positional, the Reputational and the Decisional approaches through which the rural women have emerged as leaders provides an opportunity for measuring the combined effects of integrated approaches in the emergence of rural women leadership.

Syntheses of Different Approaches

The Positional, the Reputational and the Decisional approaches may be integrated in four ways by combining any two or all the three simultaneously as follows:

1. Synthesis of Position and Reputation
2. Synthesis of Reputation and Decision
3. Synthesis of Decision and Position
4. Synthesis of Position, Reputation and Decision.

Testing of Hypothesis

Hypothesis 6: "The different types of syntheses of position, reputation and decision-making as bases of power significantly enhance the emergence of rural women leadership".

In statistical terms, the above hypothesis means that there is a positive relationship between the votes polled and the sum of the scores secured by the respondents for the power bases of Position, Reputation and Decision-making taken two by two and all the three simultaneously.

For the purpose of statistical analysis, the composite scores of the respondents falling under different types of syntheses are computed by adding the scores of the components in the respective synthesis.

Leadership vis-a-vis Position and Reputation

TABLE 5.18

VOTES POLLED VIS-A-VIS COMBINED SCORES ON POSITION AND REPUTATION

Sl. No.	*Votes Polled*	*Levels of Combined Scores*			*Total*
		Low	*Medium*	*High*	
1.	Defeated (0-49)	72 (72.7)	24 (24.3)	3 (3.0)	99 (48.1)
2.	Elected (50-100)	54 (50.5)	37 (34.5)	16 (15.0)	107 (51.9)
	Total	126 (61.2)	61 (29.6)	19 (9.2)	206 (100)

Source: Computed.

Note: Figures within parentheses are percentages.

Fig. 5.5: Combined Scores on Position and Reputation of Respondents : A Comparative Analysis.

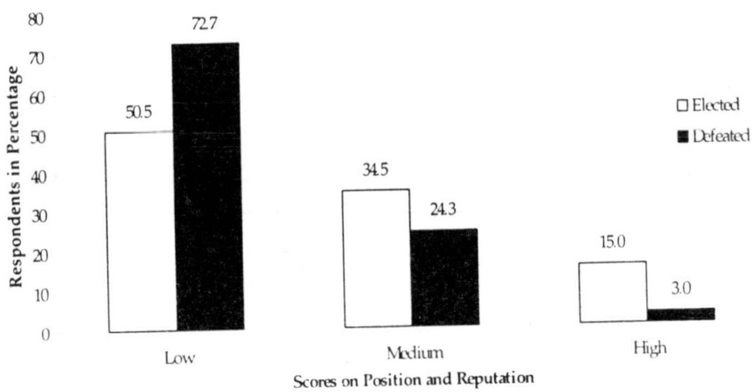

Table 5.18 reveals that 49.5 per cent of the elected respondents have secured medium or high scores for position and reputation as against 27.3 per cent of the defeated respondents and that 50.5 per cent of the elected respondents come under low composite scores of position and reputation compared to 72.7 per cent of the defeated respondents.

The statistical analysis of Table 5.18 shows that there is a positive and significant association between the votes polled and the combined scores on position and reputation of the respondents.

(χ^2 = 13.95; D.F. = 2; P<.01)

Leadership vis-a-vis Reputation and Decision-making

TABLE 5.19

VOTES POLLED VIS-A-VIS COMBINED SCORES ON REPUTATION AND DECISION-MAKING

Sl. No.	*Votes Polled*	*Levels of Combined Scores*			
		Low	*Medium*	*High*	*Total*
1.	Defeated (0-49)	66 (66.7)	30 (30.3)	3 (3.0)	99 (48.1)
2.	Elected (50-100)	35 (32.7)	54 (50.5)	18 (16.8)	107 (51.9)
	Total	101 (49.0)	84 (40.8)	21 (10.2)	206 (100)

Source: Computed.

Note: Figures within parentheses are percentages.

Fig. 5.6: Combined Scores on Reputation and Decision-Making of Respondents : A Comparative Analysis.

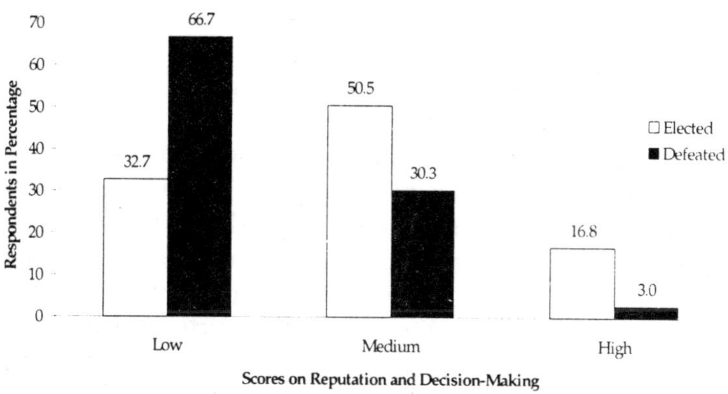

Table 5.19 makes it evident that 67.3 per cent of the elected respondents have secured medium or high levels of combined

scores on reputation and decision-making whereas only 33.3 per cent of the defeated respondents have scored at medium or high levels. On the other hand, the defeated respondents numerically outnumber the elected respondents in getting low scores by 34 per cent.

The statistical inference drawn from the above finding is that the combined effect of reputational and decisional variables has significant association with the emergence of the leadership of the respondents.

$(\chi^2 = 26.82; \text{D.F.} = 2; P<.01)$

Leadership vis-a-vis Decision-making and Position

TABLE 5.20

VOTES POLLED VIS-A-VIS COMBINED SCORES ON DECISION-MAKING AND POSITION

Sl. No.	*Votes Polled*	*Levels of Combined Scores*			
		Low	*Medium*	*High*	*Total*
1.	Defeated (0-49)	59 (59.6)	38 (38.4)	2 (2.0)	99 (48.1)
2.	Elected (50-100)	28 (26.2)	64 (59.8)	15 (14.0)	107 (51.9)
	Total	87 (42.2)	102 (49.5)	17 (8.3)	206 (100)

Source: Computed.

Note: Figures within parentheses are percentages.

It is clear from Table 5.20 that 73.8 per cent of the elected respondents come under medium or high levels of combined scores on decision-making and position, while 40.4 per cent of the defeated respondents fall under medium or high levels. Also it is found that 59.6 per cent of the defeated respondents fall under the low group as against 26.2 per cent of the elected respondents.

The statistical inference drawn from the above findings is that the impact of decisional and positional variables taken together is significantly associated with the emergence of the leadership of the respondents.

$(\chi^2 = 27.35; \text{D.F.} = 2; P<.01)$

Fig. 5.7: Combinned Scores on Decision-Making and Position of Respondents: A Comparative Analysis.

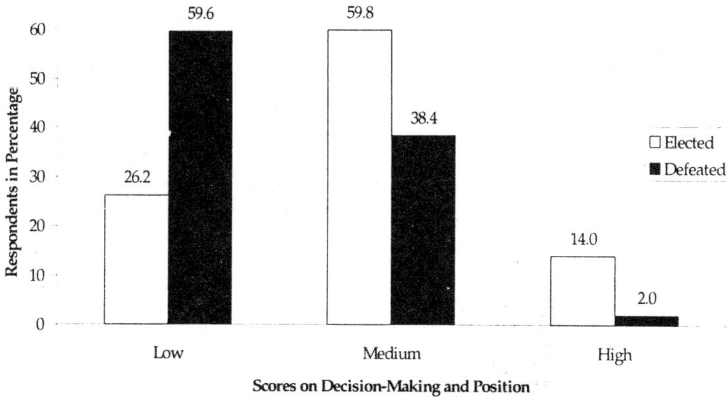

Leadership vis-a-vis Position, Reputation and Decision-making

TABLE 5.21

VOTES POLLED VIS-A-VIS COMBINED SCORES ON POSITION, REPUTATION AND DECISION-MAKING

Sl. No.	*Votes Polled*	*Levels of Combined Scores*			
		Low	*Medium*	*High*	*Total*
1.	Defeated (0-49)	72 (72.7)	25 (25.3)	2 (2.0)	99 (48.1)
2.	Elected (50-100)	47 (43.9)	41 (38.3)	19 (17.8)	107 (51.9)
	Total	119 (57.8)	66 (32.0)	21 (10.2)	206 (100)

Source: Computed.

Note: Figures in parentheses are percentages.

Table 5.21 shows that 56.1 per cent of the elected respondents have secured medium or high levels of combined scores on position, reputation and decision-making as against 27.3 per cent of the defeated respondents on the same levels. It is also seen that 72.7 per cent of the defeated respondents fall under the low group compared to 43.9 per cent of the elected respondents.

The statistical inference drawn from the above findings is that the influence of positional, reputational and decisional variables taken together is significantly associated with the emergence of the respondents as leaders.

$$(\chi^2 = 22.62;\ D.F. = 2;\ P<0.01)$$

Fig. 5.8: Combined Scores on Position, Reputation and Decision-Making of Respondents : A Comparative Analysis

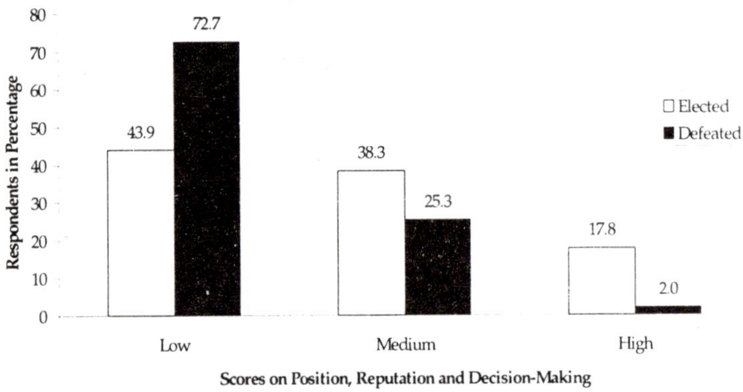

The comparative analysis of the aforesaid statistical findings reveals that the syntheses of **"Reputation and Decision-making," "Decision-making and Position"** and **"Position, Reputation and Decision-making"** influence the rural women leadership of the respondents more significantly than the combination of **"Position and Reputation".**

Overall Statistical Findings of the Three Approaches

The data in Table 5.22 reveal that the combined scores on position, with those on reputation and decision, taken two by two and all the three simultaneously are more significantly associated with the votes polled by the respondents compared to the single effect of positional scores on votes polled by the respondents.

Then again, among the combined scores, the combined scores on position and decision bear the most significant relationship with the votes secured by the respondents followed by the combined scores on all the three and those on position and reputation.

TABLE 5.22
LEADERSHIP VIS-A-VIS POSITION AND INTEGRATION OF POSITION WITH OTHER BASES OF POWER

Sl. No.	*Bases of Power*	χ^2 *(Votes vis-a-vis Bases of Power)*	*D.F.*	*P**	*R**	*Order of Effectiveness*
1.	P	6.70	2	0.05	0.18	4
2.	P+R	13.95	2	0.01	0.26	3
3.	P+D	27.35	2	0.01	0.34	1
4.	P+R+D	22.62	2	0.01	0.34	2

Source: Computed.
P - Positional scores; R - Reputational scores; D - Decisional Scores.
P* - Level of Significance; R* - Pearson's Correlation.

TABLE 5.23
LEADERSHIP VIS-A-VIS REPUTATION AND INTEGRATION OF REPUTATION WITH OTHER BASES OF POWER

Sl. No.	*Bases of Power*	χ^2 *(Votes vis-a-vis Bases of Power)*	*D.F.*	*P**	*R**	*Order of Effectiveness*
1.	R	11.08	2	0.01	0.25	4
2.	R+P	13.95	2	0.01	0.26	3
3.	R+D	26.82	2	0.01	0.36	1
4.	R+P+D	22.62	2	0.01	0.34	2

Source: Computed.
R - Reputational Scores; P - Positional Scores; D - Decisional Scores.
P* - Level of Significance; R* - Pearson's Correlation.

The data in Table 5.23 bring out that the combined scores on reputation, with those on position and decision-making, taken two by two and all the three simultaneously are significantly related with the votes secured by the respondents.

Among the combined scores, the combined scores on reputation and decision bear the most significant relationship with the votes secured by the respondents followed by the combined scores on all the three and the combined scores on reputation and position.

TABLE 5. 24
LEADERSHIP VIS-A-VIS DECISION-MAKING AND INTEGRATION OF DECISION-MAKING WITH OTHER BASES OF POWER

Sl. No.	*Bases of Power*	*χ^2 (Votes vis-a-vis Bases of Power)*	*D.F.*	*P**	*R**	*Order of Effectiveness*
1.	D	24.30	2	0.01	0.36	2
2.	D + P	27.35	2	0.01	0.34	3
3.	D + R	26.82	2	0.01	0.36	1
4.	D + P + R	22.62	2	0.01	0.34	4

Source: Computed.
D - Decisional Scores; P - Positional Scores; R - Reputational Scores.
P* - Level of Significance; R* - Pearson's Correlation.

The contents of Table 5.24 reveal that the combined scores of decision-making with those on position and reputation, taken two by two and all the three simultaneously are significantly associated with the votes secured by the respondents. Among the combined scores, those on decision-making and reputation bear the most significant relationship with the votes secured by the respondents followed by the single effect of decision-making. It is observed that the significance of the decisional score on votes secured declines whenever it is combined with position.

An overview of the statistical findings drawn from Tables 5.22, 5.23 and 5.24 lead to the consolidated conclusion that the sixth hypothesis, namely **"The different types of syntheses of Position, Reputation and Decision-making as bases of power significantly enhance the emergence of rural women leadership"** is validated affirmatively.

Categorisation of Leadership

In order to categorise the rural women leadership as positional, reputational and decisional, the mean score on each power base is considered as the cut-off point.

TABLE 5.25
DISTRIBUTION OF RESPONDENTS BY THEIR POWER BASES

Sl. No.	Pattern of Leadership	*Respondents*					
		Elected		*Defeated*		*Total*	
		No.	*%*	*No.*	*%*	*No.*	*%*
1.	Positional Leaders	69	64.5	43	43.4	112	54.4
2.	Reputational Leaders	58	54.2	26	26.3	84	40.8
3.	Decisional Leaders	71	64.4	29	29.3	100	48.5
4.	Other Leaders	8	7.5	38	38.4	46	22.3

Source: Computed.
Mean Score on Position = 9.23 out of the maximum of 42 scores
Mean Score on Reputation = 7.87 out of the maximum of 30 scores
Mean Score on Decision = 15.68 out of the maximum of 50 scores

It is evident from Table 5.25 that 54.4 per cent of the leaders possess position as a base of power, 48.5 per cent have decision - making as base of power and 40.8 per cent have reputation as base of power. It is also observed that 22.3 per cent of the respondents have emerged as leaders without any of the aforesaid bases of power.

It is also obvious that the elected respondents outnumber the defeated respondents in possessing the different bases of power.

Pattern of Emergence of Respondents' Leadership

The pattern of the emergence of the respondents as leaders is determined by taking into account the number of bases of power namely position, reputation and decision-making possessed by them. Those leaders who have all the three bases of power are classified as primary leaders, those who have only any two of the three are classified as secondary leaders and those who have only one base of power are categorised as tertiary leaders. Lastly, leaders with none of the three bases of power are classified as situational leaders.

TABLE 5. 26
LEADERSHIP PATTERN OF RESPONDENTS

Sl. No.	*Pattern of Leadership*	*Respondents*					
		Elected		*Defeated*		*Total*	
		No.	*%*	*No.*	*%*	*No.*	*%*
1.	Primary Leaders	34	31.8	8	8.1	42	20.4
2.	Secondary Leaders	31	28.9	21	21.2	52	25.3
3.	Tertiary Leaders	34	31.8	32	32.3	66	32.0
4.	Situational Leaders	8	7.5	38	38.4	46	22.3
	Total	107	100.0	99.0	100.0	206.0	100.0

Source: Computed.

It is apparent from Table 5.26 that 20.4 per cent of the respondents are primary leaders as against 25.3 per cent being secondary leaders and 32 per cent being tertiary leaders, while 22.3 per cent have emerged as situational leaders. It is important to note that the elected leaders outnumber the defeated leaders under the categories of primary, secondary and tertiary leaders.

The fact that primary leaders are minimal in number compared to secondary and tertiary leaders leads to the conclusion that there is a dispersal of power resources in the villages of Dindigul District.

Although there is overlapping of power bases among the respondents, there are some respondents having only one source of power. Their numerical identity and the exact approach through which they have emerged as leaders is displayed in the following Table:

Fig. 5.9: Venn Diagramatic Representation of Pattern of Rural Women Leadership.

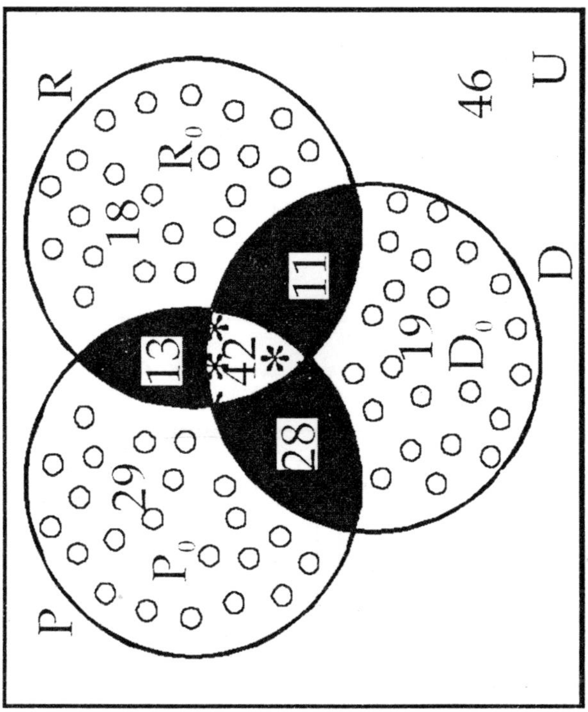

P—Set of Positional Leaders
R—Set of Reputational Leaders
D—Set of Decisional Leaders
P_0—Set of Leaders with Position only
R_0—Set of Leaders with Reputation only
D_0—Set of Leaders with Decision only

⊛ Primary Leaders
■ Secondary Leaders
⊡ Tertiary Leaders
□ Situational Leaders

Source: Computed.

Fig. 5.10: A Simple Framework of the Analysis of Leadership Pattern.

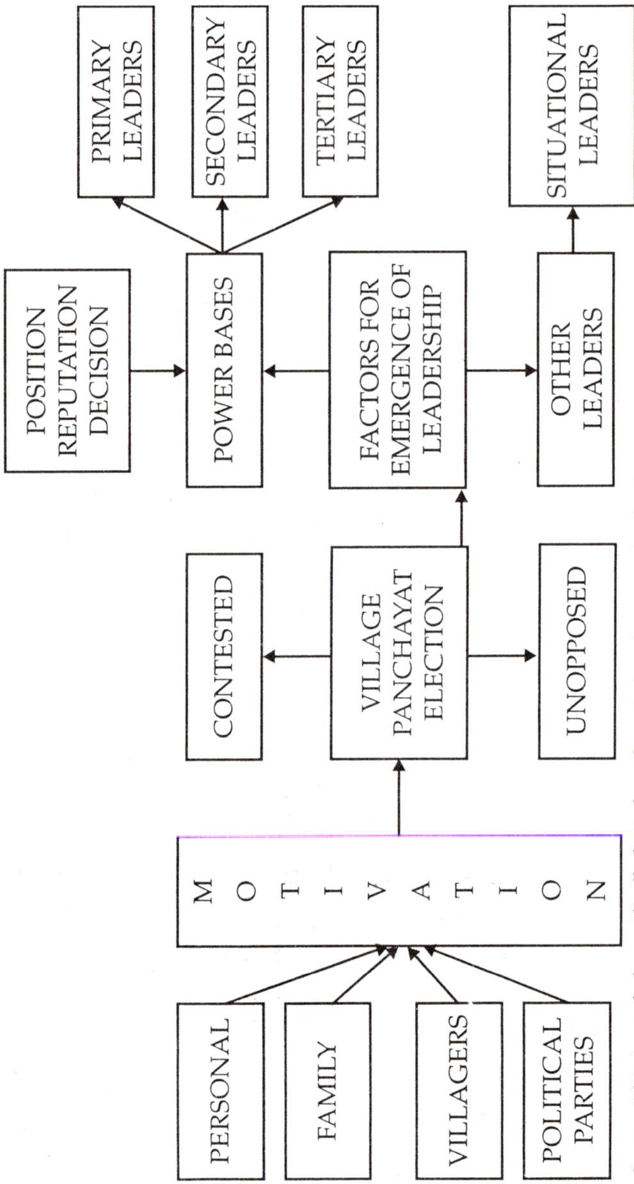

Source : This is evoled specifically based on the existing theory on leadership.

TABLE 5.27
DISTRIBUTION OF RESPONDENTS WITH SINGLE BASE OF POWER

Sl. No.	*Bases of Power*	*Respondents*					
		Elected		*Defeated*		*Total*	
		No.	*%*	*No.*	*%*	*No.*	*%*
1.	Position only	11	10.3	18	18.2	29	14.1
2.	Reputation only	10	9.3	8	8.0	18	8.7
3.	Decision-Making only	13	12.2	6	6.0	19	9.2

Source: Computed.

The data in Table 5.27 indicate that 14.1 per cent of the respondents have emerged as leaders with only position as base of power, 9.2 per cent with decision-making alone as base of power, and, 8.7 per cent with only reputation as base of power. These leaders are called the tertiary leaders.

Regression Analysis of Multi-variants

The multi-variants considered for the statistical study of the emergence of rural women leaders are the socio-economic variable (x_1), political background variable (x_2), positional variable (x_3), reputational variable (x_4) and decisional variable (x_5). The votes secured by the respondents depend upon the aforesaid multi-variants. The multi-variant regression analysis of the votes polled on the independent variants is computed as:

$$y = a_0 + a_1x_1 + a_2x_2 + a_3x_3 + a_4x_4 + a_5x_5$$

where

a_0 = 24.806918
a_1 = .171270
a_2 = .167805
a_3 = -.022622
a_4 = -.007222
a_5 = .295164 and
R^2 = .19738

The value of R^2 shows that there are some other factors which intervene in the process of the emergence of the respondents as leaders. The leaders who have emerged through **"some other factors"** are called situational leaders in this study. Peculiar situations suddenly intruding upon a political system or a community may turn to be the basis for the emergence of the new type of leaders called situational leaders.

Alliance policies of political parties, sudden phenomena causing political waves, religious, communal and inter-village animosities, sudden upheavals giving rise to anomic leaders, the dormant support of unknown influentials, caste and village affinities may be some of the peculiar situations for the emergence of situational leaders.

Freed W. Fielder[25] and his associates at the University of Illinois have suggested a contingency theory of leadership. This theory holds that people become leaders not only because of attributes of their personalities, but also because of various situational factors and the interactions between leaders and group members.

Summing up

In the beginning of this chapter, the methodological problems in identifying the influence of the three approaches, namely the Positional, the Reputational and the Decisional Approaches on the emergence of leadership were discussed. The advantages and disadvantages of the three approaches were also analysed. The methodology adopted in the present study is intended to identify the power bases through which the respondents have emerged as leaders in the Village Panchayats of Dindigul District.

A review of analysis of the data collected with regard to the position, the reputation and the decision-making of the respondents suggests the following findings:

1. Only 2.4 per cent of the respondents hold positions as office-bearers and 8.4 per cent are members in socio-political organisations other than those meant for women only; however, 37.9 per cent of the respondents are members and 26.3 per cent are office-bearers in organisations meant for women only. Contrary to the positional status of the respondents, 12.1 per cent of their family heads are office-bearers and 21.8 per cent members

in politically-oriented or caste-based village organisations, in previous Village Panchayats or in other organisations under study. However, the statistical analysis shows that the combined effect of the positions held by the respondents and their family heads has a significant and affirmative relationship with the emergence of leadership.

2. As for reputation, 23.6 per cent of the respondents have ascribed reputation because of social correlates, 22.7 per cent due to economic correlates, 53.6 per cent due to political correlates and 40.7 per cent due to community service correlates. Only 11.2 per cent of the respondents have achieved reputation. However, the integrated influence of ascribed and achieved reputation possessed by the respondents has played a significant role in their emergence as leaders.
3. As many as 13.1 per cent of respondents contested the Village Panchayat election of their own accord, while 84.5 per cent of the respondents contested the election as per the decisions of their family heads or the general public of the village and only 2.4 per cent of the respondents contested at the suggestion of political parties.

Only 16.5 per cent of the respondents have participated in different socio-political activities prior to their emergence as leaders, while 85.9 per cent of their family heads have participated in socio-political activities in order to fulfil basic amenities, developmental schemes and settling of social issues in the villages.

Further, 47.1 per cent of the family heads are polymorphic in the sense that they were instrumental in settling more than one socio-political issue, compared to 38.8 per cent who are monomorphic in the sense that they were instrumental in settling only one socio-political issue.

As many as 67.4 per cent of the family heads of the respondents have adopted more than one method of settling issues like articulating through letters, signature campaign, direct contact with authorities, demonstration, picketing and courting arrest as against 13.1 per cent of the respondents in this regard.

In respect of the promises made at the time of electioneering, 96.6 per cent of the respondents have promised the fulfilment of basic amenities, 82.0 per cent have promised Welfare Schemes and 38. 8 per cent communal harmony. Regarding the strategies for winning the elections, 58.7 per cent of the respondents are found to have harnessed the support of the influentials in the villages.

The outcome of the statistical analysis of the data on the prior socio-political activities of the respondents and their family heads reveals that decision-making has played a significant role in the process of the emergence of the respondents as leaders.

4. Of the three power bases, namely position, reputation and decision-making, decision-making has played a significant role as a power base in the emergence of the respondents' leadership followed by reputation and position.
5. The integration of position, reputation and decision-making taken two by two and all the three simultaneously enhances significantly the emergence of the respondents as leaders.
6. The findings of the comparative analysis of the integrated approaches of position, reputation and decision-making reveal that the combinations namely "Reputation and Decision-making","Decision-making and Position" and "Position, Reputation and Decision-making" influence the emergence of the leadership of the respondents more significantly than the combination of "Position and Reputation".
7. The categorisation of the rural women leadership has been carried out on the basis of the scores secured on the power bases of position, reputation and decision-making by the respondents. Those leaders who have emerged through all the three power bases are categorised as primary leaders. Those leaders who have any two of the three power bases are categorised as secondary leaders. Those who have only one power base are called tertiary leaders.

The multi-variate regression analysis brings out that there are some other factors besides the three bases of power for the emergence of rural women leadership, resulting in the emergence of a new type of leaders called situational leaders.

Since the primary leaders (20.4 per cent) are found to be less in number compared to secondary leaders (25.3 per cent), tertiary leaders (32.0 per cent) and situational leaders (22.3 per cent), there is dispersal of power resources in the villages of Dindigul District.

References

1. An excellent over view of these approaches is found in Charles M. Bonjean and David M. Olsen, "Community Leadership: Direction of Research", in William D. Hawiey and Fredric M. Wirt, (eds.), **The Search for Community Power,** Englewood Cliffs, New Jersey: Printice Hall, 1968, cited in D.C. Miglani, **Politics and Rural Power Structure**, New Delhi: Deep and Deep Publications 1993, p. 162.
2. G. Narayana Reddy, **Rural Elite and Community Work — A Socio Pclitical Perspective,** Allahabad: Chug Publications, 1986, p. 103.
3. L.C. Freeman, et al., (ed.) "Locating Leaders in Local Communities: A Comparison of some Alternative Approaches", in M. Aiken and P.E. Mott. (ed.). **The Structure of Community Power,** New York : Random House, 1970, p. 347.
4. C.M. Bonjean, and Olsen, D.M., "Community Leadership: Directions of Research", in M. Aiken, and P.E. Mott (ed.), *Ibid.*, p. 347.
5. L.C. Freeman, et al., *Op. cit.* pp 340-347.
6. C.M. Bonjean, and D.M. Olsen, "Community Leadership: Direction of Research", **Administrative Science Quartely,** Vol. 9, No. 3, December, 1974, p. 282.
7. Sheo Kumar Lal, " Approaches to the Identification of Elites" in K.L. Sharma, (ed.), **Social Inequality in India Profiles of Caste, Class, Power and Social Mobility,** New Delhi: Rawat Publications, 1995, p. 148.
8. D.C. Miglani, *Op. cit.*, p. 163.
9. C.M. Bonjean, and D.M. Olsen, *Op. cit.*, p. 204.
10. T.K. Oomen, "Myth and Reality in Indian's Communitarian Villages", in A.R. Desai (ed.), **Rural Sociology in India,** Bombay: Popular Prakashan, 1994, pp. 653-674; T.K. Oomen, "Rural Community Power Structure in India", **Social Forces,** Vol. 49, No. 2, December, 1970, pp. 226-39.
11. K. Ranga Rao, "Rural Leadership and Conflict Study of Andhra Village", **Economic and Political Weekly,** Vol. III, No. 17, April 27, 1968.
12. Yogendra Singh, "Changing Power Structure of Village Community — A Case Study of six Villages in Eastern U.P.", in A.R. Desai (ed.), Rural Sociology in India, Bombay Popular Prakashan 1994, pp. 711-23.

13. Narayana Reddy, *Op. cit.*, p. 108.
14. Manu Basker, "Women Panchayat Members in Kerala:A Profile", **Economic and Political Weekly,** Vol. XXXII, No. 17, April 1997, pp. 13-20.
15. Sharma, K.L., **The Changing Rural Stratification System,** Bangalore: Orient Longman, 1976,
16. G. Narayana Reddy, Loc. cit.
17. M.S.S. Pandian, **The Immage Trap.** New Delhi: Sage Publications, 1992. Sara Dickey, Cinema and the Urban Poor in South India, 1993, Cited in G. Palanithurai, **Perception of Gross Root Democracy and Political Performance,** New Delhi: M D Publications Pvt. Ltd., 1998, p. 186.
18. G. Palanithurai, *Ibid.*, p. 187.
19. For detail see Appendix.
20. S.R. Mehta, **Emerging Pattern of Rural Leadership**, New Delhi: Wiley Eastern Private Limited, 1972, p. 80.
21. G. Narayana Reddy, *Op. cit.*, p. 104.
22. M.E. Opler and R.D. Singh., "Economic, Political and Social Change in North Central India", **Human Organisation,** Vol. II, No. 2, Summer, 1952, pp. 5-12.
23. Robert A. Dhal, **Who Governs?,** New Heaven : Yale University Press 1961; Nelson Polsby, **Community Power and Political Theory,** New Haven: Yale University Press, 1963; and " The Sociology of Community Power", **Social Forces**, Vol. 37, March, 1959, pp. 232-36 and " Community Power", **American Sociological Review**, Vol. 24, No. 6, December, 1959, pp. 796-803.
24. Lester G. Seligman, "The Study of Political Leadership" in H. Eulau, S.J. Eldersveld and M.Janowitz, **Political Behaviour - A Reader in Theory and Research**, New Delhi: Amerind Publishing Co. Pvt. Ltd., 1972, p. 181.
25. Freed E. Fielder, **A Theory of Leadership Effectiveness,** New York: McGraw Hill, 1967, p. 151.

Six

Findings, Conclusions and Suggestions

Research studies of community leadership have been undertaken abroad and in India during the past five decades. The study of rural power structure and leadership has now become an integral part of modern political researches because of the nation's policy to strengthen the grassroots democracy.

In the present study, the emerging pattern of rural women leadership in Dindigul District of Tamil Nadu has been investigated. Besides the statistical validation of hypotheses some other major findings have also been observed in the present study.

Major Findings

Socio-Economic Status of Women Leaders

The first hypothesis of the study was with regard to the socio-economic status of the rural women in Dindigul District vis-a-vis their emergence as leaders in Village Panchayats. Through the statistical analysis, it has been established that **"the socio-economic status is a significant factor in determining the emergence of rural women leadership."**

In the discussion of the socio-economic status of the rural women in Dindigul District, the empirical data on socio-economic variables were harnessed and analysed.

In the present study, it has been found that 79.6 per cent of the rural women leaders in Dindigul District belong to the younger age group of 21-40 years with an average age of 34.4 years.

It has been observed in the current study that 63.1 per cent of the rural women leaders who have emerged are from Backward Communities and 66.0 per cent have emerged from the numerically dominant caste groups in their respective Panchayat Villages. (see Table 1.7 in the Appendix I).

In the analysis of religion as a contributory factor in the emergence of rural women leadership, it has been found that 89.3 per cent of the rural women leaders profess the Hindu faith, that 9.2 per cent are Christians and that 1.5 per cent are Muslims.

As per the government documents, the rural literacy rate of Dindigul District is 52.0 per cent as against 54.6 per cent literacy rate of Tamil Nadu. However, it is found in the present study that 99.1 per cent of the rural women leaders are literate and that 7.8 per cent are graduates. This finding reveals that education has its impact on the emergence of rural women leadership.

In respect of the educational status of the heads of families of rural women leaders, it has been observed that 98.0 per cent of the heads of families are literate while 22.3 per cent are graduates. This fact confirms that the educational levels of heads of families of rural women too plays an effective role in the emergence of the rural women as leaders.

It has been observed that 68.5 per cent of the leaders are housewives. It is also seen that 55.9 per cent of the rural women leaders hail from agricultural families. Hence, agriculture as an occupation has a bearing on the emergence of rural women leadership.

Regarding the annual income of the family, the study has found that 59.2 per cent of the rural women leaders belong to the annual income group of sixty one thousand rupees and above. It may be concluded that 59.2 per cent of the rural women leaders of Dindigul District have emerged from the higher economic strata of the rural masses.

In respect of possession of land holdings, 76.7 per cent of the rural women leaders are found to possess land holdings with river and well irrigation. This suggests that the rural women with irrigated land holdings have more opportunity to emerge as leaders than the landless and dry land owners.

Regarding the total value of assets, 62.6 per cent of the rural women leaders are found to have emerged from the asset group of Rs.6 lakh and above. This finding leads to the conclusion that possession of wealth facilitates the emergence of leadership.

As for the marital status of rural women leaders, it is observed that 96.6 per cent of the leaders are married, 3.4 per cent are widows, 0.5 per cent deserted, and, 3.4 per cent are spinsters.

It has also been found that 49.5 per cent of the rural women leaders reside in terraced houses, 93.2 per cent are residing within the panchayat limits, 66.0 per cent are from nuclear families, and, 90.8 per cent have a family size of four members (2+2) and above.

As regards the modern facilities, the families of 80.6 per cent rural women leaders own television sets. While 24.3 per cent have telephone facilities, 11.2 per cent own cars. The possession of these modern facilities is a status symbol to the rural women besides their utility and hence facilitates the emergence of the rural women leadership.

Political Background of the Women Leaders

The study has formulated the second hypothesis as: **"the higher the political background of the family, the greater will be the emergence of rural women leadership".**

The second hypothesis, referring to the impact of political background of the families of the respondents on their emergence as rural women leaders, is affirmatively validated through statistical analysis. This means that there is a significant relationship between the emergence of rural women as leaders and the political background of their families.

While testing this hypothesis, political background variables responsible for the emergence of leadership were analysed and the following major findings were arrived at.

It has been found that 75.2 per cent of the rural women leaders became aware of politics even before they attained the age of 25 years and 83.0 per cent started their political career even before the age of 40 years.

As to the sources of inspiration for political interest, 44.7 per cent of the rural women leaders have been found to have developed interest in politics through the agency of the family and the Mass Media. Political parties have been observed to be less effective agencies in inducing the political interest of the rural women in Dindigul District.

With regard to political party affiliation, 76.7 per cent of the family heads of the rural women leaders are identified to have political affiliation with parties like the DMK, the AIADMK, the TMC, the Congress (I), the CPI, the CPI(M), the BJP, the MDMK, the PMK and the DK.

It has also been observed that 27.2 per cent of the rural women leaders' family heads have affiliation with the DMK, 21.8 per cent with the AIADMK, 13.6 per cent with the TMC and 9.7 per cent with the Congress(I).

The study has also revealed that 22.8 per cent of the heads of the families of the rural women leaders hold positions as office-bearers of political parties at village or District levels whereas only 1.9 per cent of the rural women leaders themselves are office-bearers in political parties.

Concerning the political participation, 76.0 per cent of the heads of the families of the rural women leaders show active political participation, while 24.0 per cent are politically inactive.

Regarding the stimulants for political participation of the rural women leaders, it has been observed that 37.8 per cent of the leaders participated on the motivation of their family members, while 34.5 per cent participated in politics because of the stimulus of the general public. It is also observed that 23.3 per cent of the rural women leaders have resorted to political participation on their own interest and that in the case of 4.4 per cent of the rural women leaders political participation was stimulated by political parties.

In respect of political ambition, the present study has found that 59.2 per cent of the rural women leaders have static political ambition, while 27.2 per cent and 13.6 per cent have progressive political ambition and discrete political ambition respectively.

Identification of Power Bases and Categorisation of Women Leaders

Leadership vis-a-vis Position

Based on the position, the study formulated the third hypothesis as: **"the positions of the rural women leaders and their family members as bases of power have their own impact on the emergence of rural women as leaders".**

In statistical terms this hypothesis implies that there is a positive association between the votes polled and the positional scores secured by the rural women leaders.

The study has, after due statistical analysis, found that this hypothesis is affirmatively validated. While testing the hypothesis, the following findings have been observed.

Only 2.4 per cent of the rural women leaders are office-bearers and 8.4 per cent are members in socio-political organisations other than those meant for women only. However, 37.9 per cent of the rural women leaders are found to be members and 26.3 per cent are office-bearers in organisations meant for women only.

With regard to the family heads of the rural women leaders in relation to their positions, it is found that 12.1 per cent of them are office-bearers and 21.8 per cent are members in politically-oriented, caste-based village organisations, in previous Village Panchayats or in other organisations under consideration.

The statistical analysis shows that the combined effect of positions held by the rural women leaders and their family heads has a significant and affirmative relationship with the emergence of rural women leadership.

Leadership vis-a-vis Reputation

The fourth hypothesis of the study dealt with the reputation of the families of the rural women leaders and its impact on their emergence as leaders.

The statistical analysis of the study affirmatively validated the hypothesis that **"the higher the reputation of the family, the greater will be the prospects for the rural women to emerge as leaders".**

The statistical implication of this hypothesis signifies that the votes polled by the respondents in the Village Panchayat elections for the office of the chairperson has direct association with the scores secured on the reputation of the rural women leaders.

While testing this hypothesis, it has been observed that 23.6 per cent of the rural women leaders have ascribed reputation due to social correlates of reputation, 22.7 per cent due to economic correlates, 53.6 per cent due to political correlates and 40.7 per cent due to community service correlates. Only 11.2 per cent of the leaders have achieved reputation. Nevertheless, the integrated influence of the ascribed and the achieved reputation of rural women has played a significant role in their emergence as leaders.

Leadership vis-a-vis Decision-Making

The fifth hypothesis of the study was concerned with the level of involvement of the leaders and their family heads in prior socio-political activities and its influence on the emergence of their leadership.

The involvement of the leaders and their family heads in socio-political activities signifies the issue participation or the decision-making capacity of the rural women leaders. The analysis of the study of decision-making role of the leaders and their family heads has justified the hypothesis that **"Decision-making of the rural women and the family heads plays a significant role in the process of the emergence of rural women leadership".**

While testing the hypothesis, the following findings were obtained: As many as 13.1 per cent of the rural women leaders contested the Village Panchayat elections in their respective Village Panchayats of their own accord, while 84.5 per cent of the rural women leaders contested the elections as per the decisions of their family heads or the general public of the village and only 2.4 per cent of the rural women leaders contested at the suggestion of political parties.

Only 16.5 per cent of the rural women leaders have participated in socio-political activities prior to their emergence as leaders, compared to 85.9 per cent of their family heads who participated in socio-political activities in order to secure basic amenities, promote developmental schemes and settle social issues.

Based on the nature of leadership, 47.1 per cent of the rural women leaders are polymorphic in the sense that their family heads were instrumental in settling more than one socio-political issue as against 38.8 per cent of monomorphic leaders who were influentials in only one issue.

As many as 67.4 per cent of the family heads of the rural women leaders were observed to have employed more than one method of settling issues such as articulating the grievances through letters, signature campaign, direct contact with concerned authorities, demonstration, fast and road blockade as against 13.1 per cent of rural women leaders in this regard.

Regarding the promises made at the time of electioneering, 96.6 per cent of the rural women leaders made promises to fulfil the basic amenities, whereas 82.0 per cent promised welfare schemes and 38.8 per cent communal harmony.

Regarding to the strategies adopted for winning the elections, 58.7 per cent of the rural women leaders were found to be dependent upon the support of the influentials in the villages.

Integrated Approach for Emergence of Leadership

The sixth hypothesis of the study dealt with the efficacy of the three power bases of Position, Reputation and Decision-making combined two by two and all the three simultaneously towards the emergence of leadership.

The statistical analysis of the study positively validated the hypothesis that **"the different types of syntheses of Position, Reputation and Decision-making as bases of power significantly enhance the emergence of rural women leadership".**

The comparative analysis of the three approaches of Position, Reputation and Decision-making has established the fact that the combinations of **"Reputation and Decision-making", "Decision-making and Position", "Position, Reputation and Decision-making"** influence the emergence of rural women leadership more significantly than the combination of **"Position and Reputation".**

Categorisation of Leadership

On the basis of the mean scores secured on the power bases of Position, Reputation and Decision-making, the categorisation of the rural women leadership was made as Primary, Secondary and Tertiary. Those rural women leaders who had all the three power bases were categorised as **Primary Leaders** (20.4 per cent), those with any two of the power bases as **Secondary Leaders** (25.3 per cent) and those with only one of the power bases as **Tertiary Leaders** (32.0 per cent).

The Multi-variate Regression Analysis of the data has further revealed that there are some other factors besides the three power bases paving the way for the emergence of a new type of leaders called **Situational Leaders** (22.3 per cent).

It is also found that there is dispersal of power resources in the Panchayat Villages of Dindigul District based on the finding that **Primary Leaders** are less in number than the **Tertiary, Secondary and Situational Leaders.**

Conclusion

This study set out to explore answers for the questions hereunder:

1. Has the socio-economic status helped the rural women in the emergence of their leadership?
2. Has the political background of rural women and their families influenced the process of their emergence as leaders?
3. Can the positions held by the rural women and their family heads in various socio-political organisations influence the emergence of rural women as leaders?
4. Can the reputation of the rural women promote the process of achieving leadership?
5. Can the participation of rural women and their family heads in decision-making process on local community issues enable the rural women to secure the leadership?
6. Will the synthesis of different bases of power facilitate the emergence of rural women leadership ?

In the attempt to find answers to the aforesaid questions, the study first arrived at the result that there is affirmative and significant relationship between the votes polled by the rural women leaders in their Village Panchayat elections and the scores on their socio-economic status variables at 1 per cent level of significance of Chi square test.

This result implies the positive validation of the hypothesis that **"the socio-economic status is a significant factor in determining rural women leadership"**, which provides the answer to the first question.

The analysis of the study in relation to the second question showed that the association between the votes polled in the elections and the scores secured for the political background factors was validated at 1 per cent level of significance of Chi square test.

The implication of this result positively justifies the hypothesis pertaining to the second question that "**the higher the political back ground of the family, the greater will be the emergence of rural women leadership".**

The finding of the study as to the third question revealed that there was positive relationship between the votes polled and the scores secured for the positions as per the Chi square test at 5 per cent level of significance.

This finding provides the answer to the third question by positively validating the hypothesis that, **"the positions of the rural women and their family heads as bases of power have their own impact on the emergence of the rural women as leaders".**

The outcome of the study with regard to the fourth question revealed that there was significant association between the votes polled and the scores on reputation of the leaders at 1 per cent level of significance of Chi square test.

This result of Chi square test leads to the conclusion that **"the higher the reputation of the family, the greater will be the prospect for the rural women to emerge as leaders."**

The Chi square test has further established that the dependent variable, namely the votes polled, has positive association with the scores on the decision-making capabilities at 1 per cent level of significance.

Thus the answer to the fifth question is the affirmative validation of the corresponding hypothesis that, **"decision-making of the rural women and their family heads plays a significant role in the process of the emergence of rural women leadership".** On finding the answer to the last question, the following statistical inferences were arrived at.

The Chi square values of the associations between votes polled by the leaders and the scores secured by them for their Position, Reputation and Decision-making integrated two by two and all the three simultaneously, were positively significant at 1 per cent level.

This inference confirms the last hypothesis of the present study that, **"the different types of syntheses of Position, Reputation and Decision-making as bases of power significantly enhance the emergence of rural women leadership".**

These conclusions of the present study explain the pattern of rural women leadership that has emerged in Dindigul District through the Village Panchayat elections held in October 1996. To sum up, the present study has identified the emerging pattern of rural women leadership as Primary, Secondary, Tertiary, Situational leaders, Polymorphic and Monomorphic leaders.

Suggestions for Further Research

In the constitution of the Village Panchayat prior to the Seventy-third Constitution (Amendment) Act 1992, rural women were allowed only to be co-opted whenever women representatives were not elected. The co-opted women members did not enjoy the voting power and consequently their role performance was not as it ought to be. The entry of rural women into the power structure of the Village Panchayat has now been necessitated by the one-third reservation for women at all levels and for all positions of PRIs. The rural women leaders, as new entrants on the political horizon at grassroots level, may have to face various impediments in the process of their emergence as leaders. In the light of these observations, the researcher suggests that a study of the problems confronting the process of emergence of rural women leadership may be undertaken.

The present study identified the fact that there are enough rural women to contest for the office of Village Panchayat President. But these rural women were, by and large, persuaded by their male family members who could not by themselves contest in the elections in view of the reservation for women. However, after emerging as leaders, how do the rural women perceive their present position? How do they perform their roles?. These questions need to be answered and hence a research work on the role perception and the role performance of rural women leaders may be undertaken.

In the context of new Panchayati Raj Act, the spheres of powers and functions are getting enlarged and the leadership has to assume new dimensions in order to fulfil the intended expectations. New schemes and projects such as Anna Renaissance Scheme, Namakku Namae Scheme (We for Ourselves Scheme) and other developmental schemes form the core of the Time-bound Schemes of the Village Panchayats. The successful implementation of these schemes requires an enhanced capacity among rural women leaders. Can rural women leaders compete with their male counterparts in this regard? A fitting answer to this question may be provided by undertaking a comparative study of the functional abilities of rural women and men leaders.

The rural women leaders have some peculiar problems in

administering development. Their problems may vary from lack of self-confidence to the social constraints due to gender difference. These problems, have to be identified and remedied. Therefore, a research study of the problems encountered by rural women leaders in the process of their development administration is suggested.

Further, a study of the attitude of the general public to the role performance of women Village Panchayat Presidents and another study of the relationship between the officials and women leaders of PRIs may also be undertaken as they may contribute some useful and concrete suggestions towards the effective functioning of the women leaders.

In view of the fact that the social and political processes in the present day world are not constant, but ever changing, one can expect that there will always be scope for modifications in what has been observed in a research study at a particular time and in a particular geographical area. Hence, it is proposed that further research on the same subject as the one in the present study may be undertaken in varied geographical areas.

Recommendations

After having accomplished the first stage of empowerment of rural women in PRIs through reservation, there should be no question of the process getting reversed in view of the probable constraints women have to encounter therein. In this context it is the paramount duty of the leaders at the upper echelons of political parties, policy makers, bureaucrats and social workers and the general public to help the new PRIs to function on the expected lines.

In this endeavour, the first step would be to politically socialise and train the novice rural women leaders in the intricacies of the process of decision-making and in administration. Although a start has been initiated in this regard in many States including Tamil Nadu, the process has to be systematically continued in consonance with the feedback.

Through specially organised seminars and workshops, governmental organisations, NGOs and educational institutions may come forward to highlight to the rural women leaders the trends in the existing political scenario both at the state and national levels, the inter-relationships of various systems of rural power structure, community development programmes, and, the implications of political action and policies, economic and social issues.

Mere orientation cannot make rural women effective leaders. Only attitudinal changes and motivation towards leadership in its real sense can bring forth the expected results. Therefore, the attitude of male members of the society and political parties has to undergo a transformation conducive to the emergence of rural women leaders.

Political empowerment of women cannot, all of a sudden, be achieved through mere mandatory provision of one-third reservation. Sufficient exposure to politics through political parties is a prerequisite for women to accept leadership positions in the rural power structure. Naturally this exigency requires the political parties to willingly reserve leadership positions for women at all levels and to field them as candidates in the elections to the Legislatures and the Local Bodies.

The morale of rural women leaders with regard to their functional ability and ability to tackle problems may get boosted by the support and co-operation of their fellow women. Therefore, women organisations like Mahalir Mantrams and other women's pressure groups may be sensitised to the issues of rural women leaders and the significance of their support to the meaningful functioning of the rural women leaders.

The formal education, through its courses of studies and curriculum may inculcate the values of gender equality, self-respect, courage, independence etc., which would help develop the personality traits and leadership qualities of rural women.

The mass media, in its turn, may play a constructive role in enhancing women's leadership by giving wider coverage to various activities and measures taken by rural women and by highlighting their problems and prospects. Through audio-video systems, success stories of women leaders and their struggles and experiences may be portrayed to the women public so as to motivate and encourage rural women to shoulder leadership responsibilities.

The emergence of rural women leadership at the grassroots level of democracy has, as per the present study, come into being with the support base of ascribed status. Leadership will be a reality when it emerges largely through the achieved status of the leaders. With this view in mind, the family members of the rural women in particular and the society in general have to ensure women equal participation in the decision-making process, the control over resources and the mechanisms for sustaining these gains.

Glossary

Annai Velankanni	:	Mother of Lord Jesus Christ
Athiparasakthi	:	Hindu Goddess
Anna	:	Founder of the DMK party
Balwadi	:	Centre looking after children in villages organised by Government of Tamil Nadu.
Coolie	:	Low level labour/labourer
Dandi March	:	Part of Gandhiji's Freedom Movement in India
First Respect	:	The honour given to local nobles at the commencement of social and religious celebrations in villages of Tamil Nadu
Gurukkal	:	Brahmin priest of a temple
Harijan	:	Literally, children of God (an appellation used by Gandhi for the lowest castes and included in SC/ST)
Lord Ayyappan	:	Hindu God
Lord Murugan	:	Hindu God
Mandal Panchayat	:	Group of village Panchayats in Karnataka State, covering 10-12,000 persons
Nyaya Panchayat	:	Judicial Panchayat
Padayathra Pilgrims	:	Pilgrims taking a vow to visit the place of worship on foot.
Panchayat	:	Village statutory body.
Panchayati Raj	:	The term Panchatyati Raj refers to a three-tier structure of rural local self-government. The three structures are : District Panchayat, Panchayat Union and Village Panchayat.
Panchayat Union	:	Group of Village Panchayats in Tamil Nadu

Palayams : Administrative territorial unit of petty kings. under British control during pre-Independence period.

Poosari : Local temple priest.

Taluk : Administrative unit consisting of a group of revenue villages.

Tahsil : Taluk

Vedaranyam March : Part of Gandhiji's Indian Freedom Movement.

Zamindar : Royal representative of British Government with the powers of collecting taxes within a specific geographical jurisdiction.

Zilla Parishad : District Panchayat

Maniyam
Natanmai
Oor Gounder
Oor Naickar
Pannadi
Periyathanam : Tamil terms for chiefs of different Caste groups in the villages of Dindigul District in Tamil Nadu.

Interview Schedule

PART - I

Sl. No.

PERSONAL PROFILE

1.	Name of the respondent	:			
	Name of the Village Panchayat	:			
	Name of the Panchayat Union	:			
	No. of Contestants.	:			
2.	Classification of Panchayat	:	General	General Women	SC/ST
3.	Result of the Contest	:	Un-opposed	Elected	Defeated
4.	Votes Secured	:	Total	%	
5.	Difference	:			
6.	Age	:	21-30	31-40	41-50	51&above
7.	Caste	:	SC/ST	MBC	BC	FC
8.	Numerical Strength of Caste	:	Majority	Minority	
9.	Religion	:	Hindu	Muslim	Christian
10.	Numerical Strength of Religion	:	Majority	Minority	
11.	Educational Qualification	:	Illiterate	Primary	
			Secondary	Higher Secondary	
			Diploma	College	

12. Previous Occupation	:	Agricultural Coolie		
		Agriculture		
		Retired Govt. Servant		
		Housewife		
13. Marital Status	:	Single	Married	Widowed
		Divorced	Deserted	
14. Type of Family	:	Joint	Nuclear	
15. Size of Family	:	Ideal	Small	Large
16. Place of Residence	:	Within the Panchayat		
		Outside the Panchayat		
17. Are you the head of your family	:	Yes	No	
18. If no, then who?	:	Husband	Father	Son
19. Family Head's Education	:	Illiterate	Primary	
		Secondary	Higher Secondary	
		Diploma	College	
20. Family Head's Occupation	:	Agricultural Coolie		
		Agriculture		
		Retired Govt. Servant		
		Housewife		
21. Family's annual income (in ,000s)	:	upto-20	21-40	
		41-60	61-80	
		81-100	Above 100	

ASSETS:

A. *Details of land holdings*

	In acres	Value in Rs
a. River or Tank Irrigated Land		
b. Well Irrigated Land		
c. Dry Land (Manavari)		
d. Land Leased in		
e. Land Leased out		
f. Non-cultivatable Land		
g. House Sites		

B. *Household assets*

a. House Buildings	Nos	Value
Nature of House	Thatched	Tiled
	Terraced	Colony House
b. Rent from Houses	Rs.	

	Nos.	Value in Rs.
c. TV		
d. Motorbike		
e. Sewing Machine		
f. Fridge		
g. Washing machine		
h. Grinder		
i. Mixie		
j. Gas stove		
k. Phone		
l. Car		
m. Others		

C. *Livestock*

	Number	Value in Rs.
a. Cows		
b. Bullocks		
c. Buffaloes		
d. Goats		
e. Poultry		
f. Others		

D. *Machinery and other implements*

	Number	Value in Rs
a. Tractor		
b. Bullock Cart		
c. Others		

POLITICAL BACKGROUND:

1. When did you become aware of Politics?

>15	16-20	21-25	26-30	31-35

2. Age on entering Politics.

21-30	31-40	41-50	51 and above

3. What were the sources of inspiration for your political interest?

SOURCES	*Yes*	*No*
Family		
Mass Media		
Political Parties		

4. Do you belong to any Political Party? | Yes | No |

5. Do you hold any Party Positions? | Yes | No |

6. Does your family head belong to any Political Party? | Yes | No |

   If yes, mention the political party

AIADMK	BJP
CONGRESS (I)	CPI
CPI(M)	DMK
DK	MDMK
PMK	TMC

7. Does your family head hold any position in the party? | Yes | No |

8. Mention the nature of your family head's political participation

Sl.	*Political activities*	*Inactive*	*Active*	*V. Active*
1.	Voting in General Election	☐	☐	☐
2.	Attending Party Conferences and Meeting	☐	☐	☐
3.	Participating in Party Protest Activities	☐	☐	☐
4.	Contesting and Election Campaigning Work	☐	☐	☐
5.	Raising Party Funds	☐	☐	☐

9. Who stimulated your Political Participation?

Stimulants	*Yes*	*No*
a Personal Interest	☐	☐
b Family Members	☐	☐
c Villagers	☐	☐
d Political Parties	☐	☐

10. What is your future political ambition?

Ambition	*Yes*	*No*
1. To be in office for only one term.	☐	☐
2. To continue in the office for many terms.	☐	☐
3. To acquire a position higher than the present one.	☐	☐

PART - II

POSITIONAL PROFILE

Position held by the Respondents

Sl.	*Organisations*	*Office-bearer*	*Member*
1.	Mahalir Mantram		
2.	Self-help Group		
3.	Governmental Organisation		
4.	Political Party		
5.	Trade Union		
6.	Village Panchayat		
7.	Co-operative Society		
8.	Voluntary/Social Service Organisation		

Positions held by the Family Heads of Respondents

Sl.	*Organisations*	*Office-bearer*	*Member*
1.	Caste Organisation		
2.	Religious Organisation		
3.	Governmental Organisation		
4.	Political Party		
5.	Trade Union		
6.	Village Panchayat		
7.	Co-operative Society		
8.	Voluntary/Social Service Organisation		
9.	Rasigar Mantram		

PART - III

REPUTATIONAL PROFILE

Social Correlates of Reputation: *Yes No*

1. Do you belong to Periyathanam family? ☐ ☐
2. Do your family members heriditarily become your caste leaders? ☐ ☐
3. Does Your family receive First Respect at the time of your village festivals or other social functions? ☐ ☐
4. Are your family members trustees of your village temples? ☐ ☐
5. Does any of your family members act as Village Priest? (Gurrukal or Poosary) ☐ ☐
6. Are your family members highly educated (College Level) in your village? ☐ ☐
7. Do your family members hold any professional positions? (Lawyers, Engineers, Doctors, C.A., etc.) ☐ ☐

Economic Correlates of Reputation

8. Do belong to Pannaiyar Family? ☐ ☐
9. Does your family belong to high annual income group (above Rs. 60,000) in your village? ☐ ☐
10. Does your family run any Factory/Mills/Stone Crushers? ☐ ☐
11. Do you have a car and telephone connection in your house? ☐ ☐

Political Correlates of Reputation

12. Are you a relative of former or present M.L.A/M.P./Municipal/ Union Chairman/Village Panchayat President/Member? ☐ ☐
13. Do your family members having close contact with high profile leaders? ☐ ☐
14. Did your ancestors participate in the freedom struggle? ☐ ☐

Community Service Correlates of Reputation

15. Is your family admired for its social services? ☐ ☐
16. Do people of all castes and religions approach your family for donations? ☐ ☐
17. Do your family members arrange Annadhanams (free meals) in your village? ☐ ☐
18. Does your family give interest-free financial assistance to the people in your village? ☐ ☐
19. Does your family offer any free medical service (indegenous medicine) to the public? ☐ ☐
20. Do people approach your family for settling their domestic disputes? ☐ ☐

PART-IV

DECISION-MAKING PROFILE

1. Who decided your candidature? *Yes No*

   Deciding Sources

		Yes	No
a	Yourself	☐	☐
b	Villagers	☐	☐
c	Family members	☐	☐
d	Political party	☐	☐

2. Have you ever participated in any of these socio-political activities? *Yes No*

		Yes	No
a.	Basic Amenities	☐	☐
b.	Developmental Schemes	☐	☐
c.	Social Problems	☐	☐
d.	Nil Participation	☐	☐

3. Have your family heads ever participated in any of these socio-political activities? *Yes No*

		Yes	No
a.	Basic Amenities	☐	☐
b.	Developmental Schemes	☐	☐
c.	Social Problems	☐	☐
d.	Nil Participation	☐	☐

4. What was the mode of political process in settling the issues by you and your family heads?

Modes		*Your-self*	*Family Head*
1.	Articulation through letters	☐	☐
2.	Signature Campaign	☐	☐
3.	Direct contact with authorities	☐	☐
4.	Demonstration/Fast/Road Blockade	☐	☐
5.	Picketing and undergoing imprisonment	☐	☐

5. What were your promises during your election campaign? *Yes No*

	Yes	No
Basic Aminities	☐	☐
Welfare Schemes	☐	☐
Communal Harmony	☐	☐

6. What were the strategies adopted by you during electioneering?

Strategies		*Yes*	*No*
1.	Political Party Support	☐	☐
2.	Caste Support	☐	☐
3.	Influential People's support	☐	☐
4.	Personal Popularity	☐	☐

APPENDICES

Appendix - I

Data Pertaining to the Respondents are as follows:

TABLE 1.1
RESERVATION-WISE DISTRIBUTION OF VILLAGE PANCHAYATS IN DINDIGUL DISTRICT

Sl.	*Category of Panchayats*	*No. of Panchayats*	%
1.	SC/ST General	35	11.48
2.	SC/ST Women	24	7.87
3.	General Women	83	27.21
4.	General (open to all)	163	53.44
	Total	305	100.00

Source: From the records of Panchayat Election Section, Collectorate, Dindigul.

TABLE 1.2
PANCHAYAT UNION-WISE CLASSIFICATION OF THE STUDY AREA

Sl. No.	Panchayat Union	No. of Village Panchayats	Reserved for Women	G.W.	SC/ST Women
1.	Authur	22	8	6	2
2.	Batalagundu	17	6	4	2
3.	Dindigul	14	5	4	1
4.	Natham	22	8	7	1
5.	Nilakkottai	23	8	5	3
6.	Reddiarchatram	23	8	6	2
7.	Sanar Patti	21	7	5	2
8.	GujiliamParai	17	6	5	1
9.	Kodaikanal	15	5	4	1
10.	Oddanchatram	35	12	10	2
11.	Palani	21	7	5	2
12.	Thoppam Patti	38	14	11	3
13.	Vedasandur	22	8	7	1
14.	Vadamadurai	15	5	4	1
	Total	306	107	83	24

Source: Collectorate, Dindigul District.

TABLE 1.3
NUMBER OF CONTESTANTS-WISE DISTRIBUTION OF THE PANCHAYATS

Sl. No.	Number of Contestants	No. of Village Panchayats	Total of Contestants
1.	Unopposed	6	6
2.	2 Contestants	29	58
3.	3 Contestants	21	63
4.	4 Contestants	25	100
5.	5 Contestants	12	60
6.	6 Contestants	8	48
7.	7 Contestants	6	42
	Total	107	377

Source: Computed.

TABLE 1.4
NUMBER OF SC/ST WOMEN CONTESTANTS IN PANCHAYATS RESERVED FOR SC/ST WOMEN

Sl. No.	*Number of Contestants*	*No. of Panchayats*	*Total No. of Contestants*
1.	Unopposed	1	1
2.	2 Contestants	3	6
3.	3 Contestants	4	12
4.	4 Contestants	5	32
5.	5 Contestants	4	20
6.	6 Contestants	2	12
7.	7 Contestants	2	14
	Total	24	97

Source: Computed.

TABLE 1.5
VOTES POLLED BY RESPONDENTS IN PER CENT

Sl. No.	*Per Cent of Votes Polled*	*Respondents*			
		Elected		*Defeated*	
		No.	*%*	*No.*	*%*
1.	20 – 29	-	-	6	6.1
2.	30 - 39	-	-	24	24.2
3.	40 - 49	-	-	69	69.7
4.	50 – 59	65	60.7	-	-
5.	60 – 69	30	28.1	-	-
6.	70 – 79	6	5.6	-	-
7.	100	6	5.6	-	-
	Total	107	100.0	99	100.0

Source: Computed.

TABLE 1.6
COMMUNITY-WISE CLASSIFICATION OF RESPONDENTS

Sl. No.	*Community*	*Respondents*				*Total*	
		Elected		*Rivals*			
		No.	*%*	*No.*	*%*	*No.*	*%*
1	FC	-	-	1	1.01	1	0.48
2	BC	68	63.55	64	64.65	132	64.08
3	MBC	14	13.08	11	11.11	25	12.14
4	SC/ST	25	23.37	23	23.23	48	23.30
	Total	107	100.00	99	100.00	206	100.00

Source: Computed

TABLE 1.7
COMMERCIAL STRENGTH OF COMMUNITY-WISE CLASSIFICATION OF RESPONDENTS

Sl. No.	*Community*	*Respondents*				*Total*	
		Elected		*Rivals*			
		No.	*%*	*No.*	*%*	*No.*	*%*
1	Numerically Dominant Community	77	71.96	59	59.60	136	66.02
2	Numerically Minority Community	30	28.04	40	40.40	70	33
	Total	107	100.00	99	100.00	206	100.00

Source: Computed.

Appendix - II

INDICES

SOCIO-ECONOMIC STATUS INDEX

Sl. No.	*Variables*	*Scores*							
		0	*1*	*2*	*3*	*4*	*5*	*6*	*Total*
1	Caste	-	SC/ST	MBC	BC	FC	-	-	4
2	Education	Ill	Prim	Sec	Hr Sec	Diplo	College	-	5
3	Occupation	No Job	Cooly	House Wife	Farm-ing	Govt. Serv.	-	-	7
4	Heads Education	Ill	Prim	Sec	Hr Sec	Diplo	College	-	5
5	Heads Occupation	No Job	Cooly	Farm-ing	Busi-ness	Govt. Serv.	-	-	7
6	Income in Thousands	<1	1-20	21-40	41-60	61-80	81-1 lakh	1 lakh	6
7	Asset In lakh	<1	1-5	6-10	11-15	16-20	21-25	26	6
	Total Score								40

POLITICAL BACKGROUND INDEX

Sl. No.	Variables	Scores 0	1		2		3	4	Total
1	Age of Pol. Awareness	30-above	26-30		21-25		16-20	Below 15	4
2	Age of entering into Politics	60-above	51-60		41-50		31-40	21-30	4
3	Sources of Inspiration	None	Political Party		Famiy		Mass Media	-	6
4	Political Position	None	Family Heads		Respondents				
			M	OB	M	OB			(2 + 3)
			1	2	2	3			5
5	Level of Involvement	In-active	Active		Very active				(5 × 2) 10
6	Political Ambition	None	Discrete		Static		Progr-essive		3
7	Stimulant for Political Participation	Politi-cal Parties	Family		Others		Perso-nal		3
	Total Score								35

POSITIONAL PROFILE INDEX

Sl. No.	*Family Heads* — *Organisations*	*Scores* *M*	*OB*	*Sl. No.*	*Respondents* — *Organisations*	*Scores* *M*	*OB*
1	Caste	1	2	1	Mahalir Mantram	2	3
2	Religious	1	2	2	Self Help Group	2	3
3	Social Service	1	2	3	Educational Services	2	3
4	Government	1	2	4	Trade Unions	2	3
5	Trade Union/ Co-op. Society	1	2	5	Voluntary	2	3
6	Village Panchayats	1	2	6	Political Parties	2	3
7	Rasigar Mantrams	1	2	7	Village Panchayats	2	3
8	Co-operative Societies	1	2	8	Women's Societies	2	3
9	Political Parties	1	2				
	Max. Score		18				24
	Total Score = 18 + 24 = 42						

REPUTATIONAL PROFILE INDEX

Family Reputation	*Scores*	
Social Correlates of Reputation	*Yes*	*No*
1. Periyathanam Family	1	0
2. Hereditary Caste Leader	1	0
3. First Respect Family	1	0
4. Temple Trustee	1	0
5. Village Priest/Poosari/Gurukal	1	0
6. Highly Educated Family	1	0
7. Professional Positions	1	0
Economic Correlates		
8. Pannaiyar Family	1	0
9. Wealthy Family	1	0
10. Owner of Factory/Mill/Stone Crusher	1	0
11. Family with car and telephone	1	0
Political Correlates		
12. Relative/Family member of Ex V.P.P/U.C/MLA/MP	1	0
13. Contact with high profile leaders	1	0
14. Freedom fighter's family	1	0
Community Service Correlates		
15. Social Service	1	0
16. Donations to all Castes and Creeds	1	0
17. Annadhanam	1	0
18. Interest-free Financial Assistance	1	0
19. Free Medical Service	1	0
20. Settling domestic disputes	1	0
Total Score	20	

Achieved Reputation Correlates

1. Hospitality
2. Honesty
3. Helping Tendency
4. Sociability
5. Accessibility
6. Tolerance
7. Courage for Articulation
8. Intelligence
9. Self-confidence
10. Fighting Spirit

A respondent is deemed to have achieved reputation if she possesses at least any five of the afore-said correlates. A respondent with achieved reputation is given a score of 10.

Total scores for reputation = 30 (20 + 10)

DECISIONAL POFILE INDEX

1	Deciding Sources	Political Parties	Family	Villagers	Herself	Total
	Scores	1	2	3	4	4
2	Participation in Civic Amenities		Family Head	Respondent		
		Basic Facilities	1	2		
		Development Schemes	2	3		
		Social Issues	3	4		15
3	Mode of Settling Issues	Modes	Family Head	Respondent		
	Scores	1, 2, 3 4 and 5	1 + 1 + 1 2 + 2	2 + 2 + 2 3 + 3		9 10
4	Promises Made	Basic Amenities	Development Schemes	Communal Harmony		
	Scores	1	2	3		6
5	Strategies Adopted	Political Party Support	Own Caste Support	Influential People's Support		
	Scores	1	2	3		6
	Total scores					50

Bibliography

Books

Abraham, M. Francis, *Dynamics of Leadership in Village India*, Allahabad: Indian International Publications, 1974.

Aiken, M., and Mott, P.E., (eds.), *The Structure of Community Power*, New York: Random House,1970.

Allema Shamim (ed.), *Women's Development Problems and Prospects*, New Delhi: APH Publishing Corp., 1996.

Arulselvam, M., *Tamil Nadu Panchayats and Municipal Laws*, Vol. 1, Madras: Malathi Publications, 1994.

Aslana, Pratima., *Women's Movement in India*, Delhi: Vikas Publishers, 1994.

Ashok Kumar, (ed.), *Women in Comtemporary Indian Society*, Vol. 2, New Delhi: Anmol Publishers, 1992.

Bailey, F.G, *Caste and Economic Frontier*, Bombay: Oxford University Press, 1958.

Belknap, I. and Steinle, J.H., *The Community and its Hospitals: A Comparative Analysis*, Syracuse: Syracuse University Press, 1963.

Beteille, Andre, *Caste, Class and Power*, Bombay: Oxford University Press, 1966.

Bhatt, G.D., *Emerging Leadership Pattern in Rural India, An Empirical Study*, New Delhi: M D Publications Pvt. Ltd., 1994.

Bhargava, B.S., *Grassroots Leadership: A Study of Leadership in PRIs.*, New Delhi: Asish Publishing House, 1979.

Bloomberg, W.Jr. and Sunshine, M., *Suburban Power Structures and Public Education*, Syracuse: Syracuse University Press, 1963.

Carter, A., *Elite in Rural India: Political Stratification and Alliances in Western Maharashtra*, New Delhi: Vikas Publishing House, 1974.

Choudhri, Maitrayee., *Women's Movement Reform or Rivival,* Delhi: Radiant, 1993.

Chaudhry, D.S., *Emerging Rural Leadership in an Indian State, A Case Study of Rajasthan,* Rohtak: Manthan Publications, 1981.

Chauhan, S.K., *Caste, Status and Power—Social Stratification in Assam,* New Delhi: Classical Publishing Co., 1980.

Chakrabortty, K. and Bhattacharya S.K., *Leadership, Factions and Panchayati Raj: A Case Study of West-Bengal,* New Delhi: Rawat Publications. 1993.

Clark, Terry N., (ed.), *Community Structure and Decision-making: Comparative Analysis,* San Francisco: Chandler Publishing Co., 1968.

Dahl, A Robert., *Who Governs? Democracy and Power in An American City,* New Haven: Yale University Press, 1961.

Dayal Rajeswar, *Panchayati Raj in India,* Delhi: Metropolitan Book Company, Pvt. Ltd., 1970.

Dayananda Saraswati, Swami., *Sathyartha Prakash* (Light of Truth), trans. Shri. Durga Prasad, New Delhi: Jan Gyan Prakashan, 1970.

Dey, S.K., *Panchayati Raj: A Synthesis,* Bombay: Asia Publishing House, 1961.

Desai, A.R., (ed.), *Rural Sociology in India,* Bombay: Popular Prakashan, 1994.

Deb, P.C. and Agarwal,B.K., *Rural Leadership in Green Revolution,* Delhi: Researchco Publications, 1974.

Dumont, Louis, *Homo Hirarchicus,* Banglore: Vikas Publications, 1966.

Dube, Leela., *Studies on Leadership in Village India, Emerging Patterns of Rural Leadership in South Asia,* Hyderabad: National Institute of Community Development, 1965.

Dutta, Vijay Rajan., *Decision-making in Urban Government and Politics,* Allahabad: Chugh Publications, 1986.

Edwin Seligman, R.A.(ed.), *Encyclopaedia of Social Sciences,* Vol. IX and X, New York: The Macmillan Company and The Free Press,1972.

Eulau, H, Eldersweld, S.J. and Janowitz, M. (eds.), *Political Behaviour: Reader in Theory and Research,* New Delhi: Amerind Publishing Co. Pvt. Ltd., 1972.

Fielder, F.E., *A Theory of Leadership Effectiveness,* New York: Mc Graw Hill, 1967.

Ghosh, B.N., *Rural Leadership And Development,* New Delhi: Mohit Publications, 1996.

Gangrade, K.D., *Emerging Patterns of Leadership: Comparative Study of Leadership and Social Structure,* Delhi: Rachna Publications, 1974.

Gardner Lindzey, (ed.), *Handbook of Social Psychology,* New York: Addision Wesley Publishing Company,Vol. II, 1954.

Gerth, H.H., and Mills, C.W., (eds.), *Essays in Sociology,* Oxford: University Press, 1946.

Herold, Lasswell, *Psychopathology in Politics,* New York: Viking, 1960.

———, *Power and Personality,* New York: Norton, 1948,

Hutton, J.H., *Caste in India,* Cambridge: Cambridge University Press, 1946.

Hunter, Floyd., ***Community Power Structure — A Study of Decision-makers,*** Chapel Hill: The University of North Carolina Press, 1953.

———, *Community Power Succession: Atlanta's Policy Makers Revisited,* Chapel Hill: University North Carolina Press, 1980.

Inamdar, N.R., *Functioning of Village Panchayats,* Bombay: Popular Prakashan, 1970.

Indira, Mahindra, *Rebellious Home Makers,* Bombay: S.N.D.T., Women's University, 1980.

Irudayaswami, S.V., *Know Your District—Dindigul Anna District,* Kodaikanal: Aluvalar Manamakil Mandram, 1996.

Jathar, R.V., *Evolution of Panchayati Raj in India,* Dharwar: JSS Institute of Economic Research, 1964.

Jennings, M.K., *Community Influentials: The Elites of Atlanta,* London:Collier-Macmillan Ltd, 1964.

Kapadia, K.M., *Marriage and Family in India,* London: Oxford University Press, 1966.

Khan, Mumtaj Ali, *Scheduled Caste and their Status in India,* New Delhi: Uppal Publishing House, 1970.

Krech David. and Richard S. Crutchfield, *Theory and Problem of Social Psychology,* New York: McGraw Hill Book Co, 1948.

Kumari, Ranjana, *Women in Politics and Political Process—Introduction,* New Delhi: Friedrich Ebert Stiffung (FES), 1992.

Lakshminarayana, H.D, *Democracy in Rural India: Problem and Process*, New Delhi: National, 1980.

Lall, S.K., *The Urban Elite*, Delhi: Thompson Press (India) Ltd. 1974.

Lewis, Oscar, *Village Life in Northern India*, Urbana: University of Illinois Press, 1958.

Lester Millbrath, *Political Participation*, Chicago: Rand McNally, 1965.

Lipset, S.M., (ed.), *Politics and Social Sciences*, New Delhi: Wiley Eastern Private Ltd., 1972.

Lipset, S.M. and Bandix, R., *Social Mobility in Industrial Society*, Lossangels: University of California Press, 1959.

Loomis, C.P., *Social Systems: Essays on Their Persistence and Change*, New Jersey: Princeton, 1960.

MacIver, R.M. and Page, C.H., *Society: An Introductory Analysis*, London: Macmillan, 1967.

Manikayamba, P., *Women in Panchyati Raj Structure*, New Delhi: Gian Publishing House,1989.

Mathew, George, *Panchayati Raj: From Legislation to Movement*, New Delhi: Concept Publishing Company, 1994.

Mehta, Sushila, *Social Conflicts in a Village Community*, New Delhi: S. Chand and Co. (Pvt) Ltd. 1971.

Mehta, S.R., *Emerging Pattern of Rural Leadership*, New Delhi: Wiley Eastern Private Limited, 1972.

Majumdar, A.K. and Singh, Bhanwar, (eds.), *Historical and Conceptual Development of Panchayati Raj*, New Delhi: Radha Publications, 1997.

Mehta, S.R., *Emerging Pattern of Rural Leadership*, New Delhi: Wiley Eastern Private Limited, 1972.

Merriam, C.E. and Cornell, H.F., *American Party System*, New York: Macmillan Co., 1949.

Michal Rush and Dhilip Althoff, *An Introduction to Political Sociology*, London: Thomas Nelson and Sons Ltd., 1971.

Miglani, D.C, *Politics and Rural Power Structure*, New Delhi: Deep and Deep Publications, 1993.

Mills, C. Wright, *The Power Elite*, New York: Oxford University Press, 1956.

Mills, C.Wright and Ricci, D., *Community Power and Democratic Theory*, New York: Random House, 1971.

Miller, D.B., *From Hierarchy to Stratification—Changing Patterns of Social Inequality in a North Indian Village,* Delhi: Oxford University Press, 1975.

Mishra, S.N., *Pattern of Emerging Leadership in Rural India,* Patna: Associated Book Agency, 1977.

Mott. P.E. and Aiken. M., *The Structure of Community Power,* New York: Random House, 1970.

Mukhopadhyaya, Amal Kumar, *Political Sociology: An Introductory Analysis,* Calcutta: K.P. Bagchi and Company, 1980.

Narain, Iqbal, Pande, K.C. and Sharma, Mohan Lal, *The Rural Elite in an Indian State — A Case Study of Rajasthan,* New Delhi: Monohar Book Depot. 1976

Palanithurai, G., (ed.), *Caste Politics and Society in Tamil Nadu,* Delhi: Kanishka Publishers, 1994.

———, *Perception of Grass Root Democracy and Political Performance,* New Delhi: M.D. Publications Pvt. Ltd. 1998.

Pandian, M.S.S., *The Image Trap,* New Delhi: Sage Publications, 1992.

Pareek, Udai. and Trivedi, C., *Mannual of the Socio-Economic Status Scale (Rural),* Delhi: Manasayan, 1954.

Pareek, Udai (ed.), *Studies in Rural Leadership,* Delhi: Behavioural Science Centre, 1966.

Park, R.L and Tinker, G.I. (eds.), *Leadership and Political Institutions in India,* Madras: Oxford University Press, 1960.

Parsons, Talcott, *The Social System,* New York: The Free Press of Glencoe, 1964.

Polsby, N.W., *Community Power and Political Theory,* New Haven: Yale University Press, 1963.

Presthus, Robert., *Men at the Top: A Study in Community Power,* New York: Oxford University Press, 1964.

Rajput, R.S., and Maghe, D.R., *Panchayati Raj in India: Democracy at Grassroots,* New Delhi: Deep and Deep Publications, 1984.

Ranganath, *Changing Pattern of Rural Leadership in Uttar Pradesh,* New Delhi: Sindhu Publications, 1977.

———, (ed.), *Women in Decision-making,* New Delhi: Vikas Publishing House, 1992.

Reddy, G. Narayana, *Rural Elite and Community Work — A Socio-Political Perspective,* Allahabad: Chugh Publications. 1986.

Retzlaff, Ralpth H., *Village Government of India,* Bombay: Asia Publishing House, 1962.

Robin, M., *Sisterhood is Powerful,* New York: Randon House, 1970.

Ross, M.G. and Hendry, C.E., *New understanding of Leadership: A Survey and Application of Research,* New York: Association Press, 1957.

Saran, Paramatma, *Rural Leadership in the Context of India's Modernization,* New Delhi: Vikas Publishing House, 1978.

Saraswathi,S., *The Madras Panchayat System: A Historical Survey,* Vol. 1, Delhi: Impex India, 1973.

Schlesinger, Joseph A., *Ambition and Politics: Political Careers in the United States,* Chicago: Rand Mecnally, 1966.

Sen, Lalit K., and Roy, P., *Awareness of Community Development in Village India,* Hydrabad: National Institute of Community Development 1967.

———, *Opinion Leadership in India,* Hyderabad: National Institute of Community Development, 1969.

Sharma, K.L, *The Changing Rural Stratification System,* Bangalore: Orient Longman, 1976.

———, (ed.), *Social Inequality in India — Profiles of Caste, Class, Power and Social Mobility,* New Delhi: Rawat Publications, 1995.

Sharma, Mohanlal, *Dynamics of Rural Power Structure — A Study of Rajasthan,* Jaipur: Aalekh Publishers, 1984.

Shukla, N.K., *Social Structure of an Indian Village,* New Delhi: Cosmo Publications, 1976.

Sills, David L.(ed.), *International Encyclopaedia of Social Sciences,* Vol. 11 and 12, New York: Macmillan Company and the Free Press, 1972.

Singh, Harizinder, *Authority and Influence in Two Sikh Villages,* New Delhi: Sterling Publishers Pvt. Ltd., 1976.

Singh, Avtar, *Leadership Patterns and Village Structure: A Case Study of Six Indian Villages,* New Delhi: Sterling Publishers Pvt. Ltd., 1973.

Singh, Harijinder, *Village Leadership: A Case Study of Village Mohali in Punjab,* New Delhi: Sterling Publishers Pvt. Ltd., 1969.

Singh, Chandra Pal, *Dimensions of Leadership,* New Delhi: Anmol Publications, 1991.

Singh, D.R., *Rural Leadership Among Scheduled Castes*, Allahabad: Chugh Publications, 1985.

———, *Panchayati Raj and Rural Organisations*, Allahabad: Chugh Publications, 1990.

Sirsikar, V.M., *The Rural Elite in Developing Society: A Study in Political Sociology*, New Delhi: Orient Longman Limited., 1970

Sivanna, N., *Panchayati Raj Reforms and Rural Development*, Allahadbad: Chugh Publications, 1990.

Sinha, Murali M., *Modernisation and Community Power: A Comparative Study of Indian Villages*, New Delhi: Vikas Publishing House Pvt. Ltd., 1983.

Sorokin, P.A., *Social and Cultural Mobility*, Glenco: The Free Press, 1927.

Stalcup, R., *Educational Sociology*, USA: Mersill and Co., 1967.

Srinivas, M.N., *India's Villages*, Bombay: Asia Publishing House, 1960.

———, *Caste in Modern India and Other Essays*, Bombay: Asia Publishing House, 1962.

———, *Social Change in Modern India*, Berkley: University of California Press, 1966.

———, et al., (eds.), *Dimensions of Social Change*, New Delhi: Allied Publishers, 1977.

Srivastava, H.C., *Dysfunctional Para-Politics and Elite Action in India*, Varanasi: Bhartiya Vidhya Prakashan, 1967.

Stouffer, *Communism, Conformity and Civil Liberties*, Gardencity: Doubleday, 1955.

Suba, K., *Women in Local Governance*, Jaipur: RBSA Publishers, 1994.

Talcott Parson, *The Social System*, New York: The Free Press of Glencoe, 1964.

Tead, Ordway, *The Art of Leadership*, New York: McGraw Hill Book Co., 1963.

Tonnies, Ferdinand, *Community and Society*, Translated From German and edited by Loomis, P.C., New York: Harper and Row, 1963.

Venkatesan, G., *Local Self Government in India*, Madurai : Indira Pathipagam, 1982.

Venkatarangaiya, M., and Pattabhiraman, M., *Local Government in India: Select Readings*, New Delhi: Allied Publishers, 1969.

Verinder Grover, (ed.), *Political System in India,* New Delhi: Deep and Deep Publications, 1989.

Vidya, K.C., *Political Empowerment of Women at the Grassroots,* New Delhi: Kanishka Publishers, 1997.

Vidyarthi, L.P., (ed.), *Leadership in India,* Bombay: Asia Publishing House, 1967.

Whyte, Robert Orr, and Pauline Whyte, *The Women of Rural Asia,* Colorado USA.: West Wiew Press, 1982.

William D. Hawley and Fredric, M. Mirt, (eds.), *The Search for Community Power,* Englewood Cliffs, New Jersey: Printice Hall, 1968.

Article

Agger. E. Robert., "Power Attributions in the Local Community", *Social Forces,* Vol. 34, 1956.

Agnimithra, Neera, "Women in Panchayats: Empowerment or Illusion", *Gandhi Marg,* Vol. 17, No. 4, January-March, 1996.

Anderson, C.A., "Skeptical Note on the Relation of Vertical Mobility to Education", *American Journal of Sociology,* Vol. LXVI, No. 5, March, 1961.

Angell Robert Cooley., "The Moral Integration of American Elites", *American Journal of Sociology,* Part II, Vol. 61, No.1, July, 1957.

Arora,C. Subash, and Prabakhar, R.K., "A Profile of Women Contestants — A Study of Rohtak Municipal Council Elections", *Nagarlok,* Vol. XXVIII, No. 1, January-March, 1996.

Barnabas, A.P., "Who are the Village Leader?" *Kurukshetra,* Vol. VI, No. 5, February, 1958.

Barth, Earnest A.T. and Bahu, Abu-Laban, "Power Structure and the Negro Sub-Community", *American Sociological Review,* Vol. 24, 1959.

———, "Characteristics of Lay Leader in Extension Work", *Journal of the M.S. University of Boroda,* 1968.

Baskar, Manu., "Women Panchayat Members in Keral—A Profile", *Economic and Political Weekly,* Vol XXXII, No. 17, April 1997.

Bhargava, B.S. and Vidya, K.C., "Position of Women in Political Institutions — With Special Reference to Panchayati Raj System in Karnataka", *Journal of Rural Development,* Vol. II, No. 5, September, 1992.

Bhargava, B.S., "Panchayati Raj: Power to the People", *Kurukshetra,* Vol, XXXVI, No. 3, December, 1987.

Blankenship,L.Vaughn., "Community Power and Decision-Making: A Comparative Evaluation of Measurement Techniques", *Social Forces,* Vol. 4, No. 3, December, 1964.

Bohra, O.P., "Women in Decentralised Democracy," *Indian Journal of Rural Development,* Vol. 16, No. 4, October-December, 1997, Hydrabad: NIRD.

Bonjean, C.M. and Olsen, D.M., "Community Leadership: Direction of Research", *Administrative Science Quarterly,* Vol. 9, No. 3, December, 1964.

Bossard, James H.S., "Marriage as Status Achieving Device," *Sociology and Social Research,* Vol. No. 3, 29, September-October, 1944.

Desingu Setty, "A Study of Leadership in Two Valaya Communities in Tamil Nadu", *Indian Journal of Social Work,* Vol. XLII, No. 4, January, 1982.

Dube, S.C., " A Framework For the Study of Rural Leadership in Transitional Societies", *Emerging Patterns of Rural Leadership in Southern Asia,* Hydrabad: Institute of Community Development,1965.

——, "Caste Dominance in Factionalism", *Contribution to Indian Sociology,* New Series, No.11, December, 1968.

Ehrlich.H.J., "The Reputational Approach to the Study of Community Power", *American Sociological Review,* Vol. 26, No. 6, December, 1961.

Ghosh, K. Dillip, "Grassroots Women Leaders: Who are they? A Study in West Bengal District", *Journal of Rural Development,* Vol. 16, No. 2, April-June, 1997.

Herson, Lawrence, J.R. "In the Foot Steps of Community", *American Political Science Review,* Vol. 55, No. 11, November, 1961.

Hole,V., Social Effects of Planned Housing", *The Town Planning Review,* Vol. 25, No. 2, July, 1959.

Inamdar, N.R., "Panchayati Raj Leadership: Emerging Dimensions", *Journal of Rural Development,* Vol. 10, No. 5, September-October, 1991.

Jain, S.P. "Leadership among Rural Women", *Social Change,* Vol. 13, No. 3, September, 1983.

Jeyalakshmi, K. "Empowerment of Women in Panchayats Experience of Andhra Pradesh — Case Study", *Journal of Rural Development,* Vol.16, No. 2, April-June.

Jeyapal, P. and Dravidamani, "Women Panchayat Presidents" *Social Welfare,* Vol. 44, No. 1, April, 1997.

Kanango, Sukla, Deb., "Panchayati Raj and Emerging Women Leadership: An Overview", *Social Action,* Vol. 46. No. 1, January-March, 1996.

Kaushik,Susheela, "Organising Women for Panchayati Raj", *Search News,* Vol. VIII, No. 8, Land 2, January-June, 1993.

Kittur, A.T., "Emerging Pattern of Leadership: A Study of PRIs in Dharward District", *ISDA Journal,* Vol. 2, No. 4, April, 1992.

Klapp.E. Orrin. and L. Vincent Padgett, "Power Structure and Decision-Making in a Maxian Border City", *American Journal of Sociology,* Vol. 65, No. 4, January, 1960.

Mathew, George., "Will Reservation Ensure Participation", *Social Welfare,* Vol. 42, No. 5-6, August-September, 1995.

Miller, D.C., "Decision-Making Cliques in Community Power Structure", *American Journal of Sociology,* Vol. 63, No. 3, November, 1958.

———, "Town and Gown: The Power Structure of a University Town", *American Journal of Sociology,* Vol. 68, No. 4, January, 1963.

Mishra, S.N., "Dynamics and Dimensions of Panchayati Raj Elections", *The Indian Journal of Public Administration,* Vol. XXXVII, No. 3, July-September, 1991.

Murphy and Moris, "Occupational Status Subjective Social Class Identification and Political Affiliation", *American Sociological Review,* Vol. 26, 1961.

Narayana, Shashi S., "Gender Equality Through Reservation in Decision-Making Bodies", *Social Action,* Vol. 45, No. 2, April-June, 1988.

Omari, P.T., "Factors Associated with the Urban Adjustment of Rural Southern Immigrants", *Social Forces,* Vol. 35, No. 1, October, 1956.

Oomen, T.K., "Rural Community Power Structure in India", *Social Forces,* Vol. 49, No. 3, December, 1970.

Opler, M.E. and Singh, D.R., "Economic Political and Social Change in North Central India", *Human Organisation,* Vol. II, No. 2, Summer, 1952.

Palanithurai, G., "Empowerment of Women — A Novel Exercise", ***Kurukshetra***, Vol. XLII, No. 9, June, 1994.

G. Palanithurai, " Women Participation in Local Governance: A Case Analysis of Tamil Nadu", Paper presented in the National Seminar on ***Women in Local Governance: Exploring New Frontiers*** Bangalore: Institute of Social Studies Trust, From 3rd-5th February, 1999.

Panda, Snehalata., "Political Empowerment of Women — A Case Study of Orissa", *Journal of Rural Development*, Vol. 16, No. 4, October-December, 1997.

——, "Emerging Pattern of Leadership among Rural Women in Orissa", *Journal of Rural Development*, Vol. 15, No. 4, October-December, 1996.

Patnaik, Natyananda, and Laxminarayan, H.D., "Functional Politics in Village India", *Man in India*, Vol. 49, No. 2, August-September, 1969.

Polsby, N.W., "Three Problems in the Analysis of Community Power", *American Sociological Review*, Vol. 24, No. 12, December, 1959.

———, "How to Study Community Power: The Pluralist Alternative", *Journal of Politics*, Vol. 22, No. 8, August, 1960.

Rao, K.Ranga, "Rural Leadership and Conflicts Study of Andhra Village", *Economic and Political Weekly*, Vol. III, No. 17, April 27, 1968.

Radha Paul, "Women's Leadership in Welfare Work", *Social Welfare*, Vol. XXVII, No. 3, June, 1980.

Schulze. Robert, O. and Bloomberg, L.U., "The Determination of Local Power Elites", *American Journal of Sociology*, Vol. 63, No. 3,November, 1957.

Saxena, Kiran, "Empowerment of Women: The Indian Context", *The Indian Journal of Political Science*, Vol. 55 No. 4, October-December, 1994.

Singh, Mohinder, "Political Equality for Women", *Social Welfare*, Vol. 41, No. 10, January, 1995.

Soule, sJ.W, "Future Political Ambitions and Behaviour of Incumbant State Legislators", *Midwest Journal of Political Science*, Vol. XII, No. 3, August, 1969.

Ujwala S. Hiremath, "Women in Grassroots Politics", *Social Welfare*, Vol. 44, No. 2, May, 1997.

Wolfinger, Raymond E., "Reputation and Reality in the Study of Community Power", *American Sociological Review,* Vol. 25, October, 1960.

Government Reports/Documents

Government of India, Committee on Plan Projects. *Report of the Team for the Study of Community Projects and National Extension Service,* 1957, Vol. I.

Government of India, Ministry of Human Resource Development, Department of Women and Child Welfare, National Perspective Plan for Women 1988-2000 A.D. *Report of the Core Group,* New Delhi: Akashdeep Printers, 1988.

Report of the Study Team of Nyaya Panchayats, Government of India, 1962.

Shramshakti, Report of the National Commission on Self-Employed Women and Women in the Informal Sector, June 1988, in *Handbook of Policy and Related Documents on Women in India,* New Dehi: National Institute of Public-Co-operation and Child Development, 1988.

Research Projects/Reports

A Survey of Research in Sociology and Social Anthropology, Vol. II, Indian Council of Social Science Research, Bombay: Popular Prakashan, 1974.

Amarjit Kaur, "Aspirations, Concerns and Perceptions", *Convention of Women Employees,* Salem: Canara Bank Employees Union State Committee, Tamil Nadu, 23, November, 1996.

Athereya V.B. and Rajeswari, K.S., *Women's Participation in Panchayati Raj: A Case Study from Tamil Nadu* Sponsored by the National Commission for Women Co-ordinated by the Center for Development Studies and Action, Chennai: M.S. Swaminathan Research Foundation, 1998.

Goyal, S.K., "The Study of Scheduled Caste Students of College in Eastern U.P.", *Research Project* sponsored by Indian Council of Social Science Research, New Delhi: 1973-74, Department of Sociology, Banaras Hindu University, Varanasi.

Village Immerson Programme—India A World Bank Programme, *Profile of Dindigul District Booklet III,* Ganghigram: Gandhigram Rural Institute, November,1998.

News Papers

Dhinamalar, (Tamil) August 3, 1998.

Indian Express, September 29, 1998.

Indian Express, October 2, 1998.

The Hindu, October, 25, 1998.

Index

A

Abraham, F.M., 24
Adult Education, its development and advantages, 22
Agarwal, B.K., 29
Age of Women, 85 ff
Agriculture, 196
Agricultural coolies, 196
Amrit Kaur, Raj Kumari, First Health Minister in Nehru's Cabinet, a True Gandhian, 65
Arora, S.C., 34
Arya Samaj, 64
Ashok Mehta Committee, 66
Asia, 67
Atlanta's policy, 27
Authur, 204
Awtar Singh, 25, 28

B

Bahrain, 61
Baijnath Singh, 24
Balwadis, 154
Balwantrai Mehta Committee, 76
Beals, Alan, 24
Belkanap, I, 131
Bihar, 25
Blankenship, IV, 131
Bonjean, C.M., 39, 133
Brahmins, 24
Brahmo Samaj, 64
Buffaloes, breed of, 197
Business, development of, 146

C

Calcutta, 65
Caste organisation, 137
Chauhan, B., 24
Christians, 180
Community Development Programme, 21
Congress (I), 182
Cooperative societies, 137
Contracts, 146
Constitutional Amendment Act, (1992), 188
Courage, 197, 211
Cousins, Margaret, 64

D

Dams, used for irrigation purposes, 154
Dayanand, Swami, 64
Deb, P.C., 29
Desai, A.R., 25
Dhal, 39
Dhillon, H.S., 23
Dindigul, 22, 41, 43, 67, 68, 78, 134, 137 ff, 204
D.M.K., 182
Dube, S.C., a prominent anthropologist who spent much of his career in Saugar University. Later on, he became Vice-chancellor, Jammu University, 24

Dutta, V.R., 31, 52

E

Economic variables, 49
Education Department, 134, 204
Elections, the process of, 158
Europe, 61

F

Family, as a unit of society, 92
Fighting spirit, 211
Finance Commission, 74
Findings and Suggestions, 179 ff
Floyd Hunter, 27
Freeman, I.C., 131 ff

G

Gandhi, M.K., 64
Gangrade, K.D., 25, 29
Ghosh, B.N., 92
Goats, their production and breed, 197
Gokhale, G.K., 64
Governmental organisation, 137
Gram Sabha, 74
Grave-yards, 154
Grinder, 197

H

Hamid Ali, Begum, 65
Harjinder Singh, 24, 30
Harijan, 154
Hindu Faith, 180
Hiremath, U.S., 102
Hitchcock, J.T., 24
Home Rule League, 64
Honesty, 211
Hospitality, 211
Housewife, 196
Human resource, 22
Hunter, 39

I

Illinois, University of, 174
Indian politics, 61
Indian Republic, 22
Indira Singh, 24
Intelligence, 211
Iqbal Narayan, 24, 29
Irrigated land, 197

J

John Hodgsen, 75

K

Kalabhra, 70
Karnataka, 78
Kitur, A.T., 32
Kodaikanal, 68, 204
Kripalani, Mrs. Sucheta, once Chief Minister of UP and discipline of Mahatama Gandhi, 65
Kuwait, 61

L

Lall, S.K., 29
Land Reforms, 21
Leadership, 21, 141
Literature, 22
Local Bodies, 190
Lynds, R., 131

M

Madras, 75
Madhurai, 78
Mahabir Mantrams, 45, 200
Males, 119

Marital Status, 101, 196
Marx, Karl, 131
Mathew George, 33
Mehta, S.R., 25, 28
M.L.A., 147-48
M.P., 147-48
Miglani, D.C., 24
Mixie, 197
Miller, D.C., 131
Mills, C.W., 131
Mishra, S.N., 30
Munro, Thomas, 75
Mysore, 78

N

Nayaks, 78
New York, 26

O

Olsen, D.M., 39, 133
Omaris, 52
Oomen, T.K., 27-28, 133
Orenstein, H., 24
Organisations, 200
Oscar, Lewis, 23

P

Palani, 78, 204
Panchayati Raj, 21, 22, 61
Panda, S., 34
Park, R.L., 23
Political Parties, 119
Political variables, 126
Polsby, N.W., 39
Poultry, 197
Power Bases, 169
Punjab, 25, 64

R

Rajasthan, 25
Rajputs, 24
Ranchi University, 25
Rao, K. Ranga, 27, 133
Rasigar Mantras, 137
Ration shops, 154
Read, Alexander, 75
Reddy, G.N., 24, 32
Reddy, M., 65
Religion, 209
Religious organisations, 137
Robert, Lord, 75
Roy, P., 24
Roy, Rammohun, 64

S

Sanar Patti, 204
Sanitation, 154
Saran, P., 30
Schulze, R.O., 131
Self-help Group, 200
Sen, Lalit, 24-25
Sewing-machines, 197
Sharma, M.L., 25
Singh, B.N., 23
Sinha, M.M., 31
Sirsikar, V.M., 24
Social bond, 144
Social customs, 67
Social Service Organisations, 137
Special reservations, 119
Srinivas, M.N., 24, 98
Subha, K., 33
Subha, N.K., 25

T

Tamil Nadu, 21, 22, 37, 43, 61, 67, 70 ff
Tata Herabai, 64
Telephone system, 146, 197
Television, 197
Tertiary, 170

Tinker, A.I., 23
Tolerance, 211
Trade, 146
Trade Union, 200, 209

U

United Arab Emirates, 61
U.N.O., 61
U.P., 23, 25, 65
Urban development, 67
U.S.A., 61

V

Vadamadurai, 204
Vidyarthi, L.P., 24
Vijalakshimi Pandit, Former Ambassador to USSR, USSR and England; Governor of Maharashtra as well, 65
Village development, 43
Village Panchayats, 137, 188, 195
Village Priests, 21
Voluntary organisations, 137

W

Wealthy families, their contribution in our society, 146
Women, their behaviour in Indian society, 116 ff
Women, their main categories, 131 ff
Women and their Leadership in Indian society, 42, 113
Women, their socio-economic status in Indian society, 85 ff
Wright C. Mills, 25

Z

Zamindars, 21

borrow the examples of reservation quota for physically handicapped, ex-army personnel etc. in government jobs in some states. Chhattisgarh is one such example where 6% and 1% reservation is given respectively. This consideration is beyond caste and rather cuts across castes and even classes. The idea is that there is a need to interpret the provisions of article 15 and 16 along with article 14 because, the philosophy of protective discrimination after all is aimed at ensuring equality of opportunity and equal protection of laws. As long as certain sections are kept out of the purview of the article 16(4), it is but natural that the discontentment against the protective discrimination and criticism of state's affirmative action smoulders.

Equality before law is the undisputed and fully accepted principle of democratic society. But it is also a fact that the democracy with social and economic in-equalities cannot ensure freedom for its citizens because poor people can never be free. Equality of opportunity in law cannot always get itself translated into action in a society of in-equalities. Merit is synonymous to opportunity of growth. There cannot be an equal competition among in-equals. Equality of opportunity will be meaningful when the citizens are equally equipped with resources to enable them to be equal in a competition, which is an opportunity. Hence the philosophy of protective discrimination for the advancement of socially, educationally backward classes (SEBC) of India. Because these socially and educationally backward classes were historically deprived of equality in all walks of life in the name of caste hierarchy. Hence they are treated as a special class of citizens. The scheduled castes and scheduled tribes are also backward class of citizens. Apart from these tribes and castes which are scheduled, as the nomenclature goes, the state has today included the **'other backward classes'** which we know as OBCs. Nevertheless the underlying theme and criteria of social and educational backwardness continues in all the classes enlisted for affirmative action.

Vicious circle of Backwardness

The above philosophy of protective discrimination being laudable and acceptable, it however is against the basic concept of equality which is embedded in the constitution in the article 14 because the citizens are not treated equally in a system of preferential treatment in favour of some to the detriment of many. In many states, the reservations in favour of scheduled castes and scheduled tribes and Backward Classes in total has gone beyond 50% in violation of even the directions of the Supreme Court. The citizens belonging to un-reserved category have to virtually struggle un-successfully for a few Govt. jobs consigned to their fate as the reserved candidates will also be considered against the general quota displacing the un-reserved candidates in the event of the former getting selected on merit. This is a peculiar situation at least we have seen in the state of Chhattisgarh, where Backward Classes candidates got selected in the un-reserved quota as well. In a situation like this, it is not difficult to imagine that for a quarter of century from now, the Backward Classes as a special class of citizens taking advantage of the reservations can emerge as the dominant force in future with a higher educational and economic advancement. With an increasing capability and competence, they may gradually occupy most of the un-reserved posts sooner or later. In such an event, the communities belonging to un-reserved sections who are not a special class of citizens today, will have to be treated as one sooner or later. It is an irony. The philosophy which aims at bringing the backward classes to the main stream will eventually render some classes of citizens as backward in due course of time. **A class rendered backward so, may have to be treated as a special class of citizen after some time in future and need to be given the same protective discrimination to come back into main stream. It all seems to be an endless process of encouraging and discouraging different classes of citizens at different points of time which is nothing less than a *vicious circle* of backwardness.**

Putting the Cart before the Horse

It is intriguing as to why the State had to take recourse to Art.16 (4), a discretionary provision, making mandatory while Atr.15(4) in self has enough to provide in support of classified legislation. As we discussed earlier Art.15 (4) is a precursor to Art.16(4) not withstanding that Art.16(4) is complimentary to Art.15(4). In such a situation, it is but natural to arrive at a conclusion that, the state is putting the cart before the horse, because despite making a provision of reservation of jobs according article 16(4), it is not guaranteed practically that the classified class of citizens would take advantage of the same. For the simple reason that, reservation does not mean direct appointment on the posts. The stakeholders are supposed to sit for an examination for recruitment which is compulsory. It is important to realize here that within the stakeholders there happens to be competition. This is where the early birds catch the worms; in other words, the competent stakeholders naturally get selected for recruitment and the less competent are left-out. Here it is significant that there works equally the yardstick of merit even among the backwards. Therefore, the competition is among the in-equals within the classified group and it is a fact, at least in the case of recruitments in Chhattisgarh, as we have seen. The situation calls for an intervention on the part of the state to regulate the affirmation action. In other words, the backward linkages such as adequate educational infrastructure sufficient number of seats in academic institutions, special training classes for competitive exams, hostel facilities for students, proper income generating schemes for the parents of the stakeholders etc. are very much required in order to provide equality of opportunity in true sense of the term in order to ensure a reasonable though not proportional representation from at least majority of the castes within the *special class*. In the absence of such a pro-active programme or pre-emptive initiative on the part of the state, the advantage of article 16(4) would be taken away only by the dominant castes within the so-called special class of citizens which the classified legislation never intended. After all the Art. 16(4) clearly qualified for *'not adequately represented'*. Creation of infrastructure for the economic development of castes is a precondition to the provision of quota for employment or else the less advanced can not avail of the quota for employment as they are not even qualified to that end.

It is essential to know here that for Scheduled Tribes we have Tribal Sub Plan (TSB) –a separate budget allocation by Planning Commission meant for development of exclusive Tribal pocket. The same is provided for Scheduled Castes known as Special Component Plan (SCP). The State has not contemplated on the similar lines for Backward Classes till now. It is important to realise that despite enormous budgetary allocations under TSB and SCP in the State, as we have observed in the analysis, both the classes have not yet been equipped to take on the general candidates in open competition. That being factually so how can with no special development programmes for the Backward Classes (not the 'creamy layer') the most backward majority of them can even compete for jobs?

In Chhattisgarh, barring scholarships and seat reservations in academic institutions in favour of OBCs and a few hostel facilities no other structural arrangements are made or facilities provided for educational and economic advancement of Backward Classes in general. There are no sufficient number of exclusive hostels for students. No schemes of skill up gradation for income generation for most castes of the Backward Classes are taken up by the state. As a matter of fact, it is almost an open competition within the OBC for a few government jobs in the state. As we have observed in our study, 6-7 communities dominant in the state have been occupying majority of the government jobs whereas more than 80 categories/castes within the OBCs have not received any advantage. In such a situation, it is extremely difficult to conclude that reservations in favour of Backward Classes are actually helping to improve their social and economic position. However, it is not advocated here that the state should take care of each particular community in the backward classes with a view to ensure their representation in the government jobs. Nevertheless, a planned action can be initiated at least to provide equality of opportunity by providing basic infra-structures required for socio-economic development of majority of castes. Here comes the relevance of article 15(4) which is independent of article 16(4). In the absence of affirmative action in tune with the objectives of article 15(4), the provision of article 16(4) is incomplete and far from realistic.

It is not to say that the backward have not progressed; but the percentage is less because those who have already availed reservation and progressed keep getting it again and. This results in the formation of the creamy layer. Instead of having a reservation policy the emphasis of the government should be to build good schools in the rural as well as urban areas so that the poor have an opportunity to study. All kinds of encouragement from the government should be there in the implementation of such policies. The mid day meal program was a successful one and we should see more of such schemes which encourage the poor to study. The existing system has not been able to fulfil the equality clause of the constitution under Article 14 of the Constitution due to the lack of infrastructure in the rural areas where a proportionate amount of the backward classes reside. Neither has it been successful in abolishing the caste system. A disturbing sign has been the demand for inclusion by the more and more castes leading to creation of vote banks. The policy of reservation has never been subjected to a social or political audit as a matter of fact. Before including more cases, the entire policy needs to be properly examined, and its benefits over a span of nearly 60 years have to be gauged.

Some Special Classes not Included

We have discussed sufficiently, with regard to equality, equal protection of law and classified legislation in the above paragraphs. However, one crucial area, remains to be addressed still i.e. the concept of class in relation to the classified legislation. In other words we need to address the question whether the class is understood only in terms of caste or do we have enough cushion to squeeze in some classes which are not actually castes, for instance, certain groups of Buddhist faith or Christian religion or any other non-Hindu groups and even

Muslims. The constitution is very clear so far as the scheduled castes and scheduled tribes are concerned that they belong to Hindu religion and consequently they are scheduled. A historical discrimination against them has been the basis for today's preferential treatment in their favour. They are treated as special class citizens, on the basis of caste alone. The same logic has been extended by the Backward Class of Commission in recommending affirmative action even in favour of Other Backward Classes. But the question is, what if, some class of people do not belong to a caste. For instance, Christians, Buddhists and Muslims, do not have a caste system at least according to the original faith. There is economic, educational and social backwardness even among there communities even as a matter of fact. Because the majority in the country being Hindus, these minorities, often experience social backwardness and consequently, their economic status and educational progress is far from self sustaining. They do need an affirmative action in their favour. It is also a fact that quite a few State Governments in India have gone to such an extent of making provisions for reservations in favour of Christians, Muslims and neo-Buddhists. But strangely, however, while doing so, caste with in such minority was taken into account. For instance, in the OBC list we have seen in Chhattisgarh, Muslims have been included in respect of their caste and not in generic terms of backwardness whereas there is no such necessity when caste related disadvantage is only confined to Hindu society. On the contrary, it happened many times in the country that lower caste people have taken to mass-conversions into Islam and Christianity (famous case of Villupuram in Tamil Nadu) to escape the social disadvantage associated with Hinduism.

Measuring social and educational backwardness purely in terms of castes doesn't seem to be backed by sound reason. Social backwardness is not confined to caste alone; it is connected to such other factors such as religion, language, region etc. or even certain other unfortunate factors such as socially discredited professions or situations like prostitution, leprosy, AIDS, family criminal background etc. After all, the people belonging to this sort of illustrative social groups, also suffer from social backwardness not to mention of economic hardships. It is worth remembering the judgement of Supreme Court in case of '***Gaurav Jain versus Union of India***' where in special treatment in favour of prostitutes and their children in the country is suggested and relevant orders were passed by the Union of India. Here caste was not the criteria. The essence is that a class should not be determined by the social factor of caste alone. Even the constitution does not endorse the idea. It is very important today that the qualification '*special class of citizens*' be given wider meaning and its ambit extended in order to accommodate all those individuals, groups or even classes who are not strictly castes. An approach of this nature is very revolutionary and at the same time is equally pragmatic and true to the spirit of the constitution.

It is worth remembering here that there is no reservation provided in favour of minorities in the country. Do we have to conclude by this that minorities do not suffer from social and educational backwardness? But the fact is that they do. The economic factor as a criterion to define backwardness is indisputably secular in as much as this factor cuts across all faiths, castes, regions and languages. It is also interesting that even if the criteria of economic backwardness is adopted to qualify the *special class of citizens* all the so called backward classes today including scheduled castes scheduled tribes and will again be the natural beneficiaries in such an eventuality too; as economic backwardness is associated with social backwardness and social backwardness results in economic backwardness. This is a complimentary relationship. But that does not rule out logic that, not being socially backward will not result in economic or educational backwardness. For instance today the Brahmins, who enjoyed high esteem and patronage of the ruling class in the ancient India, no longer remain so. With the advent of industrial revolution, spread of education, demystification of age-old myths and with the secular character of democracy, the brahminical classes though socially advanced virtually have no source of livelihood as their traditional source of livelihood i.e. the priestly occupations have no longer been viable, especially for the new generation.

It is un-fortunate that no survey has been conducted on these lines to assess the economic status of individuals irrespective of the caste or religion. Class is a secular concept and cannot be qualified with religious connotations such as caste or creed. An approach towards egalitarian society with equality as its supreme ideal does of course require equal protection of law and this is possible by adopting a more secular yardstick to qualify all deserving citizens to be treated as *special class* to provide protection. It is sad that article 15(4) constricts the class to social and educational factors with no regard for economic indicators. It is an important question as to what happens to the lot of the so-called upper castes who are otherwise deemed to be educationally, socially not backward (the logical antonym of the socially educationally backward), when their life chances are restricted or subjected to the reservations in favour of the backward classes. In a welfare state such as India article 14 enshrines equality before law and equal protection of law and surely with in the prevalent system of protective discrimination 'the socially educationally not backward' but economically backward sections are not equally protected by law nor are they equal before law. It is also a fact that these sections are surely a minority in comparison to the backward classes, however in a democracy though the government is by the majority, it is not just for the majority; it is also for minority and for its protection. It is worth repeating the fact that in some states as U.P. even the Brahmins communities have been provided reservation in government jobs. Hence, the bottomline is class needs to be re-interpreted to qualify the term 'special class of citizens', as per the requirements of post-independent India and those of modern society.

Conclusions

On the basis of the observations made in the above discussion on various issues, the following are the conclusions:

1. Though Article 14 envisages equality before law and equal protection of law, Article 15(4) and Article 16(4) are essential for the concept of equality to be meaningful because unequals can never be equals. Hence the preferential treatment in favour of the backward classes.
2. The criteria to qualify for special class of citizens has been social and educational backwardness and these two factors are accepted by the constitution. Economic backwardness was not the criteria. However the Judiciary insisted that entomic criteria is relevant.
3. Class, though is made criteria for making special provisions, in practice the State has completely adhered to the criteria of the caste alone. This could be because of the phrases 'social and educational backwardness' and Caste is a dominant social factor. The irony is that constitution of India is strictly opposed to any adherence to caste as clearly spelt out in article 15(1) and 16(1).
4. Economic factors such as individual income, family income, ownership of land, property etc. were never taken by the State to qualify special class of citizens or so-called backward classes. As a result, as we discussed above, quite a number of social groups which cannot be strictly categorized as castes were left out of the enlistment for affirmative action.
5. Though minorities as such were also considered to be a special class of citizens in the scheme, their inclusion in the 'special class' was again on the basis of their caste identities. This is a contradiction, for social backwardness even if is considered because

of caste factor in a Hindu society, the non-Hindu minorities do not have a caste structure accepted within their religion.

6. Social backwardness was strictly attached to caste identification, thereby caste was taken as the yardstick and this perpetrated caste consciousness for eternity because when a preferential treatment is given in the name of caste though glorified in terms of criterion for identification of social backwardness, yet the caste remained a factor of identity recognized by the State; this is contrary to the intention of the constitution by letter and in spirit

7. Reservations in jobs under government employment in article 16(4) is a discretionary provision. However, the State had consciously and deliberately made it mandatory through legislation in spite of the fact that the number of posts under government are extremely limited in proportion to the population of the so-called Backward Classes of citizens. How a provision of few jobs in the Govt. result in social and educational advancement of the class of citizens has never been convincingly addressed. Even the Backward Commission headed by Mr. B.P. Mandal, while making recommendations, endorses this fact but all the same said that the affirmative action is for empowerment of the other backward classes, no matter how many jobs are available.

8. As a matter of fact, article 15(4) is broader and egalitarian in spirit for it only provides for special provisions for advancement and does not envisage job reservations. State, it seems, has paid more adherence to article 16(4) than article 15(4). It is also a fact that if a well thought out plan of action in favour of the backwards in accordance with the article 15(4) is contemplated with respect to time and to the needs of deserving classes within the backward class; article 16(4) would have become redundant. We have seen in case of Chhattisgarh that a sizeable number of Backward Classes candidates have occupied the vacancies reserved for general candidates purely on the basis of merit thanks to their relatively better economic status and standards of live.

9. Government employment was taken as an indicator of empowerment for the backwards. Article 16(4) emphasizes exclusively on *'not adequately represented'* so far as reservation of jobs are concerned. Even if an affirmative action is needed in favour of backwards, the condition of adequate representation was to be adhered to by State governments. At least in

Chhattisgarh, though data in relation to the representation of Backward Classes in general in Govt. employment is available no survey was conducted to find out caste wise representation (unlike it was done by Ramji Mahajan Committee in 1982) in support of the affirmative action. A situation of this nature led to the following aberrations :

(a) Though it is only 14% of reservation the percentage of representation in govt. jobs by Backward Classes in Chhattisgarh is not less than 30% aggregate. It, in way, questions the rationale behind the principle of special classes.

(b) Government jobs reserved for Backward Classes were seized by few dominant castes within to the neglect of the majority.

(c) Few communities have formed into a class of *self-recruiting elite* with the help of certified non-creamy layer status.

(d) Creamy layer guidelines have been amended (often manipulated) to suit the needs of these self-recruiting elite among the OBCs.

10. Many States have not conducted any survey of OBCs to ascertain their population and verify their representation in the government jobs till date; no separate Department for the welfare of the backward castes exists in Chhattisgarh and no worth mentioning substantive schemes or projects (barring scholarships and a semblance of exclusive hostels) were initiated in the State to ameliorate the conditions of Backward Classes in tune with article 15(4). The State, it seems, firmly believes that job reservations in favour of OBCs is the only panacea to uplift them from their social and educational backwardness. The absence of a concerted action with respect to Article 15(4) has led to a competition among the unequals within the Backward Classes. It is a contradiction that the provisions of article 15(4) and article 16(4) though made to give effect to the concept of equality and equal protection of law in reality these concepts were rendered meaningless, in the light of the fact that only the dominant classes (castes) within the special classes of citizens (Backward Classes) have taken best advantage of the affirmative action. The concept of equal protection of law rendered meaningless in such a situation where equally situated people are not equally treated because of an unequal competition.

11. The Preamble of the constitution contains the words, '**Democratic, Secular and Socialistic**' which characterize an egalitarian society

by the rule of majority with a view to safeguard the dignity and secure the life and liberty of the citizens. The protective discrimination in favour of Backward Classes with its negative effects as seen above is leading to a situation where one is given to understand that Democracy, Socialism and Secularism are subject to State action as the State is the supreme body. The concept of natural justice and due process of law unlike in U.S are of course not introduced in our constitution. On the contrary, it is a system of 'procedure Eestablished by Law' as understood from article 21 by the help of which the life and liberty of a citizen can be taken away. If it is so, article 21 read with article 16(4) would be anything but democratic for it does not care for principles of natural justice. Eventually, the above words of 'Democracy, Socialism and Secularism' of the constitution will be rendered mere decorative phrases far from being realistic.

12. Even the Supreme Court's power is restricted in questioning the intent of Parliament as the judicial review in India is not as per the rule of Due Process of Law unlike in America.

13. The citizens of India have constitutionally guaranteed fundamental rights which are meant for their freedom, life and liberty. Dividing citizens in the name 'special classes' with the non-secular criteria of caste, and providing some with a preferential treatment to the neglect of the rest cannot be a democratic method of governance; least so secular. If the socialistic pattern of the society is the goal of the constitution, than the immediate requirement is a classless society. When the State makes provisions, *for special class of citizens* and special provisions for their advancement, then the concept of socialism remains a farce.

14. The decisions and directions of the Supreme Court are supposed to be law binding on all Courts in the country and the State is cast with the responsibility to carry out the same. However, the subordinate legislation in the country by way of rule-making has been successful in thwarting the spirit of the judgements only to suit to the needs of the sectarian and vested interests. As we have seen many States have increased the quota of reservation more than 50%. The government orders on the creamy layer and the manipulations involved in are another example of this. Sincerity and commitment even towards the declared intentions of the legislature have disappeared to the detriment of equality, and equal protection of law.

15. But for job reservations, the State has not, for decades, contemplated on other effective steps to eradicate communal character associated with social identity of citizens. For instance, caste associations, caste related surnames, caste-based media or film presentations etc. have been flourishing in the country without check. Many lower castes tried to borrow surnames typical of upper castes only to escape from humiliating low caste identities. This syndrome is popularly is known as *sanskritisation* in the opinion of M.N. Srinivas, the veteran sociologist of the country. Successive governments have not dared even to contemplate schemes to secularize the society. State could have made stringent laws prohibiting use of surnames as a suffix depicting caste affiliation or could have banned formation of associations in the name of caste. The media and the activities of public entertainment including films, always contained insinuations of caste and virtues associated with castes. As Dr. Ambedkar expressed virtues of human beings no longer remained virtues, they have been identified with castes (*www.ambedkar.org*). The inaction of State in this respect has indirectly contributed to the perpetration of caste consciousness instead of curbing it. Politicians, and even Ministers took pride in belonging to a specific caste and openly encouraged activities connected with it. If the intention of the constitution is to improve the lot of the Backwards, the first thing required is to initiate a planned attack on the manifestations of castes which has led to social backwardness. Apart from this, State could have made legislations to encourage inter-caste, inter-religious and inter-regional marriages among citizens by introducing special schemes of incentives (few State govts. have done). Such an action on behalf of the State could have certainly led to a peaceful co-existence of castes without the presence of caste related inequalities or exploitation. Such an ideological campaign could have been the best manifestation of secularism in the country. Though caste cannot be annihilated, as Dr. Ambedkar felt, however the inequalities and ill-treatment associated with the caste could have been mitigated or controlled by a positive action on the part of the state. Unfortunately, vote bank politics in Indian democracy have got further strengthened and polarized the castes and communities. As we have seen above, a constant adherence to caste as an idiom of social identity will only perpetuate the caste consciousness for eternity.

16. Measures for improvement of the economic status of the

Backwards will have a logical consequence of enhanced self-dignity which in a way, can lead to social advancement. Unfortunately, in a mixed economy such as we have in India, except major and key sectors like defence, mines and minerals, majority of the production activities are handed over to the private sector which is largely controlled by one social group/caste i.e. the traditional Vaishyas. It is a common story in the private sector that the Backwards do not find proper employment as it is a merit based competitive organization where specialized qualifications are a must (we have discussed in detail in other chapter though in relation to Scheduled Castes). Besides, in a capitalist economy, which the private sector believes in, even corporate social responsibility is confined just to charitable purposes like public amenities, primary education, health centres etc and does not address caste based injustice. Permanent opportunities of livelihood are never reserved in favour of Backwards in Private sector. On the other hand the public sector in India was confined to mass production by mechanical techniques instead of going for production by masses; it has minimized the opportunities of skilled or semi skilled manual labour in which Backwards could have been accommodated.

17. Land reforms movement in India being a high sounding flop (except in the state of West Bengal), even cultivable land for a self-sustaining agriculture was not made available to the Backwards. It is intriguing that in an agrarian society like that of India, agriculture was never explored enough to be brought into public sector with state ownership on land. Millions of hectares of un-cultivable land was never brought under cultivation by forming state-owned organizations so that many castes in Backward Classes could be given a permanent source of income generation. With the advent of mechanized modern world household industries have miserably failed to compete with the machine-made products relegating majority of the Backwards to an existence of being manual labourers.

18. If the state was really serious about socialism as its ideal and 'classless' society to be its ultimate goal, ensuring economic equality by way of equal opportunities should have been the first priority. Instead, the State has adopted methods of piecemeal social engineering by way of Rural Development Programmes and Poverty Eradication Schemes such as NREGA, SJGRY, Indira Awaas, Jeevan Dhara. A plethora of schemes of government of

India are aimed at improving the economic status of the BPL stakeholders. Though the BPL (below poverty line) stakeholders are more than 50% even in the state of Chhattisgarh, these schemes are virtually confined to provision of daily wages for manual labour or provision of few houses or income generating activities for few families. In short, the role of the State in ensuring economic security to the Backwards has not been praise-worthy. Even the implementation of schemes of the government were often subjected to political pressures resulting in half-hearted execution associated with large-scale de-centralized corruption involving the state machinery.

19. Though the BPL category is absolutely secular, the State has taken this as criteria only for the state sponsored schemes as above while it could have employed the same criteria even for the job reservations. In such an eventuality, caste would not become a factor of identification as the BPL is generic and exhaustive enough to include almost all the Backwards in the country.

20. Modernization is defined in terms of secularism and rationality. The Tradition (of India) which harboured inequalities by way of sectarian and communal identities, was supposed to give way to Modernity in due course of time. India is one country, for example, which has been modernized in the last 100 years. Surely it speaks for the tolerance and progressive disposition of the people of India that in the post-independent era, the country has witnessed revolutionary developments such as enforcement of constitution, provisions for protective discrimination for Backwards, legislations for equal status for women, not to mention Fundamental rights and Directive principles of state policy. These epoch making happenings were unknown to traditional India. Nevertheless, the irony is, today with excessive adherence to caste criteria, the tradition seems to be sneaking back into modernity through the back door. Through out the country, we witness an increasing demand for more inclusion of castes associated with caste-related political activities holding the State for ransom. Tradition needs to be modernized; but on the contrary, in India modernity seems to be slowly getting traditionalised. If the end result of modernity is division of society in the name of caste, State sponsored inequality by way of preferential treatment in the name of Caste or a constant war among the castes for self-centred development as opposed to national development , it is in fact the Tradition which is thriving with the help of Modernity, than it being replaced,

because these maladies were congenially characteristic of Tradition. One wonders whether this is the heart, soul and the spirit of the constitution which the framers of the same intended it to be.

21. If citizens are to be classified into special classes, on the grounds of social and educational backwardness, it is intriguing as to why the constitution has not considered the one-half of the population – the Women. Women suffer from un-told situations of in-equality, humiliation and exploitation in the Indian society from ages and it continues even in the present. Actually women belong to all castes (both Forward and Backward) and all religions and all regions. The tradition has been extremely unkind to women in India as the history vouches for the facts. If social and educational backwardness was the criteria for a preferential treatment, all women in the country should have been treated as 'special class of citizens' and made eligible for preferential treatment. Even by the standards of the judgement delivered by the Supreme Court wherein 49.5% was the sealing of reservation for all backwards including SC and STs, women should have been the natural stakeholders as per the population of India; they are little less than 50%. Besides there would not be a better secular criteria to identify 'special class of citizens'. A legislation of this nature could have ushered in a great revolution in this country superseding caste consciousness and paving the way for fraternity among all. Because women belong to all castes and they are citizens of India as well. It is peculiar that the State did reflect on this aspect, of course conveniently and also made provision of reservations for women up to 30% (at least in Chhattisgarh) in government jobs. But however this 30% is not exclusively for women, rather it is horizontal within the Backward classes including SCs and STs which means the women stakeholders have to compete with their men counterparts from with in to secure their sources of livelihood. Till now we have been witnessing a war among castes but with this we wonder whether soon it is going to be a similar war-like situation between the sexes.

22. The system of reservation of jobs for Backward Classes does not seem to have a qualification of time. If the scheme is for eternity, which it seems, as per the conclusions we have arrived as above all the intentions of the constitution aimed at a classless egalitarian, socialistic, and secular society will turn void. The protective

discrimination must have a qualification of time and space. Or else sooner or later the citizens of the country will loose the identity as Indians as they prefer to choose the identity of their caste or sub-caste which is immediately beneficial to them than the broader and non-paying identity of 'Indian'.

The above being well drawn conclusions of the study, it makes us to ponder over the future action in order to preserve the unity, integrity of the country with its secular nature intact. Or else the existence of the very nation as India will be at stake not far from now. The conclusions drawn above will sensitize a true nationalistic mind to make suggestions as under:

RECOMMENDATIONS

The recommendations can be made for short term and as well for long term in tune with the priorities. To begin with we may recommend some short term measures as under:

Short Term Measures

(a) The Backward Classes as 'special class of citizens', have to be protected through affirmative action not only by way of the government jobs (with a time qualification of course) but by also improving their economic status through State sponsored schemes to that end. The traditional occupations generally associated with the OBCs need to be revived in order to ensure economic self-sustenance of these communities in the agrarian economy of India. A system of protectionism in the trades and activities of the Backward Classes in relation to the products or services is essential.

(b) Equal protection of law does not necessarily restrict to different class of citizens alone but it applies to classes within the *special class of citizens* as well. In Chhattisgarh, we have seen a few castes have been predominantly securing the government jobs with the help of reservations while majority of the castes are left-out. It is high time that the State has introduced rationing and regulated the distribution of benefits among the stakeholders. This calls for a further categorization of the most backwards among the Backwards and create the opportunities of life and growth for them. Even the Supreme Court is not against such an idea. In fact many States have done so. It could be sub-division of quota for Backward Classes or it could be a caste-wise re-allotment of quota.

(c) The census of the Backward Classes population is the responsibility of the State. The government should take it up at once and issue a white paper on the status.

(d) The reservation must not be for eternity. There has to be a specific time frame for closing the windows of protection with help of an effective monitoring mechanism.

(e) Apart from the reservation in the government jobs it is required that the general milieu and environment that the Backward Classes are living is improved by way of better infrastructure for education, for economic sustenance and for specialised knowledge.

(f) As the students are the future citizens, exclusive hostel facilities for Backward Classes with proportionate positive bias for gender is required. The academic diversification and provision of specialised knowledge avenues to compete for better jobs also needs to be provided such as coaching facilities for specialized courses or for competitive exams.

(g) An in-house survey with regard to total number of sanctioned posts in all departments of the government and the total number of Backward Classes employed thereon and the percentage of different castes appointed, needs to be compiled or updated in order to arrive at a transparent and impartial assessment of the situation and initiate required action. This helps performing a balancing act as per the requirements of the law. The backward classes commission of the State has the responsibility to perform this task.

(h) The creamy layer guidelines must be adhered to in letter and spirit to ward off the vested interests within the Backward Classes at least and to ensure that the neediest would get what they deserve.

The above recommendations are for short-term measures required to be transformed into action immediately. However, we can suggest some long term measures with regard to the system of protective discrimination in relation to basic concept of Equality and with regard to the basic structure of the Constitution as under.

Long Term Measures

I. The legislation for affirmative action in favour of Backward Classes needs a thorough review in order to make it relevant and also sufficient provisions for inclusion of certain truly secular classes as discussed above that are drawn from different castes and religions are a must. A true classified legislation has to be based on the concept of Class and not Caste. Economic classification is all that is required for it is truly secular and includes all castes and communities. Criteria of caste has of course been employed for identification of social and educational backwardness; however, it is high time in the changed socio-political scenario of 21st century, the government had given a serious thought to prefer class as criteria in place of caste. As we discussed earlier, a proper survey of economic backwardness would surely reveal that hitherto included backward classes including the SCs and STs would again be beneficiaries of protective discrimination besides making room for many other classes which are not only just castes. Or else the caste factor recognized by the State would eat up the vital foundations of Indian democracy rendering the constitution absolutely a paradise for caste politics.

II. Provisions also required for sub-classification of Backward Classes with a view to ensure equal protection of law even from within. As we have seen in the case of Chhattisgarh, it is not un-common in the rest of India as well, that dominant castes under the umbrage of Backward Classes gather maximum benefits of reservation while hundreds of other struggling castes are never in a position to compete. In few states, the governments have resorted to sub-division of quota for the Backward Classes or even for the scheduled castes. With the census of India 2010 in process, with caste-based enumeration it is time for the government of India to come up with more rational and scientific methods of law making with respect to reservations.

III. Political will in a democracy, is the most important factor in order to guide legislation towards a secular and egalitarian order. All political parties especially the national ones, should come together, thrash out their differences and thinking in unison, decide to follow a secular path by shunning adherence to idioms of caste and vote bank politics. They should realise that politics is not destroy the nation. On the contrary, it is build the nation and society.

IV. Article 15(4) is extremely relevant with regard to the advancement of Backward Classes. The State must contemplate on measure to elevate the Educational backwardness of the stakeholders by special allocations of budget so that adequate infrastructural requirements can be met. A tendency to oblige the castes by way of distributing quotas for employment taking recourse to Art.16 (4) must be discouraged. Art.15 (4) is wider and more secular in content.

V. As we have observed in the recruitments the educational advancement of Scheduled Castes and Tribes is far from satisfactory in comparison to Backward Classes. Equating the latter with the former is an ill-conceived thought. Therefore extending protection to the Backward Classes on par with is unjustified as both stands on different footing. Even the Supreme Court in *Indra Sahani has* observed the same. A sheer competition with the Scheduled Castes and Tribes for equal gains is uncalled for. On the contrary, the Backward Classes are in much better position in Chattisgarh, for an example.

VI. The Phrase '*Adequate Representation' in Art. 16 (4)* needs to be given a new meaning in order to remove the vagueness it carries with. Govt. Services are not to be interpreted in terms of personal empowerment or community advancement. They are for the service to the nation. Reserving the posts in services only for empowerment backward classes would be against the philosophy of Govt. Service. *Adequate Representation* can not be a reason for it would lead to an endless saga of empowerment. Even if the reservation is necessary it should be minimal. The Scheduled Castes and Tribes can not be equated with backward classes as it is well settled by the Supreme Court.

VII. As a long time policy measure, the government should decide to downsize government establishments for the following reasons:

(a) More than 60% of the budget of all the State. Governments are spent on the establishment, i.e. salaries, allowances and creation of infrastructure for government employees with the avowed object of governance. However, lack of control and accountability led to un-bridled corruption in the system making mockery of the government machineries all over the country.

(b) Because of increased negative advantages in government services such as extra statutory influence, un-deserving perks, lack of accountability, strong trade unionism etc., there is a strong attraction for government services in the country.

(c) Often people working in government at different levels get affiliated with political parties and involve in politics against their code of conduct and keep receiving the *Godfather* patronage.

(d) Govt. Service is meant for governance of State and for execution of its programmes and schemes. The Mandal

Commission's philosophy of empowerment of Backward Classes through Govt. Service is misconstrued for it sends a message that it is a source of empowering one self. Services under Government are not means for acquiring income or power. On the contrary the services are for the nation and society.

Downsizing government machineries and encouraging private sector or private-public participation (PPP) models will discourage the craze for government jobs. Consequently, the clamouring for inclusion for reservation will automatically die down in due course of time.

The state should encourage an all-round planned development separate from government sector whereby more number of jobs in private-sector and in self-employment can be created in a specific time frame and so that the aspiring youth can be accommodated. Unfortunately, in India government service has become the most attractive to empower oneself. This is mostly because of negative aspects (which are profitable) associated with government sector. The State should create an environment of industrial development, check the Private Sector, expand services sector and encourage entrepreneurial talents of the people so that over time, the government jobs will become less lucrative and gradually loose charm.

VIII. Dignity of labour has not received its proper place in Indian society even after decade's years of self rule. Many occupations are still associated more with status and social esteem than basic dignity of labour. Craze for officer like or white collared jobs is still dominant in the society. This is partly due to caste identification with the nature of a specific job and partly due to low wages paid against. The State should seriously contemplate on hiking the wage component of such jobs like sanitation workers, sweepers, medical menial staff, peons, etc so that the allurement of income on those jobs will have a glorifying effect and gradually the social disrespect going with the job will finally disappear. In such an eventuality even upper castes would not hesitate to take up such jobs. Over a period of time the caste associated jobs will be open for all resulting in caste tolerance in place of caste consciousness. The trend has already set in, in metros where beauty saloons, leather goods business, hotels, catering massage parlours are no longer run by the people from the ascribed castes they are traditionally associated with. The State need to involve in a loud thinking and act simultaneously.

IX. Stringent electoral reforms to check the vote bank politics of the political parties is the need of the hour. Appropriate steps are required to check caste based election campaigns, mobilisation of people on caste lines and non-secular identities. This would discourage the trend of placating the castes and appeasing non-secular demands of communities.

X. Media is the most effective way of communication in the modern world, but often it is used to whip up the passions and create hatred and mistrust among people for the sake of quick business interest. The State has the responsibility to check the negative activities of media by provision of stringent laws and uniform regulations.

XI. India is a secular country. However, the governance of the republic is not always devoid of communal and sectarian manifestations. For instance, State sponsored programmes and schemes quite often smack of communal fervour. Ministers and heads of states are often seen participating in religion-based activities or caste-specific programmes and functions. Many governments have appeased non-secular sects by doling out the lands for the purpose of association buildings, Dharamshalas etc. These are the most unwarranted things to happen in a secular Democracy and need to be curbed.

XII. Positive laws to encourage inter caste marriages with special incentives are to be enacted. All Educational curriculum and syllabi must contain secular pedagogic contents. Application Forms for Admissions and Examinations should not have caste or surname related information as mandatory.

XIII. Equality and equal protection of law being the two important aspects of our constitution, the State is entrusted with the responsibility of safeguarding these two provisions at any cost. Though classified legislation is a necessary evil for an effective realization of these two above concepts, the same should be qualified by indicators of time and space with the principle of universal inclusion and equity. Equity is more humanistic feeling than the statutory provision of equality; because all legislations guided by equity have of course the underlying principle of equality but it is not necessary that all legislations for equality have equity as part and parcel. The enormous importance given to the Concept of Equity in Law need not be explained here as it is no secret to the students of law. Constricting benefits of reservation to exclusive sections on the basis of caste alone is, certainly, not equity.

XIV. The government should take effective steps towards accountability of Govt. Servants in the running of the State machinery and stricter punishments including termination of services must be provide for against corrupt. Or else a lenient disposition would result in misuse of office encouraging unbridled corruption which becomes an attraction for the youth to seek jobs in Govt. Permanent security of tenure was often misused by maximum of the government employees across the country.

Last Word

To sum-up, we have examined, analysed, discussed various issues involved in the subject of reservation for SEBC in government services and arrived at conclusions as above in tune with the hypothesis of our research. We have discovered in the process that protective discrimination becomes a sine-qua-non for realization of the concept of equality in a society like India which is ridden with inequalities in the name of birth in a caste. However, the reservations in government services for backward classes who do not suffer from the peculiar syndrome of untouchability unlike Dalits and Tribes do, cannot be justified in the absence of qualification of time. Besides the creamy layer concept needs to be strictly enforced in order to eliminate those sections of backward classes who do not deserve the 'protection'. However, the identification of beneficiaries among the so-called backward classes should not be on the basis of caste. It should be on the basis of a secular criterion known as 'Class' for all the castes who are economically impoverished such as BPL groups will find a place in no uncertain terms. Besides, class is wider enough to include even those groups of unfortunate human beings such as destitute men and women, homeless, prostitutes, aids-victims, leprosy patients etc who have no reservation at least in government services. Similarly, women as a gender are also socially educationally backward for centuries. Concept of class is not averse to inclusion of women.

System of reservation in government services for backward classes needs to be revamped with more objective and transparent parameters of identification of beneficiaries. The basic structure of Indian Constitution needs to be protected and safeguarded in order to make equality before law a realistic concept. Political parties should rise above the politics of vote banks and sectarian affiliations and work in unison for the upkeep of unity and integrity of nation. The intention of legislature and the actions of subordinate legislation must be endowed with unity of command backed by secular and democratic spirit. The legislature should contemplate more on positive actions as envisaged by article 15(4), for the advancement of backward classes instead of resorting to quick and populist announcements of quotas in favour of one or more castes or groups. The day the schemes and programmes intended and enacted for the advancement of backward classes true to the spirit of article 15(4) , the need for reservation for anyone in government services does not arise for the social and educational backwardness will have vanished or diminished to a substantial extent by then.

From a long time perspective the State (the Executive and the Legislature) should seriously contemplate on protecting the secular fabric of the country by discouraging, through effective legislation, any manifestations of sectarian identities such as caste, religion, or creed. The political parties should exemplify themselves by shunning caste-oriented appeals or un-secular public or private acts. Reservation in the name of caste should not become an instrument of political mobilisation to the detriment of noble and lofty ideals and goals of democracy. The intention of law-makers should be to eradicate social and educational backwardness of citizens of the country in tune with the demands of modernity and certainly not by the dictates of tradition which are manifested in unscientific and inhuman institutions such as caste or creed.

Let us close by quoting Pt. Nehru once again,

> *" So these external props, as I might call them, that is reservation of seats and the rest-may possibly be helpful occasionally in the case of backward groups, but they produce a false sense of strength, and ultimately, therefore, they are not so nearly as important as real educational, cultural and economic advance which gives them inner strength to face any difficulty or any opponent".*

ANNEXURES

ANNEXURE-6.1

Government Employees & there percentage of Reserved Category in Administrative Department First Class (on 31st March 2008)

S. No.	Name of Department	Total Employees	First Class					
			SC		ST		OBC	
			No.	%	No.	%	No.	%
1	General Administration	110	18	16.36	28	25.45	140	12.73
2	Home	98	13	13.27	15	15.31	9	9.18
3	Finance & Planning	83	13	15.66	23	27.71	23	27.71
4	Revenue & P.H.E.	105	12	11.43	21	20.00	18	17.14
5	Forest	89	15	16.85	9	10.11	13	14.61
6	Mining and minerals	79	10	12.66	12	15.19	12	15.19
7	Energy & Water Resource	148	15	10.14	18	12.16	37	25.00
8	Agriculture	108	14	12.96	26	24.07	12	11.11
9	Health & Family welfare	348	45	12.93	45	12.93	94	27.01
10	Public Works, Housing, Environment, Urban Development	79	7	8.86	16	20.25	7	8.86
11	Education	599	65	10.85	62	10.35	84	14.02

Contd...

S. No.	Name of Department	Total Employees	First Class					
			SC		ST		OBC	
			No.	%	No.	%	No.	%
12	Law	154	23	14.94	33	21.43	14	9.09
13	Panchayat and Rural Development	94	8	8.51	8	8.51	17	18.09
14	Labour, Sports and Youth welfare	26	3	11.54	6	23.08	10	38.46
15	Tribal	45	8	17.78	12	26.67	12	26.67
16	Women and Child Development and Social Welfare	34	5	14.71	9	26.47	3	8.82
17	Food, Civil Supplies and Consumer Protection	18	4	22.22	4	22.22	5	27.78
18	Tourism. Culture	39	4	10.26	7	17.95	4	10.26
Total		**2256**	**282**	**12.50**	**354**	**15.69**	**388**	**17.20**

(ANNEXURE-6.2)

Government Employees and the percentage of Reserved Category in Administrative Department Second Class (on 31st March 2008)

S. No.	Name of Department	Total Employees	Second Class					
			SC		ST		OBC	
			No.	%	No.	%	No.	%
1	General Administration	218	10	4.59	19	8.72	3	1.38
2	Home	268	32	11.94	83	30.97	19	7.09
3	Finance and Planning	258	30	11.63	98	37.98	25	9.69
4	Revenue and P.H.E.	398	80	20.10	124	31.16	70	17.59
5	Forest	328	68	20.73	63	19.21	44	13.41
6	Mining and minerals	132	17	12.88	48	36.36	15	11.36
7	Energy and Water Resource	664	68	10.24	81	12.20	80	12.05
8	Agriculture	398	59	14.82	91	22.86	77	19.35
9	Health and Family welfare	1972	280	14.20	366	18.56	296	15.01
10	Public Works, Housing, Environment, Urban Development	71	20	28.17	49	69.01	21	29.58
11	Education	3260	412	12.64	611	18.74	748	22.94

S. No.	Name of Department	Total Employees	Second Class					
			SC		ST		OBC	
			No.	%	No.	%	No.	%
12	Law	170	31	18.24	34	20.00	29	17.06
13	Panchayat and Rural Development	302	45	14.90	69	22.85	67	22.19
14	Labour, Sports and Youth welfare	40	4	10.00	10	25.00	9	22.50
15	Tribal	1283	89	6.94	419	32.66	201	15.67
16	Women and Child Development and Social Welfare	128	15	11.72	50	39.06	12	9.38
17	Food, Civil Supplies and Consumer Protection	15	0	0.00	7	46.67	2	13.33
18	Tourism, Culture	23	1	4.35	1	4.35	4	17.39
Total		**9928**	**1261**	**12.70**	**2223**	**22.39**	**1722**	**17.34**

ANNEXURE-6.3

Government Employees and the percentage of Reserved Category in Administrative Department Third Class (Executive) (31st March 2008)

S. No.	Name of Department	Total Employees	Third Class (Executive)					
			SC		ST		OBC	
			No.	%	No.	%	No.	%
1	General Administration	412	42	10.19	145	35.19	50	12.14
2	Home	19918	1462	7.34	7835	39.34	3890	19.53
3	Finance and Planning	1742	109	6.26	392	22.50	312	17.91
4	Revenue and P.H.E.	3896	418	10.73	1452	37.27	1649	42.33
5	Forest	5212	345	6.62	1612	30.93	1618	31.04
6	Mining and minerals	712	84	11.80	150	21.07	150	21.07
7	Energy and Water Resource	2422	220	9.08	540	22.30	815	33.65
8	Agriculture	5112	540	10.56	1800	35.21	1020	19.95
9	Health and Family welfare	11812	1050	8.89	2255	19.09	2360	19.98
10	Public Works, Housing, Environment, Urban Development	1612	280	17.37	189	11.72	410	25.43
11	Education	28208	3420	12.12	6265	22.21	9827	34.84

Contd...

S. No.	Name of Department	Total Employees	Third Class (Executive)					
			SC		ST		OBC	
			No.	%	No.	%	No.	%
12	Law	1214	111	9.14	112	9.23	355	29.24
13	Panchayat and Rural Development	3536	322	9.11	425	12.02	940	26.58
14	Labour, Sports and Youth welfare	212	46	21.70	22	10.38	45	21.23
15	Tribal	15668	3836	24.48	7040	44.93	4000	25.53
16	Women and Child Development and Social Welfare	1790	120	6.70	412	23.02	400	22.35
17	Food, Civil Supplies and Consumer Protection	214	22	10.28	22	10.28	25	11.68
18	Tourism, Culture	172	12	6.98	10	5.81	12	6.98
Total		**103864**	**12439**	**11.98**	**30678**	**29.54**	**27878**	**26.84**

Annexure 7.1

Appendix - Five of Chhattisgarh Public Service Commission Description of exams form 01.04.2004 to 31.03.2005

S.N.	Name of Exam/ Date of Exam	Number of Applicants								
		General		Schedule Caste		Schedule Tribe		Other Backward Class		
		Female	Male	Female	Male	Female	Male	Female	Male	Total
(1)	Chhattisgarh Public Service Commission - 2003 (Exam from 26.07.2004 to 18.08.2004)									
1	Number of applicants									2169
2	Number of admit cards issued	324	779	135	234	162	291	44	177	2146
3	Number of candidates appeared in exam	277	671	125	226	143	290	43	168	1943
4	Number of qualified candidates	66	162	27	48	33	60	09	36	441
(2)	Chhattisgarh Public Service Commission - 2004 (Exam from 26.12.2004)									

Contd...

S.N.	Name of Exam/ Date of Exam	Number of Applicants								
		General		Schedule Caste		Schedule Tribe		Other Backward Class		
		Female	Male	Female	Male	Female	Male	Female	Male	Total
1	Number of applicants	1794	9148	118	520	62	291	251	1509	13693
2	Number of admit cards issued	1738	8913	113	502	61	275	244	1480	13326
3	Number of candidates appeared in exam	787	2849	107	430	44	221	186	1302	5926
4	Number of qualified candidates	754	365	45	91	46	122	32	94	949

Annexure 7.2

Appendix – Four of CGPSC Description of exams form 01.04.2003 to 31.03.2004

S.No.	Name of Exam and Year	Date of Exam	Number of applications received								
			General		Schedule Caste		Schedule Tribe		Other Backward Class		
			Female	Male	Female	Male	Female	Male	Female	Male	Total
1	Civil Judges Prelims (2003)	3-8-2003	7114	1400	561	111	259	38	1549	223	11255
2	Assistant Forest Conservator - 2003	8-10-2003 15-10-2003	317	52	140	26	186	32	240	30	1023
3	CGPSC (Pre)- 2003	21-12-2003	37836	14248	8215	2841	11543	4315	17867	5415	102280
4	Civil Judges Mains (2003)	28-12-2003	165	76	50	15	59	30	46	16	457

Annexure 7.3

Appendix – Eight Description of exams form 01.04.2006 to 31.03.2007

Description of exams under reporting

S.No.	Name of Exam and Date of Exam	Number of applications received								
		General		Schedule Caste		Schedule Tribe		Other Backward Class		
		Female	Male	Female	Male	Female	Male	Female	Male	Total
1	Civil Judges Mains (2004) exam date 24.4.2005									
	Number of applicants	154	365	45	91	46	122	32	94	949
	Number of candidates appeared in exam	-	-	-	-	-	-	-	-	906
	Number of candidates qualified for interview appeared in exam	30	69	10	18	10	25	06	18	186
2	CGPSC (Pre) – 2005 Exam Date 06.11.2006									
	Number of applicants	-	-	-	-	-	-	-	-	79953

Contd...

S.No.	Name of Exam and Date of Exam	Number of applications received								
		General		Schedule Caste		Schedule Tribe		Other Backward Class		
		Female	Male	Female	Male	Female	Male	Female	Male	Total
	Number of admit cards issued	-	-	-	-	-	-	-	-	76949
	Number of candidates appeared in exam	6944	16824	2093	6051	3201	8174	3824	13482	60593
3	Principal Hr. Sec. School Exam –2005 Exam Date 8.1.2006									
	Number of applicants	2035		489		516		974		4014
	Number of admit cards issued									3056
	Number of candidates appeared in exam	621	876	50	219	66	157	110	642	2741

(Source for Annexures 7.1 to 7.3 is the record of State Public Service Commission Chhatisgarh, Raipur)

Annexure 7.4. Sub Caste wise total number of candidates applied in different varg of Shikshakarmi Recruitment Exam 2009

VARG-1			VARG-2			VARG-3	
CASTE	TOTAL		CASTE	TOTAL		CASTE	TOTAL
5101	15561		5101	30720		5101	85366
3904	6272		3904	12129		3904	27543
6201	2830		6201	5683		4201	13264
4201	2734		4201	5436		6201	11032
2501	2112		2501	4326		1207	10266
0105	1862		0105	3569		3308	10227
3308	1783		3308	3536		2501	9941
1207	1545		1207	3274		0105	8971
0109	1466		0109	2954		0109	8594
4303	1300		4303	2434		4702	6202
4501	1229		4702	2427		4901	5913
4702	1203		4501	2403		4501	5613
4901	1092		4901	2168		4303	5580
2001	923		2001	1857		2001	5067
3201	776		3201	1481		3801	3458
3908	735		3908	1291		4203	3354
0101	646		3801	1258		0101	2901
4203	627		0101	1245		3908	2828
3801	622		4203	1231		3201	2763
3207	490		6101	915		0108	2350
0108	456		0108	914		6101	2304
0301	434		0301	890		0301	1975
6101	426		3207	878		2502	1811
2502	350		2502	702		1201	1807
3302	325		1201	678		2908	1578
8717	313		8717	586		3207	1521

Contd...

VARG-1			VARG-2			VARG-3	
CASTE	TOTAL		CASTE	TOTAL		CASTE	TOTAL
1201	311		3302	572		8722	1335
8722	302		2908	563		8717	1214
2908	268		8722	511		2004	1190
0116	208		0116	462		3305	1185
3307	197		3307	432		0116	1182
1204	191		2004	403		3302	1164
5502	187		0501	388		3307	1025
2702	186		2702	388		4701	989
3202	180		5502	371		1205	952
0501	179		3305	348		2301	931
3305	176		4701	346		5502	868
2004	171		1204	340		2702	863
4701	171		3903	333		2203	824
1203	158		1205	321		2503	771
2503	153		1203	317		3903	703
3903	153		2503	307		1204	687
1205	151		3202	306		0501	613
2301	149		2301	305		1203	598
9101	144		2003	266		2003	596
0106	143		9101	258		3202	574
3910	140		0106	242		7801	540
2003	121		3910	240		3910	522
0803	115		0404	220		0106	521
0404	113		2203	212		0404	507
2203	108		3301	192		0401	483
1901	107		1901	191		9101	475

Contd...

VARG-1			VARG-2			VARG-3	
CASTE	TOTAL		CASTE	TOTAL		CASTE	TOTAL
3606	105		3606	186		3901	437
3901	105		3901	176		0803	377
3907	100		0803	173		3301	365
0401	86		3907	166		2311	354
3301	86		7801	157		3907	328
7801	83		4803	153		3606	322
4803	81		0401	150		2101	319
0601	74		0601	137		1901	316
2901	74		0503	136		4803	310
0503	73		2901	125		8101	295
8101	72		3609	124		2901	269
2311	63		2311	122		8710	254
3609	55		8101	117		0503	234
8710	54		0904	103		0601	233
0904	50		1202	102		0904	232
1202	50		8710	100		3609	227
1902	50		1301	98		1202	203
3607	48		2101	98		0115	174
2101	47		1902	85		1301	168
1301	45		3607	83		8721	166
8721	42		8708	78		8708	164
8708	39		7501	72		7501	154
0115	37		0507	68		4202	144
2302	36		2302	64		1902	143
0507	32		0115	61		3607	134
7501	30		1904	59		2302	133

Contd...

VARG-1			VARG-2			VARG-3	
CASTE	TOTAL		CASTE	TOTAL		CASTE	TOTAL
0701	28		8721	55		6502	117
2701	27		0701	52		8706	117
3603	26		2701	49		1904	116
6001	26		3603	46		2701	114
1904	23		6001	46		3303	113
3602	23		6502	46		6001	108
8706	22		3002	45		0507	104
6502	21		8706	41		3002	103
3002	20		8711	40		1001	94
1001	19		3602	39		3603	92
2801	19		4202	38		6601	92
8711	18		1001	36		0701	87
1501	17		8901	31		1004	77
8901	17		6601	27		4401	76
0051	15		0902	25		8901	74
4401	15		1501	25		6602	70
7901	15		3205	25		3602	65
0120	14		7901	25		7901	65
1004	14		8701	25		7802	62
2504	14		3303	24		0902	61
3205	14		4401	24		1501	60
8701	14		1004	23		8711	58
8715	14		2801	23		4405	50
0902	12		7802	22		2801	47
1101	12		0120	21		0120	44
3303	12		0406	21		5701	42

Contd...

VARG-1			VARG-2			VARG-3	
CASTE	TOTAL		CASTE	TOTAL		CASTE	TOTAL
4202	12		2504	21		8701	42
6601	12		3914	21		8715	42
0406	11		6602	21		8734	41
5701	11		8715	21		2512	40
6602	11		2512	19		0051	39
7802	11		0051	18		4101	38
8734	11		1101	18		0406	34
3905	10		8714	17		0104	33
8714	10		4405	16		2504	33
2512	9		3905	15		1303	31
3914	9		4101	15		3914	31
1303	8		0110	14		0604	30
3601	8		6801	14		5105	30
4101	8		9001	14		3205	29
4405	8		1303	13		0110	28
6801	8		3601	13		3601	28
0110	7		5105	13		8714	28
4712	7		5701	13		3802	27
6501	7		8707	13		1101	26
7601	7		8734	13		3909	26
8720	7		7601	12		3401	25
0604	6		8709	11		3905	25
3608	6		0604	10		8709	23
3909	6		3608	10		3608	22
5105	6		3802	10		4102	21
5111	6		1109	9		6801	21

Contd...

VARG-1			VARG-2			VARG-3	
CASTE	**TOTAL**		**CASTE**	**TOTAL**		**CASTE**	**TOTAL**
8707	6		3906	9		3906	20
9001	6		3909	9		1002	19
1105	5		5111	9		5111	19
1106	5		1002	8		1212	18
3217	5		4712	8		8707	18
3401	5		8720	8		7601	17
TOTAL	**54936**		0104	7		9001	17
			0118	7		0118	16
			1212	7		0089	15
			2511	7		1109	15
			3003	7		2508	15
			5001	7		4712	15
			6501	7		2511	14
			0089	6		5201	14
			1105	6		6302	14
			1106	6		8720	14
			1401	6		0061	13
			2508	6		1106	13
			3101	6		3101	13
			4102	6		4511	13
			4211	6		5001	13
			5201	6		5901	13
			6302	6		1105	12
			8718	6		1401	12
			0038	5		4904	12
			0039	5		0039	11

Contd...

VARG-1			VARG-2			VARG-3	
CASTE	**TOTAL**		**CASTE**	**TOTAL**		**CASTE**	**TOTAL**
			0103	5		0117	11
			0602	5		1005	11
			0807	5		3003	11
			1005	5		3318	11
			2904	5		8718	11
			3217	5		0014	10
			3304	5		0901	10
			3318	5		0103	9
			4511	5		1302	9
			5901	5		5601	9
			TOTAL	**108296**		6501	9
						8900	9
						0038	8
						0045	8
						0602	8
						1115	8
						2904	8
						4902	8
						0016	7
						0402	7
						3304	7
						3501	7
						3504	7
						8801	7
						0808	6
						3204	6

Contd...

VARG-1			VARG-2			VARG-3	
CASTE	**TOTAL**		**CASTE**	**TOTAL**		**CASTE**	**TOTAL**
						3502	6
						4001	6
						4211	6
						4304	6
						5102	6
						5501	6
						6202	6
						6301	6
						8201	6
						8703	6
						9304	6
						0042	5
						0807	5
						0903	5
						1107	5
						2306	5
						2404	5
						2603	5
						3004	5
						3211	5
						3217	5
						3309	5
						4402	5
						4403	5
						4502	5
						4504	5

Contd...

VARG-1			VARG-2			VARG-3	
CASTE	TOTAL		CASTE	TOTAL		CASTE	TOTAL
						4707	5
						5401	5
						8705	5
						8902	5
						TOTAL	273665

Annexure 7.5. Decoding of the Sub Caste of Shikshakarmi Recruitment Exam 2009

S. No	List No.	Caste Name	Caste No.	S. No.	List No.	Caste Name	Caste No.
1	1	Ahir	0101	36	5	Kumavat	0504
2	1	Brajwasi	0102	37	5	Kumawat	0505
3	1	Gayli	0103	38	5	Varai	0506
4	1	Goli	0104	39	5	Barai (Chorasiya)	0507
5	1	Jadav(Yadav)	0105	40	6	Badai	0601
6	1	Bargahi	0106	41	6	Sutar	0602
7	1	Gargarh	0107	42	6	Davej	0603
8	1	Thethwar	0108	43	6	Kunder Vishwkarma)	0604
9	1	Raut	0109	44	7	Bari	0701
10	1	Govari(Gvari)	0110	45	8	Vasudev	0801
11	1	Gobra	0111	46	8	Vasudeva	0802
12	1	Gavari	0112	47	8	Vaasudev	0803
13	1	Nyas	0113	48	8	Vaasudeva	0804
14	1	Gapalijee	0114	49	8	Harbola	0805
15	1	Mahakul (Raut)	0115	50	8	Kapdiya	0806
16	1	Mahkul	0116	51	8	Kapadi	0807

Contd...

S. No	List No.	Caste Name	Caste No.	S. No.	List No.	Caste Name	Caste No.
17	1	Gop	0117	52	8	Gondhali	0808
18	1	Gwalee	0118	53	8	Tharvar	0809
19	1	Lingayat	0119	54	9	Bhadrbhuja	0901
20	1	Gopal	0120	55	9	Bhunjaya	0902
21	2	Asara	0201	56	9	Ghurji	0903
22	2	Asada	0202	57	9	Dhuri or Dhoori	0904
23	3	Bairagi (Vaishnav)	0301	58	10	Bhaat	1001
24	4	Banjara	0401	59	10	Charan Suthiya	1002
25	4	Banjari	0402	60	10	Salvi	1003
26	4	Mathura	0403	61	10	Rao	1004
27	4	Nayak	0404	62	10	Janmalondi	1005
28	4	Nayakada	0405	63	10	Jasondhi	1006
29	4	Ghariya	0406	64	10	Marusoniya	1007
30	4	Labhana	0407	65	11	Chhipa	1101
31	4	Lavana	0408	66	11	Bhawsar	1102
32	4	Laamne	0409	67	11	Neelgar	1103
33	5	Barai	0501	68	11	Geenagar	1104
34	5	Tamoli	0502	69	11	Nirali	1105
35	5	Tamboli	0503	70	11	Rangari	1106
36	11	Mandhav	1107	120	23	Gayari	2310
37	12	Dheemar	1201	121	23	Gadriya (Pal Baghele)	2311
38	12	Bhoi	1202	122	24	Kadere	2401
39	12	Kahaar	1203	123	24	Dhunkar	2402

Contd...

S. No	List No.	Caste Name	Caste No.	S. No.	List No.	Caste Name	Caste No.
40	12	Kahara	1204	124	24	Dhuniya	2403
41	12	Dheevar/Mallah/Nawdha	1205	125	24	Dharka	2404
42	12	Turaha	1206	126	24	Kodar	2405
43	12	Kewat (Kashyap, Nishad, Rayakwar,Botham)	1207	127	25	Kostha	2501
44	12	Keer (Except Bhopal, Raisen, Sehor District))	1208	128	25	Koshti (Dewangan)	2502
45	12	Britiya (Vrittiya)	1209	129	25	Koshta	2503
46	12	Singraha	1210	130	25	Mala Padamshali	2504
47	12	Jalari , Jalaranlu (Except Baster District)	1211	131	25	Sali	2505
48	12	Sendhiya	1212	132	25	Sutarsali	2506
49	13	Pawar	1301	133	25	Salewar Salvi	2507
50	13	Powar	1302	134	25	Dewang	2508
51	13	Bhoyar	1303	135	25	Jandra	2509
52	13	Bhoyaar	1304	136	25	Koskaati	2510
53	14	Bhurtiya	1401	137	25	Koshkathi (Lingayat)	2511
54	14	Bhutiya	1402	138	25	Gadwal	2512
55	15	Bhopa	1501	139	25	Ganewar	2513
56	15	Maanbhaw	1502	140	25	Garwar	2514
57	16	Bhatiyara	1601	141	25	Dukar	2515
58	17	Chunkar	1701	142	25	Kolhati	2516
59	17	Chunkar Kulvadhiya	1702	143	26	Dholi/Dhafhali/Dhafhli/Dholi	2601

Contd...

S. No	List No.	Caste Name	Caste No.	S. No.	List No.	Caste Name	Caste No.
60	17	Rajgir	1703	144	26	Dagami	2602
61	18	Chitari	1801	145	26	Gurav	2603
62	19	Darjee	1901	146	27	Gusai	2701
63	19	Chipee	1902	147	27	Goswami	2702
64	19	Shipee	1903	148	28	Gujar (Gurger)	2801
65	19	Mavee (Namdev)	1904	149	29	Lohar	2901
66	20	Dhobee (Except Siroj and Lateri Tahsil of Vidisha District)	2001	150	29	Luhar	2902
67	20	Batti	2002	151	29	Lohpeeta	2903
68	20	Baretha	2003	152	29	Gadhole	2904
69	20	Rajak	2004	153	29	Gadole	2905
70	21	Meena (Ravat)	2101	154	29	Hunga Lohar	2906
71	21	Deshwali	2102	155	29	Lohpata	2907
72	21	Mewatee Meena(Except Siroj & Lateri Tahsil of Vidisha District)	2103	156	29	Gadola	2908
73	22	Kirar	2201	157	30	Garpagari	3001
74	22	Kirad	2202	158	30	Nath-Jogi	3002
75	22	Dhakad	2203	159	30	Joginath	3003
76	23	Gadriya	2301	160	31	Goshi	3101
77	23	Dhangar	2302	161	32	Sonar	3201
78	23	Kurmar	2303	162	32	Sunar	3202
79	23	Hatkar	2304	163	32	Jhani	3203
80	23	Baster Hatkar	2305	164	32	Jhadi (Swarnkar)	3204

Contd...

S. No	List No.	Caste Name	Caste No.	S. No.	List No.	Caste Name	Caste No.
81	23	Gaadri	2306	165	32	Awadhiya	3205
82	23	Dhhariya	2307	166	32	Aaudhiya	3206
83	23	Dhaushi (Gadriya)	2308	167	32	Soni (Swarnkar)	
84	23	Gari	2309	168	33	Kachhi (Kushwaha, Shakya, Maurya)	
85	33	Koyari or Koiri (Kushwaha)	3302	214	43	Kalautha	4302
86	33	Panara	3303	215	43	Kolta	4303
87	33	Murai	3304	216	43	Koltha	4304
88	33	Sonkar	3305	217	44	Loniya	4401
89	33	Kohari	3306	218	44	Luniya	4402
90	33	Mali (Saini)	3307	219	44	Oad	4403
91	33	Marar	3308	220	44	Ode	4404
92	34	Joshi (Bhaddhri)	3401	221	44	Odiya Naunia	4405
93	34	Dakocha	3402	222	44	Murha	4406
94	34	Dhakota	3403	223	44	Muraha	4407
95	35	Lakhera	3501	224	44	Mudhha	4408
96	35	Lakher	3502	225	44	Kudhaha	4409
97	35	Kachera	3503	226	45	Naai (Sen, Svita, Usrete, Srivas)	4501
98	35	Kacher	3504	227	45	Mhali	4502
99	36	Thatherra	3601	228	45	Navhi	4503
100	36	Kasar	3602	229	45	Usrete	4504
101	36	Kasera	3603	230	46	Nayata	4601
102	36	Tamera	3604	231	46	Nayada	4602

Contd...

S. No	List No.	Caste Name	Caste No.	S. No.	List No.	Caste Name	Caste No.
103	36	Tambatkar Otari	3605	232	47	Panka	4701
104	36	Tamer	3606	233	47	Panika (Except Districts: Chh-attarpur, Panna, Datia, Tikamgarh, Satna, Riwa, Sidhi, Shadol)	4702
105	36	Tamrkar	3607	234	48	Patka	4801
106	36	Ghadwa	3608	235	48	Patki	4802
107	36	Jhariya Kaser	3609	236	48	Patwa	4803
108	37	Khatiya	3701	237	49	Lodhi	4901
109	37	Khathiya	3702	238	49	Lodha	4902
110	37	Khati	3703	239	49	Lodh	4903
111	38	Kumhar (Prajapati)	3801	240	50	Sikligar	5001
112	38	Kubhar (Except Chhatarpur, Datiya, Panna, Tikamgarh, Satna, Rewa, Sidhi and Sahdol Districts)	3802	241	51	Teli (Thath, Sahu, Rathore)	5101
113	39	Kurmi	3901	242	52	Turha	5201
114	39	Kurmar	3902	243	52	Tirwali	5202
115	39	Kunbi	3903	244	52	Baddar	5203
116	39	Kurmi	3904	245	53	Kisdi	5301
117	39	Patidar (Kulmee, Kulmi, Kulambi)	3905	246	53	Kasadi	5302
118	39	Kurmwanshi	3906	247	54	Vovariya	5401
119	39	Sirvi Chandrakar	3907	248	55	Rotiya	5501
120	39	Chandranahoo	3908	249	55	Routiya	5502

Contd...

S. No	List No.	Caste Name	Caste No.	S. No.	List No.	Caste Name	Caste No.
121	39	Kumbhi	3909	250	56	Mankar	5601
122	39	Gavali (Gamail)	3910	251	56	Nahal	5602
123	40	Kamriya	4001	252	57	Kotwar	5701
124	41	Korav	4101	253	57	Kotwal (Except the Districts of Bhind, Dhar, Dewas, Guna, Gwalior, Indore, Jhabua. Khargone, Mandsaur, Morena, Ujjain, Rajgarh, Ratlam, Shajapur, Shivpuri and Vidisha)	5702
125	41	Kavare	4102	254	58	Khairuwa	5801
126	42	Kalar (Jaiswal)	4201	255	59	Lodha(Tanvar)	5901
127	42	Kalal	4202	256	60	Mowar	6001
128	42	Dhadhsena	4203	257	61	Rajwar	6101
129	43	Kalauta	4301	258	62	Aghariya	6201
130	63	Toori	6301	308	87	Tadvi	8719
131	63	Turi	6302	309	87	Banjara	8720
132	64	Bharuda	6401	310	87	Mochi	8721
133	65	Sut	6501	311	87	Teli, Nayata, Pindari (Pindara), Kankar	8722
134	65	Sarthi-Sais/Sahees	6502	312	87	Pemdi	8723
135	66	Shhelanga	6601	313	87	Kalaigar	8724
136	66	Tilga	6602	314	87	Nalband	8725
137	67	Raghvi	6701	315	87	Shishgar	8726
138	68	Rajbhar	6801	316	87	Goli	8727

Contd...

S. No	List No.	Caste Name	Caste No.	S. No.	List No.	Caste Name	Caste No.
139	69	Kharol	6901	317	87	Rajgeer	8728
140	70	Sargara	7001	318	87	Daphaali	8729
141	71	Golan	7101	319	87	Ghoshi & Gavali, Goli	8730
142	71	Gavalan	7102	320	87	Sikligar	8731
143	71	Gaulan	7103	321	87	Santral, Kharadi, Kamligar	8732
144	72	Rajad	7201	322	87	Nat	8733
145	72	Rajjhjad	7202	323	87	Shekh Mehatar	8734
146	73	Jaadam	7301	324	87	Niyargar	8735
147	74	Gangi	7401	325	87	Gaddi	8736
148	75	Gayaar / Pradhaniya	7501	326	87	Mukeri, Makrani	8737
149	76	Kudmi	7601	327	87	Bhand Nakkal	8738
150	77	Mer	7701	328	88	Vaiswar	8801
151	78	Vaya Mahara / Kaushal	7801	329	89	Wani	8901
152	78	Vaya	7802	330	90	Vishnoi, Jaat	9001
153	79	Pinjra (Hindu)	7901	331	91	Rathor Jati	9101
154	80	ABONDEND					
155	81	Scheduled Castes who have embarded Christianity	8101				
156	82	Aanjna	8201				
157	83	Thoriya	8301				
158	84	Gehlota Mewada	8401				
159	85	Rewari	8501				

Contd...

S. No	List No.	Caste Name	Caste No.	S. No.	List No.	Caste Name	Caste No.
160	86	Ruaala / Ruhela	8601				
161	87	Rangrej	8701				
162	87	Bhishti	8702				
163	87	Chheepa	8703				
164	87	Hela	8704				
165	87	Bhatiyara	8705				
166	87	Dhobi	8706				
167	87	Mewati	8707				
168	87	Pinjara, Naddak, Behna, Dhuniya, Dhunkar, Fhakir, Shah, Sai, Kabrkhodu	8708				
169	87	Kujda, Raeen	8709				
170	87	Mnihar	8710				
171	87	Kasai, Kssaw	8711				
172	87	Mirasi	8712				
173	87	Mirdha	8713				
174	87	Badai (Carpenter)	8714				
175	87	Hajjam (Barber)	8715				
176	87	Hammal	8716				
177	87	Momin (Julaha)	8717				
178	87	Luhar, Nagauri	8718				

Annexure 7.6. Chhattisgarh Shikshakarmi Recruitment Exam 2010
Summary of Top 25 Candidates List for Varg - 3

Zone : (1) BASTAR, District : (14) DANTEWADA, D.ED					
	SC	ST	OBC	GEN	TOTAL
No. of Candidates	7	24	52	32	115
Percentage	6.09	20.87	45.22	27.83	
Zone : (1) BASTAR, District : (14) DANTEWADA, NON D.ED					
	SC	ST	OBC	GEN	TOTAL
No. of Candidates	35	34	204	77	350
Percentage	10.00	9.71	58.29	22.00	
Zone : (1) BASTAR, District : (17) JAGDALPUR, D.ED					
	SC	ST	OBC	GEN	TOTAL
No. of Candidates	22	120	181	116	439
Percentage	5.01	27.33	41.23	26.42	
Zone : (1) BASTAR, District : (17) JAGDALPUR, NON D.ED					
	SC	ST	OBC	GEN	TOTAL
No. of Candidates	58	129	373	140	700
Percentage	8.29	18.43	53.29	20.00	
Zone : (1) BASTAR, District : (20) KANKER, D.ED					
	SC	ST	OBC	GEN	TOTAL
No. of Candidates	19	103	95	63	280
Percentage	6.79	36.79	33.93	22.50	
Zone : (1) BASTAR, District : (20) KANKER, NON D.ED					
	SC	ST	OBC	GEN	TOTAL
No. of Candidates	14	110	157	69	350
Percentage	4.00	31.43	44.86	19.71	

Contd...

Zone : (2) SARGUJA, District : (11) AMBIKAPUR (SARGUJA), D.ED					
	SC	ST	OBC	GEN	TOTAL
No. of Candidates	18	151	189	212	570
Percentage	3.16	26.49	33.16	37.19	
Zone : (2) SARGUJA, District : (11) AMBIKAPUR (SARGUJA), NON D.ED					
	SC	ST	OBC	GEN	TOTAL
No. of Candidates	39	133	385	393	950
Percentage	4.11	14.00	40.53	41.37	
Zone : (2) SARGUJA, District : (12) BAIKUNTHPUR (KOREA), D.ED					
	SC	ST	OBC	GEN	TOTAL
No. of Candidates	5	11	30	44	90
Percentage	5.56	12.22	33.33	48.89	
Zone : (2) SARGUJA, District : (12) BAIKUNTHPUR (KOREA), NON D.ED					
	SC	ST	OBC	GEN	TOTAL
Name of Candidate	10	22	88	130	250
Percentage	4.00	8.80	35.20	52.00	
Zone : (2) SARGUJA, District : (19) JASHPURNAGAR, D.ED					
	SC	ST	OBC	GEN	TOTAL
No. of Candidates	18	102	50	45	215
Percentage	8.37	47.44	23.26	20.93	

Zone : (2) SARGUJA, District : (19) JASHPURNAGAR, NON D.ED					
	SC	ST	OBC	GEN	TOTAL
No. of Candidates	54	100	134	112	400
Percentage	13.50	25.00	33.50	28.00	
Zone : (2),SARGUJA, District : (22) KORBA, D.ED					
	SC	ST	OBC	GEN	TOTAL
No. of Candidates	37	11	143	59	250
Percentage	14.80	4.40	57.20	23.60	

Contd...

Zone : (2) SARGUJA, District : (22) KORBA, NON D.ED					
	SC	ST	OBC	GEN	TOTAL
No. of Candidates	26	15	124	85	250
Percentage	10.40	6.00	49.60	34.00	

Zone : (3) BILASPUR, District : (13) BILASPUR, D.ED					
	SC	ST	OBC	GEN	TOTAL
No. of Candidates	41	42	148	132	363
Percentage	11.29	11.57	40.77	36.36	

Zone : (3) BILASPUR, District : (13) BILASPUR, NON D.ED					
	SC	ST	OBC	GEN	TOTAL
No. of Candidates	53	19	195	233	500
Percentage	10.60	3.80	39.00	46.60	

Zone : (3) BILASPUR, District : (18) JANJGIR-CHAMPA, D.ED					
	SC	ST	OBC	GEN	TOTAL
No. of Candidates	3	4	14	3	24
Percentage	12.50	16.67	58.33	12.50	

Zone : (3) BILASPUR, District : (18) JANJGIR-CHAMPA, NON D.ED					
	SC	ST	OBC	GEN	TOTAL
No. of Candidates	82	33	210	125	450
Percentage	18.22	7.33	46.67	27.78	

Zone : (3) BILASPUR, District : (24) RAIGARH, D.ED					
	SC	ST	OBC	GEN	TOTAL
No. of Candidates	22	44	193	43	302
Percentage	7.28	14.57	63.91	14.24	

Contd...

Zone : (3) BILASPUR, District : (24) RAIGARH , NON D.ED					
	SC	ST	OBC	GEN	TOTAL
No. of Candidates	48	29	268	105	450
Percentage	10.67	6.44	59.56	23.33	
Zone : (4) RAIPUR, District : (15) DHAMTARI, D.ED					
	SC	ST	OBC	GEN	TOTAL
No. of Candidates	11	5	43	7	66
Percentage	16.67	7.58	65.15	10.61	
Zone : (4) RAIPUR, District : (15) DHAMTARI, NON D.ED					
	SC	ST	OBC	GEN	TOTAL
No. of Candidates	12	9	146	33	200
Percentage	6.00	4.50	73.00	16.50	
Zone : (4) RAIPUR, District : (16) DURG, D.ED					
	SC	ST	OBC	GEN	TOTAL
No. of Candidates	33	52	165	80	330
Percentage	10.00	15.76	50.00	24.24	
Zone : (4) RAIPUR, District : (16) DURG, NON D.ED					
	SC	ST	OBC	GEN	TOTAL
No. of Candidates	46	37	336	187	606
Percentage	7.59	6.11	55.45	30.86	
Zone : (4) RAIPUR, District : (21) KABIRDHAM(KAWARDHA), D.ED					
	SC	ST	OBC	GEN	TOTAL
No. of Candidates	10	6	63	44	123
Percentage	8.13	4.88	51.22	35.77	
Zone : (4) RAIPUR, District : (21) KABIRDHAM(KAWARDHA), NON D.ED					
	SC	ST	OBC	GEN	TOTAL
No. of Candidates	10	4	107	79	200
Percentage	5.00	2.00	53.50	39.50	

Zone : (4) RAIPUR, District : (23) MAHASAMUND, D.ED					
	SC	ST	OBC	GEN	TOTAL
No. of Candidates	19	14	129	16	178
Percentage	10.67	7.87	72.47	8.99	
Zone : (4) RAIPUR, District : (23) MAHASAMUND, NON D.ED					
	SC	ST	OBC	GEN	TOTAL
No. of Candidates	12	7	172	59	250
Percentage	4.80	2.80	68.80	23.60	
Zone : (4) RAIPUR District : (25) RAIPUR, D.ED					
	SC	ST	OBC	GEN	TOTAL
No. of Candidates	47	32	345	74	498
Percentage	9.44	6.43	69.28	14.86	
Zone : (4) RAIPUR District : (25) RAIPUR NON D.ED					
	SC	ST	OBC	GEN	TOTAL
No. of Candidates	72	33	490	155	750
Percentage	9.60	4.40	65.33	20.67	
Zone : (4) RAIPUR, District : (26) RAJNANDGAON, D.ED					
	SC	ST	OBC	GEN	TOTAL
No. of Candidates	38	48	227	76	389
Percentage	9.77	12.34	58.35	19.54	
Zone : (4) RAIPUR, District : (26) RAJNANDGAON, NON D.ED					
	SC	ST	OBC	GEN	TOTAL
No. of Candidates	39	26	263	122	450
Percentage	8.67	5.78	58.44	27.11	

(Source for the annexures Data 7.4 to 7.8 is the records of State Professional examination Board, Chhatisgarh, Raipur).

Annexures 7.7 : Over all Position of OBC, SC, ST Candidates going into General

Verge -1

Subject	Zone	Jila/Panchayat	B.Ed									Non B.Ed								
			Total	General	%	OBC	%	SC	%	ST	%	Total	General	%	OBC	%	SC	%	ST	%
Commerce	Sarguja	Ambikapur (Sarguja)	25	12	48	5	20	0	0	8	32	25	11	44	10	40	1	4	3	12
Commerce	Sarguja	Baikuntpur	12	10	83	2	17	0	0	0	0	25	22	88	2	8	0	0	1	4
Commerce	Bilaspur	Bilaspur	25	15	60	7	28	2	8	1	4	25	15	60	9	36	0	0	1	4
Commerce	Baster	Dantewada	8	3	38	4	50	0	0	1	13	25	12	48	8	32	1	4	4	16
Commerce	Raipur	Dhamtari	25	7	28	16	64	2	8	0	0	25	8	32	14	56	3	12	0	0
Commerce	Raipur	Durg	25	18	72	7	28	0	0	0	0	25	16	64	7	28	2	8	0	0
Commerce	Baster	Jagadalpur	21	14	67	4	19	0	0	3	14	25	7	28	13	52	2	8	3	12
Commerce	Bilaspur	Janjgir-Champa	25	9	36	13	52	2	8	1	4	25	7	28	16	64	2	8	0	0
Commerce	Sarguja	Jashpurnagar	0	0	0	0	0	0	0	0	0	16	8	50	2	13	6	38	0	0
Commerce	Baster	Kanker	10	5	50	3	30	0	0	2	20	25	5	20	11	44	4	16	5	20
Commerce	Raipur	Kabirdham (Kawardha)	10	4	40	4	40	2	20	0	0	25	13	52	11	44	0	0	1	4
Commerce	Sarguja	Korba	25	13	52	11	44	0	0	1	4	25	8	32	14	56	2	8	1	4
Commerce	Raipur	Mahasamund	18	8	44	9	50	1	6	0	0	25	9	36	16	64	0	0	0	0
Commerce	Bilaspur	Raigarh	23	8	35	13	57	0	0	2	9	25	10	40	11	44	3	12	1	4
Commerce	Raipur	Raipur	25	15	60	8	32	1	4	1	4	25	8	32	16	64	1	4	0	0
Commerce	Raipur	Rajnandgaon	25	16	64	6	24	1	4	2	8	25	12	48	12	48	0	0	1	4
Commerce		**Total**	**302**	**157**	**52**	**112**	**37**	**11**	**4**	**22**	**7**	**391**	**171**	**44**	**172**	**44**	**27**	**7**	**21**	**5**

Subject	Zone	Jila/Panchayat	B.Ed									Non B.Ed								
			Total	General	%	OBC	%	SC	%	ST	%	Total	General	%	OBC	%	SC	%	ST	%
Agriculture	Sarguja	Ambikapur (Sarguja)	3	2	67	1	33	0	0	0	0	19	6	32	5	26	1	5	7	37
Agriculture	Sarguja	Baikuntpur	0	0	0	0	0	0	0	0	0	3	2	67	1	33	0	0	0	0
Agriculture	Bilaspur	Bilaspur	1	1	100	0	0	0	0	0	0	10	8	80	0	0	0	0	2	20
Agriculture	Baster	Dantewada	0	0	0	0	0	0	0	0	0	11	4	36	2	18	0	0	5	45
Agriculture	Raipur	Dhamtari	0	0	0	0	0	0	0	0	0	9	4	44	2	22	1	11	2	22
Agriculture	Raipur	Durg	0	0	0	0	0	0	0	0	0	6	2	33	4	67	0	0	0	0
Agriculture	Baster	Jagadalpur	0	0	0	0	0	0	0	0	0	10	2	20	5	50	0	0	3	30
Agriculture	Bilaspur	Janjgir-Champa	0	0	0	0	0	0	0	0	0	3	1	33	0	0	2	67	0	0
Agriculture	Sarguja	Jashpurnagar	0	0	0	0	0	0	0	0	0	7	2	29	3	43	1	14	1	14
Agriculture	Baster	Kanker	0	0	0	0	0	0	0	0	0	5	0	0	3	60	0	0	2	40
Agriculture	Raipur	Kabirdham (Kawardha)	0	0	0	0	0	0	0	0	0	1	0	0	1	100	0	0	0	0
Agriculture	Sarguja	Korba	0	0	0	0	0	0	0	0	0	5	1	20	1	20	2	40	1	20
Agriculture	Raipur	Mahasamund	0	0	0	0	0	0	0	0	0	1	1	100	0	0	0	0	0	0
Agriculture	Bilaspur	Raigarh	0	0	0	0	0	0	0	0	0	0	0	0		0	0	0	0	0
Agriculture	Raipur	Raipur	0	0	0	0	0	0	0	0	0	4	2	50	2	50	0	0	0	0
Agriculture	Raipur	Rajnandgaon	0	0	0	0	0	0	0	0	0	10	2	20	6	60	2	20	0	0
		Total	**4**	**3**	**75**	**1**	**25**	**0**	**0**	**0**	**0**	**104**	**37**	**36**	**35**	**34**	**9**	**8.7**	**23**	**22**

Subject	Zone	Jila/Panchayat	B.Ed									Non B.Ed								
			Total	General	%	OBC	%	SC	%	ST	%	Total	General	%	OBC	%	SC	%	ST	%
Biology	Sarguja	Ambikapur (Sarguja)	25	15	60	8	32	0	0	2	8	25	11	44	8	32	0	0	6	24
Biology	Sarguja	Baikuntpur	18	15	83	1	6	1	6	1	6	25	17	68	5	20	1	4	2	8
Biology	Bilaspur	Bilaspur	25	12	48	11	44	2	8	0	0	25	15	60	6	24	1	4	3	12
Biology	Baster	Dantewada	8	7	88	0	0	1	13	0	0	25	8	32	5	20	7	28	5	20
Biology	Raipur	Dhamtari	20	7	35	9	45	3	15	1	5	25	5	20	17	68	3	12	0	0
Biology	Raipur	Durg	25	10	40	14	56	0	0	1	4	25	11	44	8	32	3	12	3	12
Biology	Baster	Jagadalpur	25	18	72	6	24	1	4	0	0	25	9	36	11	44	3	12	2	8
Biology	Bilaspur	Janjgir-Champa	25	6	24	12	48	6	24	1	4	25	8	32	9	36	6	24	2	8
Biology	Sarguja	Jashpurnagar	11	4	36	4	36	2	18	1	9	25	6	24	7	28	7	28	5	20
Biology	Baster	Kanker	9	1	11	6	67	0	0	2	22	25	1	4	10	40	1	4	13	52
Biology	Raipur	Kabirdham (Kawardha)	5	2	40	2	40	1	20	0	0	25	9	36	12	48	2	8	2	8
Biology	Sarguja	Korba	25	11	44	10	40	3	12	1	4	25	10	40	5	20	7	28	3	12
Biology	Raipur	Mahasamund	13	2	15	9	69	2	15	0	0	25	7	28	15	60	2	8	1	4
Biology	Bilaspur	Raigarh	25	6	24	19	76	0	0	0	0	25	5	20	15	60	2	8	3	12
Biology	Raipur	Raipur	25	13	52	10	40	1	4	1	4	25	7	28	7	28	7	28	4	16
Biology	Raipur	Rajnandgaon	17	8	47	6	35	2	12	1	6	25	10	40	10	40	4	16	1	4
		Total	**301**	**137**	**46**	**127**	**42**	**25**	**8**	**12**	**4**	**400**	**139**	**35**	**150**	**37.5**	**56**	**14**	**55**	**14**

Subject	Zone	Jila/Panchayat	B.Ed									Non B.Ed								
			Total	General	%	OBC	%	SC	%	ST	%	Total	General	%	OBC	%	SC	%	ST	%
Chemistry	Sarguja	Ambikapur (Sarguja)	18	14	78	3	17	0	0	1	6	25	10	40	7	28	5	20	3	12
Chemistry	Sarguja	Baikuntpur	10	8	80	2	20	0	0	0	0	23	18	78	3	13	1	4.3	1	4.3
Chemistry	Bilaspur	Bilaspur	25	21	84	2	8	2	8	0	0	25	12	48	10	40	2	8	1	4
Chemistry	Baster	Dantewada	3	3	100	0	0	0	0	0	0	4	3	75	1	25	0	0	0	0
Chemistry	Raipur	Dhamtari	9	4	44	5	56	0	0	0	0	25	4	16	17	68	2	8	2	8
Chemistry	Raipur	Durg	25	13	52	12	48	0	0	0	0	25	12	48	8	32	4	16	1	4
Chemistry	Baster	Jagadalpur	16	8	50	8	50	0	0	0	0	25	13	52	8	32	1	4	3	12
Chemistry	Bilaspur	Janjgir-Champa	25	6	24	17	68	2	8	0	0	25	10	40	10	40	5	20	0	0
Chemistry	Sarguja	Jashpurnagar	1	1	100	0	0	0	0	0	0	22	6	27	8	36.4	6	27	2	9.1
Chemistry	Baster	Kanker	1	1	100	0	0	0	0	0	0	18	6	33	7	38.9	5	28	0	0
Chemistry	Raipur	Kabirdham (Kawardha)	1	1	100	0	0	0	0	0	0	8	4	50	1	12.5	3	38	0	0
Chemistry	Sarguja	Korba	25	16	64	6	24	2	8	1	4	25	11	44	7	28	5	20	1	4
Chemistry	Raipur	Mahasamund	5	3	60	2	40	0	0	0	0	25	5	20	18	72	2	8	0	0
Chemistry	Bilaspur	Raigarh	13	8	62	1	8	4	31	0	0	25	11	44	18	72	2	8	4	16
Chemistry	Raipur	Raipur	25	20	80	4	16	0	0	1	4	25	12	48	11	44	1	4	1	4
Chemistry	Raipur	Rajnandgaon	6	5	83	1	17	0	0	0	0	25	13	52	8	32	2	8	2	8
		Total	**208**	**132**	**63**	**63**	**30**	**10**	**5**	**3**	**1**	**350**	**150**	**43**	**142**	**41**	**46**	**13**	**21**	**6**

Subject	Zone	Jila/Panchayat	B.Ed									Non B.Ed								
			Total	General	%	OBC	%	SC	%	ST	%	Total	General	%	OBC	%	SC	%	ST	%
Physics	Sarguja	Ambikapur (Sarguja)	10	6	60	3	30	1	10	0	0	25	14	56	11	44	0	0	0	0
Physics	Sarguja	Baikuntpur	7	6	86	1	14	0	0	0	0	6	4	67	0	0	0	0	2	33
Physics	Bilaspur	Bilaspur	25	20	80	5	20	0	0	0	0	25	13	52	10	40	2	8	0	0
Physics	Baster	Dantewada	0	0	0	0	0	0	0	0	0	3	2	67	0	0	0	0	1	33
Physics	Raipur	Dhamtari	4	0	0	4	100	0	0	0	0	16	10	63	3	19	36	225	0	0
Physics	Raipur	Durg	25	13	52	12	48	0	0	0	0	25	8	32	12	48	5	20	0	0
Physics	Baster	Jagadalpur	3	3	100	0	0	0	0	0	0	11	5	45	2	18	1	9.1	3	27
Physics	Bilaspur	Janjgir-Champa	19	10	53	0	0	0	0	0	0	25	7	28	15	60	2	8	1	4
Physics	Sarguja	Jashpurnagar	0	0	0	0	0	0	0	0	0	7	1	14	3	43	2	29	1	14
Physics	Baster	Kanker	2	0	0	2	100	0	0	0	0	7	2	29	5	71	0	0	0	0
Physics	Raipur	Kabirdham (Kawardha)	1	0	0	1	100	0	0	0	0	3	2	67	0	0	1	33	0	0
Physics	Sarguja	Korba	12	6	50	4	33	2	17	0	0	25	14	56	7	28	3	12	1	4
Physics	Raipur	Mahasamund	6	4	67	2	33	0	0	0	0	18	7	39	10	56	1	5.6	0	0
Physics	Bilaspur	Raigarh	7	4	57	3	43	0	0	0	0	25	8	32	10	40	5	20	2	8
Physics	Raipur	Raipur	19	9	47	10	53	0	0	0	0	25	10	40	14	56	1	4	0	0
Physics	Raipur	Rajnandgaon	3	1	33	1	33	1	33	0	0	17	9	53	4	24	3	18	1	6
		Total	**143**	**82**	**57**	**48**	**34**	**4**	**3**	**0**	**0**	**263**	**116**	**44**	**106**	**40**	**62**	**24**	**12**	**5**

Subject	Zone	Jila/Panchayat	B.Ed									Non B.Ed								
			Total	General	%	OBC	%	SC	%	ST	%	Total	General	%	OBC	%	SC	%	ST	%
Mathematics	Sarguja	Ambikapur (Sarguja)	21	11	52	10	48	0	0	0	0	25	8	32	13	52	2	8	2	8
Mathematics	Sarguja	Baikuntpur	8	5	63	2	25	0	0	1	13	16	12	75	3	18.8	1	6.3	0	0
Mathematics	Bilaspur	Bilaspur	25	14	56	11	44	0	0	0	0	25	14	56	11	44	0	0	0	0
Mathematics	Baster	Dantewada	5	5	100	0	0	0	0	0	0	18	6	33	11	61.1	1	5.6	0	0
Mathematics	Raipur	Dhamtari	23	6	26	16	70	1	4	0	0	25	3	12	20	80	2	8	0	0
Mathematics	Raipur	Durg	25	8	32	17	68	0	0	0	0	25	7	28	16	64	2	8	0	0
Mathematics	Baster	Jagadalpur	19	12	63	5	26	0	0	2	11	25	13	52	9	36	0	0	3	12
Mathematics	Bilaspur	Janjgir-Champa	25	8	32	17	68	0	0	0	0	25	5	20	19	76	0	0	1	4
Mathematics	Sarguja	Jashpurnagar	3	2	67	1	33	0	0	0	0	25	7	28	12	48	3	12	3	12
Mathematics	Baster	Kanker	8	2	25	2	25	2	25	2	25	25	9	36	9	36	1	4	6	24
Mathematics	Raipur	Kabirdham (Kawardha)	6	4	67	2	33	0	0	0	0	25	11	44	11	44	2	8	1	4
Mathematics	Sarguja	Korba	25	19	76	5	20	0	0	1	4	25	9	36	13	52	0	0	3	12
Mathematics	Raipur	Mahasamund	20	4	20	15	75	0	0	1	5	25	4	16	20	80	0	0	1	4
Mathematics	Bilaspur	Raigarh	25	8	32	16	64	1	4	0	0	25	4	16	16	64	3	12	2	8
Mathematics	Raipur	Raipur	25	11	44	13	52	1	4	0	0	25	8	32	14	56	3	12	0	0
Mathematics	Raipur	Rajnandgaon	25	12	48	11	44	2	8	0	0	25	11	44	11	44	2	8	1	4
		Total	**288**	**131**	**45**	**143**	**50**	**7**	**2**	**7**	**2**	**384**	**131**	**34**	**208**	**54**	**22**	**6**	**23**	**6**

Subject	Zone	Jila/Panchayat	B.Ed									Non B.Ed								
			Total	General	%	OBC	%	SC	%	ST	%	Total	General	%	OBC	%	SC	%	ST	%
Pol. Sc.	Sarguja	Ambikapur (Sarguja)	25	8	32	17	68	0	0	0	0	25	9	36	12	48	0	0	4	16
Pol. Sc.	Sarguja	Baikuntpur	25	15	60	7	28	2	8	1	4	25	13	52	8	32	3	12	1	4
Pol. Sc.	Bilaspur	Bilaspur	25	5	20	17	68	1	4	2	8	25	11	44	9	36	3	12	2	8
Pol. Sc.	Baster	Dantewada	25	2	8	14	56	3	12	6	24	25	8	32	13	52	1	4	3	12
Pol. Sc.	Raipur	Dhamtari	13	2	15	10	77	0	0	1	8	25	4	16	20	80	1	4	0	0
Pol. Sc.	Raipur	Durg	25	8	32	14	56	2	8	1	4	25	3	12	20	80	2	8	0	0
Pol. Sc.	Baster	Jagadalpur	25	6	24	10	40	4	16	5	20	25	6	24	15	60	1	4	3	12
Pol. Sc.	Bilaspur	Janjgir-Champa	25	7	28	10	40	6	24	2	8	25	4	16	15	60	5	20	1	4
Pol. Sc.	Sarguja	Jashpurnagar	24	2	8	0	0	1	4	21	88	25	6	24	5	20	1	4	13	52
Pol. Sc.	Baster	Kanker	25	4	16	5	20	0	0	16	64	25	2	8	10	40	2	8	11	44
Pol. Sc.	Raipur	Kabirdham (Kawardha)	25	10	40	10	40	3	12	2	8	25	7	28	15	60	2	8	1	4
Pol. Sc.	Sarguja	Korba	25	13	52	7	28	4	16	1	4	25	7	28	11	44	5	20	2	8
Pol. Sc.	Raipur	Mahasamund	9	2	22	5	56	2	22	0	0	25	7	28	14	56	2	8	2	8
Pol. Sc.	Bilaspur	Raigarh	25	2	8	19	76	2	8	2	8	25	7	28	13	52	1	4	4	16
Pol. Sc.	Raipur	Raipur	25	3	12	16	64	5	20	1	4	25	4	16	16	64	4	16	1	4
Pol. Sc.	Raipur	Rajnandgaon	25	9	36	9	36	4	16	3	12	25	8	32	14	56	2	8	1	4
		Total	**371**	**98**	**26**	**170**	**46**	**39**	**11**	**64**	**17**	**400**	**106**	**27**	**210**	**53**	**35**	**9**	**49**	**12**

Subject	Zone	Jila/Panchayat	B.Ed									Non B.Ed								
			Total	General	%	OBC	%	SC	%	ST	%	Total	General	%	OBC	%	SC	%	ST	%
History	Sarguja	Ambikapur (Sarguja)	25	11	44	11	44	2	8	1	4	25	13	52	9	36	0	0	3	12
History	Sarguja	Baikuntpur	8	6	75	1	13	0	0	1	13	25	8	32	12	48	0	0	5	20
History	Bilaspur	Bilaspur	25	7	28	10	40	5	20	3	12	25	10	40	8	32	3	12	4	16
History	Baster	Dantewada	20	7	35	6	30	3	15	4	20	25	12	48	9	36	1	4	3	12
History	Raipur	Dhamtari	7	0	0	6	86	0	0	1	14	25	6	24	12	48	4	16	3	12
History	Raipur	Durg	25	10	40	11	44	1	4	3	12	25	7	28	13	52	1	4	4	16
History	Baster	Jagadalpur	25	9	36	12	48	1	4	3	12	25	5	20	10	40	3	12	7	28
History	Bilaspur	Janjgir-Champa	19	6	32	11	58	2	11	0	0	25	5	20	15	60	4	16	1	4
History	Sarguja	Jashpurnagar	5	1	20	0	0	0	0	4	80	25	7	28	6	24	3	12	8	32
History	Baster	Kanker	16	5	31	2	13	2	13	7	44	25	1	4	10	40	1	4	13	52
History	Raipur	Kabirdham (Kawardha)	14	6	43	6	43	2	14	0	0	25	10	40	15	60	0	0	0	0
History	Sarguja	Korba	25	11	44	9	36	4	16	1	4	25	8	32	12	48	4	16	1	4
History	Raipur	Mahasamund	2	0	0	2	100	0	0	0	0	25	3	12	17	68	3	12	2	8
History	Bilaspur	Raigarh	8	5	63	3	38	0	0	0	0	25	6	24	17	68	0	0	2	8
History	Raipur	Raipur	25	11	44	14	56	0	0	0	0	25	9	36	10	40	2	8	4	16
History	Raipur	Rajnandgaon	17	12	71	5	29	0	0	0	0	25	14	56	9	36	2	8	0	0
		Total	**266**	**107**	**40**	**109**	**41**	**22**	**8**	**28**	**11**	**400**	**124**	**31**	**184**	**46**	**31**	**8**	**60**	**15**

Subject	Zone	Jila/Panchayat	B.Ed									Non B.Ed								
			Total	General	%	OBC	%	SC	%	ST	%	Total	General	%	OBC	%	SC	%	ST	%
Economics	Sarguja	Ambikapur (Sarguja)	25	8	32	15	60	2	8	0	0	25	9	36	15	60	0	0	1	4
Economics	Sarguja	Baikuntpur	23	20	87	1	4	1	4	1	4	25	13	52	8	32	0	0	4	16
Economics	Bilaspur	Bilaspur	25	17	68	7	28	0	0	1	4	25	10	40	10	40	4	16	1	4
Economics	Baster	Dantewada	25	5	20	13	52	1	4	6	24	25	9	36	11	44	2	8	3	12
Economics	Raipur	Dhamtari	12	1	8	7	58	2	17	2	17	25	7	28	14	56	2	8	2	8
Economics	Raipur	Durg	25	11	44	10	40	3	12	1	4	25	7	28	16	64	1	4	1	4
Economics	Baster	Jagadalpur	25	3	12	14	56	2	8	6	24	25	4	16	14	56	1	4	6	24
Economics	Bilaspur	Janjgir-Champa	17	7	41	8	47	2	12	0	0	25	6	24	17	68	2	8	0	0
Economics	Sarguja	Jashpurnagar	9	3	33	0	0	1	11	5	56	25	9	36	6	24	2	8	8	32
Economics	Baster	Kanker	21	1	5	5	24	5	24	10	48	25	3	12	13	52	1	4	8	32
Economics	Raipur	Kabirdham (Kawardha)	25	12	48	11	44	1	4	1	4	25	10	40	11	44	2	8	2	8
Economics	Sarguja	Korba	25	13	52	6	24	3	12	3	12	25	13	52	8	32	3	12	1	4
Economics	Raipur	Mahasamund	12	1	8	8	67	1	8	2	17	25	1	4	21	84	3	12	0	0
Economics	Bilaspur	Raigarh	25	5	20	10	40	4	16	6	24	25	8	32	13	52	1	4	3	12
Economics	Raipur	Raipur	25	9	36	15	60	1	4	0	0	25	8	32	11	44	3	12	3	12
Economics	Raipur	Rajnandgaon	25	7	28	15	60	1	4	2	8	25	9	36	11	44	3	12	2	8
		Total	**344**	**123**	**36**	**145**	**42**	**30**	**9**	**46**	**13**	**400**	**126**	**32**	**199**	**50**	**30**	**8**	**45**	**11**

Subject	Zone	Jila/Panchayat	B.Ed									Non B.Ed								
			Total	General	%	OBC	%	SC	%	ST	%	Total	General	%	OBC	%	SC	%	ST	%
Geography	Sarguja	Ambikapur (Sarguja)	25	5	20	12	48	7	28	1	4	25	8	32	11	44	2	8	4	16
Geography	Sarguja	Baikuntpur	2	0	0	1	50	0	0	1	50	25	9	36	8	32	0	0	8	32
Geography	Bilaspur	Bilaspur	25	9	36	11	44	2	8	3	12	25	6	24	11	44	3	12	5	20
Geography	Baster	Dantewada	10	0	0	2	20	2	20	6	60	25	4	16	9	36	3	12	9	36
Geography	Raipur	Dhamtari	3	0	0	3	100	0	0	0	0	25	1	4	16	64	2	8	6	24
Geography	Raipur	Durg	25	11	44	6	24	5	20	3	12	25	4	16	13	52	6	24	2	8
Geography	Baster	Jagadalpur	25	11	44	2	8	5	20	7	28	25	2	8	12	48	0	0	11	44
Geography	Bilaspur	Janjgir-Champa	3	1	33	0	0	2	67	0	0	25	4	16	13	52	7	28	1	4
Geography	Sarguja	Jashpurnagar	6	1	17	0	0	1	17	5	83	25	10	40	4	16	4	16	7	28
Geography	Baster	Kanker	22	1	5	9	41	0	0	12	55	25	1	4	16	64	0	0	8	32
Geography	Raipur	Kabirdham (Kawardha)	25	6	24	13	52	5	20	1	4	25	5	20	9	36	5	20	6	24
Geography	Sarguja	Korba	25	6	24	6	24	12	48	1	4	25	5	20	15	60	3	12	2	8
Geography	Raipur	Mahasamund	5	0	0	4	80	0	0	1	20	25	1	4	11	44	6	24	7	28
Geography	Bilaspur	Raigarh	25	3	12	16	64	2	8	4	16	25	2	8	17	68	3	12	3	12
Geography	Raipur	Raipur	25	4	16	18	72	2	8	1	4	25	5	20	18	72	2	8	0	0
Geography	Raipur	Rajnandgaon	11	2	18	8	73	0	0	1	9	25	8	32	10	40	6	24	1	4
		Total	**262**	**60**	**23**	**111**	**42**	**45**	**17**	**47**	**18**	**400**	**75**	**19**	**193**	**48**	**52**	**13**	**80**	**20**

Subject	Zone	Jila/Panchayat	B.Ed									Non B.Ed								
			Total	General	%	OBC	%	SC	%	ST	%	Total	General	%	OBC	%	SC	%	ST	%
English	Sarguja	Ambikapur (Sarguja)	25	13	52	7	28	3	12	2	8	25	15	60	6	24	2	8	2	8
English	Sarguja	Baikuntpur	14	11	79	1	7	1	7	1	7	25	20	80	3	12	0	0	2	8
English	Bilaspur	Bilaspur	25	17	68	5	20	3	12	0	0	25	14	56	9	36	1	4	1	4
English	Baster	Dantewada	7	6	86	0	0	1	14	0	0	25	13	52	6	24	3	12	3	12
English	Raipur	Dhamtari	22	10	45	11	50	1	5	0	0	25	10	40	12	48	2	8	1	4
English	Raipur	Durg	25	12	48	13	52	0	0	0	0	25	13	52	11	44	0	0	1	4
English	Baster	Jagadalpur	25	19	76	6	24	0	0	0	0	25	9	36	10	40	2	8	4	16
English	Bilaspur	Janjgir-Champa	25	15	60	9	36	1	4	0	0	25	4	16	15	60	6	24	0	0
English	Sarguja	Jashpurnagar	15	4	27	2	13	1	7	8	53	25	6	24	14	56	2	8	3	12
English	Baster	Kanker	5	4	80	1	20	0	0	0	0	25	7	28	9	36	2	8	7	28
English	Raipur	Kabirdham (Kawardha)	8	3	38	4	50	0	0	1	13	25	15	60	5	20	5	20	0	0
English	Sarguja	Korba	25	16	64	9	36	0	0	0	0	25	14	56	8	32	3	12	0	0
English	Raipur	Mahasamund	25	8	32	12	48	4	16	1	4	25	6	24	17	68	1	4	1	4
English	Bilaspur	Raigarh	25	9	36	14	56	1	4	1	4	25	4	16	16	64	2	8	3	12
English	Raipur	Raipur	25	11	44	11	44	3	12	0	0	25	9	36	11	44	4	16	1	4
English	Raipur	Rajnandgaon	25	18	72	6	24	1	4	0	0	25	9	36	11	44	2	8	3	12
		Total	**321**	**176**	**55**	**111**	**35**	**20**	**6**	**14**	**4**	**400**	**168**	**42**	**163**	**41**	**37**	**9**	**32**	**8**

Subject	Zone	Jila/Panchayat	B.Ed									Non B.Ed								
			Total	General	%	OBC	%	SC	%	ST	%	Total	General	%	OBC	%	SC	%	ST	%
Sanskrit	Sarguja	Ambikapur (Sarguja)	20	5	25	10	50	0	0	5	25	25	6	24	14	56	0	0	5	20
Sanskrit	Sarguja	Baikuntpur	6	5	83	1	17	0	0	0	0	25	21	84	4	16	0	0	0	0
Sanskrit	Bilaspur	Bilaspur	25	10	40	13	52	1	4	1	4	25	7	28	14	56	2	8	2	8
Sanskrit	Baster	Dantewada	6	1	17	2	33	0	0	3	50	14	6	43	5	35.7	1	7.1	2	14
Sanskrit	Raipur	Dhamtari	25	6	24	17	68	1	4	1	4	25	3	12	18	72	2	8	2	8
Sanskrit	Raipur	Durg	25	13	52	12	48	0	0	0	4	25	9	36	12	48	3	12	1	4
Sanskrit	Baster	Jagadalpur	14	9	64	5	36	0	0	0	0	25	13	52	7	28	1	4	4	16
Sanskrit	Bilaspur	Janjgir-Champa	25	10	40	11	44	4	16	0	0	25	6	24	17	68	1	4	1	4
Sanskrit	Sarguja	Jashpurnagar	3	0	0	2	67	0	0	1	0	25	1	4	6	24	18	72	0	0
Sanskrit	Baster	Kanker	5	0	0	1	20	0	0	4	20	25	5	20	8	32	3	12	9	36
Sanskrit	Raipur	Kabirdham (Kawardha)	14	6	43	7	50	0	0	1	29	25	17	68	8	32	0	0	0	0
Sanskrit	Sarguja	Korba	25	13	52	8	32	4	16	0	4	25	8	32	12	48	3	12	2	8
Sanskrit	Raipur	Mahasamund	13	5	38	7	54	1	8	0	0	25	10	40	13	52	2	8	0	0
Sanskrit	Bilaspur	Raigarh	20	9	45	9	45	1	5	1	0	25	7	28	16	64	1	4	1	4
Sanskrit	Raipur	Raipur	25	6	24	12	48	6	24	1	4	25	4	16	17	68	3	12	1	4
Sanskrit	Raipur	Rajnandgaon	25	14	56	7	28	2	8	2	4	25	8	32	16	64	0	0	1	4
		Total	**276**	**112**	**41**	**124**	**45**	**20**	**7**	**20**	**1**	**389**	**131**	**34**	**187**	**48**	**40**	**10**	**31**	**8**

Subject	Zone	Jila/Panchayat	B.Ed									Non B.Ed								
			Total	General	%	OBC	%	SC	%	ST	%	Total	General	%	OBC	%	SC	%	ST	%
Hindi	Sarguja	Ambikapur (Sarguja)	25	7	28	15	60	3	12	0	0	25	11	44	10	40	4	16	0	0
Hindi	Sarguja	Baikuntpur	25	18	72	7	28	0	0	0	0	25	11	44	6	24	1	4	7	28
Hindi	Bilaspur	Bilaspur	25	11	44	10	40	4	16	0	0	25	12	48	11	44	2	8	0	0
Hindi	Baster	Dantewada	25	11	44	10	40	1	4	3	12	25	5	20	15	60	4	16	1	4
Hindi	Raipur	Dhamtari	25	2	8	22	88	1	4	0	0	25	7	28	15	60	1	4	2	8
Hindi	Raipur	Durg	25	10	40	13	52	2	8	0	0	25	9	36	14	56	2	8	0	0
Hindi	Baster	Jagadalpur	25	7	28	11	44	2	8	5	20	25	3	12	19	76	1	4	2	8
Hindi	Bilaspur	Janjgir-Champa	25	7	28	16	64	2	8	0	0	25	0	0	24	96	0	0	1	4
Hindi	Sarguja	Jashpurnagar	25	4	16	2	8	0	0	19	76	25	9	36	12	48	0	0	4	16
Hindi	Baster	Kanker	23	6	26	4	17	0	0	13	57	25	3	12	15	60	1	4	6	24
Hindi	Raipur	Kabirdham (Kawardha)	25	9	36	7	28	5	20	4	16	25	11	44	12	48	1	4	1	4
Hindi	Sarguja	Korba	25	13	52	9	36	3	12	0	0	25	8	32	16	64	0	0	1	4
Hindi	Raipur	Mahasamund	25	0	0	22	88	1	4	2	8	25	3	12	17	68	3	12	2	8
Hindi	Bilaspur	Raigarh	25	7	28	11	44	3	12	4	16	25	4	16	14	56	4	16	3	12
Hindi	Raipur	Raipur	25	7	28	18	72	0	0	0	0	25	7	28	16	64	2	8	0	0
Hindi	Raipur	Rajnandgaon	25	7	28	15	60	2	8	1	4	25	5	20	12	48	5	20	3	12
		Total	**398**	**126**	**32**	**192**	**48**	**29**	**7**	**51**	**13**	**400**	**108**	**27**	**228**	**57**	**31**	**8**	**33**	**8**

Subject	Zone	Jila/Panchayat	B.ed									Non B.ed								
			Total	General	%	OBC	%	SC	%	ST	%	Total	General	%	OBC	%	SC	%	ST	%
Other	Sarguja	Ambikapur (Sarguja)	25	10	40	11	44	3	12	1	4	25	5	20	18	72	0	0	2	8
Other	Sarguja	Baikuntpur	6	2	33	2	33	0	0	2	33	25	8	32	8	32	4	16	5	20
Other	Bilaspur	Bilaspur	25	11	44	8	32	4	16	1	4	25	10	40	12	48	3	12	0	0
Other	Baster	Dantewada	15	5	33	5	33	1	7	4	27	25	5	20	13	52	4	16	3	12
Other	Raipur	Dhamtari	5	1	20	4	80	0	0	0	0	25	5	20	18	72	1	4	1	4
Other	Raipur	Durg	25	7	28	14	56	2	8	2	8	25	7	28	15	60	3	12	0	0
Other	Baster	Jagadalpur	17	6	35	7	41	1	6	3	18	25	5	20	13	52	2	8	5	20
Other	Bilaspur	Janjgir-Champa	25	5	20	16	64	4	16	0	0	25	7	28	11	44	5	20	2	8
Other	Sarguja	Jashpurnagar	9	5	56	0	0	0	0	4	44	25	9	36	10	40	3	12	3	12
Other	Baster	Kanker	3	1	33	1	33	0	0	1	33	25	4	16	12	48	2	8	7	28
Other	Raipur	Kabirdham (Kawardha)	13	6	46	4	31	3	23	0	0	25	10	40	9	36	2	8	4	16
Other	Sarguja	Korba	28	6	21	10	36	5	18	2	7	25	6	24	12	48	3	12	3	12
Other	Raipur	Mahasamund	8	2	25	6	75	0	0	0	0	25	7	28	17	68	0	0	1	4
Other	Bilaspur	Raigarh	3	1	33	2	67	0	0	0	0	25	8	32	9	36	3	12	5	20
Other	Raipur	Raipur	25	7	28	14	56	4	16	0	0	25	6	24	12	48	4	16	3	12
Other	Raipur	Rajnandgaon	6	1	17	2	33	3	50	0	0	25	11	44	9	36	1	4	4	16
		Total	**238**	**76**	**32**	**106**	**45**	**30**	**13**	**20**	**8**	**400**	**113**	**28**	**198**	**49.5**	**40**	**10**	**48**	**12**

ANNEXURE 7.8

Subject	Zone	Jila/Panchayat	B.Ed									Non B.Ed								
			Total	General	%	OBC	%	SC	%	ST	%	Total	General	%	OBC	%	SC	%	ST	%
Vyayam	Sarguja	Ambikapur (Sarguja)	11	2	18	0	0	0	0	9	82	25	7	28	4	16	0	0	14	56
Vyayam	Sarguja	Baikuntpur	2	1	50	1	50	0	0	0	0	21	9	43	6	29	1	5	5	24
Vyayam	Bilaspur	Bilaspur	5	4	80	1	20	0	0	0	0	11	7	64	3	27	1	9	0	0
Vyayam	Baster	Dantewada	2	0	0	2	100	0	0	0	0	4	2	50	0	0	1	25	1	25
Vyayam	Raipur	Dhamtari	13	4	31	4	31	2	15	3	23	25	4	16	18	72	1	4	2	8
Vyayam	Raipur	Durg	25	13	52	9	36	1	4	2	8	25	9	36	14	56	1	4	1	4
Vyayam	Baster	Jagadalpur	1	1	100	0	0	0	0	0	0	22	7	32	6	27	1	5	8	36
Vyayam	Bilaspur	Janjgir-Champa	25	6	24	13	52	5	20	1	4	25	8	32	8	32	8	32	1	4
Vyayam	Sarguja	Jashpurnagar	1	0	0	0	0	0	0	1	100	17	4	24	0	0	0	0	13	76
Vyayam	Baster	Kanker	0	0	0	0	0	0	0	0	0	3	0	0	1	33	0	0	2	67
Vyayam	Raipur	Kabirdham (Kawardha)	4	1	25	1	25	1	25	1	25	25	8	32	10	40	5	20	2	8
Vyayam	Sarguja	Korba	2	0	0	1	50	1	50	0	0	25	13	52	10	40	1	4	1	4
Vyayam	Raipur	Mahasamund	5	1	20	3	60	1	20	0	0	25	3	12	17	68	2	8	3	12
Vyayam	Bilaspur	Raigarh	0	0	0	0	0	0	0	0	0	3	2	67	1	33	0	0	0	0
Vyayam	Raipur	Raipur	25	9	36	13	52	3	12	0	0	25	10	40	11	44	1	4	3	12
Vyayam	Raipur	Rajnandgaon	2	1	50	0	0	0	0	1	50	17	7	41	8	47	2	12	0	0
		Total	**123**	**43**	**35**	**48**	**39**	**14**	**11**	**18**	**15**	**298**	**100**	**34**	**117**	**39**	**25**	**8**	**56**	**19**

Subject	Zone	Jila/Panchayat	B.Ed									Non B.Ed								
			Total	General	%	OBC	%	SC	%	ST	%	Total	General	%	OBC	%	SC	%	ST	%
Music	Sarguja	Ambikapur (Sarguja)	1	0	0	0	0	0	0	1	100	8	5	63	2	25	1	13	0	0
Music	Sarguja	Baikuntpur	0	0	0	0	0	0	0	0	0	3	3	100	0	0	0	0	0	0
Music	Bilaspur	Bilaspur	2	2	100	0	0	0	0	0	0	7	2	29	3	43	2	29	0	0
Music	Baster	Dantewada	0	0	0	0	0	0	0	0	0	5	4	80	0	0	0	0	1	20
Music	Raipur	Dhamtari	0	0	0	0	0	0	0	0	0	1	1	100	0	0	0	0	0	0
Music	Raipur	Durg	5	4	80	1	20	0	0	0	0	23	17	74	4	17	1	4	1	4
Music	Baster	Jagadalpur	0	0	0	0	0	0	0	0	0	5	1	20	1	20	0	0	3	60
Music	Bilaspur	Janjgir-Champa	0	0	0	0	0	0	0	0	0	3	0	0	2	67	1	33	0	0
Music	Sarguja	Jashpurnagar	0	0	0	0	0	0	0	0	0	23	8	35	8	35	6	26	1	4
Music	Baster	Kanker	0	0	0	0	0	0	0	0	0	1	1	100	0	0	0	0	0	0
Music	Raipur	Kabirdham (Kawardha)	1	0	0	0	0	0	0	1	100	4	0	0	3	75	0	0	1	25
Music	Sarguja	Korba	2	2	100	0	0	0	0	0	0	12	5	42	5	42	1	8	1	8
Music	Raipur	Mahasamund	0	0	0	0	0	0	0	0	0	0	0	0	0	0	0	0	0	0
Music	Bilaspur	Raigarh	0	0	0	0	0	0	0	0	0	2	2	100	0	0	0	0	0	0
Music	Raipur	Raipur	4	3	75	1	25	0	0	0	0	22	16	73	4	18	1	5	1	5
Music	Raipur	Rajnandgaon	1	1	100	0	0	0	0	0	0	19	12	63	5	26	2	11	0	0
		Total	**16**	**12**	**75**	**2**	**13**	**0**	**0**	**2**	**13**	**138**	**77**	**56**	**37**	**27**	**15**	**11**	**9**	**7**

Subject	Zone	Jila/Panchayat	B.Ed									Non B.Ed								
			Total	General	%	OBC	%	SC	%	ST	%	Total	General	%	OBC	%	SC	%	ST	%
Tabla	Sarguja	Ambikapur (Sarguja)										11	4	36	6	55	0	0	1	9
Tabla	Sarguja	Baikuntpur										3	2	67	1	33	0	0	0	0
Tabla	Bilaspur	Bilaspur										2	1	50	1	50	0	0	0	0
Tabla	Baster	Dantewada										2	2	100	0	0	0	0	0	0
Tabla	Raipur	Dhamtari										0	0	0	0	0	0	0	0	0
Tabla	Raipur	Durg										5	1	20	4	80	0	0	0	0
Tabla	Baster	Jagadalpur										4	0	0	2	50	0	0	2	50
Tabla	Bilaspur	Janjgir-Champa										1	0	0	0	0	1	100	0	0
Tabla	Sarguja	Jashpurnagar										4	0	0	3	75	1	25	0	0
Tabla	Baster	Kanker										1	0	0	1	100	0	0	0	0
Tabla	Raipur	Kabirdham (Kawardha)										0	0	0	0	0	0	0	0	0
Tabla	Sarguja	Korba										3	0	0	2	67	0	0	1	33
Tabla	Raipur	Mahasamund										0	0	0	0	0	0	0	0	0
Tabla	Bilaspur	Raigarh										0	0	0	0	0	0	0	0	0
Tabla	Raipur	Raipur										8	2	25	5	63	0	0	0	0
Tabla	Raipur	Rajnandgaon										3	1	33	2	67	0	0	0	0
		Total										**47**	**13**	**28**	**27**	**57**	**2**	**4**	**4**	**0**

Subject	Zone	Jila/Panchayat	B.Ed									Non B.Ed								
			Total	General	%	OBC	%	SC	%	ST	%	Total	General	%	OBC	%	SC	%	ST	%
Commerce	Sarguja	Ambikapur (Sarguja)	25	14	56	11	44	0	0	1	4	25	11	44	12	48	1	4	1	4
Commerce	Sarguja	Baikuntpur	14	12	86	2	14	0	0	0	0	25	17	68	6	24	0	0	2	8
Commerce	Bilaspur	Bilaspur	25	20	80	5	20	0	0	0	0	25	14	56	10	40	0	0	1	4
Commerce	Baster	Dantewada	7	5	71	2	29	0	0	0	0	25	7	28	11	44	2	8	5	20
Commerce	Raipur	Dhamtari	14	5	36	9	64	0	0	0	0	25	10	40	12	48	3	12	0	0
Commerce	Raipur	Durg	25	17	68	7	28	1	4	0	0	25	15	60	9	36	1	4	0	0
Commerce	Baster	Jagadalpur	25	15	60	6	24	0	0	4	16	25	5	20	13	52	2	8	5	20
Commerce	Bilaspur	Janjgir-Champa	25	11	44	12	48	2	8	0	0	25	8	32	15	60	2	8	0	0
Commerce	Sarguja	Jashpurnagar	3	1	33	0	0	0	0	2	67	25	10	40	9	36	1	4	5	20
Commerce	Baster	Kanker	15	8	53	4	27	1	7	2	13	25	3	12	11	44	2	8	9	36
Commerce	Raipur	Kabirdham (Kawardha)	4	1	25	2	50	1	25	0	0	25	11	44	12	48	1	4	1	4
Commerce	Sarguja	Korba	25	14	56	11	44	0	0	0	0	25	7	28	14	56	2	8	2	8
Commerce	Raipur	Mahasamund	18	7	39	10	56	0	0	1	6	25	11	44	13	52	1	4	0	0
Commerce	Bilaspur	Raigarh	17	9	53	7	41	0	0	1	6	25	12	48	12	48	1	4	0	0
Commerce	Raipur	Raipur	25	14	56	10	40	1	4	0	0	25	6	24	17	68	0	0	2	8
Commerce	Raipur	Rajnandgaon	25	18	72	6	24	0	0	1	4	25	16	64	7	28	0	0	2	8
		Total	**292**	**171**	**59**	**104**	**36**	**6**	**2**	**12**	**4**	**400**	**163**	**41**	**183**	**46**	**19**	**5**	**35**	**9**

Subject	Zone	Jila/Panchayat	B.Ed									Non B.Ed								
			Total	General	%	OBC	%	SC	%	ST	%	Total	General	%	OBC	%	SC	%	ST	%
Art	Sarguja	Ambikapur (Sarguja)	25	12	48	13	52	0	0	0	0	25	15	60	10	40	0	0	0	0
Art	Sarguja	Baikuntpur	25	20	80	4	16	0	0	1	4	25	17	68	6	24	1	4	1	4
Art	Bilaspur	Bilaspur	25	9	36	13	52	1	4	2	8	25	13	52	9	36	2	8	1	4
Art	Baster	Dantewada	25	3	12	19	76	1	4	2	8	25	5	20	16	64	3	12	1	4
Art	Raipur	Dhamtari	25	2	8	22	88	0	0	1	4	25	10	40	10	40	4	16	1	4
Art	Raipur	Durg	25	13	52	9	36	2	8	1	4	25	5	20	16	64	3	12	1	4
Art	Baster	Jagadalpur	25	7	28	13	52	3	12	2	8	25	6	24	13	52	2	8	4	16
Art	Bilaspur	Janjgir-Champa	25	7	28	10	40	7	28	1	4	25	5	20	13	52	1	4	6	24
Art	Sarguja	Jashpurnagar	25	5	20	1	4	3	12	16	64	25	10	40	6	24	2	8	7	28
Art	Baster	Kanker	25	8	32	6	24	2	8	9	36	25	5	20	12	48	1	4	7	28
Art	Raipur	Kabirdham (Kawardha)	25	9	36	15	60	1	4	0	0	25	7	28	16	64	1	4	1	4
Art	Sarguja	Korba	25	13	52	11	44	1	4	0	0	25	14	56	9	36	1	4	1	4
Art	Raipur	Mahasamund	25	5	20	19	76	1	4	0	0	25	7	28	14	56	1	4	3	12
Art	Bilaspur	Raigarh	25	7	28	17	68	0	0	1	4	25	7	28	15	60	1	4	2	8
Art	Raipur	Raipur	25	12	48	12	48	1	4	0	0	25	9	36	15	60	1	4	0	0
Art	Raipur	Rajnandgaon	25	9	36	11	44	2	8	3	12	25	9	36	13	52	2	8	1	4
		Total	**400**	**141**	**35**	**195**	**49**	**25**	**6**	**39**	**10**	**400**	**144**	**36**	**193**	**48**	**26**	**7**	**37**	**9**

Subject	Zone	Jila/Panchayat	B.Ed									Non B.Ed								
			Total	General	%	OBC	%	SC	%	ST	%	Total	General	%	OBC	%	SC	%	ST	%
Science	Sarguja	Ambikapur (Sarguja)	25	15	60	10	40	1	4	1	4	25	13	52	10	40	2	8	1	4
Science	Sarguja	Baikuntpur	25	19	76	4	16	1	4	1	4	25	16	64	6	24	2	8	1	4
Science	Bilaspur	Bilaspur	25	17	68	5	20	3	12	0	0	25	14	56	6	24	4	16	1	4
Science	Baster	Dantewada	25	18	72	4	16	3	12	0	0	25	8	32	15	60	2	8	0	0
Science	Raipur	Dhamtari	25	5	20	19	76	1	4	0	0	25	3	12	18	72	3	12	1	4
Science	Raipur	Durg	25	10	40	14	56	1	4	0	0	25	7	28	14	56	2	8	2	8
Science	Baster	Jagadalpur	25	13	52	11	44	1	4	0	0	25	14	56	7	28	1	4	3	12
Science	Bilaspur	Janjgir-Champa	25	9	36	15	60	0	0	1	4	25	7	28	16	64	1	4	1	4
Science	Sarguja	Jashpurnagar	25	8	32	4	16	1	4	10	40	25	5	20	8	32	6	24	6	24
Science	Baster	Kanker	25	10	40	12	48	0	0	3	12	25	8	32	9	36	1	4	7	28
Science	Raipur	Kabirdham (Kawardha)	25	7	28	13	52	4	16	1	4	25	11	44	9	36	3	12	2	8
Science	Sarguja	Korba	25	8	32	13	52	3	12	1	4	25	10	40	12	48	2	8	1	4
Science	Raipur	Mahasamund	25	6	24	18	72	1	4	0	0	25	3	12	21	84	1	4	0	0
Science	Bilaspur	Raigarh	25	12	48	12	48	0	0	1	4	25	6	24	15	60	3	12	1	4
Science	Raipur	Raipur	25	10	40	13	52	1	4	1	4	25	6	24	12	48	6	24	1	4
Science	Raipur	Rajnandgaon	25	12	48	9	36	3	12	1	4	25	6	24	13	52	5	20	1	4
		Total	**400**	**179**	**45**	**176**	**44**	**24**	**6**	**21**	**5**	**400**	**137**	**34**	**191**	**48**	**44**	**11**	**29**	**7**

Subject	Zone	Jila/Panchayat	B.Ed									Non B.Ed								
			Total	General	%	OBC	%	SC	%	ST	%	Total	General	%	OBC	%	SC	%	ST	%
Mathematics	Sarguja	Ambikapur (Sarguja)	25	9	36	14	56	1	4	1	4	25	11	44	12	48	0	0	2	8
Mathematics	Sarguja	Baikuntpur	25	24	96	1	4	0	0	0	0	25	18	72	4	16	1	4	2	8
Mathematics	Bilaspur	Bilaspur	25	19	76	6	24	0	0	0	0	25	14	56	10	40	1	4	0	0
Mathematics	Baster	Dantewada	9	7	78	1	11	0	0	1	11	25	11	44	13	52	0	0	1	4
Mathematics	Raipur	Dhamtari	25	5	20	20	80	0	0	0	0	25	3	12	21	84	1	4	0	0
Mathematics	Raipur	Durg	25	5	20	19	76	0	0	1	4	25	9	36	15	60	0	0	1	4
Mathematics	Baster	Jagadalpur	25	12	48	12	48	0	0	1	4	25	9	36	11	44	1	4	4	16
Mathematics	Bilaspur	Janjgir-Champa	25	8	32	16	64	1	4	0	0	25	8	32	17	68	0	0	0	0
Mathematics	Sarguja	Jashpurnagar	8	5	63	2	25	0	0	1	13	25	2	8	14	56	3	12	6	24
Mathematics	Baster	Kanker	14	3	21	6	43	2	14	3	21	25	4	16	15	60	2	8	4	16
Mathematics	Raipur	Kabirdham (Kawardha)	25	9	36	14	56	1	4	1	4	25	10	40	14	56	1	4	0	0
Mathematics	Sarguja	Korba	25	10	40	14	56	0	0	1	4	25	12	48	11	44	0	0	2	8
Mathematics	Raipur	Mahasamund	25	5	20	20	80	0	0	0	0	25	7	28	18	72	0	0	0	0
Mathematics	Bilaspur	Raigarh	25	11	44	13	52	1	4	0	0	25	4	16	18	72	2	8	1	4
Mathematics	Raipur	Raipur	25	4	16	21	84	0	0	0	0	25	5	20	18	72	2	8	0	0
Mathematics	Raipur	Rajnandgaon	25	9	36	15	60	1	4	0	0	25	10	40	14	56	0	0	1	4
		Total	**356**	**145**	**41**	**194**	**54**	**7**	**2**	**10**	**3**	**400**	**137**	**34**	**225**	**56**	**14**	**4**	**24**	**6**

Subject	Zone	Jila/Panchayat	B.Ed									Non B.Ed								
			Total	General	%	OBC	%	SC	%	ST	%	Total	General	%	OBC	%	SC	%	ST	%
Urdu	Sarguja	Ambikapur (Sarguja)	5	3	60	2	40	0	0	0	0	14	12	86	2	14	0	0	0	0
Urdu	Sarguja	Baikuntpur	1	1	100	0	0	0	0	0	0	7	6	86	1	14	0	0	0	0
Urdu	Bilaspur	Bilaspur	1	1	100	0	0	0	0	0	0	6	3	50	5	83	0	0	0	0
Urdu	Baster	Dantewada	1	0	0	1	100	0	0	0	0	0	0	0	0	0	0	0	0	0
Urdu	Raipur	Dhamtari	0	0	0	0	0	0	0	0	0	0	0	0	0	0	0	0	0	0
Urdu	Raipur	Durg	3	2	67	1	33	0	0	0	0	21	10	48	11	52	0	0	0	0
Urdu	Baster	Jagadalpur	0	0	0	0	0	0	0	0	0	1	0	0	1	100	0	0	0	0
Urdu	Bilaspur	Janjgir-Champa	0	0	0	0	0	0	0	0	0	1	1	100	0	0	0	0	0	0
Urdu	Sarguja	Jashpurnagar	1	1	100	0	0	0	0	0	0	1	1	100	0	0	0	0	0	0
Urdu	Baster	Kanker	0	0	0	0	0	0	0	0	0	1	1	100	0	0	0	0	0	0
Urdu	Raipur	Kabirdham (Kawardha)	0	0	0	0	0	0	0	0	0	0	0	0	0	0	0	0	0	0
Urdu	Sarguja	Korba	1	1	100	0	0	0	0	0	0	3	2	67	1	33	0	0	0	0
Urdu	Raipur	Mahasamund	0	0	0	0	0	0	0	0	0	1	1	100	0	0	0	0	0	0
Urdu	Bilaspur	Raigarh	0	0	0	0	0	0	0	0	0	2	2	100	0	0	0	0	0	0
Urdu	Raipur	Raipur	2	0	0	2	100	0	0	0	0	15	14	93	1	7	0	0	0	0
Urdu	Raipur	Rajnandgaon	1	0	0	1	100	0	0	0	0	8	6	75	2	25	0	0	0	0
		Total	**16**	**9**	**56**	**7**	**44**	**0**	**0**	**0**	**0**	**81**	**59**	**73**	**24**	**30**	**0**	**0**	**0**	**0**

Subject	Zone	Jila/Panchayat	B.Ed									Non B.Ed								
			Total	General	%	OBC	%	SC	%	ST	%	Total	General	%	OBC	%	SC	%	ST	%
English	Sarguja	Ambikapur (Sarguja)	25	17	68	3	12	0	0	5	20	25	15	60	6	24	1	4	3	12
English	Sarguja	Baikuntpur	8	6	75	0	0	1	13	1	13	25	16	64	8	32	1	4	0	0
English	Bilaspur	Bilaspur	25	21	84	3	12	1	4	0	0	25	17	68	4	16	2	8	2	8
English	Baster	Dantewada	6	5	83	0	0	0	0	1	17	25	13	52	9	36	1	4	2	8
English	Raipur	Dhamtari	11	7	64	3	27	1	9	0	0	25	10	40	9	36	6	24	0	0
English	Raipur	Durg	25	17	68	6	24	1	4	1	4	25	14	56	8	32	2	8	1	4
English	Baster	Jagadalpur	18	12	67	4	22	0	0	2	11	25	10	40	7	28	3	12	5	20
English	Bilaspur	Janjgir-Champa	25	11	44	8	32	6	24	0	0	25	10	40	9	36	6	24	0	0
English	Sarguja	Jashpurnagar	12	3	25	0	0	2	17	7	58	25	10	40	8	32	4	16	3	12
English	Baster	Kanker	2	0	0	2	100	0	0	0	0	25	9	36	7	28	9	36	0	0
English	Raipur	Kabirdham (Kawardha)	4	3	75	1	25	0	0	0	0	25	17	68	7	28	1	4	0	0
English	Sarguja	Korba	25	17	68	4	16	1	4	3	12	25	9	36	8	32	5	20	3	12
English	Raipur	Mahasamund	12	2	17	6	50	2	17	2	17	25	4	16	18	72	2	8	1	4
English	Bilaspur	Raigarh	14	9	64	5	36	0	0	0	0	25	5	20	14	56	2	8	4	16
English	Raipur	Raipur	25	14	56	7	28	3	12	1	4	25	8	32	8	32	8	32	1	4
English	Raipur	Rajnandgaon	25	20	80	4	16	0	0	1	4	25	5	20	15	60	2	8	3	12
		Total	**262**	**164**	**63**	**56**	**21**	**18**	**7**	**24**	**9**	**400**	**172**	**43**	**145**	**36**	**55**	**14**	**28**	**7**

Subject	Zone	Jila/Panchayat	B.Ed									Non B.Ed								
			Total	General	%	OBC	%	SC	%	ST	%	Total	General	%	OBC	%	SC	%	ST	%
Sanskrit	Sarguja	Ambikapur (Sarguja)	25	8	32	13	52	1	4	3	12	25	5	20	19	76	0	0	1	4
Sanskrit	Sarguja	Baikuntpur	5	5	100	0	0	0	0	0	0	25	13	52	9	36	0	0	3	12
Sanskrit	Bilaspur	Bilaspur	25	14	56	11	44	0	0	0	0	25	10	40	12	48	1	4	1	4
Sanskrit	Baster	Dantewada	3	3	100	0	0	0	0	0	0	25	7	28	10	40	1	4	7	28
Sanskrit	Raipur	Dhamtari	7	1	14	4	57	2	29	0	0	25	9	36	10	40	4	16	2	8
Sanskrit	Raipur	Durg	25	11	44	10	40	1	4	3	12	25	9	36	7	28	6	24	3	12
Sanskrit	Baster	Jagadalpur	12	6	50	2	17	0	0	3	25	25	4	16	9	36	1	4	11	44
Sanskrit	Bilaspur	Janjgir-Champa	19	6	32	8	42	5	26	0	0	25	3	12	19	76	3	12	0	0
Sanskrit	Sarguja	Jashpurnagar	4	0	0	1	25	1	25	2	50	25	1	4	11	44	9	36	4	16
Sanskrit	Baster	Kanker	7	0	0	1	14	1	14	5	71	25	2	8	8	32	2	8	13	52
Sanskrit	Raipur	Kabirdham (Kawardha)	13	5	38	5	38	1	8	2	15	25	11	44	10	40	2	8	2	8
Sanskrit	Sarguja	Korba	17	12	71	4	24	1	6	0	0	25	6	24	11	44	6	24	2	8
Sanskrit	Raipur	Mahasamund	5	2	40	2	40	1	20	0	0	25	8	32	14	56	0	0	3	12
Sanskrit	Bilaspur	Raigarh	14	3	21	10	71	0	0	1	7	25	5	20	18	72	0	0	2	8
Sanskrit	Raipur	Raipur	25	11	44	10	40	3	12	1	4	25	7	28	17	68	1	4	0	0
Sanskrit	Raipur	Rajnandgaon	16	5	31	5	31	4	25	2	13	25	6	24	13	52	3	12	3	12
		Total	**222**	**92**	**41**	**86**	**39**	**21**	**9**	**22**	**10**	**400**	**106**	**27**	**197**	**49**	**39**	**10**	**57**	**14**

Subject	Zone	Jila/Panchayat	B.Ed									Non B.Ed								
			Total	General	%	OBC	%	SC	%	ST	%	Total	General	%	OBC	%	SC	%	ST	%
Hindi	Sarguja	Ambikapur (Sarguja)	25	2	8	21	84	2	8	0	0	25	7	28	14	56	3	12	1	4
Hindi	Sarguja	Baikuntpur	25	14	56	8	32	1	4	2	8	25	11	44	8	32	3	12	3	12
Hindi	Bilaspur	Bilaspur	25	15	60	6	24	3	12	1	4	25	12	48	7	28	3	12	3	12
Hindi	Baster	Dantewada	25	8	32	11	44	2	8	4	16	25	6	24	14	56	2	8	3	12
Hindi	Raipur	Dhamtari	18	6	33	11	61	0	0	1	6	25	6	24	16	64	1	4	2	8
Hindi	Raipur	Durg	25	13	52	12	48	0	0	0	0	25	10	40	13	52	1	4	1	4
Hindi	Baster	Jagadalpur	25	9	36	9	36	2	8	5	20	25	6	24	16	64	1	4	2	8
Hindi	Bilaspur	Janjgir-Champa	25	4	16	18	72	3	12	0	0	25	2	8	20	80	3	12	0	0
Hindi	Sarguja	Jashpurnagar	25	11	44	7	28	1	4	6	24	25	4	16	19	76	0	0	2	8
Hindi	Baster	Kanker	16	4	25	2	13	4	25	6	38	25	3	12	14	56	2	8	6	24
Hindi	Raipur	Kabirdham (Kawardha)	25	11	44	8	32	4	16	2	8	25	11	44	12	48	0	0	2	8
Hindi	Sarguja	Korba	25	13	52	7	28	4	16	1	4	25	8	32	15	60	2	8	0	0
Hindi	Raipur	Mahasamund	25	2	8	20	80	2	8	1	4	25	4	16	19	76	2	8	0	0
Hindi	Bilaspur	Raigarh	25	4	16	14	56	6	24	1	4	25	3	12	16	64	3	12	3	12
Hindi	Raipur	Raipur	25	5	20	19	76	1	4	0	0	25	5	20	17	68	2	8	1	4
Hindi	Raipur	Rajnandgaon	25	14	56	9	36	2	8	0	0	25	6	24	17	68	1	4	1	4
		Total	**384**	**135**	**35**	**182**	**47**	**37**	**10**	**30**	**8**	**400**	**104**	**26**	**237**	**59**	**29**	**7**	**30**	**8**

Subject	Zone	Jila/Panchayat	B.ed									Non B.ed								
			Total	General	%	OBC	%	SC	%	ST	%	Total	General	%	OBC	%	SC	%	ST	%
Other	Sarguja	Ambikapur (Sarguja)	19	8	42	1	5	0	0	10	53	25	5	20	16	64	1	4	3	12
Other	Sarguja	Baikuntpur	3	2	67	0	0	0	0	1	33	25	10	40	6	24	4	16	5	20
Other	Bilaspur	Bilaspur	15	7	47	3	20	3	20	2	13	25	11	44	6	24	4	16	4	16
Other	Baster	Dantewada	2	0	0	1	50	0	0	1	50	25	4	16	9	36	4	16	8	32
Other	Raipur	Dhamtari	3	1	33	1	33	0	0	1	33	25	6	24	15	60	2	8	2	8
Other	Raipur	Durg	25	15	60	6	24	2	8	2	8	25	13	52	9	36	2	8	1	4
Other	Baster	Jagadalpur	9	2	22	1	11	1	11	5	56	25	4	16	9	36	1	4	11	44
Other	Bilaspur	Janjgir-Champa	5	1	20	2	40	2	40	0	0	25	6	24	12	48	5	20	2	8
Other	Sarguja	Jashpurnagar	4	0	0	0	0	1	25	3	75	25	4	16	11	44	2	8	8	32
Other	Baster	Kanker	5	0	0	0	0	1	20	4	80	25	3	12	10	40	1	4	11	44
Other	Raipur	Kabirdham (Kawardha)	2	1	50	0	0	0	0	1	50	25	13	52	7	28	1	4	4	16
Other	Sarguja	Korba	20	12	60	0	0	5	25	3	15	25	6	24	11	44	5	20	3	12
Other	Raipur	Mahasamund	2	0	0	2	100	0	0	0	0	25	3	12	15	60	4	16	3	12
Other	Bilaspur	Raigarh	16	2	13	3	19	3	19	8	50	25	4	16	10	40	6	24	5	20
Other	Raipur	Raipur	20	5	25	10	50	3	15	2	10	25	11	44	8	32	3	12	2	8
Other	Raipur	Rajnandgaon	5	2	40	1	20	0	0	2	40	25	11	44	11	44	1	4	2	8
		Total	**155**	**58**	**37**	**31**	**20**	**21**	**14**	**45**	**29**	**400**	**114**	**29**	**165**	**41**	**46**	**12**	**74**	**19**

Bibliography

1. Constitutional Assembly Debates (C.A.D) Vol. VII.
2. Lipson, Leslie: The Great Issues of Politics, Jaico Publishing House, Bombay, 1973.
3. Sills, David, L. (ed): International Encyclopedia of the Social Sciences, Vol. V, The Macmillan Company and The Free Press, U.S.A., 1968.
4. Singh, Sukhvir, A History of Political Thought, Vol. I (Rastogi & Company, Meerut-2, 1973, p. 276.
5. Singh, Sukhvir, A History of Political Thought, Vol. I (Rastogi & Company, Meerut-2, 1973, p. 504.
6. Deanel, Herbert, A.: The Political Ideas of Harold J. Laski, Columbia University Press, New York, 1955.
7. Kering, "Marxism, Communism and Western Society", Vol. III, A Comparative Encyclopedia (1972), Herder and Herder, p. 209.
8. Lenin, V.I. : Collected Works, Vol. 29 (Progress Publishers, Moscow, 1966).
9. *Yajur Veda* - XXXVI-2.
10. Veni Samharam Natakam (Sahitya Bhandar, Meerut, 2nd Ed. 1967).
11. Harsha, Shri (Shastri, Dr. Shiva Raj – Commentator), Naishadh Mahakavya, Sahitya Bhandar, Subhash Bazar, Meerut, 1972.
12. Majumdar, R.C. and Others: An Advanced History of India (Macmillan and Co. Ltd., St. Martin's Street, London, 1950.
13. Jayaswal, S.R. (ed.): Nehru on Society, Education and Culture, Vinod Pustak Mandi, Agra, 1965.
14. Bright, J.S. (ed.): Selected Writings of Jawahar Lal Nehru 1916-1950, The Indian Printing Works, New Delhi.

15. Anil Bhatt, 1975 : 'Caste Class and Politics' Manohar Book Service, New Delhi, p. 40

16. Dumont, Louis, 1970 : Homo-hierarchus : An Essay on the Caste System, Chicago : The University of Chicago Press.

17. F.G. Bailey, Caste and the Economic Frontier (Manchester: Manchester University Press, 1957).

18. M.N. Srinivas, *Caste in Modern India and Other Essays*, Bombay: Asia Publishing House, 1962.

19. L. Dumont, *Religion, Politics and History in India,* The Hague: Hague Press, 1970.

20. The Modernity of Tradition: *The Political Development in India*, M.N. Srinivas, New Delhi: Orient Longman.

21. V.A. Pai Panandiker, ed., *The Politics of Backwardness*: *Reservation Policy in India,* New Delhi 1997.

22. Radhakrishnan, P., 1996: Backward Class Movements in Tamil Nadu in M.N.Sreenivas (ed).: Caste: Its Twentieth Century Avatar, New Delhi: Viking.

23. Pandian J., 1987: *Caste, Nationalism and Ethnicity*, Bombay: Popular Prakashan.

24. E.F.Irschick: 1969: Politics and Social Conflict in South India: The Non-Brahmin Movement and Tamil Separation (1916-29): California: University of California Press.

25. Beteille, Andre,: *Caste Old and New*, London: Asia Publishing House: 1969.

26. Rajagopal Indhu: *The Tyranny of Caste*, New Delhi: Vikas Publishing House,1985.

27. Pandian J: Caste, *Nationalism and Ethnicity*, Bombay: Popular Prakashan, 1987.

28. "Why I am not a Hindu" by Illaiah Kanchan (Kanchan:1997:214)

29. Robin Jeffrey, *The Decline of Nayar Dominance,* London, 1976.

30. Anirudh Prasad, Reservation, *Policy and Practice in India*, New Delhi 1991.

31. Constitutional Assembly Debates (C.A.D) Vol. II.

32. Nehru. The First Sixty Years (ed.) Dorothy Norman. Asia Publishing House, Bombay 1965.

E

Economic
  And Social Backwardness, 190
  Backwardness, 82, 206
  Order, 93
  Problems, 19
  Social and Political Inequalities, 17
Economically Backward Class, 45
Economy, 16, 40, 191, 206
Educational
  And Labour Market, 18
  Backwardness, 95, 164
    Report on-, 164
  Conference at Simla, 1901, 138
  Institutions, 45, 63
  Opportunities, 93
Educationally Backward Class, 24, 25, 71, 99
Endogamy, 37
Equal Protection of Law, 71, 77
Exploitation, 87

F

Farming, 16
First Backward Class Commission, 51-52
Freedom Fighters, 87
Fundamental Rights, 24, 69, 71, 72, 87, 99
  Against Discrimination, 71

G

Gandhi, Mrs Indira, 91
Gandhi, Rajiv, 91
Golaknath Vs State of Punjab, 99
Gonvindraj, Marathi Poet, 37
Government Basic Training Institute, 138
Group Mobilization, 18
Gujarat, 43
Gujjar Agitation, 2007, 45, 46
  Highlights of-, 46
Gujjars, 101
  In Rajasthan, 45
Guru Ghasidas, 140

H

Hartog Committee, 49
Health Centres, 318
Hidimba, 35
Hindu
  And Indian Society, 40
  Community, 57
  OBC, 58
  Social Order, (HSO), 14, 19, 20, 22, 41, 44,
  Society, 36, 37, 40, 191, 198
Hinduism, 13, 16, 190
History of Renaissance, 22

I

Impact of Manu on Indian Society, 40
Important Personalities Bio-Sketches, (IPB), 198
  Bilasa Bai Kewaten, 198
  Chandulal Chandrakar, 201
  Chandulal Chandrakar—Bannibai Sonkar, 202
  Danganpat Singh, 199
  Hiralal Kavyapadhayay, 198
  JA Barchhiha, 200
  Kakah Bai, 200
  Khoobchand Baghat, 200
  Ramaprasad Deshmukh, 199
  Rohini Bai Parganiha, 199
  Ramaprasad Deshmukh, 199
  Rohini Bai Parganiha, 199
India's Population, 91
Indian
  Caste System, 36
  Central Committee, 49

Culture and Civilization, 35
Franchise Committee, 49, 50
National Congress, 141
Population, 14
Society, 13, 16, 20, 28, 36, 47, 305
Impact of Manu On-, 40
Statutory Commission, 49
Indira Sahni Case Vs UOI, 31, 90
Industrialization
And Employment, 43
And Work Forces, 43
Industrialized States, 41
Gujarat, 41
Karnataka, 41
Madhya Pradesh, 41
Maharashtra, 41
Rajasthan, 41
West Bengal, 41
International Monetary Fund, 112
Islam, 37

J

Jainism, 13
Jana Dal, 95, 98
Janam Bhoomi Controversy, 98
Judicial Legislation, 95
Judiciary, 17, 18, 295

K

Kaka Kalelkar Commission, 55, 90
Brief, 55
Report, 17
Kalachury Dynastry, 137
Kanshi Ram, BSP Supremo, 98
Karn, A Great Warrior, 35
Kerala, 43
Keshavanand Bharati Case, 100
Kevat Caste, 277
Krishna, 35
Krishnamachari, TT, 90
Kurmi—Sonar, 278

L

Labour Movement of Chhatisgarh, 141
Land Reform Movement, 318
Laws of Manu, 36, 37, 40
Legislation, 13, 30, 40, 64, 82, 88, 99, 133, 296

M

Madhya Pradesh, 203
Act, 2000, 139
State, 20, 21
Vidhan Sabha, 139
Maharaja of Kolhapur, 48
Maharashtra, 43
Maikal Range, 21
Major Beneficiaries, (MB), 233
Bhoi, 233
Chandrakar, 233
Devagana, 233
Goswami, 233
Maurya, 233
Sam, 233
Soni, 233
Vishvakarma, 233
Yadavs, 233
Mandal, BP, 56, 57, 62, 306, 314
Mandal Commission, 56, 58, 62-66, 91, 93-96, 105, 110, 298, 301
Brief, 56, 57
Recommendations, 60-64, 96-98, 204
Report, 17, 20
Views, 58-60
Mandal's Recommendations, 204
Manu, 20, 38, 40, 41
Manu's Laws as Shudras, 15
Manusmriti, 38, 39
Maoist Naxal Operations, 21
Maratha Administration, 137
Marxism, 98

Mass Conversion to Islam and Christianity, 311
Medicine, 16
Mining Department, 211
Ministry of
  Social Justice, 125
  Welfare, 110
Minorities, 31, 88, 89
  Christianity, 31, 89
Muslims, 31, 89
Minority
  And Backward Class, 49
  Quota, 99
Monolithic Identity, 13
Muslim OBC, 65, 66
Muslims, 13

N

National
  Commission for Backward Classes, (NCBC), 125
  Democratic Alliance, 139
  Front, 96, 97
  Front Government, 93
  Movement in Chhatisgarh, 141
  Parties, 22
    Bhartiya Janta Party (BJP), 22
    BSP, 22
    Congress, 22
Nehru, Pandit Jawahar Lal, 87, 91

O

OBC (Other Backward Castes), 19, 20, 21, 22, 24, 30, 50, 55, 56, 61-63, 65, 66, 77, 90, 101, 105-110, 125-127, 132, 146, 149, 163,165, 166, 168, 189-194, 196-198, 206, 209, 211, 215, 216, 229, 232, 235, 237, 239, 241, 243, 248, 249, 276, 283, 284, 298, 299, 301-305, 309, 315
Communities, 149
Creamy Layer, 31, 110
  Exclusion of-, 110
  Gujjars, 91
  In Government, 203
  In Government Jobs, 24
  List, 311
  Muslims, 278
  Population, 301
  Population, 66
  Recruitment, 232
  Recruitment Findings, 232
  Reservation Laws, 105
  Reservations, 22, 91, 20, 125
Occupational Diversity of OBC in Chhatisgarh, 190
Occupations, 14, 16, 40

P

Panchayati Raj Institutions, (PRIs), 88, 191
Pandian, J, Justice, 128, 129
Paramilitary Forces, 113
Patel, Kurmi, Devagans, 229
Pillai, GK, Union Home Secy., 46
Plantations, 114
Political Parties, 17, 44, 75, 95, 101
Power Structure, 19, 20
Preamble of the Constitution of India, 23, 315
Pre-Manu Hindu Society, 35
Primary Education, 138, 318
Primary English Education, 138
Primary Vernacular Education, 138
Protective Discrimination (PD), 25, 27, 29, 87, 98, 295, 298, 308, 318
Public Sector
  Banks, 106
  Undertakings (PSU), 105, 106, 113

Q

Quota, 194, 297
  For Minorities, 99

Of A-B-C-D Group, 63

R

Raipur District, 166
Rajasthan
  High Court, 45
  Police, 46
Rajendra Case, 83
Ram
  Janam Bhoomi, 97, 98
  Temple in Ayodhya, 97
Ramji Mahajan Commission, 296, 297, 301, 303, 315
Report, 277
Rashtriya Swayam Sevak Sangh (RSS), 97
Ratanpur (Present Bilaspur), 137
  Ancient Capital of –Chhatisgarh, 137
Rath Yatra by LK Advani, 97
Recruitments, 239
Recruitments in Chhatisgarh, 309
Regulatory Mechanism, 300
Relaxation in Examination, 107
Religious
  Groups, 16
  Movement, 37
Reservation, 17-19, 20, 35-68, 45, 71, 88, 90, 94, 97, 98, 100, 105, 109, 132, 133, 295, 308
  For Backward Class, 26
  For Muslims, 18
  For OBC, 61
  For Scheduled Tribes, 239
  In Educational Institutions, 126
  In Government Service, 54
  In Jobs, 314
  In the Public Employment, 89
  Laws, 18, 105-135
  Of Backward Class, 204
  Of Jobs, 17
  Of Seats for SC/ST, 89
  Policy, 17, 18, 28, 29, 54, 101
  Protection against Caste Society, 35-68
  Quota, 61, 307
Reserved
  And Unreserved Class Comparison, 247
  Classes, 193, 194
  Classes In Government Sector, 194
Right to Equality, 90
Rigvedic Aryans, 35
River
  Mahanadi, 21
  Sheonath, 21
Rosaiah, K, CM, 99
Rules of Natural Justice, 109
Rural
  India, 16
  Schools, 138
Russel Castes details in Chhatisgarh, 143-146

S

Salauddin Ahmed, Rajasthan Chief Secretary, 46
Sant Guru Ghasidas, 22
Sardar Patel, 88
Sarguya District, 166
Sarva Samaj Samiti, 142
Satnam Faith, 22
Satnamis, 22
  Reservation in Jobs, 22
Scheduled Castes, 22
Seats in Educational Institutions, 22
Scheduled Caste/Scheduled Tribes, 15, 24, 41-43, 55, 58, 60, 61, 63, 66, 69, 71-74, 77, 78, 88, 90, 91, 94, 100, 105, 108, 109, 165, 166, 191, 193, 194, 196-198, 204, 216, 232, 235, 237, 241, 243, 285, 299, 307, 311

INDIAN TOURISM BUSINESS
A
Legal Perspective

by

Manohar Sajnani

GYAN

Author

All rights reserved. No part of this work may be reproduced, stored, adapted, or transmitted in any form or by any means, electronic, mechanical, photocopying, micro-filming, recording or otherwise, or translated in any language, without the prior written permission of the copyright owner and the publisher. The book is sold subject to the condition that it shall not, by way of trade or otherwise, be lent, resold, hired out, or otherwise circulated without the prior publisher's written consent in any form of binding or cover other than that in which it is published.

The views and opinions expressed in this book are author(s) own and the facts reported by them have been verified to the extent possible, and the publishers are not in any way liable for the same.

ISBN: 978-81-212-0650-1(HB)
First Published,
Published, 2019
Published by

Gyan Publishing House
5, Ansari Road
Daryaganj, New Delhi-110002
Phone: 011-47034999, 9811692060
www.gyanbooks.com
E-mail: books@gyanbooks.com

Printed at: G. Print Process, Delhi.

CONTENTS

List of Annexures 7

List of Cases 8

Preface 9

Acknowledgments 11

1. Tourism: Concepts and Forms 13
2. Indian Tourism: A Quantitative and Qualitative Glance 19
3. Incorporation of Business in India 23
4. Social Responsibility and Business Ethics in Tourism 33
5. Need for Tourism Laws and Regulations 49
6. Regulatory Laws for Tourism Business in India 53

   Part A - Regulations for Travel Agencies in India 53

   Part B - Regulations Regarding Documentections Procedures Facilitation 67

   Part C - Regulatory Laws for Accommpdation Sector 86

   Part D - Cargo Regulations 100
7. Comparative Study of Tourism Regulations in the United States and Canada 105
8. A Taxonomy of Tourism Legislations 125

   Part A - Legislations Related to Travel Agency, Business 126

   Part B - Legislation Regarding Hotel Industry 148

   Part C - Laws Relating to Wildlife Preservation 159

Part D - Laws Relating to Airline Sector 174

Part E - Legislations Related to Surface Transport Business 184

Part F - Legislations Relating to Forest Preservation 202

Part G - Consumer Protection Act. 220

Part H - Legislations Releting to Constitutional Remedies 228

Part I - Antiquities and Art Treasures Act., 1972 253

Part J - Laws Relating to Preservation of Cultural Heritage 257

LIST OF ANNEXURES

1. Specimen of Application form for IATA approval 58
2. Specimen of Application form for PATA approval 62
3. List of Indian Missions and FRRO's 72
4. Visa Requirements and formalities 73
5. List of Visas Offices for Neighbouring Countries 79
6. List of Restricted/Protected areas 80
7. Comparative Analysis of Public Complains on zonal railways 191
8. List of Authorities under Antiquities Act 261

LIST OF CASES

1. Cases Related to Travel Agency Sector : 145
   (a) M/s Four ways Travels and Tours and Ans V/S. Mr. K.N. Nagomantcam 146
   (b) Girikand Travels V/S Dr. A N Pujari 147
2. Cases Related to Accommodation Sector : 154
   (a) Controversy of Raddisson, New Delhi 154
   (b) East India hotels Ltd. V/s Mittlebachart, Lufthansa Copilot 156
   (c) M.S. Shoes V/s Hudco. 158
3. Case related to wildlife Protection Act: 172
   (a) Conviction against going around in a restricted place with loaded gun 172
4. Cases Related to Airline Sector: 181
   (a) Mrs. Ranjana Wahi V/s Indian Airlines Ltd. 181
   (b) Mrs. Maria D'souza V/s Air India Ltd. 182
   (c) Mr. B.L. Kachru V/s Lufthansa 183
   (d) Dr. Jiteswarahir V/s Indian Airlines 183
5. Cases Related to Road ways :
   (a) R.S.R.T. Corp. V/s Kailash Nath Kothari and Ors. 195
   (b) K.S.R.T. Corp. V/s B. Shennoy 200
   (c) Dolphin Travel V/s Mr. K. Suryanaryan 200
6. Cases Related to Railways : 195
   (a) Union of India V/s United India Insurance Co. Ltd.,
   (b) Mrs. Meenaksh Sundram V/s. Southern Railways 201
   (c) Union of India V/s United India Insurance Co. Ltd., 201
7. Cases Related Sea Transport :
   (a) Baltic Shipping Co. V/s Mrs. Dhillons and Ors.
8. Cases Related to Forest Preservation:
   (a) A case of appeal of reserved forest 213
   (b) T.N.G. Thirumulkpad V/s Union of India 215
9. Cases Related to Consumer Protection Act.
   (a) Air India V/s Y.H. Parekh and Ors. 225
   (b) Geeta Arts V/s Modiluft 227
   (c) Wg. Cdr. P.S. Sandhu and Ors V/s Union of India 228
10. Cases Related to Constitutional remedies:
   (a) Gopalan V/s state of Madras 238
   (b) Maneka Gandhi V/s Union of India 240
   (c) Smt. Charanjit Kaur V/s Union of India 241
   (d) S.S. Sawhney V/s Govt. of India 242
   (e) State of Orrissa V/s Dr. Binapani 243
   (f) R.D. Shetty V/s I.A.A.I 247
   (g) K.S. Abdullah V/s Enforcement Directorate 250
   (h) Order of Kerda high court on Airport Tax. 252

PREFACE

Tourism is neither a theme nor a situation. There are no longer two distinct classes of people, on mobile and another static. We are all tourists to some extent or otherwise. In the world of today, few of us stay but all the time and most of us have had the experience of being visitors in other people's villages, towns, cities, regions and countries. Other people, in turn, come as tourist to our areas. There is nothing new in this. Afloating population of explorers, pilgrims and traders have been moving about the earth since ancient times. What is new is the rapidly increasing speed of travel and growing volume of travellers.

Today, travel and tourism industry is the largest individual industry in the world and the biggest contributor to global economic development. Annually 595 million tourists across the world purchases worth US$ 3.6 trillion that is 3.6 followed by eleven zeroes, i.e., 10.69 per cent of gross global product. Tourism also provides or creates jobs worldwide, every 2.54 seconds or to put it another way 25 jobs a minute or 1500 jobs an hour, 36000 new jobs a day.

It is due to the immense importance of this encompassing industry as well as growing number of colleges and universities that offer courses or degrees in Travel and Tourism management, the author opted for a textbook that would interest a cross-section or readership, viz., teacher and students of tourism management, commerce, economics as well as law. It will also serve the interest of legislators, business executives, enterprenuers, investors and other interested in Indian tourism business.

Until now none of available material on tourism business laws combined practical occupational skills with essential academic qualities, i.e., where legal taxonomy is supported with related cases. Therefore, the author has attempted in his way to provide a textbook which will be of equal value to professional travel employees as well as the students. Collection of cases may also serve as a check point for those in the travel business who want to improve their skills by arguing the knowldege of what is legally correct and ethical and what is not? What could be the repercussions of such an act which is unethical or unlawful.

ACKNOWLEDGMENTS

Acknowledgements are many,
but lines are few
A gratitude so deep
that words would not do!

This is to acknowledge some of the people, for their help, effort and guidance.

First of all I would like to express my immense gratitude to Prof. Vinod Batura, Director, Institute of Management Studies, Ghaziabad, who besides being my Director has always inspired me in hours of distress and goaded me to achieve my long cherished goal.

I am also extremely grateful to my research guide Prof. S.C. Bagri, Prof. of Indian Institute of Travel and Tourism Management, Gwalior for sparing his valuable time in giving final shape to this text.

I wish to thank my parents and my wife Madhu who has inspired and stood with me always without any grudge.

I am indebted to Dr. G. Ravindran, Dy. Director Gen., Dept., for Tourism, for his expert guidance in completing this work.

A lot of credit also goes to Mr. Shekhar Ghose, Director, Head, Indian Airlines Ltd. who helped me in many ways to complete this work. A very special debt of gratitude is also due to Ms. Neena Rao, Head of Dept., Tourism, College of Vocational Studies, Delhi University, Dr. Sangeeta Jain, Dean, Academics. Institute of Management studies Ms. Timira

Shukla, Head of Dept., Business Management, Mrs. Ruchi Kapur Faculty member, Tourism Dept. Ms Anita Singh, Sr. Faculty B.B.A.; and many other colleagues at Institute of Management studies, Ghaziabad who also deserve my heartfelt thanks for their help at various stages of the prepration of this text.

I also express my gratitude to the editors, authors and compilers from whose works I culled some materials to be used in the present study. Besides, I am indebted to Mr. Sushil Kumar, who has enabled the present work to see the light of the day.

Last but not the least my students also deserve a pat for without their co-operation the work would not have attained it's persent form.

1

TOURISM: CONCEPTS AND FORMS

The word "Tourism" has its origin in a Latin word *Tornos* meaning a tool for describing a circle or turners wheel. This refers to a pin at the end of a stretched string used to describe a circle. From the same Latin word, terms like "roundtour" or a "packagetour" have emerged to give essence to tourism. However, this term has evolved from an ancient Greek word referring to a circular arrangement *(Webster New International Dictionary, The Oxford English Dictionary)*. But this etymology does not explain how "tour" came to mean particular types of trips among various trips where itineraries are circular. A possible explanation is given that "tour" meaning a trip evolved from "tower" meaning castle and referred as to leisurely relaxing and sight-seeing while going around the parapets of tower. It was only by early eighteenth century that tour in modern sense of a temporary trip away from home for some pleasurable purpose had become well established. Defoe's "A tour through the whole Island of Britain" provides the best example to testify this fact.

It was in late eighteenth century that one Scottish Professor, Adam Smith, a prominent writer on social and economic themes after completing grand tour of Europe along with a young aristocrat as a tutor, got the idea of suffixing "Ist" to 'tour' and thereby coined a new expression.

Adam Smith's unconscious idea had evolved in many subtle and shifting notions in modern popular consciousness there upon rendering specialized meaning. Emergence of research on this term has evolved the following three sets of meanings to this term (Neil Leipero).

(1) **Popular Notion:** It comprises of meanings used in everyday communication and consciousness.

(2) **Heuristic Definition:** It intends to clarify understanding, in which popular notions are refined into academic conepts. This definition has the following three components.

(a) distance covered in trips,

(b) duration, and

(c) purpose or motivation.

When we combine all these components it comes out to be,

"Tourist is defined as a visitor who visits in a region for atleast one night to less than a year, whose main purpose of visit is other than earning money against what he expenses within region visited."

With specific behaviouristic role of tourist, he is defined as: "a person travelling away from their normal residential region for a temporary period, staying away at least for one night but not permanently, to the extent that his behaviour involves a search for leisure experienced from interaction with features or environmental characteristics of the places he chooses to visit."

Jafári (1989) with an analytical anthropological approach suggested seven components in touristic process:

- Corporation (entangled forms and forces of everyday ordinary life).
- Emancipation (distancing oneself from the ordinary world).
- Animation (experiences in non-ordinary conditions).
- Repatriation (leaving the spatial, temporal and cultural zones of non-ordinary conditions).
- Incorporation (getting back into ordinary existence).
- Omission (ordinary current that flows in spite of tourist's absence from home).

(3) **Technical definition:** It applied for quantitative research for statistical uses as well as for legal applications such as in case of immigration administration.

The term "Tourist" coined consciously in 18th century, was also extended to "Tourism". Oxford English dictionary in 19th century defines tourism as "behaviour of tourists".

After this, the practiced and popular meaning of tourism taken was "theory and practice of touring, travelling for pleasure. A new dimension and popular notion was added by Webster as "the guidance or management of tourists as a business or governing function".

Third notion was added by Random House Dictionary when it explains tourism as "promotion of tourist travel, especially for commercial purposes".

However, the first accepted conceptual definition of tourism is given by Prof. Hunzikar and Krapt in 1940, when they defined tourism as:

"Sum of the phenomena and relationships arising from the travel and stay of non-resident, in so far as they do not lead to any permanent residence and aren't connected with any earning activity."

Other school of researchers have attempted to define tourism as an industry (Burkart 1981), as a market (Kaul 1985), as a system for which a holistic approach is required (Mill and Morrison 1985).

No other subject involve so many views about the same term as is "Tourism". This is primarily because of the fact that different researchers have tended to define tourism in term of their own discipline or personal perspective. For example, an economist defines tourism as an economic activity which needs an industry to exist; marketeers see tourism as a market where buyers (consumers) and suppliers meet; environmentalists focus upon environmental aspect and thereby talk about sustainable growth of tourism; holistic view holders (system theorists) treat this term as an integrated field of study; social scientists tend to see the human perspective in it. Therefore, there are as many definitions of tourism as are the uses of this term.

But these different perspectives give rise to three important dimensions in the form of: Tourism Market; Tourism Industry; and Tourism System.

TOURISM MARKETS

The range of tourism market is huge as well as distinct. In both cases market can be defined as identifiable collection of persons who are willing and able to buy, consume, use or experience some category of goods or services offered for exchange. Therefore, within broader of tourism markets, marketeers identify tourists whom they wish to cater.

In certain cases an individual tourist who may be a targeted market to a business organisation by the same individual tourist may be an incidental market to the departmental store of the city where this business organisation is located.

TOURISM INDUSTRY

Since tourism is an amalgamation of various sectors, thereby tourism industry assumes a complex structure comprising of a wide variety of business and other organisations, touching virtually all spheres of our economy. But some scholars like Kaiser, Helber (1978), and Kaul (1981) are in the opinion that there exists nothing of sort like Tourism industry, what really lies under that appellation is collection of separate industries with different kinds of links with tourists, for instance, with some perceived and aimed and with others incidental.

However, an alternative and balance approach is proposed by Leiper (1979). According to him, it is true that some of the identifiable sets of tourists are catered by segments like travel agents, tour operators, airlines and hotel in a non-fragmented manner but other components like restaurant and general stores, though do nothing in this manner, but they may be important and perhaps vital, to the region, as a tourist destination to provide complete satisfaction and to give value to tourist for the money they spend here. This alternative approach helps in understanding the notion that tourism tends to be partially industrialised and partially not.

TOURISM SYSTEM

Tourism, due to its being trans-disciplinary subject, has been accepted as a complex subject.

Fifty research scholars like Jafari (1989) and Leiper (1990) have adopted a comprehensive approach. A system can be defined as a set of elements interacting with one another; whereas in an open system elements and system as a whole are also interacting with the environment. This is truly applicable for the study in this field as that of Leiper (1990) who has suggested a model to study tourism system as a very open system with different elements.

ENVIRONMENTS: HUMAN, SOCIO-CULTURAL, PHYSICAL, ETC.

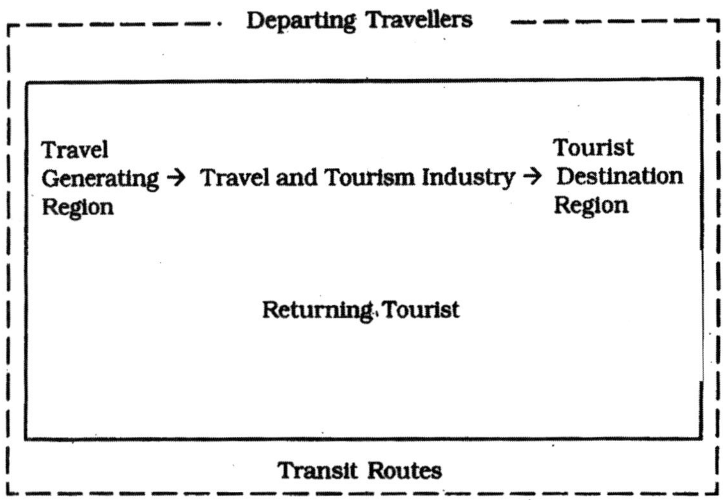

(a) Travel Generating Region—where travel begins and ends, i.e. one per trip, location where motivation forces are tried, resources to be spent on trip are accumulated and where pre-trip arrangements are made.

(b) Transit Routes—are paths along which a traveller must go to reach his destination.

(c) Touristic Destination—which may be one or more in one trip itself where normally these visitors are connected as tourist.

(d) Departing traveller—once they have enjoyed their holidays at the destination, travellers return to region of their origin.

(e) Travel and Tourism Industry—is most vital element of the model which comprises of organizations in the business of tourism located all along the itinerary of tourist. In the place of origin this may include travel agents and tour operators. Along transit routes it may include airlines, other modes of carriers as well as transit from a accommodation. At destination it includes accommodation, local tour operators restaurants, specialist retailers, and entertainment elements of tourist market.

2

INDIAN TOURISM: A QUANTITATIVE AND QUALITATIVE GLANCE

Tourism industry is a limitless industry with immense growth potential. It ranks number two, next to oil industry and third in India next to Gems and Garments. It has tremendous positive impacts on the economic and social aspects in developing countries. This is why every country is trying with each other to woo more domestic and international tourist and India is not an exception though her achievements are not astonishing. If we see the figures available we can see that tourists arrivals have increased manifold between 1960 and 1997, i.e., from a meagre figure of 16,829 to 23,74,094.

A detailed analysis of immense importance as available statistics reveal that during 1997, 19,73,647 foreign tourists were of other than the nationals of Pakistan and Bangladesh. This figure of foreign tourist arrival in India during this period constitute to be only 0.39 per cent of global tourist arrivals, which stood at 627 million during the year under consideration. Tourism industry earned foreign exchange to the tune of Rs. 11051.43 crore (US $ 3151.70 million). Total foreign exchange receipts of India during the same year were Rs. 11263.88 crore (US $ 3172.93 million). At the point of time when economies of several developing and developed nations are banking on the contribution of tourism industry. India is able to receive only 0.71 per cent of world tourism receipts. (US $ 443.8 million).

Foreign tourist arrivals in the country (including the nationals of Pakistan and Bangladesh) registered on of 3.8 per cent from 22,87,860 in 1996 to 23,74,094 in 1997. The arrival (excluding the nationals of Pakistan and Bangladesh) increased from 19,23, 695 in 1996 to 19,73,647 in 1997, registering a growth of about 2.6 per cent. A summary of international tourist traffic to India has been given in Table 2.1.

Table 2.1: Summary of International Tourist Traffic to India

Year	*Excluding Nationals of Pakistan and Bangladesh*		*Including Nationals of Pakistan and Bangladesh*	
	Number	*% change*	*Number*	*% change*
1981	853148	6.6	1279210	—
1982	860178	0.8	1288162	0.7
1983	884731	2.9	1304976	1.3
1984	835503	-5.6	1193952	-8.5
1985	836908	0.2	1259384	5.5
1986	1080050	29.1	1451076	15.2
1987	1163774	7.8	1484290	2.3
1988	1239992	6.5	1590661	7.2
1989	1337232	7.8	1736093	9.1
1990	1329950	-0.5	1707158	-1.7
1991	1236120	-7.1	1677508	-1.7
1992	1434737	16.1	1867651	11.3
1993	1442643	0.6	1764830	-5.5
1994	1562016	8.3	1886433	6.9
1995	1762228	12.8	2123683	12.6
1996	1923695	9.2	2287860	7.7
1997	1973647	2.6	2374094	3.8

Nationals of the United Kingdom with an arrival figure of 3,70,567 continued to occupy the first position in the tourist arrival to India during 1997 and accounted for 18.8 per cent of total tourist traffic as against an arrival figure of 3,60,686 (18.7 per cent) during 1996. The United Kingdom was followed by the U.S.A. with 2,44,239 tourist arrivals during 1997 accounting 12.4 per cent as compared to 2,28,829 (11.9 per cent) arrivals in 1996. The other major Countries whose relative shares in total tourist traffic were significant, include Sri Lanka (1,22,080 or 6.2 per cent), Germany (1,05,979 or 5.4 per cent) and Japan (99,729 or 5.1 per cent). Tourists from France, Canada, Malaysia, Italy and Singapore each constituted between 4.6 per cent and 2.6 per cent of total traffic during 1997. The top ten market generating tourist arrivals to India are summarised in Table 2.2.

Table 2.2 : Summary of Top Ten Markets Generating Arrivals to India

				% change		*% change*		
Nationality	*1995*	*1996*	*1997*	*1996/95*	*1997/96*	*1995*	*1996*	*1997*
U.K.	334827	360686	370567	7.7	2.7	19.0	18.7	18.8
U.S.A.	203343	228829	244239	12.5	6.7	11.5	11.9	12.4
Sri Lanka	114157	107351	122080	-6.0	13.5	6.5	5.6	6.2
Germany	89040	99853	105979	12.1	6.1	5.1	5.2	5.4
Japan	76042	99018	99729	30.2	0.7	4.3	5.1	5.0
France	82349	93325	91423	13.3	-2.0	4.7	4.9	4.6
Canada	63821	74031	78570	16.0	6.1	3.6	3.8	4.0
Malaysia	50039	53370	60401	6.7	13.2	2.8	2.8	3.1
Italy	53015	49910	53854	-5.9	7.9	3.0	2.6	2.7
Singapore	48632	47136	52004	-3.1	10.3	2.8	2.5	2.6
Others	646963	710186	694801	9.8	-2.2	36.7	36.9	35.2
Total	1762228	1923695	1973647	9.2	2.6	100	100	100

Analysis of tourist arrivals by the country of residence [19,67,696 tourists] shows that Western Europe accounted for bulk of traffic [8,32,153 or 42.2 per cent] followed by North America [3,23048 or 16.4 per cent]. South Asia [1,83,704 or 9.3 per cent], East Asia [1,46,784 or 7.4 per cent], South East Asia [1,46,459 or 7.4 per cent], West Asia [1,13,141 or 5.7 per cent], Africa [1,01,695 or 5.2 per cent], Australasia [65,172 or 3.3 per cent], East Europe [45020 or 2.3 per cent] and Central and South America [16,471 or 0.8 per cent].

Tourist arrivals were highest during the month of December while lowest number of arrivals were recorded in May. Over the years the tourist arrivals tend to establish increasing trends. However, the factors like global economic situation, political instability, tourism facilities, touristic image, etc., Introduce distorting trend and produce short-term variations. There are also seasonal variations, which produce identical patterns during corresponding months of successive years. A month-wise variations in tourist arrivals in India are given in Table 2.3.

Table 2.3 : Month-wise Variations in Tourist Arrivals in India.

Nationality	*Lean Months*	*Peak Months*	
U.K.	May	November	Oct.-Dec.
U.S.A.	April	December	Oct.-Dec.
Sri Lanka	June	September	Jun-Mar.
Germany	June	November	Oct.-Dec.
France	May	November	Oct.-Dec.
Japan	June	February	Jan.-Mar.
Italy	June	November	Oct.-Dec.
Canada	June	December	Oct.-Dec.
C.I.S.	April	September	Jan.-Mar.
Singapore	May	December	Oct.-Dec.
U.A.E.	April	July	Oct.-Dec.
Australia	June	December	Oct.-Dec.
Malaysia	April	December	Oct.-Dec.
Switzerland	June	November	Jan.-Mar.
Netherland	May	November	Oct.-Dec.

3

INCORPORATION OF BUSINESS IN INDIA

Business can be defined as an activity with which one occupies himself to earn his livelihood, for example, village farmer tills his land and sells his produce, shoemaker who makes shoes on order, various kinds of shops in the markets of urban and rural are as dealing in various articles and commodities in demand, restaurants and small time caterers who cater to the needs of different class of population, banks, insurance, companies, and transporters, etc., all are different types of businesses.

But to incorporate a business is an important question which comes up in that of organizing business operation. Whether incorporation of a business is done by an individual (sole proprietorship) or a group of individuals (partnership) to inquire legal title to assets for the purpose of controlling them and to enjoy the gains or profits from their possessions and use. From this point of view there are the following four possible alternatives to incorporate a business:

(a) Sole proprietorship
(b) Partnership
(c) Co-operative society
(d) Joint stock company.

Sole proprietorship is a form of business organization in which an individual introduces his own capital, uses his own skill and intelligence in the management of its affairs and is solely responsible for the results of its operations. This is the oldest and simplest form of organization. All that is required, is that the individual concerned should decide to carry on some particular business and find the required capital for which he may depend solely on his savings or else he may borrow a part of it from his friends or relatives.

There are no legal formalities to be gone through except those required for a particular type of business. For example, if one wants to start a restaurant or a guest house or a clinic, one has to obtain license / permission from concerned authorities like Municipal Corporations, Health Dept., or Medical Association, etc.

The law makes no distinction between firm and a proprietor. In other words, the owner's personal property is also liable to the liabilities of the firm, for example, if business prospers owners enjoy all the profits but if it doesnot do well, he bears the whole loss even by liquidating all his assets.

This form of organisation is least regulated. Restrictive laws are limited only to those kinds which are affecting all citizens equally. A sole proprietor doesnot have to comply with tax and labour laws like other establishments but there is no legal regulation of formation or dissolution for this form of organisation. Any person enjoying the capacity to contract can set up such an organisation.

PARTNERSHIP FORM OF ORGANISATION

When sole proprietorship organisation proved unsatisfactory to ever expanding businesses, which called for enhancement of risks involved. So more capital was called for, as well as for more managerial abilities which were beyond the capabilities of an individual as an owner/master of sole proprietor firm.

They give a kind of stimulation to associations among individuals. For example, if one person has money to invest and other has managerial abilities to look after the business and to make invested money multiply. These two individuals join hands for a common interest to earn profits, keeping in view the social interest of ordinary public.

The formation and management of partnership organisation is governed by provisions of *Indian Partnership Act, 1932*. Section 4 of this act defines the term 'partnership' as "The relation between persons who have agreed to share profits of a business carried on by all or any of them acting for all."

There are a number of conditions which should be satisfied to constitute partnership. For example,

- It can be executed when it is meant to do some kinds of business.
- There should be minimum of two persons. For maximum, Act doesn't say anything specifically but at one place it is stated that a partnership consisting of more than 20 persons for a general business and 10 partners for a banking business would be illegal. Thus, it can be regarded as upper limit of partners in partnership.
- There should be contractual relationship for a person who is minor and is not competent to enter into an agreement, If so he cannot be a partner.
- There should be profit motive and there must be an agreement to share the profit. Although in some cases manager may also be getting part of profit as his share but he connot be treated as a partner.
- There should be principal agent relationship the business must carried on by all or one or more acting on behalf of all the partners. Thus every partner is an agent of other partners of the firm.
- Partnership agreement provided unlimited liability to each partner in respect of firm's debts. For example, if firm assets are insufficient to cover dues of creditior, any partner's or assets of all partners can be attached or liquidated to meet the requirements.
- There should exist utmost good faith. Each partner should be transparent in his activities to other members.

FORMATION OF PARTNERSHIP

Though, rests on a contract among persons, but doesnot involve any special legal formalities or problems. In normal conditions a partnership deed is prepared stating terms and conditions of partnership and also mentioning rights, obligations and duties of partners.

Law doesnot make it necessary to register a partnership firm but registration of a firm becomes important to protect the mutual interests. This registration of partnership deed can be done by Registrar of Firms. So, it may be considered as a part of formation procedure for partnership organisation.

FINANCING OF PARTNERSHIP FIRM

Financing consists of capital contributed by all partners. This contribution maynot be in proportion to their profit sharing ratio. Even someone with exceptional managerial skills may be incorporated as a partner without any capital investment. In partnership firm initial finances may be augmented by borrowings which will depend upon strength of security of the firm's property and of private/personal property of partners.

Control in a partnership firm is shared by all partners. Major decisions can be made only with the consent of all members. In some cases where one or two partners remain more active and others play the sleeping role or domant partners, even in this case rights of these domant partners cannot be denied.

Management of a partnership firm is conferred by law to every partner. Pattern of management is chosen in line with an agreement among all members. Either one managing partner looks after the firm as chief executive or in another case management members allocate departments amongst themselves. For example, one may look after office, other factory, third one purchases fourth one sales, fifth one finance, sixth one liaisoning with different governmental and non-governmental departments. But in such a case decisions on major issues of objectives, policies are made by all-together.

Duration of such an agreement expires when any of the partners dies, retires, or becomes insolvent. But if other members decide to continue business under the same name, style, firm it wouldnot be dissolved and will continue the business.

Indian Partnership Act gives certain circumstances when firm will be disolved. For example, either when the business becomes illegal or when all the partners become insolvent. In other cases, court of law is empowered to order dissolution of firm. Partnership agreement is written down in the form of partnership deed wherein rights and duties of partners are detailed.

Although Partnership Act lay down certain duties and right of partners in an ideal partnership situation but it comes into force only when there is no written agreement. It is because of this reason that before any partnership is formed, all mutual rights, power, and obligation should be discussed and incorporated in a written agreement. The following points are normally covered in a partnership deed:

- Name of business.
- Place where it will be carried on.
- Duties, rights and obligation of partners.
- Whether loans will be acceptable from partner and at what rate of interest.
- The amount to be allowed as private drawings for each partner and interest to be charged on such drawings.
- The method by which a partner may retire and arrangement for payment dues of a retired or a deceased partner.
- Method of valuation of good-will of retiring or deceased partner.
- Whether expulsion of partner is possible? If so, the procedure.
- The circumstances/conditions for dissolution of deed and in case of dissolution, who will be custodian of books, and
- Arbitration in case of disputes among partners.

REGISTRATION OF A FIRM

Indian Partnership Act does not make it compulsory for firms to get themselves registered with Registrar of Firms. But because of certain benefits like in area of income tax there is a growing tendency of registering partnership firms. If firm is not registered, tax will be charged on the whole of its income but if it is registered income tax authorities will have to divide the profits among partners and charge tax on the income of partners individually. Moreover, it is only registration of a firm which can file suits and enforce rights against third parties if such rights arise out of contract.

For registration, application is sent on a prescribed form along with the fees which vary from state to state. But registration of a firm must be done within six months from the date of formation of a partnership.

JOINT STOCK COMPANY

When the needs of modern industry and commerce cannot be met by sole proprietorship or partnership firm of organisations, a new alternative was looked for. As a result concept of joint stock company appeared to facilitate the full utilisation fo technical and other innovations brought about by the industrial revolution.

A company can be defined as "an artificial person recognised by law, with a distinctive name, common seal, a common capital comprising of transferable shares of fixed value carrying limited liability and having a perpetual succession."

Formation of a company can be divided into the following two stages:

(i) Promotion (ii) Incorporation.

Promotion is a process of exploration, investigation and organisation of necessary resources with the objective of initiating business under corporate ownership.

Incorporation is the legal process through which the separate corporate entity of a company is given recognition by law. To secure incorporation, promoters prepare and submit the following documents to the Registrar of Joint Stock Companies:

- Memorandum of Association, i.e., the charter of company laying down the objective and capital of the company.
- The Articles of Association, i.e., rules and bye-laws governing the internal, working of the company.
- Written consents of persons who have agreed to serve as directors of the company.
- Notice of registered office of the company (which may even be filed after 28 days of registration).
- Statutory declaration by the Secretary.
- Proposed company or a solicitor to the effect that all provisions regarding incorporation have been compiled with.

VARIOUS KINDS OF COMPANIES

Classification of companies is based upon different point of views, viz.

1. From point of view of incorporation
2. From point of view of nationality
3. From point of view of liability
4. From point of view of public interest.

First point of view includes companies to be incorporated:

- Under a special charter — this kind of chartered companies do not exist at present because now there is no monarchy.
- Under a special Act of parliament — this is done in special cares where conduct of company is required to be regulated for some specific purposes. Best example of such companies is like LIC, IFCI, etc.
- Under the provisions of Companies Act, 1956— which specifically details the procedure by which a company can be brought into existence. Up till now largest number of companies are incorporated under this category.

Second point of view includes companies like :

- National companies which operate whithin the boundaries of the country.
- Multi-national companies, operating across the world.

Third point of view includes companies with :

Limited liability in the form of guarantees by the members in order to pay the creditors of the company. This additional amount of share is laid down in Memorandum Article of Association. This type of company is normally formed in case of its being non-profit making in nature. Best available example is that of Chamber of commerce.

- Unlimited liability of members as in the case of sole proprietorship or partnership wherein members can be called upon to pay creditors even from their private estates to satisfy them.

- Limited liability by shares being held by members. In other words if member 'A' holds 10,000 shares of Rs. 300/- each of which he has already paid Rs. 200/- each. So he can be called upon to pay only Rs. 100/- per share. Most of companies formed today are of this nature.

Fourth point of view includes companies like:

- Private Company
- Public Company
- Government Company.

Table 3.1 : Basic Distinctions Between Private and Public Companies

Basic distinctions	*Public Company*	*Private Company*
1. No. of members	Minimum 7, maximum no limit	minimum two, maximum 50 (excluding past and present employee shareholders)
2. Invitation for public subscription	Invitation to public is done	No public offer either for shares or debentures
3. Transfer of shares.	Transfer of shares is allowed subject to the procedurs and conditions laid down in its article.	Transfer of shares is restricted.

Government company is called so under section 617 of the Companies Act 1956, when at 51 per cent of its share capital is held by the Central Government, or a State Government or jointly by Centre with any numer of State Governments.

FORMS OF ORGANISATIONS IN TRAVEL TRADE

In Travel Trade field, a travel agency plays the most important role to bring consumer close to producer. Travel agents assist individual or groups who wish to undertake travel in planning, costing and finalishing their itineraries. That is why at times his job is compared with that of an architect or a lawyer who possesses a great deal of specialised technical knowledge along with training and ability to consult correct references and sources for the arrangement of client's requirements.

The forms of organisation in travel trade remain the same, viz.,

(i) Proprietorship
(ii) Partnership
(iii) Corporate.

Table 3.2 : The Summary of Differences Amongst Three Forms of Organisation Can be Listed As

Proprietorship	*Partnership*	*Corporate*
1. One owner	Two or more owners	Min. 2 in private com. min 7 in public com.
2. Owner personally liable	Partners equally liable	Libality is limited to the face value of shareholding
3. Total income is proprietor's income	Each partner is taxed on his/her share of profit	Profits distributed to shareholders as dividend
4. Self-employment individual slab rates are applicable since status is that of an individual	All income status is that of a firm's personal income	Shareholders elect board of Directors status is that of a company
5. Tax to be paid by proprietors.	Paid by firm and partner.	Paid only by company.

Organization of a small agency

Owner Mgr.

- Sales
  - Sales agents
- Finance and accounting
  - Finance and accounting specialist

Organization of a medium sized agency

Owners/President

General Mgr.

- Sales
  - Supervisors, Agents and trainers
- Finance and accounting
  - Finance and accounting specialist
- Outside sales
  - Supervisors, finance and Accounting executives

Organization of large size agency

President/Chairman

Executive Vice-President

- Vice-President operation
  - Sales
  - Finance and accounting
  - Agent supervisors, commercial sales, Leisure sales
- Vice-President marketing
  - Advertising Director,
    - Sales manager finance and accounting specialist, executive

4

SOCIAL RESPONSIBILITY AND BUSINESS ETHICS IN TOURISM

The terms social responsibility, business ethics and management ethics appear frequently in popular and technical literature. Everyday, newspapers report business activities considered by some people to be socially irresponsible and unethical. Yet others think such actions are quite proper, both from a social and ethical standpoints.

Social problems are dysfunctions of society and at least potentially-degenerative diseases of the body politics. But, for business management they represent challenges. They are major sources of opportunity. It is the function of business to satisfy a social need and at the same time serve their institution, by making resolution of a social problem into a business opportunity.

DEFINITION AND MEANING

Social responsibility is implied, enforced as felt obligation of managers, acting in their official capacity, to serve or protect the interest of groups other than themselves.

The meaning of social responsibility can be classified into the following three general categories as:

(i) Social obligation

(ii) Social reaction

(iii) Social responsiveness.

Social Responsibility as Social Obligation

This view holds that a corporation engages in socially responsible behaviours when it pursues profit only within the constraints of law. Because, society supports business by allowing it to exist, business is obligated to repay society by making profits. Thus, legal behaviours in pursuit of profit is socially responsible behaviour, and any behaviour that is illegal as not in pursuit of profit, is socially irresponsible.

According to economist Milton Friedman, "There is one and only one social responsibility of business to use its resources and engage in activities designed to increase its profit as long as it stays within the rules of the game, which is to say, engages in open and free competition without deception as fraud."

The proponents of social responsibility as social obligation offer the following primary arguments in support of their view:

(1) Businesses are accountable to their shareholders, the owners of the corporation.

(2) Socially responsible activities such as social improvement programmes should be determined by law, by public policy and by the actions and contributions of private individuals.

(3) If management allocates profits to social improvment activities, it is abusing its authority.

(4) These actions by management may work to the disadvantage of society.

Although, many people disagree with this meaning, social responsibility can refer to behaviours directed exclusively (but legally) towards the pursuit of profit. A manager can depend on some justification, stating that he has discharged his obligation to society by creating goods and services in exchanges for profit within the limits defined by law.

Social Responsibility as Social Reaction

A second meaning of social responsibility is behaviour that is in reaction to "currently prevailing social norms, values and performance expectations." This emphasises that society is entitled to more than the mere provisions of goods and services. At minimum, business must be accountable for the ecological, environmental and social costs incurred by its actions. At maximum, business must react and contribute to solving society's problems.

According to Keith Davis, "A firm is not being socially responsible if it merely complies with the minimum requirements of the law. Social responsibility goes one step further. It is a firms' acceptance of social obligation beyond the requirements of the law." A firm that accepts social obligation only in reaction to pressure group, consumer's boycotts, as adverse publicity, it not socially responsible factor.

Social Responsibility as Social Responsiveness

According to this view, socially responsible behaviours are anticipatory and preventive, rather than reactive and restorative. The characteristics of socially responsive behaviours include taking stands on public issues, accounting willingly for actions to any group, anticipating furture needs of society and moving towards satisfying them, and communicating with the government about existing and anticipated socially desirable legislation.

The social responsiveness is the broadest meaning of social responsibility. It places managers and their organisations in a position for removed from the traditional one of singular concern with economic means and ends. This view rests on the following two premises:

(i) Corporations should be involved in preventing as well as solving social problems.

(ii) Corporations are perhaps the most effective problem solving organisation in a capitalist society.

Table 4.1 A Continuum of Social Responsibility

	Primary Emphasis
Socially obligated behaviours	The organisations' legal and economic responsibility.
Socially reactive behaviour	The organisations' economic, legal and social responsibilities.
Social responsive behaviour	The organisations' economic, legal social and citizenship responsibilities.
Social obligation	Reflects only the firms' economic and legal responsibilities.
Social reaction	Behaviour demanded by groups with a direct stake in the organisations' actions.
Social responsiveness	Reflects anticipatory, proactive and preventive expectations.

As mentioned before, one aspect of social responsibility is felt obligation of managers but obligations differ from individual to individual and from organisation to organisation.

Obligations to Individuals

Individuals often find healthy outlets for their energies through joining organisations. To some degree, most of society still subscribe to the notion that the customer is king. To the extent that individuals expectations are acknowledged as responsibilities by the organisation, they become part of the social contract.

Obligation to Other Organisations

Managers must be concerned with relationships involving with other organisations—both organisations that are like their own, such as competitors and very different ones.

Obligations to Government

Government is an important party to the social contract for every kind of organisation. Under the auspices of government, companies have a license to business, along with patent rights, trade-marks and so forth.

Obligations to Society in General

The traditional view of business responsibility has been that business should produce and distribute goods and services in return for a profit. Businesses have performed this function effectively, handshaking with the US, one of the highest overall standards of living in the world. Some goals of the businesses expected to help society are as follow:

(i) Elimination of poverty.

(ii) Provision of quality health care.

(iii) Preservation of environment by reduction in the level of pollution.

(iv) Provision of a sufficient numbers of jobs and paves opportunities for all members of the society.

(v) Improvement in the quality of working life of empolyees.

(vi) Provision of safe, liable communications with good housing and efficient transportation.

IMPLICATIONS

Thus, by understanding the meanings of social responsibility, we recognise that it changes with time and circumstances. To understand the implications of social responsibility and ethics, the whole subject can be divided into two parts:

(1) Society's expectations for corporate and managerial behaviours.

(2) Changing business ethics.

CHANGING VALUES AND SOCIAL RESPONSIBILITY

Numerous associations of respected business leaders, including the American Management Association and the Committee for Economic Development, have encouraged corporations and managers to become involved in socially responsible activities. In a climate of changing social values, these groups have stressed such programmes as the following:

(i) Better jobs and promotion opportunities for minorities and women.
(ii) Financial support for education.
(iii) Financial and managerial help aimed at improving health and medical care.
(iv) A safe working environment.
(v) Leadership and financial support for urban renewal.
(vi) Reduction of environmental pollution.

A DOWN TO EARTH APPROACH

Some companies have started programmes of community involvement not only for their won employees and managers but also for the whole society. It is important that top-level managers of reputed organisations set the example. Some examples of social responsibility are as follows :

(1) Escorts Heart Research Centre of Escorts Group is completely a socially committed organisation. It gets funds from the commercial activities of all the business organisations of Escorts Group. Thus, it is working for a good cause of the society and for the nation as a whole.

(2) TATA Cancer Research Centre of TATA Group is also working for the development of medical science of India and in turn helping the society. It also gets funds from business activities of TATA Group of Companies.

(3) Environmentally conscious Iron Exchange Enviro Farms Ltd., has decided to employ only bio-intensive farming as chemical free farming. This will greatly help in growing fruits in the four locations in Maharashtra, Tamil Nadu and Andhra Pradesh.

CRITICAL APPROACH

Thus, we see that many companies have understood their responsibility towards the society and are working in that direction. But still there are some which are playing a negative role in the improvement of society. A very important field where industries have not understood their responsibility is of pollution. In spite of governments' repeated reminders and Supreme Court's warnings to install effluent treatment plants to reduce pollution, industries were not paying any attention to them. As a result, nearly 500 of the total 869 tanneries had been shut down in April, 1996, in Tamil Nadu. And recently Supreme Court ordered the closure of over 100 refineries and other industries in Uttar Pradesh. But agian, it is the society which has to bear the consequences. When these industries are operating without ETPs, they are creating pollution and when they have been shut down, society has to bear the price hikes of the goods manufactured by these industries.

BUSINESS ETHICS

Business ethics is the application of ethical principles to business relationships and activities. It is concerned with truth and justice and has a variety of aspects such as expectations of society, fair competition, advertising, public relations, consumer autonomy and corporate behaviours in the home country as well as abroad.

Business ethics has become a topic of concern because businesses are reliazing that ethical misconduct by management can be extremely costly affair for the company and the society as a whole. At the same time, the dynamics of ethics in management, decision making is an often complex phenomenon. Everyday, managers face ethical problems that have no easy, solutions. What, for example, is a 'fair' profit? What is a 'just' price for a product? How 'honest' should a company be with the press? Thus, deciding what is ethical is often difficult. One upcoming ethical controversy in the U.S. business is the projected future use of 'genetic testing' by employees.

Testing proponents assert that employees should be tested in businesses where they are exposed to chemicals and other potential hazards in the workplace. This would reduce chances of running the high risk of illness and lower the company's health costs.

However, many observers oppose genetic screening. They argue that the tests are an invasion of privacy and it would cause the denial of employment and dismissals.

Thus, we see how genetic testing is ethical for some and unethical for others. Some view it as a step in the direction of welfare and development of workers while others consider it unjust and unfair and an invasion onto one's personal life.

ETHICAL THEORIES

In organisations, managers compete for information, influence and resources. The potential for conflicts in selecting the ends as well as the means to the ends is easy to understand, and the question of what criteria should guide ethical behaviours become acute.

The following three basic types of moral theories in the field of normative ethics have been developed:

(1) Utilitarian Theory: It suggests that plans and actions should be evaluated by their consequences. The underlying idea is that plans and actions should produce the greatest good for the maximum number of people.

(2) Rights Theory: It holds that all people have basic rights, such as the right to freedom of speech, conscience, due process and so on.

(3) Theory of Justice: It demands that decision makers be guided by fairness and equity as well as impartiality.

INSTITUTIONALISING ETHICS

Managers and especially top managers do have a responsibility to create an organisational environment that fosters ethical decision making by institutionalising ethics. By this we mean, applying and integrating theoretical concepts into daily action. Theodore Purcell and James Webes suggest that this can be accomplished in by the following three ways:

(i) Company policy as a code of ethics.

(ii) A formally appointed ethics committee, and

(iii) The teaching of ethics in management development programmes. Management Development Programmes dealing with ethical issues are very seldom used, although companies such as Allied Chemical, Internet Business Machines and General Electric have instituted such programmes.

FACTORS THAT RAISE ETHICAL STANDARDS

The two factors that raise ethical standards according to the respondents are as follow:

(i) Public disclosure and publicity;

(ii) The increased concern of a well-informed public.

To make ethical codes effective, provisions must be made for their enforcement. Unethical managers should be held responsible for their actions. This means that privileges and benefits have to be withdrawn and sanctions have to be applied.

Another factor that could raise ethical standards is the teaching of ethics and values in business and other schools and unversities. The Harvard Business School has come under severe criticism by its own president, Derek Bok for the lack of teaching of human values.

CRITICAL ANALYSIS

Thus, we see that many ethical theories have been evolved and a large numbers of ethical codes have been formulated, but for what reason? Are these theories being evolved and conducts being formulated just to be taught in business schools and to be written in bold letters on the notice boards of organisations? Because, in our daily life, we hardly come across any ethical conduct followed by management of any organisation. No doubt, business organisations are there to make profits and to judge. What is ethical or unethical is a million dollar question but in broad terms, when it comes to the question of society, the management of organisations can make ethical decisions sacrificing a small amount of their profits.

The need for improvement of ethical behaviour has become evident by way of some widely publicised cases. Take for example, the adulteration of food products. It may be ethical in the eyes of those who do it as it helps them to make some profits but it is totally unethical from society's point of view.

Some experts believe businesses are accepting their social responsibilities and that managers are becoming more ethical. According to social theorist Archie. B. Croll, however, the demands made on business and the expectations of what is considered proper conduct have risen faster than the ability of business to raise its standards. Caroll suggests that ethical level of "actual business practices" will continue to rise but not as quickly as "society's expectations of business." In order to meet the expectations of society, future managers will need to strive to be more ethical and socially responsible.

In summary, managers operate in a complex environment. They are being affected and to some extent influenced by the economic, technological, social, political, legal and ethical environment. The concept of social, political, legal and ethical environment. The concept of social responsibility is still evolving. To determine the appropriate relationship between various organisations and society, is not an easy task. Nevertheless, many corporations and organisations are making serious efforts to establish an environment beneficial to individuals, business and society.

PRINCIPLES OF BUSINESS ETHICS IN TOURISM

In travel trade work habits and attitudes are highly influential in a close-working environment such as that of a travel agency. If the majority of the employees are basically honest, the largest part of ethic battle is already won or otherwise a travel agency to ensure ethical conduct, must create an environment that is conducive to such conduct.

Results of one survey conducted to identify important ethical issues confronting the hospitality and tourism industry-results are as follow:

Table 4.2

Ranks	*Issues*	*Responses Rate (%)*
1.	Solid waste disposal	37
2.	Conditions of employment	32
3.	Non-specific discrimination	29
4.	Race	27
5.	Employee theft	26
6.	Sex discrimination	24
7.	False advertising	15
8.	Sexual harassment	11
9.	Vendors honesty	11
10.	Sanitation violation	10
11.	AIDS discrimination	09

Government's Legal Moral Regulations can be rejected as means of Business moralisation. It was in 1983, that Christopher Stone showed that laws are inadequate to keep corporations within socially desirable bounds. Because laws are the results of a slow, reactive process and law-makers generally act after the problem becomes a public issue.

In same year Norman Bowie provided a legal criticism of legal regulation by giving conditions that any good legal system must fulfil:

(1) While Government Regulations must be general in practice they tend to be developed incrimentally.

(2) Government Regulations can be hidden and changed spontaneously.

(3) Government Regulations threaten firms with *ex-post facto* punishment such as in case of environmental damages when firm had no way of knowing that some of its' activities were in fact causing environmental damage.

(4) Regulations shallnot be expensive, so that non-productive legal staff is not necessary.

(5) Contradictory regulations shallnot exit.

- Consider the client's interest first in all transactions. Be receptive for counsel from vendors and colleagues.
- Recommend and purchase travel products without prejudice, seeking to obtain the maximum value for every client.
- Seek constantly to expend your knowledge of travel products, prices, and options.
- Adhere to and work for honesty and truthfulness in recommending, purchasing, and selling, and if necessary, place the client's interest above those of agency.
- Extend promptness and courtesy in all dealings with the public and with vendors.
- Counsel and assist other travel agents in performing of their duties, whenever the occasion permits.
- Co-operate with all organisations and individuals engaged in activities designed to enhance the professional standing of the travel industry.
- The following enlists the American Society of Travel Agents' principles of professional conducts and ethics.

PRINCIPLES OF PROFESSIONAL CONDUCT AND ETHICS—IDEAL EXAMPLE OF ASTA MEMBERS

Preamble

We live in a world where travel has become both increasingly important and complex in its variety of modes and choices. Travellers are faced with a myriad of alternatives as to transportation, accommodations, and other travel services. Travellers must depend on travel agencies and other industries has for honesty and competent guidence. Similarly, carriers, hotels, and other suppliers must provide to the traveller the product as it was advertised. All ASTA members pledge themselves to observe this spirit in all their activities and to conduct their business in accordance with the following principles of professional conduct and ethics:

Responsibilities of All Members

1. All ASTA members shall be factual and accurate when providing information about their services and the services of any firm to which they represent. They will not use misleading or deceptive practices which could be damaging to the consumer or the travel industry.
2. All ASTA members shall remit any undisputed funds under their control within the specified time limt. Reasons for any delay in providing funds will be communicated to the claimanant in a timely manner.
3. All ASTA members will provide complete details about terms and conditions of any travel service, including, but not limited to, cancellation and service free policies, prior to non-refundable payment being accepted for the booking.
4. All ASTA members will not make use of improperly obtained client lists or other confidential data obtained from agency to which they rendered their service earlier.
5. All ASTA members will co-operate with any inquiry conducted by ASTA to referred in writing to ASTA's Consumer Affairs Department.
6. All ASTA members shall consider every transaction for a client as a confidential matter and not disclose any information without permission of the client, unless such disclosure is required by law.
7. ASTA members operating tours shall provide all components as specified in their brochure or written confirmation, or provide alternate services of equal or greater value, or appropriate compensation.
8. ASTA members operating tours shall promptly advise the agent or client who reserved the space, of any change in itinerary, services, features and/ or price. If substantial changes are made that are within the control of the operator, the client shall be offered the opportunity to cancel without penalty.

9. ASTA members shall stand behind any programme in which their names and/or logo are used with their permission for advertising or promoting travel.
10. ASTA members will falsely not represent a person's affiliation with their firm.

Adherence to the principles of professional conduct and ethics signifies competence, fair dealing, and high integrity. Failure to adhere to these principles may subject a member to disciplinary action, as set forth in ASTA's by laws.

This is unethical on part of agents when they misrepresent friends/relatives as an employee of agency for purpose of obtaining discounting travel.

BIBLIOGRAPHY

1. Ivaneevich "Management"
2. R. Wayne Mondy, Arthur Sharplin. Shane R. Premeaux "Management-Concepts, Practices and Skills"
3. Peter. F. Drucker "Management-Tasks, Responsibilities and Practices."
4. Horold Koontz and Heinz Weihrich "Management"
5. Heinz Weihrich Harold Koontz "Management- A Global Perspective"
6. Business India July 29 - Aug 11 - 1996.
7. Business India May, 1996

5

NEED FOR TOURISM LAWS AND REGULATIONS

Tourism as a product is made up of dreams, passion and challenges of delivering dreams. Hence as we are delivering services which are intangible, perishable and also uncontrollable in nature. There comes the need for business laws, i.e., a set of rules and regulations to govern tourism business. Their existence becomes all the more imperative because tourism industry is interdisciplinary and transdiciplinary in its approach, since this industry in India, is all set to expand more and more. Expansion is directed and governed not only by national organisations but also by multinational enterprises. There are chances of arising legal conflicts in relation to investment and management of tourism enterprises.

Indian constitution provides no special provisions and treatments for tourism industry. So at present we have to pick up and assemble laws from different subjects and to apply them to specific situations arising in the field of travel and tourism.

- A tourism product is an amalgamation of different components like transportation, accommodation, locale, entertainment and experience, which qualifies the satisfaction level of tourists. As rightly put by Middleton, one of leading tourism marketing analyst that in practice, ability to engineer intangible service product on paper and to promise satisfaction in brochure and in advertising often exceeds a destination or producers, ability to deliver the satisfaction at the time of consumption. Because the tourism products are the mere concepts at the time of purchase. Tourist's experiences are more extensive, more complex and more difficult to regulate than physical components themselves. Difficulties in measuring tourist's experiences are due to the facts that:

- Tourist's experience depends upon the expectations. In this market no two individuals can perceive the things alike because we are selling dreams. When one embarks on a journey, individuals have a set of expectation, when these expectations donot turn into reality, this leads to dissatisfaction and comes up the need of laws to settle the issue.
- There exists attitude problems. Different people have different kinds of attitudes. Attitudes of provider/supplier of services depend upon situations as well as the background and mood. This results in service gap (λδ). Therefore, in such a case where formulating of intangible product is concerned, and formulation of a code of conduct is almost impossible, cases can be dealt with established laws and procedures than on personal judgments.
- Tourism product is intangible and perishable. Since package tours are merely ideas at the time of purchase, either on brochures or on videotapes. So, traditional common law's remedies for breach of contract, negiligence or misrepresentation are grossly insufficient for tourism products because producers themselves are not aware of conditions that will prevail at the time of delivery of tourist's experiences.
- Tourism product is of consumable nature. Once a package is bought out from a travel agent it has to be consumed, if finds unsatisfied, nothing is left to return, or to repair. If person A and B had waited whole year for vacation to come, when it came, they set out on their holiday, but when they reached at

the destination, it was found nothing existed, what was all promised by travel agent. Here the main focus is on time value, which is different for different category of society, for which no compensation is feasible.

- It is international in nature. So, legal problem arises when two or more then two states are involved in a contract. It is very difficult to take guarantee of tour operator for conditions at the destination, there are all the chances of breach of any promise in such a contract.
- Process of manufacturing, delivery of tourism product is subject uncontrollable variables or unforeseen factors which play a crucial role in widening the gap between expectation and satisfaction level. There may come up unalterable situations, like if it starts raining during a trip, of a political upheavel or military coup takes place at the destination or may be the case as is mentioned in the case of the following:

A example of case Related to sea transport :-

Baltic Shipping Co. Vs Dhillon the 'Mikhail Lermontov' (1993). 176 CLR 344

Mrs. Dhillon was a passenger on a 14-day pleasure cruise aboard the Mikhail Lermontov which struck a shoal off New Zealand and sank on the tenth day. Baltic Shipping refunded A $ 788 of the A $ 2,205 fare and arranged alternative transportation back to Sydney and subsequently procured her executive of a full release in exchange for an *ex-gratia* payment of A $ 4,786. Mrs. Dhillon brought proceedings in her own name and on behalf of 122 other passengers claiming damages for personal injuries, loss of personal belongings, disappointment and return of the balance of the fare. At the trial she succeeded on all claims and was awarded a further $ 51,396 made up as follows :

• Restitution of balance of fare	1417
• Loss of items of personal property	4265
• Compensation for disappointment at the loss of enjoyment	5000
• Damages for personal injuries (including emotional trauma)	35000
• Interest	10500
• Less paid	4746
• Total	A $ 51.396

On appeal by the shipping company to the New South Wales Court of Appeal, the majority held *inter alia* that:

- The contract of carriage was made when the ticket was issued and the limitation clauses contained in the ticket did not form part of the contract as the defendant did not do all that was necessary to draw them to her attention.
- The release was void for unconscienability under the Contract Review Act, 1980 (NSw) having regard for the insufficiency of sum paid, inequality of bargaining power and diminished capacity of the plaintiff. (See now s 51 AB Trade Practices Act, 1974 (Cth).
- The contract of carriage was an entire contract and there had been a total failure of consideration thereby entitling the plaintiff to restitution of the full fare.
- The plaintiff was entitled to compensation for disappointment and distress at the loss of the entertainment and facilities for enjoyment which the defendant had promised.

On appeal by the shipping company to the High Court of Australia special leave to appeal on the first two questions was rescinded and the appeal proceeded on the third and fourth grounds. The full bunch of the High Court ultimately held unanimously that:

- re 3: The plaintiff was not entitled to restitution of the fare as: (i) the contract of carriage was not and entire contract; (ii) there had not been a total failure of consideration as the plaintiff and derived the benefit of the first nine days of crusing; and (iii) restitution could not be recovered in addition to compensation for disappointment.
- re 4: The plaintiff was entitled to compensation for disappointment. Each judge cited with approval the following passage from Bingham LJ in Watts Vs Morrow (1991) 1 WLR at 1445:

Where the very object of a contract is to provide pleasure, relaxation, peace of mind or freedom from molestation, damages will be awarded if the fruit of the contract is not provided or if the contrary result is procured instead.

6

REGULATORY LAWS FOR TOURISM BUSINESS IN INDIA

Throughout the world, the formation of regulatory laws is the task performed by the respective governments applicable in respective countries. Diverse activities are controlled systematically as activities of tourism business are done.

Regulations are required not only for checking the faulty procedures and bringing them to correct position but also to perform an important task of setting up a comprehensive and logical system to encourage the activities by giving incentives or to curb the activity by enforcing restriction in the interest of general public.

Tourism Sector can be Illustrated Through A Diagram

Tourism Sector

Dynamic activities;	Static activities;
Travel agencies	Hotels
Tour operators	Catering agencies
Carriers	Organisations

PART-A : REGULATIONS FOR TRAVEL AGENCIES IN INDIA

Not before 1963, importance of regulatory law for travel agencies and tour operation was realised. It was for the first time in United Nation's Conference on International Travel and Tourism at Rome, experts discussed at length on this topic and came to the conclusion that regulations and legislations should be internationally uniform. Main lines of discussions focussed on recognition of travel agents to upkeep the working environment of tourism business

REGULATIONS FOR SETTING UP A TRAVEL AGENCY

Procedure for setting up of a Travel Agency in India is similar to that of setting up of any business organisation. The company must be registered with Registrar of Companies in accordance with Indian Companies Act, 1950. Once the iniliable stage is crossed over now the agency will need various recognitions in form of approvals from authorities like Department of Tourism, International Air Transport Association, Universal Federation of Travel Agents Association to assure their subscribers/patrons about quality of their services.

REGULATIONS FOR APPROVAL FROM DEPARTMENT OF TOURISM

1. The firm in consideration must have at least one year's experience of handling tourist traffic.
2. The firm must keep full-time staff members who would be in a position to provide up-date information on customs and currency regulations along with issuing air and rail tickets.
3. Firms have to furnish yearly statement about volume of tourist traffic handled and other activities rendered by the agency.
4. The applicant agency must have minimum paid up capital of rupees 1 lakh.
5. Applicant for grant of recognition by Department of Tourism must also have the following:
   (a) Approval of I.A.T.A.
   (b) Approval of M.E.A. (Ministry of External Affairs)_ to handle travel documents like visas, etc., and to interact with passport offices.

(c) Reserve Bank of India's approval to book foreign passenger.

(d) Registration under local Shops and Establishment Act.

6. The recognition may or may not be extended to whole country.
7. For sale of railway tickets, Railway Board's approval is to be furnished.
8. The decision of Department in this matter would be final.

With the objective of encouraging more and more travel agents and tour operators to get themselves recognised and registered with D.O.T., (Department of Tourism), latter offers number of incentives. For example, in the Export Policy of Government of India announced in 1985, effective till 1988, specifically mentioned incentives to be rendered to recognised travel agents and tour operators like any travel agent may be granted import license for a value of up to 2.5 per cent of net foreign exchange earned by them in preceding year on account of rendering services to guests up to a maximum limit of Rs. 7.5 Lakhs for import of equipments and other professional requirements for tourist use. Travel agent is only required to furnish a bank certificate stating net foreign exchange earned during the period under consideration.

Another important incentive in the same period is in form of granting of permission by R.B.I. to spend foreign currency for tourist promotion and travel abroad if the particular case is recommended by Director General, D.O.T., New Delhii.

REGULATIONS FOR RECOGNITION OF IATA

International Air Transport Association (IATA) is the organisation of scheduled airlines. It's members (135 airlines) carry the bulk of world's scheduled air traffic under the flags of over 100 nations. For the airlines, IATA provides machinery for findings joint solution and problems beyond the resources of any single company. It has become the means by which they knit their individual network into a worldwide public service system, despite differences in languages, currencies, laws and measurements.

Since no airline can afford to set up sales offices in every city of the world, so the airline industry has traditionally been relied on sales agents as intermediaries in the market place. Over the years IATA has built up a working relationship with both UFTAA (Universal Federation of Travel Agents Association) and FIATA (Federation of Freight Forwarders Associations). As the commercial environment has evolved so has the Agency Programme. Today there are over 70,000 passenger agencies location listed in IATA programme worldwidely and about 4300 for cargo. IATA has divided the world into ,the following three broad geographical regimes referred to as Conference Areas.

Conference Area I: It includes all of North and South American continents, Central America, Greenland, Denmark, the West Indies, Island of Caribbean Sea, Hawaiian Islands.

Conference Area II : It includes Europe, the Middle East, Africa, Ascension Island, and Western Asia, including Iran.

Conference Area III: It includes Far East, Australia, Newzealand, and Pacific Islands (except Hawaii, Midway and Palmyra).

IATA has simplified procedures for accredition and has developed conditions tailored to meet local requirements. Agency's investigation agency consists of IATA members located and operating out of a country where applicant agency is located. These requirements are :

Financial: IATA requires a bond or an irrevocable letters of credit. The bond is a performance or a financial guarantee type of bond. The irrevocable letter of credit is a guarantee of payment issued by a Federally insured lending institution. The minimum amount required of IATA bond or irrevocable letter of credit is $ 20,000 or equivalent. An IATA bond is obtained through a surety of a bonding company, while an irrevocable letter of credit is obtained through a bank. An attorney can provide advice concerning these procedures, and a bank may also provide advice with respect to irrevocable letter of credit.

Personnel: IATA requires that location shall have at least one trained person who is a full-time employee and on payroll of the applicant. This person must have had, within past 3 years full-time experience in airline passenger ticketing and possess each of following qualifications :

(a) Exercises daily supervision of and responsibility for the operation of that agency location and has the authority to make management decisions.

(b) Demonstrates a working knowledge of Industry's Agent's handbook by completing a written questionnaire.

(c) Has had at least two full years experience in either selling general travel services to the public or supervising the operations of a business offering such services.

Location: The location of the Travel Agency must be freely accessible and clearly identified to the public. The office must be primarily engaged in sale of passenger transportation, there are exceptions to accessibility requirements for restricted access and customer premises/ locations.

Other requirements: Other IATA requirement for inclusion cover includes the following:

- Identification of agency to the general public;
- Name of agency shouldnot be misleading;
- Citizenship of the applicant;
- Financial integrity;
- Information regarding change of agency ownership;
- Information regarding change of agency's bank account;
- A separate license is required for commissions to be payable on the sale of services of IATA members;
- Application has to be made (format is enclosed) on applicant's stationary (in triplicate) to AIP;
- AIP (2 members panel) has no executation authority but it mayn't forward the particular application when it fails to meet the requisite standard for the approval. But reasons for non-recommending are stated in writing.

Most important benefit which permeates from IATA approval is that one gets the privilege of holding International Air Ticket Stocks of IATA member companies to earn commission on such sales.

ANNEXURE-I

SPECIMEN OF APPLICATION FOR IATA APPROVAL

1. Name.................. Date ....
   Are you a cargo agent ....
2. Type of Business Sole proprietor ....
   Partnership ....
   Association ....
   Corporation ....
3. What is the Principal Business of your organisation
   ....
4. Is your organisation engaged in other types of business
   ....
5. Full address of the principal office of your organisation
   ....
6. Specify:
   Regd. Capital Rs. ....
   Paid-up Capital Rs. ....
   Minimum Paid-up Capital Rs. ....
   Regd. by the Law of the Country ....
   State Shareholder ....
7. Date of Establishment ....
8. If your organisation is cured by another organisation, answer the following in respect of parent organisation:
   Address and Name ....
   Principal Business ....
   Current Financial Statement ....
9. Trade Regd. No. ....
10. Specify the date and type of Govt. Licence required to operate your Travel Agency. ....
11. State the name of Regd. Office which is to appear on IATA. ....
12. Address of Branch Office. ....
13. If approval is required for a Branch Office. ....
14. Date of Commencement of Business. ....
15. Length of time owned ....

16. Name of Director/Managers ....
    IATA/UFTAA Training Course ....
    Extent of participation ....
    Other Business Interest ....
17. Qualifications of Staff ....
    Bankruptcy ....
    Default ....
    Attach photographs of Interior/Exteriors ....
    Entirely to sale-promotion of transportation ....
    1. Floor ....
    2. Surface area ....
    3. Space for IATA ....
    4. Means of access ....
18. How is it separated from other business ....
19. What are display facilities available for advertisement number of show windows ....
20. Located in a Hotel/Club ....
21. GSA ....
22. Profits of GSA/IATA agency ....
23. Any customer has interest in the Agency ....
24. Are you acting GSA of an Airline ....
25. Non IATA Airline ....
26. Approved as an Agent for Transportation Conference ....
27. Statement of Sales ....
    Ist year ....
28. Production Agency will materialise ....
29. Need for seeing Ticket stocks ....
30. You would be liable for loss ....
31. Adequate facilities for storing ticket stock Steel fireproof cabinet. ....
32. Step to secure stocks. ....
33. Signature ....

STATEMENT OF INTERNATIONAL SALES

- Financial Qualifications:
  - Availability of adequate liquid funds to meet normal Trading Circumstances
  - Capital is commensurate with fixed assets
  - Evidence of ability to trade profitably
  - Existence of charges and
- Arbitration US $750
- IATA numeric ticket
- IATA applicant standing
- One year in business

2 staff Members = 2 years' experience
at an approved in International Ticketing
IATA Agent — Fare constructions

1. Working knowledge of IATA documentation
2. Fare construction principles
3. Currency
4. Cheer Rules
5. Interpret principles of excursion fare regulations
6. Related fares
7. Reroute, revision, revalidate

- No-under applicant
  - GSA for Agents
  - GSA for more than/Airlines
  - Located at an Airport
  - Located at Club/hotels
  - Similarity to name of other Agent
  - Unsatisfactory Record
- Head Office
  - Branch Office
  - Non-qualified staff
  - Direct with Airlines

1. New Business-non-diluting
2. Adequate premises
3. Good display Windows
4. Good decorations
5. Adequte staff
6. Knowledge of Air Ticketing and Reservation
7. Procedures Healthy Airlines Business
8. Capital 10,000/20,000
9. Total Revenue Earned.

UNIVERSAL FEDERATION OF TRAVEL AGENTS ASSOCIATION (UFTAA)

Universal Federation of Travel Agents Association (UFTAA) was founded in 1966, by merger of the International Federation of Travel Agencies (IFTAA) and Universal Organisation of Travel Agents Association (UOTAA). It now forms the only global federation of travel agents association and thus represents throughout the world.

UFTAA membership is made up of National Travel Agents Association or organisations from every country of the world. UFTAA has a present about 35,000 travel agencies. Full-time members of UFTAA are National Travel Agents Association or organisations. Besides the full members, the Secetary General of UFTAA may register individually any travel agency which is:

- A member of National Association which has membership of UFTAA.
- A member of National Association in a country which doesn't have UFTAA membership.
- Located in a country where there is no National Association.
- Any individual firm, company or other legal entities such as airlines, hotels or car rental operators, whose activities are allied to those of travel agents, may obtain registration on the same terms laid down for Registered Agents.

REGULATIONS FOR MEMBERSHIP OF PACIFIC ASIA TRAVEL ASSOCIATION (PATA)

Membership Criteria

(a) PATA membership can be held in only one category.

(b) PATA membership is held by an organization, not an individual (except those listed on page 11 of the PATA membership Structure booklet).

(c) Where an organization engages in several activities, such as selling air and/or cruise line tickets (Travel Agency), conducting sightseeing tours for incoming visitors and packaging and selling tours to places within the Pacific-Asia area (Wholesale Tour Operator), the category of membership for which the applicant's eligibility is determined on the basis of the highest PATA dues category.

(d) If more than one category of membership is indicated on an application form, the highest dues category is assigned.

(e) For any category requiring that an applicant has been engaged in business for a minimum of two years, the applicant may request that one of the two years be waived if the application is accompanied by a letter supporting that the management staff has at least 15 years of appropriate experience.

(f) Please Note: There is a one-time administration fee for new members in the amount of US$ 150. This is in addition to the regular dues amount.

Note : Government and Carrier member applicants should not fill out this form. A letter of intent will suffice.

ANNEXURE-II

Application is hereby made to PATA for membership in the one category checked below:

I. Government and Carrier Members:
Should not fill out this form. Instead a letter of intent will suffice.

II. Corporate Members:

Corporate Category: (Granted only to organisations with revenue of US$ 1 Billion or over).

III. Industry / Associate Industry Members :

A. Industry Members

❑ Head Office

❑ Wholesale Tour Operator

( ) Gross annual volume of business: US$ 1,000,000 or

( ) Gross annual volume of busines: less than US$ 1,000,000

❑ Sightseeing operator

( ) Gross annual volume of business: US$ 1,000,000 or over

( ) Gross annual volume of business: less than US$ 1,000,000

❑ Hotel

( ) 500 rooms or more ( ) 100-199 rooms

( ) 200-499 rooms ( ) 1 to 99 rooms

❑ Travel Trade Association

❑ Tourist Attraction

❑ Representative

❑ Travel Agency

❑ Branch Office

Name of PATA industry member of which you are a branch:

__________Member Number__________

B. Associate Industry Members :

❑ General

❑ Media

❑ Education

- ❑ Associate Branch Office
  Name of PATA associate industry member of which you are a branch:
  ____________Member Number____________

PLEASE RETURN THIS APPLICATION FORM TO:

PACIFIC TRAVEL ASSOCIATION
I Montgomery Street, Telesis Tower, Suite 1750
San Francisco, California 94104
You will be invoiced upon receipt and approval,
USA
Fax: (415) 986-3458

FORMALITIES FOR PATA MEMBERSHIP

1. A prime requisite for PATA membership is the recognition accorded by the Department of Tourism, Government of India.
2. It is imperative to first become a member of the international PATA body headquartered at San Francisco. On obtaining their Membership, you will be invited to join the India Chapter Membership.
3. Your PATA HQ membership application form as well as "particulars of the Applicant" should be fully completed and returned along with the relevant documents to the PATA India Chapter Secretariat, New Delhi.
4. Your application will be examined by the Executive Committee of PATA India Chapter who will then formally sponsor and recommend the same to PATA HQ, San Francisco. The India Chapter Secretariat will subsequently forward your documents to San Francisco. PATA HQ, San Francisco will not entertain any Membership Applications sent to them directly without the India Chapter's formal sponsorship. On confirmation of your membership with PATA HQ, they will send you their invoice which is to be paid in the US Dollars directly to PATA, San Francisco.
5. We charge a Sponsorship Fee of US$ 50 in its equivalent Indian Currency. A cheque for this amount, made out in favour of PATA India Chapter, must accompany your application.

6. Please do not omit to attach documents that have been specifically asked you for.
7. In case of any further clarification on the membership formalities, please do not hesitate to contact to:

   Executive Secretary
   PATA India Chapter Secretariat
   # 509 Mercantile House, 5th Floor
   15 Kasturba Gandhi Marg, New Delhi-110001
   Phone: 3325156 Fax: 3325156

PARTICULARS OF APPLICANT

1. Name of the firm.
2. When established.
3. Full address, Telephone nos, Telegraphic/telex addresses of the office making this application.
4. Name of individual/s who will represent the firm.
5. State whether the applicant has a sole proprietorship, partnership, a private limited company or a public limited company.
6. Give the name/s of the proprietor, partner, or Directors of the Company as the case may be. Indicate holdings.
7. State the paid-up capital as on date. (In case of proprietorship or partnership, state the capital invested).
8. State whether the applicant is a Travel Agency/ Tour Operator/Hotel.
9. (a) State whether Travel Agency/Tours/Hotel is your principal business and how long has this business been established.
   (b) Are you General Sales Agents of any airlines or shipping companies or any Hotel Chain.
   (c) What special arrangements you have for booking hotel accommodation
10. State places where you have Branch Offices with their full addresses and names of Managers.

RECOMMENDED BY THE FOLLOWING TWO MEMBERS OF PATA INDIA CHAPTER

(1) Name

Designation

Organisation

Signature Date :

Stamp of Company

---

(2) Name

Designation

Organisation

Signature Date :

Stamp of Company

PATA INDIA CHAPTER DUES STRUCTURE

1. Annual Subscription (AS)

A flat rate of Rs. 15/- is charged per member. The bills are raised at the beginning of the financial year, i.e. 01 April of each year.

2. Promotional Fees (PRL)

Subsequently, a bill for promotional fees is raised which helps finance various activities conducted by the Chapter, administrative expenses, etc. A prescribed formula is followed on the basis of which these bills are raised in the proportionate share of travel agents, airlines, hotels, Central government, State governments, etc. The share of the travel agents segment is Rs. 550/- and the hotels segment is Rs. 650/- each per year. The bills are raised in the month of July each year.

PATA INTERNATIONAL MEMBERSHIP DUES

Category	*1993/94 (3.5%) 94/95*
Industry:	**US$**
Corporate	5,175
Head Office	1,345
Operator:	
Tour/Sightseeing/Equipment	
(Vol US$ 1,000,000 or over)	1,345
(Vol less than US$ 1,000,000	620
Hotel Member :	
(500 rooms or more) #	1,345
(200 to 499 rooms) #	930
(100 to 199 rooms) #	570
(1 to 99 rooms) #	440
Travel Trade Associations:	830
Tourist Attraction	620
Representative	500
Travel Agency/Branch Office/Individual	440
Associate Industry:	
General/Media	620
Education/Branch Office	440
Government/Carrier:	
Associate Government/Associate Carrier	2,370

PART B : REGULATIONS REGARDING DOCUMENTATION/FACILITATION

Tourist Information Booklet of India an itinerant tourist is described as a "land of stupendous dimensions—colourful, exotic, traditional, modern—with her varied topography, picturesque valleys, high mountain peaks and cascading rivers. She never ceases to surprise tourists with her caleidoscopic attractions.

Undoubtedly, this information/description excites the imagination of a tourists. Matched by the unfailing warmth and hospitality of our people. India should naturally become a hot destination among tourists from all parts of the globe. But soon the excitement subsides and gives way to a realism that evokes a different rather altogether different response, i.e. India is a land of disorder where laxity in all kinds of regulations is a norm. This image perhaps is based on partial truth due to lack of information or to some extent disinformation regarding legal, regulatory and control practices in the country.

Thus, becomes mandatory for a student of this field to obtain and master comprehensive information on the regulations regarding documentation. So that itinerant tourist may be guided properly to create a positive image of our country.

THE MAJOR DOCUMENTATION AREAS LIKE

(a) Passport
(b) Tourist card
(c) Visa
(d) Special papers :
   (i) Police certificate of good conduct
   (ii) Letter of recommendation
   (iii) A ticket to leave a particular country
(e) Health Certificate:
   (i) Vaccination
   (ii) Re-vaccination
(f) Customs and Migrations.

Passport: According to Passport Act, 1967, a passport is defined as a official document issued by a competent public authority to nationals or to alien residents (mostly stateless persons) of the issuing country. It establishes the bearer's identity and nationality as well as authorises the holder to travel abroad.

The passport may include the spouse of bearer, unmarried minor children, less than 13 years of age of bearer, unmarried minor brothers or sisters of the bearer. A person who is included in the passport of bearer may not use the passport for travel unless he is accompanied by bearer or with his authorising letter.

KINDS OF PASSPORTS

(1) White colour passport or official passport is issued to every person who is going abroad for any assignments of Government of India.
(2) Red passport or diplomatic passport is issued only to Ministers, Secretaries, Joint Secretaries or Deputy Secretaries.
(3) Blue colour passport or ordinary passport is issued to any Indian citizen going abroad.
(4) Alien passport which is valid only for 2 years.
(5) International Red Cross Passport is issued to employees or project awardees of UNESO projects.

(I) How to Obtain a Passport

All regional passport officers are in authority to issue a passport to any Indian citizen by proving his/her residence in India for at least 2 years without a break. To obtain a passport one must provide duly:

- Filled up E A (P) form, a prescribed, passport application form.
- Seven passport size photographs two of which attested by a gazetted officer.
- Proof of date of birth, either from SSLC certificate or LIC policy etc.
- Proof of residence, either through ration card or passbook of an Indian nationalised bank with continuous transactions.
- For students, a bonafide student certificate from their institution.

- Degree certificate for attestation of their qualification.
- A fees (non-refundable) of Rs. 300/-.
- In case of minor, a signed declaration by parent or local guardian with legal guardianship affidavit duly executed on non-judicial stamp paper of Rs. 2/- before a Notary public or a first class magistrate.

(II) How to Get Passport Renewed

For renewal of Vailidity of Existing passports one must fill up EA (P) 6 form, a prescribed form to get one's passport revalidated for a further period of 5 years from the date of it's initial validity. For revalidation of existing passport one must apply within two years from original date of expiry, otherwise a fresh passport can only be applied for.

(III) Replacement of Passports

Replacement of passport can take place when there is a change in name/surname, as in the case of female applicants after marriage, or if there is a change in appearance/specimen signatures. In the former case applicant is required to fill up EA (P) 6 form along with passport size photographs duly attested on reverse in the married name together with a fees of Rs. 60/- and marriage certificate or marriage invitation card as well as an affidavit called "deed poll" duly executed on a notary public or a first class magistrate. Of course all these must be submitted to regional passport office along with existing passport held in maiden name.

In latter case, form EA (P) 6 must be filled up with a fees of Rs. 50/- along with 2 passport size photographs duly attested on reverse by Local Station House Officer (SHO)/ Gazetted Officer/or Magistrate.

(IV) Miscellaneous Requirements

- Inclusion of child's name: certified copies of birth certificate/school certificate containing the name of child, place and date of birth, sex and relationship with applicant should be submitted along with duly filled up EA(P) and form.
- Change of Name/Surname: Along with EA(P) 6 form applicant must submit 2 newspaper clippings or gazette notification issued by competent authority

in support of change of name and an affidavit called "deed poll" along with 5 passport size photographs duly certified on reverse in changed name.

- Lost and damaged passports: In both the cases duplicate passports are issued, when applicants apply on EA(P) 10 form with following requirements:
- Original copy of FIR lodged with police station in case of lost passport.
- Personal particulars form, in duplicate duly certified. 5 passport size photographs in case of damaged passports.
- An affidavit on nonjudicial stamp paper of Rs 2/- denomination duly executed before a Notary Public or a Magistrate containing information on how passport got lost/damaged, whether holder has travelled on the damaged passport, if so, please give the last date of re-entry into India or whether the applicant has availed any of Custom/Repatriation/FTS/concession. If so, please give details on the date and place of availing such a concession, amount of concession and name of office from where the concession was obtained.

(V) Circumstances under which an application can be rejected:

- If applicant is not a citizen of India.
- If the applicant during preceding 5 years from the date of submission of application has been convicted by a court of law in India for any offence involving in moral tumultuation and has been sentenced for not less than 2 years.
- If proceedings are pending in the criminal court but due to unavoidable reasons applicant needs to go abroad, court issues an order to permit the applicant to leave the country for a limited period.
- If any warrant/summon has been issued by the court for not allowing the applicant to leave the country.
- If the applicant has been repatriated and hasnot reimbursed the course of repatriation.

Tourist Card: A document issued to prospective tourists as a prerequisite for entry and departure is called tourist card. It is only the document required by issuing country. In other words no passport is sufficient without tourist card.

Visas: Visa is an endorsement placed in a passport or in a documents issued in lieu of passport by authority of originating country. This endorsement is done by the Consular other country's government. It indicate that this official document has been examined by such an official. This is required to be obtained before departure for that particular country. Therefore, this is an important step in total itinerary preparation. Application for visas should be done correctly while fulfilling all requirements mentioned to avoid unnecessary and unwanted delay or rejection by the Consular. Visa, indicates dates of travel and cities of entry and exit allowed during the course of travel. Any change in the programme would make visa invalid.

Visas may be grouped into different categories on the basis of purpose of visit such as:

– Tourist Visa	Immigration Visa
– Student Visa	Single entry"
– Business Visa	multiple"
– Transit Visa	double"

Long-term Visa (max. duration of 5 years. multiple entry).

The maximum duration of Visa is 180 days. But if a visa is issued for a lesser period, application for extension should be made within 180 days for which no extra fee is charged. The only requirement is submission of a set of identical passport photographs. There is also provision for extension of Visa beyond 180 days but this is exceptionally operated. In such cases fee charged varies within a fix scale:

- Visa can be renewed in all state capitals and district headquarters on an application made to district police chief. (Commissioner of Police/S.S.P./S.P.). Visa, extension/renewal cases in cities of New Delhi/Bombay/Calcutta are handled by F.R.R.O. (Foreigners Regional Registration Officers). In Madras by Chief Immigration Officer (CIO). Appendix lists the address of major Indian Consular offices abroad, FRRO and CIO in India.

ANNEXURE-III
INDIAN MISSIONS AND FRRO'S

Australia	3-5 Moonah Place, Yarralumla, Act 2600, Tel: (062) 733999
Bangladesh	120 Road 2, Dhanmodi Residential Area, H.No.129. Dhaka, Tel: 507670
Canada	10 Springfield Road, Ottawa KIM 109, Tel: 7443451
Japan	2-11, Kudan Minami 2-Chome, Chiyodaku, Tokyo, Tel: 2622391
Kenya	Jeevan Bharati Building, Harambee Avenue, Nairobi, Tel: 22566
Malaysia	United Asian Bank Building, 19, Malacca Street, Kuala Lumpur, Tel: 221766
Myanmar	545-547, Merchant Street, Yangoon, Tel: 15933, 16381
Nepal	Lainchaur, GPO Box 292, Kathmandu, Tel: 211300
Netherlands	Buitenrustwg 2, The Hague, Tel: (070) 469771
New Zealand	180, Molesworth Street, Princess Towers, Wellington, Tel: 736390
Pakistan	482-F, Sector G-6/4, Islamabad, Tel: 821049
Singapore	India House, 31 Grange Road, Singapore, Tel: 7376777
Sri Lanka	3rd Floor, State Bank of India Building, 18-3/1 Sir Baron Jayatilaka Mawatha, Colombo. Tel: 21604, 22788
Switzerland	Weltportstr 17, 3015 Berne, Tel: (031) 440193
Thailand	46, Soi Prasarmitra, Sukhumvit 23, Bangkok, Tel: 2580300
UK	India House, Aldwych, London WC2B4NA, Tel: 8368484
USA	2107, Massachusetts Ave NW, Washington DC 20008, Tel: 9397000
Germany	Adenaverrallee 262, 5300 Bonn, Tel: 54050
Foreigners'	Regional Registration Offices (FRROs) in New Delhi, Bombay and Calcutta and the Chief Immigration Officer in Madras handle visa renewals as well as permits for Restrict Areas, viz., Andaman Islands, Sikkim, Assam, Ladakh, Lahaul Spiti, etc.
New Delhi	FRRO, 1st floor, Hans Bhawan, Near Tilak Bridge, Bahadur Shah Zafar Marg, New Delhi-110 002, Tel: 3319781, 3318179
Bombay	FRRO, Office of the DCP, Special Branch II, CID Head Office (Annex 2), Crewford Market, Bombay-400 034 (Tel: 2620455, 2621169)
Calcutta	FRRO, 237, Acharya Jagdish Bose Road, Calcutta-700 020 (Tel: 443301, 440549)
Madras	Chief Immigration Officer, 9 Village Road Nungambakkam, Madras - 600 034 (Tel: 477036)
Tourism Ind.	Visas can also be renewed in all State Capitals and District Headquarters by an application to the Police Commissioner's Office/Senior Superintendent of Police/Superintendent of Police.

Visas 1

ANNEXURE–IV

Destination	Issuing Authority									Valdity of Visa maximum stay permitted	Fee
Afghanistan	Bombay 115, Walkeshar Road Bombay-400 006 Tel: 3633777/361228€ New Delhi-110 021 Tel: 606628/603328	Delhi Plot No. 5, Block-50F Shantipath Chanakyapuri	Valid for 3 months after the expiry of visa	1	1	R/O,F	*	Afghanistan 200	3 months 10 day stay		
Argentina	B/8-9, Vasant Vihar New Delhi-110 057 Tel: 671345/671348		*	1	2	R/O,F		Visa for onward destination	US $13	3 months multiple entry	Rs. 768
Australia	16th Floor, Maker Tower E-Block Cuffe Parade Bombay-400 005 Tel: 2181071, 2181072 (Only Business Visas issued)	1/50 G, Shantipath Chankyapuri New Delhi-110 021 Tel: 6888223/6888228	*	1	1			Leave certificate from employer, Proof of sufficient funds			Gratis forless than 90days; above 3 months Australian $30
Bangladesh (Visas issued at Calcutta and Agartala also)		56 Ring Road Lajpat Nagar-III, New Delhi-110 024 Tel: 6834668/9209/3550	*	2	2	US$5 per day				30 days	
Belgium (Visas issued at Calcutta also)	Morena 11 M.L. Dahanukar Marg Cumballa Hills, Bombay-400 025 Tel: 4918101/4939261	50, N. Shantipath Chanakyapuri, New Delhi-110 021 Tel: 608295/608067	*	1	1	R/O	*	Proof of funds visa for onward destination		90 days; 30 days stay	1 month Rs. 1,152, 1-3 mon. Rs. 1536 above 3 months Rs. 1,920
Brazil		8, Aurangzeb Road New Delhi-110 001 Tel: 3017301	valid for over 6 months	2	2	R/O		Proof of Sufficient funds	Depends on airport of departure	3 months validity and stay	Tourist Rs. 800; Business Rs. 2,400
Canada	41/42, Maker Chamber 6 Jamnalal Bajaj Marg Nariman Point, Bombay-400 021 Tel: 2876027	7/8, Santipath, Chanakyapuri, New Delhi-110 021 Tel: 6876560	*	1	3	R/O	*	Proof of sufficient funds, leave certificate from employer			Rs. 400 extra through travelagent single entry

China	Madhuli, Flat 23, floor Opp. Nehru Planetarium Dr. A. Besant Road Worli, Bombay-400 018 Tel: 4921773	50-D, Shantipath, Chanakyapuri, New Delhi-110 021 Tel: 606682, 600328, 600329	*	1	1	R/O		Confirmed hotel reservation, traveler's cheques endorsed by the people's Bank China	Chinese Ren Bi Men 60 (Ren Bi Men=Rs 5.37)		Rs. 1,265 multiple entry Rs. 1,955 Rs. 175. There are additional charges if visa is required urgently
Denmark (Personal appearance necessary)	L and T House Ballard Estate Bombay-400 038 Tel: 2614462, 2618181	11 Aurangzeb Road, New Delhi-110 011 Tel: 3010900, 3010002	Valid for 6 months beyond stay	3	2	R/O	*	Proof of sufficient funds	Danish Kroner 200	270 days; 90 day stay	
Egypt	Benhur Narayan Dhabolkar Marg, Bombay-400 006 Tel: 3676422/ 3676407	1/5, M Niti Marg, Chanakyapuri, New Delhi-110 021 Tel: 602074, 608904	Valid for 2 months	1	1	R/O	*	Proof of funds	Egyuption pounds 14.50		Single entry Rs. 860; Double entry Rs. 1,310; Countesy fee Rs. 170
			Valid for 6 months beyond stay			R/O				7 day stay	
France* (Visa issued at Calcutta and Pondicherry also)	Datta Prasad Bldg., IInd Floor, 19 Nowroji Gamadia X Rd. Bombay-400 026 Tel: 4950918/2289/1870	Tel: 605409/605205 2/50 E Shantipath Chanakyapuri, New Delhi-110 021 Tel: 604300	Valid for 3 months beyond expiry of visa	1	1	R/O,F		Confirmed hotel ooking and visa for next destination leave certificate from employer, stay I Text statement of 3 years		Tourist- 3 months; 15 day stay, business 1 year, 6 months	Up to 3 months Rs. 1,320; 1 years Rs. 3,960 and Industry
Russian Federation (Visa issue date Calcutta and Madras also)	Palm Beach 42 L Jagmohan Das Marg OldNepean Sea Road, Bombay-400 034 Tel: 3633627/3633628	Shantipath, Chanakyapuri, New Delhi-100 021 Tel: 605545, 600022, 606558, 606026	*	1	3	R	*	Confirmed accommodation in Moscow			Gratis; urgent visa Rs. 1,500

Singapore (Visa issued at Calcutta and Madras too)	94, Sankar Bhawan, 9th Flr. 30 Nariman Point, Bombay-400 021 Tel: 2043205/2043211	E-6, Chandragupta Marg, Chanakyapuri, New Delhi-110 021 Tel: 6895659/ 6886506	Valid for 3 months beyond stay	1	*	R/O		Proof of funds, visa for next destination	Sing $ 10 from Seletar and S.$ 15 from Changi airport	3 months; 14 day stay	Rs. 350
South Africa	Mr. Jacques De Vos/Ashwin C/oHotel President Room No. 602, Bombay-400 021 Tel: 2150808	Rep. office of S. Africa Hotel Hyett Regency Bhikaji Cama Place, New Delhi-110 016 Tel: 6881234/35	*	1	1	R	*	Proof of funds, confirmed hotel accommodation			Gratis
Spain		12 Prithviraj Road, New Delhi-110 011 Tel: 3792085/82/74	Valid for 3 months beyond the issue of visa	3	3	R/O	*	Proof of sufficient funds; visa for next destination		2 months; 30 days stay	Tourist Rs. 704 Business Rs. 1,408
Sri Lanka (Visas issued at Madras and Calcutta also)	Sri Lanka House 34, Homi Modi Street Fort, Bombay-400 001 Tel: 2045861, 2048303	27, Kautilya Marg, Chanakyapuri, New Delhi-110 021 Tel: 3010201/02/03	Valid for 2 months beyond expiry of visa	1	1 Signed on back	*	*	Proof of sufficient funds	LKR 500	30 day stay	Rs. 140
Switzerland	Bhupesh Gupta Bhawan, 85 Sayani Road, Prabhadevi, Bombay-400 0255 Tel: 4360493	Nyaya Marg, Chanakyapuri New Delhi-110 021 Tel: 604225, 604226	Valid for 6 months beyond expiry of visa	1	1	R/O,F	*	Visa for next destination			Rs. 650; minor Rs. 275
United Kingdom* (Visas issued at Calcutta and Madras also. Personal appearance necessary for first time applicant)	4 Maker Chamber IInd Floor Jamnalal Bajaj Marg Nariman Point, Bombay-21 Tel: 2832330, 2833602, 2830517	Shantipath, Chanakyapuri, New Delhi-110 021 Tel: 6872161	*	1	2	*	*				single entry under 25 years Rs. 910; single above 25 years Rs. 1,815; multiple (6 months) Rs. 2,475 (multiple) (2 years)

USA* (Visas issued at Madras and Calcutta also, Personal appearance necessary for first time applicant)	Lincoln House 78, Bhulabhai Desai Road, Bombay-400 026 Tel: 3633611-18	Shantipath, Chanakyapuri, New Delhi-110 021 Tel: 600651	Valid for 6 months beyond entry	A non refun-dable pay order of US$ 20 must accom-pany the from (Rs. 640)	1	R/O signed on back	*	Proof of sufficient funds	means of travel expenses, proof of property copy of income tax returns; leave certificate, copy of bank statement		Rs. 3,575 multiple (5 years) Rs. 7,150 Rs. 800 for 6 months

* The British High Commission also issues visas for Anguila, Bermuda, British Antarctic Territory, British Indian Ocean territory, Cayman Islands and Dependencies, Hong Kong, Montserrat, Pitcaim, Henderson, Ducies and Oeno Islands, St. Helena and Dependencies, Turks and Caicos Islands, Virgin Islands and the Soverign Base Areas of Akrotiri and Dhekelia.

** AUS visa is also valid for Puetro Rico, Guam, Virgin Islands (USA) and Samoa (American).

Germany (Visas issue at Madras and Calcutta also)	Hoechst House 10th Floor, Nariman Point Bombay-400 021 Tel: 2832422, 2832661, 2832517	50/N Shantipath, Chanakyapuri, New Delhi-110 021 Tel: 604861	Valid for 3 months beyond stay	1	1	R/O,F		Proof of employment, leave certificate, covering letter explanning purpose of visit, Proof of funds	Deutsche mark 11 (from Berlin only)	3 months	3 months Rs. 470; above 3 months Rs. 820
Greece* (Visas issued at Madras and Calcutta also)	Mehta Mahal, 11th Floor 15, Mathew Road Opera House, Bombay-400 004 Tel: 3612539/3837066	16, Sundar Nagar, New Delhi-110 003 Tel: 64178004	*	1	1	R/O,F		Sufficient funds, leave certificate, visa for next destination, I.Tax papers	(Greece) GRD 2500-5000	3 months	Rs. 140

Indonesia (Visas issued at Madras and Calcutta also)	49 Altamount Road Cumballa Hills Bombay-400 036 Tel: 3868678/3868388	50-A, Chanakyapuri New Delhi-110 021 Tel: 602352/54/43/48/ 05/06/07	Valid for 6 months from the date of issued of visa	2	2	R,F		Proof of sufficient funds 2 covering letters	Depends upon airport of departure	Tourist 3 months; 14 day stay; Business 30 day stay	Single entry Rs. 800 Multiple entry Rs. 1,550

* The French Consulate also issues visas for French Guiana, French Polynesia the Central African Republic, Maceritania, Monaco, New Caledonia, Dijibouti, Gabon and Togo.
** Photographs have to be pasted.

Israel	Kailash, 50 G Deshmukhi Rd. Bombay-400 026 Tel: 3862793/94/95	Gopal Das Verma Bhavan, 15th Floor, 2B Barakhamba Rd. New Delhi-110 001	Valid for 3 months beyond expiry of visa	2	2	R/O	*	Visa for next destination; leave certificate from employer	Rs. 365		
Italy (Visas issued at Calcutta also)	Kanchenjunga 72G Deshmukh Rd. Bombay-400 026 Tel: 387407/72/73	50-E, Chandragupata Marg, Chanakyapuri New Delhi-110 021 Tel: 600071	Valid for 4 months after the issue of visa	2	2	R/O,F		Proof of employment, leave certificate, proof of funds visa for next destination; I. Tax. returns, covering letter		90 days Tourist-10-15 day stay, Business 8-day stay	Rs. 960
Japan (Visas issued at Calcutta also)	1, Babasaheb Dahanakar Marg Cumbala Hill, Bombay-400 026 Tel: 4934610/4933857	4/50, Shantipath, Chanakyapuri New Delhi-110 021 Tel: 6876581/2/ 36876564/6876581	*	1	1	R/O	*	Proof of sufficient funds		90 days	Tourist Rs. 240; Business Rs. 260
Kenya		66, Vasant Vihar, New Delhi-110 057 Tel: 6876538/39/40	*	1	2	R/O		Should prossess US$ in hard currency	US$20	90 days; multiple entry visa granted on request	Rs. 960 single entry
Malaysia* (Visas issued at Madras also)		50 M Satya Marg Chanakyapuri New Delhi-110 021 Tel: 601291/92	Valid for 3 months beyond stay	3	3	R		Proof of funds	Ringgit 20	90 days; 15 days stay	Rs. 247
Malta		Rep. Mr. O.P. Kathpalia Hanorary	*	2		R		Proof of sufficient funds	Malta £10 on arrival		Rs. 350

		Consulate of Malta, 1, Haile Road New Delhi-110 001 Tel: 3329090	and a Photocopy								
Mauritius	Mittal Towers 'C' Wing Nariman Point Bombay-400 021 Tel: 2825127, 2844165	5, Kautilya Marg Chanakyapuri New Delhi-110 021 Tel: 3011113, 3011112	Valid for 3 months beyond stay	1	2	R/O		Proof of sufficient funds, photocopy of passport/ticket confirmed hotel booking	Mauritian Rs. 100	90 days	
Myanmar (Burma)*		3/50 F Nyaya Marg Chanakyapuri New Delhi-110 021 Tel: 600251, 600252	*	3	3	R/O		US$ 4		90 days, 7 day stay	Rs. 840
Netherlands	The Internatinoal, 3rd flr. 16, Maharishi Karve Road, Churchgate, Bombay-400 020 Tel: 2016911	6/50 Shantipath Chanakyapuri New Delhi-110 021 Tel: 6885852, 6884951	Valid for 6 months beyond date of issue	1	1	R/O,F		Proof of sufficient funds; visa for next destination; confirmed hotel booking		90 days; 30 days	Rs. 955 upto one month, Rs. 1,320 upto 3 months; Rs. 1,660 for 1 year
New Zealand***		50 N, Nyaya Marg Chanakyapuri New Delhi-110 021 Tel: 6883170	Valid for 3 months beyond stay	1	1	*		Proof of NZ $1000 per months of stay or US$500 if staying with relatives, leave certificate from employer	NZ$ 20 from Christ-church	90 days	US$ 40 only in foreign exchange
Pakistan	Anjuman-i-Islam High School, Dr. D.N. Road, Bombay-400 001 (Temporary visa office established every 3 months)	2/50 G, Shantipath Chanakyapuri New Delhi-110 021 Tel: 600601/600603	*	4	4	R	*	Visa only for blood relatives; application through travel agents not entertained	First class pax Pak Rs. 400; business pax Pak Rs. 300; economy pax Pak Rs. 200	1 months	

* Children above 7 years travelling on a joint passport need separte applications. Travel to and from Myanmar Should be via sea or air only.

** Dependants must have individual passports.

ANNEXURE-V

VISA OFFICES FOR NEIGHBOURING COUNTRIES

Afghanistan	From the Embassy at 5/50-F, Shantipath, New Delhi 110 021 (Tel: 603331 Telex : 031- 72253)
Bhutan	Bhutan Tourism Corporation, P.O. Box. No. 159, Thimphu, Bhutan which organises group tours of six or more members will also take care of visa formalities.
Myanmar	From the Embassy at 3/50-F, Nyaya Marg, New Delhi - 110 021 (Tel: 600251 Telex: 0317224 Mend In)
Nepal	From the Royal Nepalese Embassy, Barakhamba Road, New Delhi-110 001 (Tel: 3329969 Telex: 031- 66283 NEMB IN Fax: 332 6857)
Thailand	From the Embassies in New Delhi and Calcutta: 56-N, Nyaya Marg, New Delhi-110 021 (Tel: 607807 Telex: 031-72275 THAI INN Fax: 6872029), 18-B Mandeville Garden, Ballygunj, Calcutta-700 019 (Tel: 460836)
Sri Lanka	Most westerners do not need a visa.

SPECIAL PAPER'S RELATED REGULATIONS

This requirement includes a police certificate issued by police station Incharge of local police station of area where applicant is living or working. This certificate certifies that applicant bears good moral character and that he has never booked under any charges or no complaint has ever been lodged against him/her.

If applicant is in service a letter of recommendation from employer can facilitate the process. If applicant is not in service, for example, self-employed in such a case a letter of recommendation from renowned personality of the location can also facilitate the procedure. Although, there is no restriction on Indian and foreign nationals for movement within India. But in case of border states and two groups of islands (Andaman and Lakshadweep Islands) there are some restrictions.

Visitor requires a special entry permit which is valid for a period of 15 days only. For group tourist the application must be made at least two weeks in advance to the appropriate authority.

List of Restricted/prohibited areas of authorities for assuring permission given in Annexure:

Annexure-VI Places Open in Restricted/Protected Areas

Sl. No. *Name of State*	*Whether individual tourists permitted*	*Authority who can grant permit*	*For how-many days*	*Remarks*
1	*2*	*3*	*4*	*5*
Restricted/Protected Area				
1. Assam				
(i) Kaziranga National Park (ii) Manas Bird Sanctuary (iii) Guwahati City and Kamakhya Temple (iv) Sibsagar (v) Jatinga Bird Sanctuary	No	MHA and All F.R.R.Os. All Indian Missions abroad, Commr., Assam, Resident Commr., Assam Government, New Delhi and Trade Adviser Government	5 10	(i) Entry up to Guwahati by air only (ii) Journey to Sibsagar by national highway and Jatinga by train
2. Meghalaya				
(i) Shillong (ii) Barapani (iii) Cherapunji (iv) Mawsyram (v) Jakeran (vi) Raniker (vii) Thadlaskein (viii) Nartiang (ix) Tura and (x) Siju	No	MHA and All F.R.R.Os, All Indian Missions abroad, Home Commr., Meghalaya	10	(i) Journey up to Guwahati by air only
3. Manipur				
Loktak Lake, Imphal, Mourang INA Memorial, Keibul Deer Sanctuary and Waithe Lake	No	All India missions abroad All F.R.R.Os and MHA, state government of	5	(i) Calcutta to Imphal by air only Manipur (home commr. Manipur)
4. Andaman and Nicobar Island				
(i) Municipal Area, Port Blair (ii) Havelock Island (iii) Long (iv) Neil Island (v) Jolly Buoy (vi) Cinque (vii) Red Skin (viii) Mayabunder (ix) Diglipur (x) Rangat (xi) Mt. Harriet and (xii) Madhuban	Yes	MHA and All F.R.R.Os. all Indian missions abroad, immigration officer, Port Blair	30	(i) Places for (i) to (vii) day and night allowed Places for (viii) to (xii) day visit allowed
5. Lakshadeep				
Bangaram	No	Administrator, Lakshadweep MHA	7	

6. Sikkim				
(i) Gangtok, Rumtek Phodang and Pemayangtse	Yes	Indian missions abroad, immigration officers at airports at Bombay, Calcutta, Madras and	15	MHA, All F.R.R.Os, all New Delhi. Chief secretary/home secretary/secetary (tourism) government of Sikkim, Gangtok, T.G. of Police. Gangtok Asst. Director (tourism), government of Sikkim, Silliguri, Dy. Director (tourism) Sikkim Government of New Delhi, resident commr. Government of Sikkim, Calcutta, tourism officer, Rengpo, dy. commr. Darjeeling, dy. secretary home department., government of West Bengal, Calcutta
(ii) Zongri in West Sikkim	No	HA and all issuing	15	For trekking authorities of government of Sikkim and its representatives at Calcutta and Silliguri and Rangpo
7. Mizoram				
Vairangte, Thingdawl and Aizawl	No	Home commr. Government of Mizoram Aizawl, all F.R.R.Os at Delhi,	10	Tourist groups are to travel on the identified tour circuits only Bombay and Calcutta, Chief immigration officer, Madras all India missions abroad
8. Himachal Pradesh				
(i) Poo-Khab-Sumdo-Kaja	No	MHA/Government of Dhankar-Tabo-Gompa-Concerned/ITBP		For trekking H.P./DM/SDM
9. Arunachal Pradesh				
Itanagar, Ziro, Along, Pasighat, Miao, Namdapha and Tipi	No	Home commr.Government of Arunachal Pradesh, Itangar, all F.R.R.Os	10	Tourist groups are to travel on the identified tour, tour circuits only at Delhi, Bombay, Calcutta, chief immigration
10. Uttar Pradesh				
(i) Nanda Devi Sanctuary, Niti Ghati and Kalindi Khal in Chamoli and Uttar Kashi Districts	No	MHA/Government of U.P./Dm/SDM Concerned/ITBP		
(ii) Adjoining areas of Milam Glaciar	No	MHA/Government of U.P./DM/SDM Concerned/ITBP		

HEALTH CERTIFICATE REGULATIONS

W.H.O. has published a handbook which is circulated amongst all member countries of the United Nations. This handbook contains detailed information about health certificates and formalities required to be fulfilled.

Health protection of travellers is viewed from a dual standpoint including preventive and curative measures. Vaccination is the internationally accepted form of preventive health care. Curative measures are based on the particular circumstances related to climate, environment and disease factors at the destination.

A standard format has been developed for vaccination certificate so that the procedure of one country is recognised in other countries. This is an excellent example of international co-operation in the prevention of diseases.

All travellers are advised/must be advised to contact their local health department, physician or private agency minimum two weeks prior of departure to obtain information on vaccination or revaccination. Bureau of Epidemiology and Centre for Diseases Control publish *Blue Sheet* a weekly report giving current details of all countries, if they are infected with some quarantinable diseases (Cholera, small pox, and yellow fever).

The validity of vaccination certificate and incubation period, recommended by Department of Epidemiology is as follows:

FOR VACCINATION

Small Pox: not less than 8 days from departure and not more then 3 years old. Incubation period–14 days.
Cholera: not less than 6 days and not more than 6 months old. Incubation period–5 days. For Revaccination.
Small Pox: certificate becomes valid from the date of revaccination.
Cholera: Vaccination to be done within six months of previous vaccination then vaccination becomes valid immediately.
Yellow Fever: Revaccination must be done within 10 days. Then vaccination becomes valid immediately.

CUSTOM AND MIGRATION

On coming back to country of origin, for example, India, all passengers must show their passport when clearing immigration. After immigration every traveller must clear customs, where their bags may be opened because all articles acquired in abroad and brought in India are subject to pay duty and internal revenue tax. But as a returning resident one is entitled for certain exemptions from paying duty on items obtained during their trip abroad. These concessions and exemptions are discussed in the Baggage Rules, 1994.

The combined value of all goods purchased abroad, which may be imported duty-free should not exceed a certain limit of a amount for person. This list of duty-free goods may include 200 cigarettes or 50 cigarettes or 250 gm. of tobacco, or alcoholic liquor and wine upto one litre and 50 cartridges of fire arms within the overall permissible monetary limit.

FOR TOURIST OF FOREIGN ORIGIN, EXEMPTION

From duty on personal effects are listed in the Baggage Rules, 1994, which are subject to amendment from time to time and these changes are publicly notified for upgradation if informations of travel agents to advise their client to avoid duty hastles.

Rule 11 of Baggage Rules lays down conditions of personal effects of a tourist which shall be allowed to be imported temporarily without duty if:

- Personal effects are for the personal use of tourist;
- They are part of baggage accompanied by tourist;
- There is no reason to fear misuse; and
- These personal effects, after consumption whatever is left would be reimported by tourist to country of his/her origin.

Note: Expression that 'personal effects' would carry the meaning to all clothings, all articles—new or used, which a tourist may personally and reasonably acquire during his trip to several countries.

A tourist may bring an important item like audiovisual aids including slides, cameras, and films for demonstrations and instructional purposes, so, with an undertaking to re-export all these items on TBRE from tourist can get exemption from duty on these item. Re-export permission is granted by customs authorities only when they are convinced that articles are meant for bonafide use of tourist. But if tourist fail to fill up of BRE form either incidentally or intentionally and make an attempt to pass through Green channel, which is meant for passenger, carrying goods within free allowance or for passengers not carrying dutiable baggage. If such a passenger is stopped by custom officer for interrogation all such items which are even meant for re-export would be dutiable no exemption can be sought by tourists (Rule 7 of Baggage Rule, 1995):

- Baggage Rules also allow foreign tourist and import-free of duty, at the discretion of proper officer, articles of personal use free of duty intended to be given as gifts. The maximum amount limit of such an item/article is Rs. 600/- (Rule 1 of Baggage Rules, 1994).
- Tourists of Indian origin but who are residing abroad and whose stay in India is for more than 24 hours, may be allowed, at the discretion of proper officer, to import articles of personal use free of duty intended to be given as gift. The list of such items may include:
- Watch, tools and equipments required for study/ research, equipment and raw films, transistors; portable television set, dry fruits, and antiquities, etc.

  (Rule 5 of Baggage Rule, 1995).
- For the temporary import of private road vehicles or the components. Thereof exemption from custom duty through a notification from Department of Revenue, Ministry of Finance, Government of India, Circular No. 53-cus-dated, May 1st, 1997, providing that such vehicles are required to be re-exported within permitted period failing which such imported vehicles will be subject to custom duty under Customs Act 1962.

  (Article 1 of Customs Convention).

Foregin Exchange Regulations:

These regulations and restrictions are mentioned in Foreign Exchange Regulations Act (FERA) amended in 1993, applied to all citizens of India, outside India and to branches and agencies outside India of companies or bodies corporate, registered or incorporated in India. These regulations can be enforced by:

- Director of Enforcement
- Additional Director of Enforcement
- Dy. Director of Enforcement
- Asst. Director of Enforcement
- Other such officers appointed by Directorate of Enforcement for the effective enforcement of this Act.

This act also provides authorisation to agencies to deal with foreign currency exchange. Most vital role in this direction is played by Reserve Bank of India who authorises any person or an agency to deal with foreign exchange. Sub-section 1 of this act provides that no person other than authorised dealer shall in India, and no person residing in India other than an authorised dealer shall outside India purchase or otherwise acquire or borrow from, or sell or otherwise transfer or lend to or exchange with any person not being on authorised dealer, any foreign exchange.

REGULATION REGARDING INSURANCE

Insurance companies active in the field of movement of persons and travel have become increasingly involved in the provision of insurance to protect the client as well as the agents, or the operator of tourism services, so now travel trips are enjoyable with a vacation travel insurance. Which assures protection against unforeseen disasters, financial distress and mental agony which could be the result of disturbance to the most carefully planned vacation. Agencies are selling the following three sets of covers:

(1) Personal effects and baggage insurance,
(2) Trip cancellation insurance,
(3) Air passenger insurance.

Personal Effects and Baggage Insurance

Insurance covers the entire trip, 24 hours a day at every place in air or on roads. Exception is to damage caused by normal wear and tear, hostile or war-like action, deterioration, illegal act, insurrection, rebellion, revolution, radioactive or nuclear contamination, confiscation by the order of law authorities, animals, artificial teeth limbs, contact lenses, credit cards, documents, furniture, vermin insects, money, rugs of any, type securities, tickets, automobiles, auto-equipments, boats, motors, etc., while checked as baggage with common carrier.

As per the terms and conditions of Insurance Cover, immediate reporting of loss or damage in writing should be made to proper authorities; failure to this will invalidate any claim to this effect.

Trip Cancellation Insurance

Insurance is provided to the maximum amount selected by client for non-refundable portion of travel expenses like airfare, land and water common carriers such as boat, train, etc., and hotel and other accommodations pre-arranged by self or by an agency.

Air Passenger Insurances

This is also referred to as Travel Accident Insurance. This covers injuries suffered by a passenger while on board of a scheduled airline's flight. According to this cover amount is payable on the policy obtained for the following:

- Loss of life, limb, sight.
- Accident medical expenses, and
- Hospital sickness benefits.

PART-C: REGULATORY LAWS FOR ACCOMMODATION SECTOR

Accommodation Laws

The accommodations/lodging sectors of the tourism industry are highly fragmented with more than 50,000 establishments operating in the United States, ranging from small roadside motels to resort casinos with more than 3,000 rooms. Included within the lodging industry are inns, hotels, motels, spas, taverns, restaurants, casinos, and resorts.

Common Law Duties in General

Hotels and motels have to duty a provide accommodations without discrimination to all those who request them and to take reasonable care in the operation of the property as well as in satisfying the guest by offering services of high quality to prevent unreasonable risks of harm to the guests and their property. Generally, innkeepers have a duty to: (1) receive and accommodate travellers; (2) provide safe accommodations; (3) protect guests from harm; (4) protect the property of guests; (5) provide good quality of food; and (6) ensure privacy. It has long been recognised that an innkeeper assumes these duties upon holding out to the traveller hotel accommodations.

Regulations for accommodation sector in India can be referred to at two stages:

- Approval stage
- Classification stage.

Guidelines for Approval of One to Five-Star Hotel at the Project/Planning Stage:

Approval 1. The hotel industry is entitled to various benefits including, among other things, income tax concessions under the Income Tax Act and priority consideration of its various requirements like telephone, telex, LPG, etc., by the government authorities at Municipal, State and Union levels or a semi or a quasi-government body. To be eligible for these benefits, a hotel has to be approved by the Department of Tourism. Such approval is granted from the point of view of the suitability of a hotel for foreign tourists and approved hotels are required to maintain certain minimum level of standards of service and amenities.

Approval 2. The approval can be applied for at the project/ planning stage. A hotel approved at the project stage is eligible for allocation of foreign exchange for its essential imports of equipment and provisions. On completion and becoming functional, like other functioning hotels, it also gets worldwide publicity through tourism literature published by the Department of Tourism and distributed through its offices in India and overseas. Approved hotel projects are also eligible to apply to the Industrial Finance Corporation of India and Tourism Finance Corporation of India and the respective State Finance Corporation for the grant of loan. The application for loan is considered by these financial corporations in the context of detailed feasibility studies, etc., and the project approval by the Department of Tourism should not in any way be considered as an assurance for the grant of any loan thereto.

Application: The application for approval of a hotel at the project/planning stage should be submitted in the prescribed form complete in all respects, to the Director General of Tourism, C-I Hutments, New Delhi-110011 in the case of hotel projects planned for the 4 and 5-Star categories; and to the Regional Director of the concerned Government of India Tourist Office at Delhi/Mumbai/Calcutta/Chennai in the case of 1,2 and 3-Star categories. A copy of the application should be endorsed to the Director/Manager of the nearest Government of India Tourist Office and to the Director (Tourism) of concerned State Government.

Requirements

Various documents and information to be furnished about hotel projects when applying for project approval are given in detail in the application form. However, the basic requirements are given below and these should be sent along with the application:

(i) A project report establishing the feasibility of the proposed hotel, describing the amenities to be provided at the hotel particularly mentioning any special or distinctive features and indicating the star category which the establishment is being planned for. The criteria applied in determining the star category of a hotel on classification by the Hotel and Restaurant Approval and Classification Committee as a functioning unit, are briefly described later in these guidelines.

(ii) The site selected should be suitable for the construction of a hotel intended for foreign tourists. While selecting the site such aspects as its accessibility from airport/railway station/shopping areas, etc., making it a convenient location, may be kept in mind as also that its environs that it is not crowded, noisy, unhygienic, etc.

(iii) A land-use certificate from the concerned State/local authority certifying that it is permissible to construct a hotel on the site selected. Blue prints of the sketch plans of the project (including front and side elevation) indicating the areas, with dimensions of the rooms/bathrooms/public rooms, etc., duly signed by the architect and the promoter. The Department has prescribed certain minimum area standards for guest rooms and attached bathrooms and it should be ensured that none of the guest rooms/attached bathrooms fall short of the prescribed minimum carpet areas limits which are given below:

Type of Hotel	*Star U*	*Single Room*	*Double Room*	*Attached Bathroom*
(1) City Hotel	5-Star Deluxe	180 sq.ft.	200 sq.ft.	45 sq.ft
	5-Star	180 sq.ft.	200 sq.ft.	45 sq.ft.
	4-Star	120 sq.ft.	140 sq.ft.	36 sq.ft.
	3-Star	(AC and N-AC).	(AC and N-AC)	
	2-Star	100 sq.ft.	120 sq.ft.	30 sq.ft.
	1-Star	(AC and N-AC).	(AC and N-AC)	
(2) Resort	5-Star	180 sq.ft.	200 sq.ft.	45 sq.ft.
Hotel	4-Star	120 sq.ft.	140 sq.ft.	36 sq.ft.

(iv) Ownership Deed of the Land.

(v) Urban Land Ceiling Certificate, if applicable.

(vi) Approval of International Airports Authority of India/Director General of Civil Aviation if hotel project is near an airport.

(vii) Name and business antecedents of the promoters.

(viii) Proposed ownership structure, giving full details as to whether the new undertaking will be owned by individual(s) or a firm or a company.

(ix) Estimated cost of the project and the manner in which it is proposed to raise the funds to meet the cost.

(x) The Department has prescribed regulatory conditions to be adhered to by promoters of furnish the acceptance of these regulatory conditions and the form of their acceptance appears later in these guidelines.

Regulatory Conditions for Approval of Hotel Projects

All hotels approved by the Department of Tourism are required to furnish the following information:

(1) Documents relating to its legal status, i.e. if the company is incorporated under the companies Act, a copy of its Memorandum and Articles or Associations, if it is a partnership firm, a copy of the partnership deed and the certificate of registration under the partnership Act, if it is a proprietory concern name and address of the proprietor etc.

(2) Any licence and/or approvals required from the local administration/police and/or other concerned authorities for the construction/operation of the hotel should be obtained directly by the promoters from the concerned authorities. The approval by the Department will not, in anyway, substitute for them. This Department's approval will be deemed to have withdrawn in case of violation of this condition as and when brought to its notice.

(3) In the event of the promoters making any change in the plans of the project as submitted earlier, the

approval of this Department will have to be applied for afresh.

(4) Officers of the Department of Tourism or any other officer deputed by the Department to inspect the hotel premises from time to time will be allowed free access with or without prior notice.

(5) As a project which has been approved from the point of view of its suitability for foreign tourists the promoters will be eligible for grant of loan from Central/State Financial Institutions and priority in the procurement of building material, telephone and telex connections, etc. However, this approval should not in any way be construed as an assurance for the grant of these facilities since this would fall within the jurisdiction of the concerned authorities.

Conditions to be Fulfilled after the Hotel becomes Functional

1. The hotel must immediately inform to the Department of Tourism the date from which it became functional, and apply for classification within 2 months thereafter.
2. The hotel will submit the following information to the Director General, Department of Tourism so as to reach on or before 31st May, each year for the preceding financial year:

(a) A bank certificate regarding foreign exchange deposited by the hotel;

(b) Total bed capacity offered by the hotel as given under:
Single Rooms
Double Rooms
Suites.

(c) Number of rooms occupied on a permanent/semi-permanent basis by residents/staff officers, etc.;

(d) A specimen copy of the current tariff card;

(e) List of the names of the Senior Executives with their designation, experience, etc. (Department-wise);

(f) Total number of persons employed indicating separately the number of Indian and foreign staff;

(g) Annual report of the hotel and a statement showing the audited balance sheet and profit and loss account within 4 months of the close of the financial year;

(h) Statistical returns regarding the number of guests, rooms, occupancy, income and employment on regular basis as prescribed by the Department of Tourism from time to time.

3. The Regional Director/Director/Manager of the Government of India, Tourism Offices of the region and the Director General, Department of Tourism should be kept informed from time to time about the facilities introduced or withdrawn and of any additions or alterations made regarding the bed capacity of the hotels.

4. The hotel tariff should be prominently displayed in each room. This card shall also indicate all taxes, service charges, etc.

5. If a hotel confirms a booking at a particular rate, it will be honoured at the same rate even if accommodation at higher rates only is available at the time of the guest's arrival. Alternatively, if accommodation at a lower rate only is available and the guest elects to use it, the lower rate should be charged.

6. Normally, no rooms will be let out for purposes other than residential. However, with the prior approval of the Department of Tourism not more than 10 per cent of the rooms in the hotel will be let out to any person or company for residential or commercial purposes.

7. In case, the hotel is required to provide guides for tourists, only those guides who have been approved by the Department of Tourism should be employed in places where such guides are not available.

8. The hotel should at all times adhere to the high standard of maintenance and services for which it has been recognised and in all dealings with its guests observe practices worthy of an establishment of repute.

9. The officers of the Department of Tourism or any other officer deputed by it to inspect hotel premises from time to time will be allowed free access with or without prior notice.

In the event of breach of any of the above conditions by the hotel, the Department of Tourism shall have the right to withdraw approval.

REGULATION REGARDING ACCOMMODATION

Classification State

Department of Tourism with a classification committee comprising of members belonging to Federations of Hotels and Restaurant Association of India, deals with the classification of Hotels. This committee is called HRACC (Hotels and Restaurants Approvals and Classification Committee). Based on the recommendation of this committee deserving hotels are awarded the appropriate star category and are placed on the approved list of Department. Approved hotels become eligible for various fiscal reliefs and benefits. The Department interceded on behalf of such hotels whenever necessary to ensure that their needs get priority consideration from various concerned authorities.

These hotels also get worldwide publicity through tourism literature published by Department of Tourism and distributed by their offices in India and abroad. Approved hotels become eligible for foreign exchange for import of essential equipments and provisions and for their advertising, publicity and promotion under the import entitlement scheme in export-import policy.

To be eligible to apply for classification a functioning hotel must fulfil the following minimum basic requirements and all hotels should adhere to these strictures strictly in order to get the required classification.

FIVE STAR CATEGORY

General Features

The facade, architectural features and general construction of the hotel building should have the distinctive qualities of a luxury hotel of this category. The locality, including the immediate approach and environs should be suitable for a luxury hotel of this category, and there should be adequate parking space for cars. The hotel should have at least 25 lettable bedrooms, all with attached bathrooms with long baths or the most modern shower chambers. All public rooms and private rooms should be fully air-conditioned and should be well-equipped with superiors quality carpets, curtains, furniture, fittings, etc., in good taste. It would be advisable to employ the services of professionally qualified and experienced interior designers of repute for this purpose. There should be an adequate number of efficient lifts in the building of more than two stories (including the ground floor) with 24 hour services. There should be a well-designed and properly equipped swimming pool. There should be a well-appointed lobby and ladies and gentlemen cloak-room equipped with fittings and furniture of the highest standard.

Facilities

There should be a reception, cash and information counter attended by highly qualified trained and experienced personnel and conference facilities in the form of one each or more of the conference rooms and banquet halls, and private dining rooms. There should be a bookstall, a beauty parlour, a barber shop, recognised travel agency, money changing and safe deposit facilities, left luggage room, a florist and a shop for toilet requisites and medicines on the premises. There should be a telephone in each room for the use of guests and visitors and provision for a radio or relayed music in each room. There should be a well-equipped well-furnished and well-maintained dining room/restaurant on the premises and wherever permissible by law, there should be an elegant, well-equipped bar/permit room. The pantry and cold storage should be professionally designed to ensure efficiency of operation and should be well-equipped.

Services

The hotel should offer both international and Indian cuisine and the food, and beverage services should be of the highest standard. There should be professionally qualified, highly trained, experienced, efficient and courteous staff in smart, clean uniforms, and the staff coming in contact with guests should be flare and fluent in English. The supervisory and senior staff knowing at least one continental language should be rotated on duty at all times. There should be 24 hours service for reception, information and telephones. There should be provision for reliable laundry and dry-cleaning services. Housekeeping at the hotel should be of the highest possible standard and there should be plentiful supply of linen, blankets quality available. Each bed room should be provided with a good vacuum jug/ thermos-flask with ice cold, boiled drinking water except where centrally chilled purified drinking water is provided. There should be special restaurant/dining room where facilities for dancing, orchestra are provided.

FOUR STAR CATEGORY

General Features

The facade, architectural features and general construction of the building should be distinctive and the locality including the immediate approach and the environs should be a suitable for a hotel of this category. There should be adequate parking facilities for cars. The hotel should have at least 25 lettable bed rooms, all with attached bathrooms. At least 50 per cent of the bathrooms must have long baths or the most modern shower chambers, with 24 hours service of hot and cold running water. All public and private rooms should be fully air conditioned and should be well-furnished with carpets, curtains, furniture, fittings, etc., in good taste. It would be advisable to employ the services of professionally qualified and experienced interior designers of repute for this purpose. There should be an adequate number of efficient lifts in building of more than two storeys (including the ground floor). There should be a well-appointed lobby and ladies and gentlemen's cloakrooms equipped with fittings of a standard befitting a hotel of this category.

Facilities

There should be a reception, cash and information counter attended by trained and experienced personnel. There should be a book stall, recognized travel agency, money changing and safe deposit facilities and a left luggage room on the premises. There should be a telephone in each room and telephone for the use of guests and visitors and provision for a radio or relayed music in each room. There should be a well-equipped, well-furnished and well-maintained dining room/restaurant on the premises and wherever permissible by law, there should be an elegant, well-equipped bar/permit room. Kitchen, pantry, cold storage should be professionally designed to ensure efficiency of operation and should be well-equipped.

Services

The hotel should offer both international and Indian cuisine and food,and beverage services should be of the highest standard. There should be professionally qualified, highly trained, experienced, efficient and courteous staff in smart, clean uniform and the staff coming in contact with the guests should be fluent and flare of English. It will be desirable for some of the staff to possess knowledge of a foreign language and staff knowing at least one continental language should be rotated on duty at all times. There should be provision of reliable laundry and dry-cleaning services. House keeping at the hotel should be of the highest possible standard and there should be a plentiful supply of linen, blankets, towels, etc., which should be of the highest quality available. Each bedroom should be provided with a vacuum jug/flask with ice cold, boiled drinking water. There should be a special restaurant/dining room where facilities for dancing, orchestra are provided.

THREE STAR CATEGORY

General Features

The architectural features and general construction of the building should not be of a very good standard and the locality, including the immediate approach and environs should be suitable for a very good hotel and there should be adequate parking facilities for cars. The hotel should have at least 20 lettable bedrooms, all with attached bathrooms having bath tubs and/or showers which should be modern in design and equipped with fittings of a good standard, with hot and cold running water. At least 50 per cent of the rooms should be air-conditioned and the furniture and furnishings such as carpets, curtains, etc., should be of a very good standard and design. There should be adequate number of lifts in buildings with more than two storeys (including the ground floor). There should be a well-appointed lounge and a separate ladies and gentlemen's cloakroom equipped with fittings of a good standard.

Facilities

There should be a reception and information counter attended by qualified and experienced staff, and a bookstall, a recognised travel agency, money changing and safe deposit facilities on the premises. There should be a telephone in each rooms (except in seasonal hotels where there should be a call bell in each room and a telephone on each floor for the use of hotel guests) and a telephone for the use of guests and visitors to the hotel. There should be a well-equipped and well-maintained air-conditioned dining room/ restaurant and wherever permissible by law, there should be a bar/permit room. The kitchen, pantry and cold storage should be clean and organised for orderliness and efficiency.

Services

The hotel should offer good quality cuisine both Indian as well as continental, and the food and beverage service should be of good standard. There should be qualified, trained, experienced, efficient and courteous staff in smart and clean uniforms and the supervisory staff coming in contact with the guests should understand English. There should be provision for laundry and dry-cleaning service. Housekeeping at the hotel should be of a very good standard and there should be adequate, supply for linen, blankets, towels, etc., of good quality. Similarly, cutlery, crockery and glassware should be of good quality. Each bedroom should be provided with a vacuum jug/thermos-flask with cold, boiled drinking water. The hotel should provided orchestra and ball room facilities and should attempt to present specially choreographed Indian cabaret.

TWO STAR CATEGORY

General Features

The building should be well-constructed and the locality and environs including the immediate approach should be suitable for a good hotel.

"The hotel should have at least 10 lettable bedrooms of which at least 75 per cent should have attached bathrooms with showers and a bathroom for every four remaining rooms. All bathrooms should have modern sanitation and running cold water with adequate supply of hot water, soap and toilet paper. At least 25 per cent of the rooms should be air-conditioned and all rooms should be properly ventilated, clean and comfortable with all the necessary items of furniture. There should be a well-furnished tongs.

Facilities

There should be a reception counter with a telephone. There should be a telephone or call bell in each room and there should be a telephone on each floor unless each room has a separate telephone. There should be a well-maintained and well-equipped dining room/restaurant serving good, clean wholesome food, there should be a clean, hygienic and well-equipped kitchen and pantry.

Services

There should be experienced courteous and efficient staff in smart and clean uniforms. The supervisory staff coming in contact with guests should understand English. There should be provision for laundry and dry-cleaning services. House-keeping at the hotel should be of a good standard and clean and good quality linen, blankets, towels, etc., should be provided. Similarly crockery, cutlery and glassware should be of good quality.

ONE STAR CATEGORY

General Features

The general construction of the building should be good and the locality and environs, including immediate approach should be suitable. The hotel should have at least 10 lettable bedrooms of which at least 25 per cent of the bathrooms should have western style WCs. All bathrooms should have modern sanitation and running cold water with adequate supply of hot water, soap and toilet paper. The rooms should be properly ventilated and should have clean and comfortable bed and furniture.

Facilities

There should be a reception counter with a telephone and a telephone for the use of guests and visitors. There should be a clean and moderately well-equipped dining room/restaurant serving clean wholesome food, and there should be a clean, well-equipped kitchen and pantry.

Services

There should be experienced, courteous and efficient staff in smart and clean uniforms and the senior staff coming in contact with guests should possess a working knowledge of English. Housekeeping at the hotel should be of a good standard and clean and good quality linen, blankets, towels, etc., should be supplied. Similar crockery, cutlery and glass-ware should be of good quality.

A classification fee at the following rate is payable by the hotel applying for classification:

- 1-Star - Rs. 2,000
- 2-Star - Rs. 3,000
- 3-Star - Rs. 4,000
- 4-Star - Rs. 6,000
- 5-Star - Rs. 8,000
- 5-Star Deluxe - Rs. 10,000

The classification fee is payable by means of a demand draft drawn in favour of the Pay and Accounts Officer, Department of Tourism, New Delhi. For reclassification, fee will be 50 per cent of the above fee.

- The Department of Tourism has introduced a new category of *Heritage Hotel's*. It covers running hotels in places/castles/forts/havelies/residences of any size, which were built prior to 1950. The fee payable for classification in the heritage category is Rs. 5,000 and for reclassification Rs. 2,500.

Application form for Heritage, 4,5, and 5-Deluxe categories can be had from the Member Secretary, HRACC, Department of Tourism, Government of India, C-I Hutments, Dalhousie Road, New Delhi-110 011.

> The powers to classify hotels in 1, 2 and 3 star categories have been delegated to the respective Regional Directors of the Government of India Tourist Offices with effect from 1.1.93.

A hotel applying for 1, 2 and 3 star category is, therefore, required to approach the concerned Regional Office of the Department of Tourism at Delhi, Mumbai, Calcutta, and Channai.

PART-D: CARGO REGULATIONS

1. Regulations: Carriage of cargo is governed by conditions of contract under International and Non-international Carriage of cargo (other than Baggage and Mail) regulations as amended from time to time, the conditions of contract are printed on Consignee's copy of Air Waybill and are also available in Indian Airlines/Agents offices.

2. Instructions for Despatch of Goods: Shippers are required to complete and sign the instructions for despatch of goods which is available at Airlines/Agents offices.

3. Advance Arrangement: The following shipments/ commodities may be accepted with advance arrangements:

(a) Shipments of unusual shape and size
(b) Human remains
(c) Perishables
(d) Valuable cargo
(e) Livestock
(f) Dangerous goods
(g) Shipment and concentrated weight exceeding aircraft floor limitation
(h) Any other shipment requiring special handling/ care.

4. Packing: Shipments are required to be packed so as not to injure or damage persons or other cargo, properties and to ensure safe carriage with ordinary care in handling.

(a) Dangerous goods are required to be packed in accordance with IATA Dangerous Goods

Regulations. The articles must be listed with proper shipping name. The shipper is also required to sign shippers certification as required under IATA Dangerous Goods Regulations.

(b) Shipments containing liquids are required to be packed in containers strong enough to prevent breakage or damage in transit or caused by pressure or altitude.

5. Marking: Shippers are required to address legibly and durably the consignee/consignor's name, city, address, contact telephone number (if any) on each shipment. Delete and/or obliterate the old marking from the package.

6. Labelling: For the carriage of dangerous goods, the shippers have to attach to each package containing such articles the appropriate label(s). Where space permits, labels shall be adjacent to the consignee's address. Remove and/or obliterate the old labels.

7. Contract of Carriage: Contract of Carriage as evidenced by Air Waybill will automatically be terminated once the delivery is effected.

8. Check list for acceptance of cargo:

(a) Shippers letter of instructions for Despatch of Goods is invariably obtained duly filled in.

(b) Before acceptance the cargo should ensure that packing of goods is strong enough to withstand the normal transportation. Also should ensure that there is no evidence of any damage/leakage.

(c) Ensure that proper markings are given on the packages that is consignor's consignor's full postal address including telephone number (if any).

(d) Ensure that necessary labels are affixed to the packages specially with "Dangerous Goods" and "Live Animals" shipments.

Cargo Rates and Charges

1. Minimum Charges:

(i) Minimum charges for any consignment shall be charged for each one kg. at under 45 kg. at the rate of Rs. 20 whichever is higher.

(ii) When applicable weight or volume charged for a consignment is lower than the minimum charges established by the carrier, the minimum charge shall apply.

(iii) Minimum charge published does not include other charges.

(iv) There is separate minimum charges for certain other charges.

(v) For minimum charges on International Shipments, shippers may contact Indian Airlines/Agent office.

(vi) Minimum freight charge on valuable cargo is Rs. 40.

2. General Cargo Rate (GCR): The rate established for cargo in general also known as "General Commodity Rate" They are as follow:

(i) Basic freight—rate generally expressed as a normal under 45 kg rate.

(ii) Quantity Discount (Bulk) Rate(s) based on specified quantities of consignment on specified sectors/route(s) and is generally offered for weight breaks of 40 kg and above.

3. Specific Commodity Rate (SCR): The rate(s) applicable for carriage of specifically designated commodity from/to "Specifically Designated" points to promote the growth of "Specified Commodities".

4. Class Cargo Rate(s): A rate applicable for carriage of "Specifically" designated class of goods. This is generally expressed as a percentage of a normal rate and takes precedence over all other rate(s). The following commodities shall be treated as class cargo on Indian Airlines Domestic Services:

(i) Live animals

(ii) Valuable cargo

(iii) Newspapers, magazines, books, etc.

(iv) Human Remains.

Rates for Class Cargo

(i) Live animals will be carried at 200 per cent of the basic freight rate per kg subject to minimum charge of Rs. 50 with certain exceptions.

(ii) Valuable cargo shall be charged at 200 per cent of basic freight rate per kg in addition to valuation charge.

(iii) Newspapers, magazines, books, etc., are carried at a discount rate of 33.3 per cent of the under 45 kg. rate.

(iv) Human remains are carried on normal basic freight rate on weight or volume basis.

5. Other Charges: The following are the other charges established by the Indian Airlines:

(i) Documentation Charges:

(a) Rs. 10 per shipment for domestic transportation.

(b) Rs. 40 for domestic-cum-international transportation for Afganistan, Nepal, Bangladesh, Srilanka, Maldiv Islands, Pakistan and other countries.

(ii) Cartage Charge:

(a) A minimum cartage of Rs. 6 on all consignments weighing up to and including 5 kg shall be charged whether the shipment is carried in IA transport in one direction that is city to airport or vice versa or in both directions that is city to city.

(b) For consignments weighing over 5 kg., a charge of 60 paise per kg or part thereoff will be levied as cartage charge in case the cargo is carried on IA transport city to city.

(c) For consignments over 5 kg., 30 paise per kg or part thereoff will be charged as cartage charge in case the cargo is carried on IA transport one way that is city to airport or vice versa.

(d) Maximum cartage charge for a single consignment shall be Rs. 350.

(e) The above cartage charge will also supply on domestic-cum-international shipments when booked at inland points.

(iii) Dumerage charge:

(a) If freight is not collected within seven days from the date of arrival of the goods, a dumerage charge of Rs. 0.60 per kg per day shall be levied from the eight day up to including the 14th day.

(b) If freight even on the 15th day after arrival, a charge of Rs. 1.50 per kg. per day shall be levied from the 8th day itself.

(c) A minimum charge of Rs. 30 shall be leviable on every consignment 8th day onwards.

(d) Dumerage charges shall be levied on the actual weight or volumetric weight, whichever is higher.

(iv) Charge Collect Fee:

A shipment may be accepted on charge collect (to pay) provided the freight and valuation charges, if any, are Rs. 500 or more and does not contain the following:

(a) Perishables items,

(b) Newspapers,

(c) Human remains,

(d) Unaccompanied baggage/personal effect,

(e) Where the resale value of goods would be less than the total amount to be collected.

(f) Livestock.

A charge collect fee @ 4 per cent of freight and valuation charges, if any, will be levied on such shipments subject to minimum of Rs. 50.

7

COMPARATIVE STUDY OF TOURISM REGULATIONS IN THE U.S. AND CANADA

The job of regulating tourism in other countries also is assigned to public sector which plays a crucial role in issuing regulation most required for sustainable development of tourism in their respective countries. To make the study simpler and extensive we can take up examples of few countries like the U.S. and Canada, to undertake indepth study of their regulations. Besides and beyond national regulations there are also International Regulations to affect tourism. Most important of them are related to civil aviation discipline which calls for bilateral or multilateral agreements among countries located in different geographical regions.

Just like our country, in other countries also classification of laws and regulations is done on the basis of functional areas they are meant for, e.g., for Accommodation Sector on the following:

- Classification and grading-rating of hotels and other establishments types.
- Fire safety regulations.
- Health safety regulations.
- Building and zoning regulations.
- Licensing regulations for liquors, etc.
- Liability regulations for guests and their belongings.
- Labour and taxation laws.

For travel trade on:

- Regulation and licensing of travel agents, tour wholesellers and operators.
- Regulation of promotions.
- Labour and taxation legislation.

For Transport sectors on:

- Controls of fares and tariffs.
- Licensing of carriers.
- Regulation of safety procedures.
- Control of route entry and exit.
- Limitation of weight and capacities.
- Negotiations of services.
- Subsidisation of routes.
- Labour and taxation legislations.

In the U.S. role of preparing legislation and regulation related to tourism, is assigned to the U.S. Federal Government reflecting the country's national interest in tourism and its interrelationship with other aspects of the U.S.-Soviet and businesses. The U.S. senate committee on Commerce has identified the following five areas of interests:

- Health and other aspects of quality of life.
- Tourism as an economic activity.
- Meeting business travel demand.
- Facilitation of International Tourism.
- Tourism's impact on publicly owned lands.

In addition to recognising tourism's direct impact and interrelationship with those five areas of interest, the committee has also recognised that tourism interacts with the national economy, the functioning of transport system, system of social and eco-statistics, the forms of environmental protection, clearance of International visitors, the public revenue and forms of consumer protection.

The most comprehensive analysis of federal legislation in the U.S. was completed in 1976, as part of National Tourism Policy study, when it was realised that on orderly system of law is crucial and the development of the U.S. travel and tourism industry of the Senate Commerce Committee seprated the existing tourism legislation in the U.S. into two main categories:

(a) Federal Tourism Legislations Covering

- Tourism promotion and development legislation.
- Tourism resource legislation.

(b) Federal Tourism Related Legislations

- Interstate transport investment and regulation.
- Non-immigrant visa and custom regulations.
- Economic development legislation.
- Environment quality control legislation.
- Energy legislation.
- Land use legislation.
- Tax legislation.

In the U.S., government uses two methods for enforcing of regulations either by establishing regulatory agencies like: Civil Aeronautics Board (CAB), Federal Aviation Administration (FAA).

Interstate Commerce Commission (ICC).

Federal High Way Administration (FHWA).

National High Way Traffic Safety Administration (NHWTSA).

Federal Maritime Commission (FMC).

United States Coast Guards (USCG).

Federal Trade Commission (FTC).

Or by utilising regulatory techniques.

Many of the regulatory agencies existing in the U.S. have been created as a result of passing of Federal Tourism related legislation. For example, CAB was established in 1938, in order to protect the safety of public and to maintain the viability of the U.S. Airline Industry. With this objective in focus CAB, like DGCA in India, was given full authority to determine which airline could operate on what routes and charging what fares in the U.S., so since it's inception it has been the most influential regulatory agency in the U.S. with respect to its impact on tourism within the country. But with the passing of Airline Deregulation Act in 1978, process of winding up of CAB started because it has not only gone too far in trying to maintain the viability of Airline Industry, but also because of its tardiness in responding to proposals presented by individual airline companies. But due to long time-lag either the companies changed their minds or they lost the benefit of the marketing opportunity they were seeking. By 1983, it lost its authority on scheduling time tables of airlines and fixing up of tariffs.

Federal Aviation Administration (FAA) is responsible for regulating the manufacturing, operation and maintenance of aircrafts to determine and certify the technical proficiency and physical fitness of flight areas as well as to certify airports by inspecting from time to time their navigation facilities.

Interstate Commerce Commission (ICC) primarily regulates rail roads, water carriers and express agencies in interstate commerce.

Federal High Way Administration (FHWA) is responsible for developing highway safety standards, to keep accident prone areas under scrutiny, to involve itself in highway designing, construction and maintenance and to run safety education programme.

National High Way Traffic Safety Administration (NHWTSA) is to regulate the vehicle safety standards. Federal Trade Commission is like our consumer forums which are primarily concerned with preventing deceptive advertising, application of unethical means/practices in business, etc.

Public sector besides appointing regulatory agencies, it also applies regulatory techniques. Normally these are concerned with use of land in fixing up of user's quota based on a resources carrying capacity, putting restrictions of an ownership transfer of land, and establishing reservation systems and by using an eminent domain in the U.S. which allows the U.S. Federal Government to take over endangered lands and historic sites. Just like Federal Government State Governments have also different regulatory powers. For example, to protect the interest of consumers in Rhodes Islands, a Travel Agency Act was passed which permits State Governments to issue licences to agents at state level too, as well as regulations regarding protection of state parks and state owned lands.

At a minimum level in the U.S., tourism law creates and defines the following basic concepts:

- Travelling as a basic right.
- Reliable and safe transportation must be readily available.

- Safe and adequate accommodation must be available for travellers.
- All travellers should have access to such transportation.
- Cost of travelling and accommodation must be reasonable.
- Regulation of travel tourism may be necessary.
- Redress for transgression of rights and regulations is necessary.

These concepts form the foundation of various federal and state laws relating to different segments of the U.S. tourism industry. In short the U.S. tourism law draws from a variety of sources beyond just "Court of Law". It is also derived from Federal Estate Constitution and Statutes, Federal Estate Regulatory Agencies from treaties whether bilateral or multilateral.

There are various types of laws in effect in the United States. These types may be grouped into four categories:

(A) Substantive V/s Procedural Laws

- Substantive includes all those rules defining, describing and regulating conducts or creating some legal obligation for state laws which establishes health regulations for restaurants or liability standards for innkeepers are substantive laws.
- Procedural laws are concerned with method and process for enforcing rights, duties and obligations imposed by substantive laws.

(B) Public V/s Private Law

Public Law governs the relationship between individual and government. Administrative Law in as example where authority for conducting food service and restaurant inspection by state and local public health departments are derived from state statutes.

Private Law deals with rights, obligations and legal relationship arising from 'arms-length' transactions and agreements between individuals. For example, a traveller who sues a motel for failure to provide accommodation at a previously agreed upon prices and time period is within the realm of private law.

(C) Criminal V/s Civil Law

Criminal Law is concerned with establishing standards of conduct and for prosecuting offences committed by an individual against public at large. For example, most states have enacted penal statutes making it a crime for a person to leave a hotel/motel with the intention to avoid payment for lodging. Once established the "skipper" can be prosecuted under Criminal Law.

Whereas Civil Law deals with a branch of a legal duty created by a statute to define conducts, rights and obligations between individuals or between individuals and their governments. In this law suit one party tries to make other party comply with a duty of care or pay the damage caused by the failure to comply with.

(D) Contract V/s Tort Law

Both of these types have their origin in common law. Both of these deal with standards of conduct and provide a means for imposing civil liability for wrongful acts.

Contract law regulates the creation and enforcement of agreements between persons, corporation or government. It is a promissory agreement indicating what offer will give in return for a specific promise. For example, in travel and tourism industry Contract Law is prevalent in providing the underspinning for employment contract and for sale of goods and services like transportation, hotel/motel accommodations, food service and entertainment.

Tort Law establishes the standards of conduct to protect the public against unreasonable risks of harm. Tort is a civil wrong, other than breach of contract, aiming at providing compensation to individuals who suffer because of dangerous or unreasonable conduct of others. Damages caused by negligence in travel and tourism are most common lawsuits under Tort Law.

THE U.S. LAWS ON TRANSPORTATION

Transportation sector referred to as "common-carrier" includes airlines, bus companies, railroads and cruiselines. Over the last 30 years most crucial role is played by transportation by providing low cost public transportation furnished by these common carriers all over the world. So, there appeared a sudden need of laws and statutes to regulate and control the activities of businesses providing public transportation.

For airlines, prior to 1978, i.e., before the passing of Airline Deregulation Act 1978, disputes between passengers and airlines were usually resolved according to Federal Regulatory Laws but State Rules of Laws were not applied in spite of best effort of plaintiffs. Once the Airline Deregulation Act was passed it not only changed the manner in which domestic air transportation is marketed and delivered to public but it also changed fundamental rules of law governing obligations and disputes between airlines and passengers. Now these obligations and regulations came to be known as "contract of carriage" covering areas of disputes on—ticket purchase, overbooking, flight delays and cancellation, lost, stolen, or damaged, baggage/luggage, personal injury, liability, etc.

Buses and Railroads which are largest mass transporters of travellers unlike Airlines which is transportation leader in sales revenue. Buses in the U.S. are grouped into two segments: (a) intercity buses travelling along designated routes, and (b) escorted bus tours for recreation and sight-seeing. In the first category, biggest role players are: Greyhound and Trailways operating more than 20,000 buses over a route network of 2,13,000 miles. In the second category the most popular name is Graylines which is offering more than 3000 sight-seeing excursions normally. For these carriers, Interstate Commerce Commission (ICC) is the regulatory agency to issue permit to new company, to allow to add on or and drop any service by the existing company and even to give permission to change the route. Regulations are also provided to establish terms and conditions for contract of carriage. Deregulation of bus service took place in 1982, through Bus Regulatory Reform Act. Thereby easing the entry and exit of bus companies into market as well as to give companies rate freedom. Bus companies are free to select routes of their choice, to choose the pick up points of their preference with set fares. Only regulations existing is about limiting the liability for lost or damaged baggage.

For ship transportation, which is one of the oldest forms of travel, but yet cruise ships are known to be new on waterbed because these companies are more in entertainment business than in pure transportation whereas ships used to provide only "destination-to-destination" travel. Since two destinations are involved in travel by sea too, complex jurisdictional questions arise, i.e., what law to apply whether-foreign, federal or State and where to file the lawsuit. These complexities have cropped up because Maritime Law (Law of Sea) often governs disputes with cruiseships. Under this law a vessel at sea is considered to be part of country under whose flag it flies and all on board are subject to law of that foreign country. Further this Law also provides a provision in contract containing jurisdiction clause mentioning that disputes can be resolved in the court of the country where ship is registered.

Some legal problem related area of the U.S. transportation sector can be earmarked as:

(a) Ticket Sales.
(b) Disclaimers of liability.
(c) Failure to honour ticket reservation/overbooking.
(d) Travel delays/changes/cancellations.
(e) Delayed damaged/lost luggage.
(f) Physical injury/death.

(A) In transportation sector tickets/passage of right are sold to public either through direct sales, retail travel agents or through wholesalers who use these seats as part/component of total four package. When an individual buy a ticket from supplier, enters into contract of carriage on specific conditions which are printed on ticket. For details of these conditions individual may contact carriers ticket counter, which are periodically reviewed and modified. So, it is advisable to collect and read them periodically.

(B) This contract of carriage includes liability disclaimers, limiting their liability to a fixed monetary amount to cover reservation, dishonour, overbooking, lost or damaged luggage claims, travel delays and passenger injury or death claims.

(C) The main cause of dishonour of reservation is overbooking which is a breach of contract because carrier knows that it won't be possible to deliver a seat to passenger when he/she turns up to board the carrier.

In case of airlines, Deregulation Act, 1978, provides that airline must use auction method in which 'bumped' passenger may get a seat if another passenger voluntarily gives up his/her seat. To attract and encourage volunteers, airline may offer incentives ranging from cash to free airline ticket. But if such that a situation comes, number of volunteers are insufficient, in such a case airline may apply boarding priority rules to deny boarding facility to some passengers for which they are entitled for compensation. The rules governing payments of such compensations and each airlines boarding priorities, are available at all airport ticket counters. Of all airlines, we can read one example for such a compensation.

One old woman was travelling from Phoenix to Washington with one sub-station. When she arrived at the airport she found that flight is overbooked. Some of the passengers might be bumped and unfortunately she was one of them. She was told by officials at airport ticket counter that she has options like: either she may get 200 per cent of remaining value of ticket up to maximum amount of the US $ 400, if airlines arranges for travel on another flight and passenger arrives within two hours of departure original flight, which to late due to bad weather, the compensation is half of the amount of ticket up to a maximum amount of the US $ 200.00.

In case of buses and cruiselines this problem of overbooking is not very common. But if breach of contract, negligence or fraudulent, misrepresentation is proved passenger is entitled to award of compensation against damages.

(D) Timely transportation is the cornerstone of carriage contract between supplier and user. If any deviation from schedule is proved, it may expose the carrier to liability to passenger.

In airlines, if flight is cancelled or delayed for long hours, airline may be liable for passenger's costs associated with alternative transportation, which may even be more expensive. To avoid such situations some airlines limit all or some of their liabilities by disclaiming in contract of carriage responsibility for flight delays or cancellations by offering a defuse to the delay. For example, bad weather, mechanical malfunction, safety concern, air traffic controller delay, nonconnections and improper scheduling by tour operators.

In case of buses and railroads tickets contain legally enforceable disclaimers that carrier is not liable for delay because it is very difficult to overcome it. But if passenger proves that he/she has lost business income and personal discomfort caused by available delay, carrier may be liable to pay penalty.

In case of cruiselines brochures advertise ports of call during a particular cruise so, one selects a particular cruise considering list of events at one or more ports of call, which may include shopping, fair or participation in sports activities. But when there is deviation in departure from one port of call causing delay in arrival at subsequent port of call, defeats the whole purpose for selecting this particular cruise. As a way to protect themselves from liability from itinerary changes cruiselines often adds on disclaimer in their ticket stating:

"Neither the company nor the ship......shall be or be held liable for..........damage arising from......any defect or breakdown in the ship, machinery, gear or fittings whether existing before or at the time of sailing or otherwise or preventory or delaying the sailing....for arising from defaults or errors in navigation or in the management of the ship."

By such a disclaimer cruiselines donot seek to absolve itself from all liabilities but objective is to limit liability to a specified amount of damage.

(E) Claims for delayed, damaged or lost luggage run in million. The common carrier considered to be the insurer of a passenger's luggage so is liable to pay compensation for delay, damaged or lost luggage.

Federal rule in case of lost or damaged baggage fixes the liability of carrier to the US $ 1,250 per passengers under normal circumstances. But in some exceptional cases with extenuating circumstances the court of law may deviate from established rule. For example, one passenger was flying to France with his skiing kit, but airline mishandled his luggage containing special clothing and skiing kit and he received them only when vacation was over. But he purchased second set of same to enjoy his vacation. When he filed a case against the airline, court of law ordered damages as compensation for all his out of pocket expenses plus an additional amount for diminished value of ski package.

In case of buses and railroads carriers can limit the limitation by incorporating disclaimers in its tariff application as a result of what when a passenger books his luggage worth the U.S. $ 1,500 he is entitled and a compensation of only the U.S. $ 500. But if these disclaimers in tariff application arenot approved by Interstate State Commission (ICC), the court could ignore the disclaimer and follow Common Law Liability standards.

Cruiselines donot rely on a tariff system to limit liability. So they use ticket disclaimers and deny or to limit their liability. Disclaimers for total liability is subject to criticism by court in many cases but courts normally upheld disclaimers to reduce liability.

(F) Since travel has never been risk free, accidents may happen anywhere and at any time and we hear of several hundreds of tourists have been killed. So, Law does impose on operators a high standard of care to protect the life and luggage of their passengers. In case of an airline, the liability of an airline carrier for passengers injury or death is based on negligence and Common Carrier Law. As a general rule, an airline is liable to pay compensation in case of death/injury caused by negligence in maintenance and operation of aircraft. Accidents are not just caused by poor maintenance of aircrafts but also by negligence of air crew members by operating flights on low lying, flying into storm or ignoring weather conditions, aircraft overloading, error in judgement of route, etc.

Warsaw convention of 1929, has provided disclaimers in case of International flights.

WARSAW CONVENTION, 1929

If the passenger's journey involves an ultimate destination on stop in a country other than the country of departure the Warsaw Convention may be applicable and the convention governs, and in most cases limits the liability of carrier for death or personal injury and in respect of loss of or damage to baggage.

Conditions of Contract

1. As used in this contract 'ticket' means the passenger ticket and baggage check of which these conditions and the notice form part, carriage in equivalent to 'transportation' 'carrier' means all air carriers, that carry or undertake to carry passenger or his baggage hereunder or perform any other services incidental to such air carriage. 'Warsaw Convention' means the convention for the unification of certain rules relating to International carriage by air, signed at Warsaw, 12th September, 1955, whichever may be applicable.
2. Carriage hereunder is subjected to the rules and limitations relating to liability established by Warsaw Convention unless such carriage is not 'International Carriage' as defined by the convention.

3. To the extent not in conflict with the foregoing carriage and other services performed by each corner are subjected to the following:
   (i) Provisions contained in the ticket.
   (ii) Applicable tariffs.
   (iii) Carrier's conditions of carriage and related regulations which are made part hereof (and are available on application at the offices of carrier), except in transportation between a place in the United States or Canada and any place outside thereof to which tariff in force in those countries apply.
4. Carrier's name may be abbreviated in the ticket, the full name and its abbreviation being set forth in carrier's tariffs, conditions of carriage, regulations or timetables carrier's address shall be the airport of departure shown opposite the first abbreviation of carriers name in the ticket. The agreed stopping places are those places set forth in this ticket or as shown in carrier's timetables as schedule stopping place on the passenger's route.
5. An air carrier issuing a ticket for carriage over the chest of another air carrier does so only as its agents.
6. Any exclusion or limitation of liability of carrier shall apply be for the benefit of agents, servants and representatives of carrier and any person whose aircraft is used by carriage and its agents, servants and representatives.
7. Checked luggage will be delivered to bearer of the baggage check. In case of damage to baggage moving in an International carrier complaint must be made in writing to carrier forthwith after discovering of damage and at the latest, within seven days from receipt; in case of delay, complaint must be made within 21 days from the date of baggage was delivered.
8. This ticket is good for carriage for one year from date of issuee except as otherwise provided in this ticket, in carrier's tariffs, conditions of carriage, or related regulations. The fare for damage hereunder

is subjected to change prior to commencement of carriage, carrier may refuse transportation. If the applicable fare has not been paid.

9. Carrier undertakes to use its best efforts to carry the passenger and baggage with reasonable dispatch. Times shown in timetables or elsewhere arenot guaranteed and form no part of this contract, carrier may without notice substitute alternate carrier or aircraft and may alter or omit stopping places shown on the ticket in case of necessity. Schedules are subject to change without prior notice. Carriers assume no responsibility for making connections.
10. Passenger shall comply with government travel requirements, present exit, entry and other required documents and arrive at airport by time fixed by carrier or, if no time is fixed, early enough to complete departure procedures.
11. No agent, servant or representative of carrier has authority to alter, modify or waive any provision of this contract.

Baggage Liability Limitations

Liability for loss, delay, or damage to baggage is limited as follows unless a higher value is declared in advance and additional charges are paid. For most international travel (including domestic portions of international journeys) the liability limit is approximately the US $ 20.00 per kilo for checked baggage and $ 400.00 per passenger for unchecked baggage for travel wholly between US points Federal rules required any limit on airline's baggage liability to be at least the US $ 1,250.00 per passenger.

Excess valuation may be declared on certain types of articles. Some carriers assume no liability for fragile, valuable or perishable articles. Further information may be obtained from the carriers.

Advice to International Passengers on Limitation of Liability

Passengers on a journey involving an ultimate destination or a stop in a country other than the country of origin are advised that applicable laws and rules to the entire journey, including any portion entirely within the country of origin or destination must be understood thoroughly. For such passengers on a journey to from or with an agreed stopping place in the United States of America, the convention and special contracts of carriage embodied in applicable tariffs provide that the liability of certain carrier's parties to such special contracts, for death of passenger's not to exceed the US $ 75,000 per passenger, and that this liability up to such limit shall not depend on negligence on the part of the carrier.

For such passengers travelling by a carrier not a party to such special contracts or on a journey not to, from, or having an agreed stopping place in the United States of America, liability of the carrier for death or personal injury to passengers is limited in most cases to approximately the US $ 10,000 or US $ 20,000.

The names of carriers, parties to such special contracts, are available at all ticket offices of such carriers and may be examined on request.

Additional protection can usually be obtained by purchasing insurance from a private company. Such insurance is not affected by any limitation of the carrier's liability under the Warsaw Convention or such special contracts of carriage. For further information please consult with the representative of your airline or insurance company.

Note: The limit of liability of the US $ 75,000 above is inclusive of legal fees and costs except that in case of a claim brought in a state where provisions is made for separate award of legal fees and costs, the limit shall be the sum of the US $ 58,000 exclusive of legal fees and costs.

In case of bus and railroad carriers disclaimers defences have not been allowed by court to disclaim liability for passenger's injury or death.

In case of cruiselines, under the rules of governing common carriers, cruise lines have a contractual duty to transport passengers safely to their destination. If failed, companies are liable to play for passengers injury or death resulting from negligence in the maintenance and operation of the ship and its equipment. We have a very good example in case of Mrs. Dhillon V/s Baltic Shipping Co. already discussed in Chaper 4.

The U.S. Laws on Accommodation

As a law of common duties hotels and motels have to provide accommodation without discrimination to all those who promise to pay for services consumed during their stay. Although these common law duties are very old but today a combination of common law and statutory duties are imposed on innkeepers to protect the public, traveller and guests. These are as follow:

(A) duties to receive and accommodate travellers,
(B) protect guests from harm and to provide safety,
(C) provide safe, fit and hygienic food to eat,
(D) protect property of guests,
(E) to provide privacy.

(A) Since hotels and motels are in business to earn profit, they have a common law duty to receive and accommodate travellers until the facility is at capacity. This obligation remains effective 24 hours a day, 7 days a week and 365 days a year. In other words, no property owner can refuse accommodation due to laterion of the hour or late time of the week. Nor does the property owner can limit his obligation to receive only those who are in a position to contract, i.e., even the minors who are children unaccompanied by their parents are also required to be received and accommodated by innkeepers.

It is the Federal Civil Rights Act of 1964, which prohibits places of "public accommodation" from discriminating against any person on grounds of race, colour, religion or national origin. The expression "public accommodation" refers to hotels, motels, inns, taverns, bars, restaurants, roadhouses, beauty parlours as well as other types of service establishments.

An innkeeper can refuse accommodation only when:

- The hotel in full and has no room available.
- The guest appears to be intoxicated or drug influenced conditions.
- Person seeking accommodation has a commu-nicable disease.
- Person appears to be disorderly or is likely to be a threat to other guests.
- Person has no luggage or has property consisting of banned articles like skin of wild animals, snakeskin, firearms, etc.
- Person appears to be destitute and unwilling to pay or there is a reasonable ground to believe that person is seeking accommodation to commit a criminal act.

(B) Though the hotel is not the insurer of guests' safety but it must exercise utmost care to protect guest from any harm caused due to the following:

- Negligence of hotel employees under "respondent superior" the act of employee, bonafide or matafide became the acts of employer and subjecting employer to liability.
- Acts of other guests, since innkeeper is peacekeeper and so, must reasonably control the conduct of all guests in the premises.
- Acts of non-guests committed on premises for example in a discotheque or in a restaurant which is open to guest's as well as to non-guests also. It becomes obligation of innkeeper to protect their guests from any assault or criminal acts from non-guests or otherwise.

Not only this innkeeper, though not an insurer, yet is also responsible to provide safe accommodation to guests. In one of leading cases Ms. Connie Francis, one of renowned entertainer, was awarded the to US $ 2-5 million for an alleged assault and rape that occurred while rapist allegedly entered in the room from an unsecured sliding glass door.

(C) Hotel or a restaurant is to provide safe and hygenic food to its guests. Normally the food served has to be of a standard which is considered fit for human consumption.

(D) Common law makes innkeeper liable for the full value of lost or damaged goods. But state statues have divided limited liability into the following three sections:

(i) Money valuable for which hotels have to maintain a safe to allow guest to keep their valuables in this safe and to let known guests their availability in the safe.

(ii) For losses from fire; liability of hotel is limited until negligence of innkeeper is established and if it is then hotel is liable for full value of guest's property, which is generally the case.

(iii) For losses to property in transit; possession and control of guest's property during transit make it liable to pay for full value of loss.

(E) A general proportion is that a guest expects privacy in his/her room and so innkeeper's duty is to prevent disturbance caused by any unregistered guest or by third party. Moreover, it is responsibility of innkeeper not to allow search/seizure of any property of any guest by warrantless policemen.

REGULATIONS AND LEGISLATION IN CANADA

Prior to 1978, when sector task free on Canadian Tourism Industry submitted its report, there were lots of regulations and legislations at both Federal, Provincial and Municipal level having direct relationship with tourism. But when sector task force recommended that industry could be effective economically when many or at least of some of these laws or regulations would be updated. It was only after this that Government of Canada established IDCT (Interdepartmental Committee on Tourism) as well as Canada's NTO. It was realised that main goals of IDCT shall be to upbring co-operation and co-ordination between public and private sector as well as to consult and liaise with other federal agencies.

There are several regulatory agencies within Canada whose activities have direct impact on Tourism. Most important among these is Canadian Transport Commission (CTC) which has parallel organisation to the US CAB (Civil Aeronautics Board) in Air Transport Committee (ATC), a specific task group within CTC to make regulatory decisions. But the airline scenario in Canada was quite different from the US because Air Canada, being a national carrier had less of complexities. But with gradual passage of time regulation were eased to allow private airline companies to provide scheduled services within Canada. Thus, in Canada we see regulated competition as contrast to the US open market situation.

Canadian Tourism Committee is also responsible for regulation of railways and merchant shipping in Canada. It is the duty of Coast Guard under Transport Canada to check regulate the activities of non-merchant boats and ships on Canadian waters including those of recreational cruise/ sight-seeing vessels.

8

A TAXONOMY OF TOURISM LEGISLATIONS

Before specific tourism legislations are described, it will be better to classify them, as are commonly found in most of the countries. One method of classification is to group the tourism legislation into functional areas such as those related to the protection of environment, those related to economic development, those related to frontier controls and so on [for example, as in the U.S.]. Another method of classification of legislation is to group them on an industry sector basis by identifying the legislation that relate to airlines, hotels, travel agents, wildlife, customs and foreign exchange, etc. In this respect both 'horizontal' legislations, which effect every industrial sector, be it tourism or nontourism as income tax, labour legislation as well as "specific" legislations, which are related directly to one industrial sector. The following chart illustrates commonly found tourism legislation in India classified on a sectorial basis:

- Laws related to Travel Agency
- Laws related to Accommodation
- Laws related to Wildlife Preservation and Protection
- Laws related to Airlines Industry
- Laws related to Surface Transport
- Laws related to Forest Preservation
- Laws related to Constitutional Remedies
- Laws related to Protection and Preservation of Monuments, Ancient Arts and Antiquities.

Secondary sector of tourism industry in India includes retailers, car rental agencies, commercial attractions operators and other allied businesses which have their own specific legislations and regulations in addition to the horizontal laws and regulations that apply to all.

PART-A: LEGISLATIONS RELATED TO TRAVEL AGENCY, BUSINESS

Travel Agencies play a vital role in the travel and tourism field. They assist individuals or groups, wishing to take trips, in planning their itineraries, providing the facilities like hotel and transportation reservations, obtaining or preparing ticket and performing ancillary services too. At the times it seemed a travel would have been cumbersome without a travel agent.

Law of Agency

Agency is based on the principle that a business or a place of business rendering service on behalf of some firms or organisations. According to this principle, all acts which a person can do or is bound to do except those which from their very nature can only be performed personally, can be done through an agent. The principal is bound by the acts of his agent and can get the benefit of such acts as if he had done them himself. However, no person can effectively do through an agent what he himself is legally incompetent to do personally.

Meaning of the Term 'Agent'

According to Sec. 182 of the Contract Act; "an agent is a person employed to do an act for another or to represent another in dealings with third persons". The person for whom such act is done or who is so represented is called the 'principal'. The relationship between the agent and the principal is called 'agency'.

Thus an agent is a link between the principal and third parties and thereby establishes a privity of contract between them.

Test of Agency

It may be emphasised that the use of the word 'agent' is not conclusive for determining the correct relationship between the parties. In fact, the phrase 'to do any act for another' used in Sec. 182 is very wide. Apparently, the implication of these words would be to constitute even a servant or a casual employee as an agent, which is somewhat very correct.

Whether a particular relation between the two persons is existed, depends upon the words or expressions used in the contract. It has to be gathered from the terms and conditions of the contract and the functions and responsibilities of the person employed to do any act or to represent a person in dealings with third persons. The essential element of agency is the exercise of delegated authority to do a lawful act on behalf of another and establish privity of contract between such persons and a third party.

AGENCY DISTINGUISHED FROM OTHER RELATIONS

(A) Agent and Servant

Historically, the relation of principal and agent developed from the relation of master and servant. However, the status of agent is different from that of servant due to the following reasons:

(i) Servant has no representative character. He acts under the direction and control of his employer. He is not concerned with employer's business transactions with third parties.

The agent has the authority to act on behalf of his principal and has power to create legal relations between the principal and third person.

(ii) A principal has the right to direct what the agent has to do but a master has not only that right but also the right to say how it is to be performed. In other words, agent has discretion as to the time and manner of performance.

(iii) The master is responsible for the servant's wrong doings in the course of his employment. In the case of principal-agent relationship, however, the principal is liable for the acts of the agent provided those acts are within the scope of agent's authority.

(iv) Agent gets commission while the servant renders his service for wage or salary.

(v) An agent may work for a number of principals at the same time whereas a servant works for one master at a time.

(B) Agent Vs Bailee

A person can be called bailee so long as he has the possession of goods of the bailor. Possession is essential for relationship of bailment. But a person may act as an agent of another without having the possession.

Moreover, an agent represents the principal in his dealings with third parties which is not the case with the bailee.

Capacity to Appoint Agent and to Become Agent

Agency is designed to bring the principal into contractual relationship with the third parties. It means to the principal must have the contractual capacity as is evident from Sec. 183 which provides that, any person who is of the age of majority according to the law to which he is subject and who is of a sound mind may employ an agent.

On the contrary, it is immaterial whether or not the agent has legal capacity to make a contract. As per Sec. 184, any person who is not even of the age of majority can bring about contractual relation between the principal and third party. But he will not be responsible to the principal. It implies that if a minor who is an agent, misconducts himself, the principal can not claim any compensation from him.

Consideration

Contract of agency needs no consideration. Sec. 185 provides that 'no consideration is necessary to create an agency.' Actually, the detriment to the principal in consenting, to be represented by the agent, is sufficient to support the contract.

Creation of Agency

Agency may be created in any of the following ways:

1. **Expressly (Sec. 187):** When an agent is appointed by words, spoken or written, his authority is said

to be expressed. A power of attorney is the usual form of a written contract of agency whereby a specified person is empowered to act on behalf of the person appointed.

Agents appointed to execute a deed of conveyance of property, to sign the prospectus of a company, to act as proxy for a shareholder, etc., should be authorised in writing.

2. **Impliedly (Sec. 187).** Agency which arises from the conduct of the parties, or inferred from the circumstances or ordinary course of dealings between the parties, is said to be implied. In an implied authority, the principal will not be entitled to limit the implied authority of the agent without notice to the third party so as to adversely affect his rights.

Implied agency may be any of the following kinds:

(i) Agency by estoppel (Sec. 237)

When an agent has, without authority, done acts or incurred obligations to third person on behalf of a principal, the principal is bound by such acts and obligations if he has, by words or conduct, induced such third person to believe that such acts and obligations were within the scope of agent's authority.

In other words, the conduct of the principal makes room for the application of the principal of estoppel and the person who is permitted to act as agent is deemed in law to have been permitted by the principal to act as such. The person who deals with him are entitled to assume that the agent has the authority to represent the principal. Such authority is known as 'ostensible authority'. The principal cannot later on deny such authority of the agent. For instance, A says to B in the presence and within the hearing of C that he is C's agent. C remains silent. B supplies goods to A taking him as C's agent. Then C is responsible for the payment of the price of those goods.

(ii) Agency by ratification (Sec. 196-200)

Ratification means subsequent adoption of an act by the principal, originally done by the agent without authority. This is an agency ex-past-factor. An agent who possesses limited authority but exceeds his authority, may bind the principal if the act done in excess of authority is later ratified by the principal. According to Sec. 197 *Where acts are done by one person on behalf of another, but without his knowledge or authority, he may elect to ratify or to disown such acts. If he ratifies them, the same effect will follow as if they had been performed by his authority.* The unauthorised act is converted in an authorised act from the moment the act was done and not from the date of ratification.

According to Sec. 197, ratification may be expressed or implied. For instance, A without authority buys goods for B. Afterwards B sells them to C on his own account. B's conduct implies ratification of the purchase made from him by A.

Condition of ratification: Ratification becomes valid if the following conditions are satisfied:

(a) *The agent must have purported to act for a principal:* The act must be done for or on account of the principal. Though it is not necessary to name the principal, he must be identifiable by designation and agent should purport to act on his behalf. There can be no ratification of an act which the agent has done in his own name. For instance in Keighley Maxsted and Co V Durant 1901, R authorised by K to buy wheat at a certain price exceeded his authority and bought at a higher price for D.R bought in his own name but intended to buy for K. K agreed with R to take the wheat at the price but failed to take delivery. Hence, K was not responsible to D as he could not ratify R's contracts.

(b) *The principal must be in existence:* For ratification to become valid, the principal must have been in existence at the time the contract was made. Accordingly, a company can not ratify pre-incorporation contracts made by the promoters since it was not in existence on the date when contract was made.

(c) *The principal should have contractual capacity:* Principal can ratify the acts of the agent provided he was competent to contract on the date the act sought to be ratified was done.

(d) *The act should be capable of ratification:* The act must be legal which the principal must be competent to do. Transactions void *ab initio* cannot be ratified. There can be no valid ratification of illegal or void acts. Similarly, a company cannot ratify unauthorised acts of directors which are beyond the scope of memorandum.

(e) *Full knowledge of material facts:* Ratification must be made with full knowledge of all the material facts. Ratification by a person whose knowledge of the facts of the case is materially defective, shall be bad in the eyes of law and will not bind the parties to the contract (Sec. 198).

(f) *Ratification cannot be partial (Sec. 199):* Ratification must relate to the whole of the act and not a part of it. Ratification of a part of the act will not be valid.

(g) *Ratification must not put a third party to lose (Sec. 200):* An act which is unfavourable to the interests of a third person, cannot be ratified. For instance, A holdes a lease from B terminable on three month's notice. C, an unauthorised person gives notice of termination to A. The notice can not be ratified by B so as to be binding on A.

(h) *Ratification should be done within a reasonable time:* Ratification must be made either within the time fixed or within a reasonable time after the contract was made by the agent. Ratification made after the expiry of time fixed for ratification will not be valid.

(iii) Agency by Necessity

Where a person is entrusted with the property of another and in an emergency it is necessary to do something for the preservation of the property and it is impossible to communicate with the owner, the person entrusted with the property becomes an agent of necessity with implied authority to do what is necessary to save the property. To constitute a valid agency by necessity, following conditions must be satisfied:

(a) It should be impossible to communicate with the principal.
(b) There should be an actual and definite commercial necessity.
(c) The agent of necessity must act in the interests of all the parties concerned.
(d) The agent should have adopted the most reasonable and practicable course under the circumstances, and
(e) The agent must have been in possession of the goods belonging to his principal and which are the subject of contract.

Illustration

The master of the ship, on finding that the cargo is rapidly perishing, is entitled to dispose it off at the best price available so as to bind the consignor as an agent by necessity.

Wife as an Agent of Necessity

(A) Where the husband and wife are living together in a domestic establishment of their own:

In such a case, the wife shall have an implied authority to pledge the credit of her husband for necessities except in the following circumstances:

(a) Where the husband has expressly forbidden the wife from borrowing money or buying goods on credit, or
(b) The article purchased did not constitute necessities, or
(c) He had given sufficient funds to the wife for purchasing the articles she needed to the knowledge of the seller, or
(d) The creditor has been expressly told not to give credit to wife.

(B) Where the husband deserts his wife without any of her fault:

She has an implied authority to bind the husband for necessaries, if he does not provide for her maintenance. The husband cannot escape liability by telling her wife not to ledge his credit by telling the tradesmen not to supply her necessaries on credit. But if the wife lives apart of her own will and without any justification, she cannot be treated as an agent of her husband and cannot bind her husband even for necessities.

Kinds of Agents

On the basis of extent of authority, agents are divided into the following three classes:

(i) **Special Agent:** A special agent is one who is appointed for a particular purpose. He is invested with limited powers and cannot bind the principal in respect of any other act, contract or transaction than for which he is employed, i.e., if a person is employed to purchase a house, his authority comes to an end as soon as house is purchased.

(ii) **General Agent:** A general agent has the authority to do all such acts as are connected with a particular kind of business or trade. Third parties are entitled to assume that the agent has the authority to do everything that is necessary in the course of the business.

(iii) **Universal Agent:** He is one who enjoys unlimited powers to do all such acts as could be delegated and which the principal himself could lawfully perform. Such agents are generally appointed by businessmen who owing to their physical condition want to retire by giving a blanket power of attorney to the agent to do anything that has to be done while he is in service.

(iv) **Mercantile Agent:** Mercantile agent has, in the customary course of his business, authority to sell goods, to consign goods for the purpose of sale or to buy goods or raise money on the security of goods on behalf of his principal. When a mercantile agent in possession of goods with the consent of real owner sells them in the ordinary course of his business to a bona fide buyer for value, the buyer will get better title to goods even though the mercantile agent had no authority to sell.

We may distinguish the following types of mercantile agents:

(a) **Factor:** He is a mercantile agent who is in actual possession of goods belonging to the principal. He can sell or consign the goods in the customary course of business. He may not only sell the goods on the terms he deems fit, but do it in his own name, receive the payment and give a valid discharge to the buyer. He may pledge the goods and receive money on them. He has lien on the goods for a general balance of account with the principal.

(b) **Broker:** Like a factor, he is also an agent appointed by a person to buy or sell goods on his behalf. But he does not have the possession. He merely negotiates a contract and acts as intermediary between two contracting parties. Neither he can sue in his own name nor can he exercise lien on the goods since he does not have possession thereof.

(c) **Commission Agent:** He is an agent employed to buy or sell goods on behalf of his principal. He is paid commission for his services.

(d) **Del Credre Agent:** He is an agent who guarantees the solvency of those whom he introduces to his principal. In consideration of an extra commission, the del credre agent guarantees his principal that third parties with whom he contracts will honour their financial obligation. He is thus an agent and a surety at the same time.

(e) **Auctioneer:** An agent appointed by the seller to sell his goods at the public auction for a reward in the form of commission is known as an auctioneer. He is primarily the agent of seller. Even if he sells the goods below the reserve price either inadvertantly or contrary to principal's instructions, the sale will be binding on the principal. He can receive the price of the goods sold and sue for the same in his own name.

Delegation of Authority

The general principal is "Delegatus non potest delegare", i.e., a delegate cannot further delegate. An agent himself being the delegate of his principal cannot further delegate his powers. This is specifically provided in Sec. 190. But delegation is permitted if there is ordinary custom of trade, or delegation becomes necessary owing to the nature of the agency. Other exceptions allowing delegation include the following:

(i) Express permission of the principal
(ii) Conduct of the principal
(iii) Unforeseen emergency, and
(iv) Ministerial work.

The person to whom delegation is made may be either a 'sub-agent' or 'substituted agent'.

Sub-agent: A sub-agent is a person employed by and acting under the control of the original agent in the business of agency (Sec. 191). Sub-agent may be appointed in the following cases unless expressly forbidden:

(a) When the ordinary custom of trade permits the appointment of a sub-agent.
(b) When the nature of business requires the appointment of a sub-agent.
(c) When the principal agrees to the appointment of sub-agent.
(d) When the act to be done is purely ministerial and involves no exercise of discretion or confidence.
(e) When some unforeseen emergency has arisen.

Where the sub-agent is properly employed, the principal, so far as regards third person is represented by the sub-agent and is bound by and responsible for his acts as if he was an agent originally appointed by the principal. Principal is bound by the acts of a properly appointed sub-agent. But sub-agent is not responsible for his acts to the principal but only to the agent who appointed him. In turn, the agent is responsible to the principal for the acts of sub-agent.

However, as per Section 192 the principal has a right of action against the sub-agent in the case of fraud or wilful wrong committed by him. Of course, the principal has the choice of suing either agent or sub-agent for such acts.

Where the sub-agent is improperly appointed, the relation between the agent and the sub-agent is that of principal and agent. As such, the agent is responsible for the acts of the sub-agent both to the principal and to the third parties. Since the principal is not represented by such a person, he is not responsible to the third parties. The sub-agent is not responsible to the principal even for fraud or wilful wrong.

Substituted Agent

According to Sec. 194, where an agent holding an express or implied authority to name another person to act in the business of the agency has accordingly named another person, such a person is called the substituted agent. The substituted agent is taken as agent of the principal for such part of the work entrusted to him. For instance, A directs B, his solicitor to sell his estate by auction and to employ an auctioneer for the purpose. B names C, as an auctioneer to conduct of sale. C is not a sub-agent but A's agent for the conduct of sale.

It should be noted that as soon as the substitute is appointed, the agent gets out of picture making room for the substitute to perform the act for which he is appointed. The substituted agent is responsible to the principal for duly discharging his duties as if he was appointed by the principal himself.

In selecting substituted agent for his principal, an agent is bound to exercise the same amount of discretion as a man of ordinary prudence would exercise in his own case and if he does this he is not responsible to the principal for acts of negligence of the substituted agent.

> ***Illustration:*** A instructs B, a merchant, to buy a ship for him. B employed a ship surveyor of good reputation to choose a ship for A. The surveyor makes the choice negligently and ship turns out to be an unseaworthy and is lost. B is not liable to A. Rather it is surveyor who is responsible to A.

Difference between a Sub-agent and a Substituted Agent

1. A substituted agent is only named by the agent but acts under the direct control of the principal. A sub-agent works under the control of the agent.
2. There is no privity of contract between sub-agent and the principal. Neither of them can sue the other. But both can sue the agent. However, in the case of substituted agent, there is privity of contract between the principal and the substituted agent and both can sue each other.
3. The agent is responsible to the principal for the acts of sub-agent but not for those of the substituted agents.

EFFECT OF AGENCY ON CONTRACTS MADE BY THIRD PARTIES

The consequences of agent's acts done in the course of his employment, in relation to third parties can be studied under the following three heads:

I. When the Agent Contracts for a Named Principal:

(a) **Acts within the authority of the agent:** The principal is bound by the acts done by the agent within his actual authority. He will also be liable to third parties for the acts of the agent which may be beyond his actual authority but which come within his ostensible authority unless the third party knows of the limitations on the agent's apparent authority. For example, A leaves a watch with B, an auctioneer with the instruction that it is not be sold below Rs. 100. B sells the watch to C for Rs. 80 who does not know about the special instruction. A can not set aside the contract.

(b) **Acts beyond agent's authority:** Where the agent acts in excess of his authority, actual or ostensible, the principal may ratify them and in such a case the acts of the agent become the acts of the principal and principal becomes liable to third parties for such acts of the agent as are provided in Section 196.

In case, the principal does not ratify the unauthorised acts of the agent and it is possible to separate what is within authority of the agent from what is beyond his authority, the principal becomes bound and hence liable to third parties only for what is within agent's scope of authority (Sec. 227).

Illustration: A being an owner of a ship and cargo authorises B to procure an insurance for Rs. 4,000 on the ship. B procures a policy of Rs. 4,000 on the ship and another for the like sum on the cargo. A is bound to pay the premium for the policy on the ship but not the premium for the policy on the cargo.

Where an agent does more than he is authorised to do and what he does beyond the scope of his authority can not be separated from what is within it, the principal is not bound to recognise the transaction (Sec. 228). For instance, A authorises B to buy 500 sheep and 200 lambs for the sum of Rs. 6,000. A may repudiate the whole transaction.

(c) **Liability of the principal inducing belief that agent's unauthorised acts were authorised:** Section 237, which incorporates the doctrine of estoppel, provides that where the principal holds out a person to be authorised by him, the person dealing with him is entitled to assume that his acts are within the scope of his employment. For instance, A consigns goods to B for sale and instructs him not to sell below a certain price. C being ignorant of B's instructions enters into a contract with B to buy the goods at a price lower than the reserve price. A is bound by the contract.

(d) **Doctrine of constructive notice:** Under Section 229, knowledge of the agent is deemed to be the knowledge of the principal provided. The knowledge of the agent was obtained in the course of business transacted by him for the principal. For instance, while buying goods from C on behalf of B, A an agent comes to know that goods really belonged to D. B is ignorant of the fact, B is not entitled to set off a debt owing to him from C against the price of goods.

(e) **Misrepresentations or fraud by an agent:** According to Sec. 238, principal is liable for misrepresentation or fraud of the agent committed in the course of the employment or within the scope of agent's apparent authority. It is immaterial for whose benefit such fraud or misrepresentation has been done. The liability of the principal will not, however, exclude the personal liability of the agent. He may also be sued.

Obviously the principal is not responsible for misrepresentations made or fraud committed by his agent in matters which do not fall within agent's scope of authority.

Illustration: A being B's agent for the sale of goods induces C to buy them by misrepresentation which he was not authorised by B to make. The contract is voidable as between B and C at the option of C.

(f) **Admission made by agent:** The law considers the principal and agent as one person, and therefore, any admission made by the agent in the course of agency business will be taken to have been made by the principal and the principal will be bound.

II. When the Agent Contracts for an Unnamed Principal (Sec. 226)

When the agent discloses his representative character but does not name or disclose the identity of the principal, the principal is said to be unnamed. The third parties can proceed only against the principal not against the agent. However, if the agent declines to disclose the identity of his principal when so required by the third parties, they can sue him personally also.

III. When the Agent Contracts for an Undisclosed Principal

When an agent contracts with a person without disclosing the existence of principal the principal is said to be undisclosed. The position of respective parties in such a case is noted below:

(a) If the third party comes to know of the existence of the principal before obtaining judgement against the agent, he may sue either the principal or the agent or both. If he decides to sue the principal, he must allow the principal to enjoy benefit of all payments received by him from the agent (Sec. 231).

 Example : A contracts with B to sell him 10 bales of cotton and receives Rs. 500 in advance from B. Afterwards A discovers that B was acting as agent for C. A may sue C but he must give credit to C for Rs. 500 paid by his agent B to him.

(b) The principal, if he likes, may intervene and sue the third party. In such a case he can show such a performance subject to the rights and obligations existing between the agent and the other party in the contract (Sec. 232).

The right of intervention of the undisclosed principal is subject to the condition laid down in the second para of Sec. 231. According to this para, the other party is given the right of repudiating the contract before performance on coming to know who the principal is. Thus, if the principal intervenes and discloses himself, the other contracting party may refuse to fulfil the contract if he can show that he would not have entered the contract, had he known who the principal was or that agent was not the principal.

RIGHTS AND DUTIES OF AN AGENT

Rights of Agent

(a) **Rights of retainer (Sec. 217):** Agent has the right to retain out of money received on behalf of the principal, money advanced or expenses properly incurred in conducting the agency business.

(b) **Right to receive remuneration (Sec. 219):** The agent is entitled to remuneration against his services unless he has consented to act gratuitously. The amount of remuneration depends on the terms of the contract if there is an express agreement to that effect. In the absence of any such contract, the right to receive remuneration and the conditions under which the same is payable are dependent on the custom or usage of particular business in which the agent is employed. In this context Sec. 219 lays down that the remuneration is payable only after the completion of the act in regard to which the remuneration is payable. According to Sec. 220 of the Act, an agent who is guilty of misconduct in the business of agency is not entitled to any remuneration in respect of that part of the business which he has misconducted.

(c) **Right of lien (Sec. 221):** Section 221 confers upon agent the right of particular lien on both movable and immovable property of the principal unless the amount due to him for commission, disbursement and services have been paid unless the contracts otherwise provide.

(d) **Right of indemnification for injuries caused by principal's negligence:** The agent is entitled to be idemnified by the principal against the consequences of all unlawful acts done by him in the exercise of his authority conferred upon him.

(e) **Right of indemnification against consequences of acts done in good faith:** An agent has a right to be indemnified by the principal for any compensation which he may be required to pay to third parties for injuries caused to them by his wrongful acts within the scope of his actual authority done in good faith (Sec. 223).

A Duties of an Agent

1. To follow the instructions of the principal in conducting business (Sec. 211).
2. To act with skill and diligence (Sec. 212).
3. To render proper accounts (Sec. 213).
4. To communicate with the principal in cases of difficulty (Sec. 214).
5. Not to deal with his own account (Sec. 215).

6. Not to make secret profits (Sec. 216).
7. Not to delegate authority (Sec. 190).
8. To protect and preserve the principal's interest (Sec. 209).

Personal Liability of the Agent

The general rule is that the agent can neither sue nor be sued upon a contract entered into with a third party on behalf of his principal. Section 230 of the Act clearly provides that the agent can neither personally enforce the contracts entered into by him, nor is he personally bound by them. The immunity from personal liability of an agent is subject to certain exceptions noted below:

(i) **Where the agent acts for a foreign principal:** When the contract is made for the sale or purchase of goods for a resident abroad, in case of breach of contract, the third party can make the agent personally liable. The presumption of law in case of such contracts is that credit has exclusively been given to the agent and not to the foreigner.

(ii) **Where the agent acts for an undisclosed principal:** Where an agent contracts with another without disclosing either his representative character or the name of the principal, he becomes personally liable to the contract. The personal liability of the agent arises only if the other contracting party neither know, nor has means to know that the agent is not the principal. If later on, he comes to know about existence of the principal, he may elect to hold either the agent or the principal or both of them liable to the contract.

(iii) **Where the principal can not be sued:** Where the principal, though, disclosed can not be sued owing to his incapacity for being a minor, a foreign sovereign ambassador, unregistered body or the principal is disqualified from contracting though otherwise competent to contract and this inability of the principal was not communicated to the third party at the time of contracting, he can hold the agent personally liable.

(iv) **Personal liability by agreement:** Where the agent expressly or impliedly undertakes personal liability or signs the deed in his own name, he becomes personally liable to third parties for the contracts madc with them.

(v) **Agent's liability for breach of warranty of authority:** When the agent acts without authority or beyond the scope of his real or apparent authority in such a case he becomes personally liable to the third party with whom he has contracted.

(vi) **Liability of a pretended agent:** According to Sec. 235 of the Act, if a person untruly represents himself to be the authorised agent of another and thereby induces a third party to deal with him as such agent, he becomes personally liable to third parties for loss caused to them. However, no liability will attach if the principal ratifies his acts or if the third party knows the agent to be a pretended agent.

(vii) **Agency coupled with interest:** Where the contract of agency relates to a subject matter in which the agent has a special interest, agent shall be personally liable to the extent of his interest since he shall be reckoned as a principal for that interest.

(viii) **Misrepresentation or fraud:** Where the agent commits misrepresentation or fraud he becomes personally liable.

(ix) **Trade usage or custom:** In the absence of a contract to the contrary, any usage or custom of trade may also make the agent personally liable.

Termination of Agency

Agency may be terminated in any of the following ways:

I. By acts of the parties

A contract of agency can be terminated by mutual agreement like any other contracts as follow:

(a) By agreement between the principal and agent.

(b) By revocation of agency by the principal after giving reasonable notice. Nonetheless, the principal shall have to pay compensation to the agent for any premature revocation.

(c) By renunciation of business by the agent after giving reasonable notice.

II. Termination by operation of law

(a) Completion of agency business or the accomplishment of the object for which agency was formed.

(b) Efflux of time, i.e., expiry of the time for which agency was created irrespective of whether the work has been completed or not.

(c) Death or insanity of agent or principal.

(d) Insolvency of the principal terminates agency when the fact of his insolvency comes to the knowledge of the agent. Insolvency of agent does not terminate the agency.

(e) Destruction of the subject matter of agency.

(f) Principal becoming an alien enemy.

According to Section 210, the termination of the authority of an agent causes the termination of all sub-agents appointed by him.

Irrevocable Agency

Although Sec. 201 empowers the principal to revoke the authority conferred upon the agent by his unilateral action, he cannot revoke the authority of the agent in the following cases:

(I) Where the agency is coupled with interest

According to Sec. 202 where the agent has an interest in the property which forms the subject matter of agency, the agency cannot be terminated to the prejudice of such interest. Even the death or insanity of the principal will not terminate the authority of the agent. However, an express agreement between the principal and agent may provide for an exception to this rule.

To constitute agency coupled with interest the following elements must be present:

(a) The interest of the agent in the subject matter of contract of agency must be substantial. Mere prospect of earning remuneration is not a sufficient ground.

(b) The interest of the agent must exist at the time of creation of agency.

(c) The primary object of giving power to the agent should be to secure an interest of the agent.

Interest of the agent in the subject matter may arise when the principal has contracted to give something to a person and has appointed the latter as an agent to collect it for himself. For instance, A gives authority to C to sell A's land and to pay himself out of the proceeds the debt due to him form A. A neither can revoke his authority, nor can it be terminated by his death or insanity.

(II) Where authority has been partly exercised by the agent

Accoring to Sec. 204, where the agent has partly exercised his authority, the principal can not revoke the agent's authority, so far as such act and obligations arise from such an exercise of authority. For instance, A asks B his agent to pay out of A's funds a sum of Rs. 1000 to C in two equal instalments. By a subequent letter, A revokes B's authority. Before this revocation B had already paid a sum of Rs. 500 to C. A is bound by this payment.

(III) Where agent has incurred personal liability

The principal cannot revoke agent's authority if the agent has, in the exercise of his authority, incurred any personal liability. For instance, A authorises B to buy 1000 bales of cotton on account of A and to pay for it out of A's money remaining in B's hands. B buys 1000 bales of cotton in his own name so as to make prevent himself against being held personally liable for the price towards discontentment of dissatisfied guests. A can not revoke B's authority so far as regards payment for the cotton.

CASES RELATED TO LEGISLATIONS ON TRAVEL AGENCY SECTOR IN INDIA

Present: Hon'ble Mr. Justice V. Balakrishna Eradi, president; **Mr. Justice B.S. Yadav and Dr. (Mrs.) R. Thamarajakshi, Members.**

M/s Four Ways Travel and Tours and ANR (Appellants) Versus M.K.N. Nagamanickkam (Respondent).

Complaint paid in advance full fare for an Air Ticket to USA—opposite party failed to purchase the ticket and returned the money by cheque which was dishonoured. Complainant filed a complaint before a Criminal Court and also filed the present complaint for compensation. State Commission allowed the complaint. Hence appeal—Whether the complainant is entitled to the refund?

When the counsels of both sides were carefully heard and records were thoroughly studied and no documentary evidence by way of receipt from the Appellants for the disputed amount of Rs. 48,570/- was available in the records, the opposite parties have themselves submitted in the counter statement before the State Commission that the complainant paid to them a sum of Rs. 48,570/- for purchase of a ticket to the USA. The averment of the opposite parties that this ticket was for Miss Hema Latha, is however, contradicted by the fact that the fare specified on the ticket for the said passenger who travelled in June, 1991, was only Rs. 32,399/-. The Appellants have tried to confuse by giving different explanations about the dishonoured cheque. They have averred before the State Commission that it was given by way of security for the refund claim for return fare of the relative of the complainant. In the appeal, they have mentioned that they stated before the State Commission that the cheque was towards the refund of return fare as also the commission for the tickets booked by them for the Respondent in June, 1991; How could all these add up to Rs. 48,570/- has, however, not been shown by Appellants.

From the aforesaid statement, it emerges that there has been payment made by the respondent to the Appellants for purchase of an air ticket to the USA in August, 1991. The Appellants failed to purchase this ticket, although the cheque dated 29.8.91 issued by the Appellants to the Respondents for this amount, has been dishonoured, and the money has been with the Appellants. We, therefore, concur with the State Commission that the Appellants should return the amount of Rs. 48,570/- with interest at per annum with effect from 29.8.1991. However the order of the State Commission does not contain any discussion of the basis on which has awarded a compensation of Rs. 10,000/- to the complainant. We are of the view that the facts and circumstances of the case do not justify the award of compensation to the complainant. We, therefore set aside the order of the State Commission in this regard.

GIRIKAND TRAVELS V/S DR. A.N. PUJARI

In this case Dr. A.N. Pujari filed a case when his travel agent, failed to arrange accommodation and taxi service for which agency's services were hired and paid for. This complaint was filed in the court of District Forum, Kohlapur. The District Consumer Disputes Redressal Forum ordered that the travel agency should pay Dr. Pujari Rs. 12,142/- out of total payment Rs. 15,630/- paid to the agency as compensation for the loss and inconvenience suffered. The travel agency appealed against this order before the Maharashtra State Consumer Disputes Redressal Forum based at Bombay, which uphold the order of District Forum. According to travel agency, the period of the travel was during Diwali vacations and therefore, the hotel reservations and taxi services were not available. The agency also blamed the arrest of Mr. L.K. Advani and the subsequent disturbances for the deficiencies in services and said that it could not be held responsible more so it had already returned Rs. 3,827 to the client as the final settlement of their claim. The court, however, did not accept this argument and said a travel company while arranging the schedule has to visualise and anticipate eventualities which may occur during the tour, thus the claim of the agency that schedule of the tour got upset due to political disturbances and so the agency is not liable to payments of compensation, is not acceptable by the court. In this case, the State Forum also observed that the entire schedule of the tour was not completed by Girikand travels and so the petitioner has to face number of difficulties for hotel bookings and taxi services that is why the State Forum upheld the decision given by the lower court and ordered that the agency should pay a compensation of Rs. 12,142 to the petitioner.

Source: *Ethical, Legal, Regulatory Aspects of Tourism Business, Satyender Malik,*

PART-B: LEGISLATION REGARDING HOTEL INDUSTRY

Tourism is the single largest worldwide industry growing at a faster pace than that of world economy. As a matter of fact, the hotel industry, a major component of tourism industry, is one of the most important foreign exchange earners, i.e., more than 55 per cent of hotel foreign exchange earnings constitute more than 40 per cent of total tourist expenditure. Hotel industry is also bestowed with vast scope for employment opportunities. In fact due to their increasing importance hotels are becoming centres of a wide gamut of social, commercial, cultural, governmental, diplomatic and entertainment activities. Therefore, hotel industry can rightly be referred to as the backbone of tourism industry.

Till date, the union government and only 14 states have accorded tourism, the status of an industry. However States of Punjab, Rajasthan, Orissa and West Bengal have gone a step ahead to accord 'hotels', the status of an industry. But hotel industry has not only been facing a lot of problems in availing themselves of concessions, incentives, exemptions and benefits extended to other types of industries but it is also facing a lot of legal problems and confrontations which no other industry has. Various laws, relevant to hotel industry are discussed below:

1. The Urban Land Ceiling Act, 1976

This Act was passed with a view to prevent the concentration of urban land in few person's hands for speculation and profiteering activity. However, the objectives set out are not yet met out.

National Commission's report on urbanisation reveals that out of total *of 1,66,920, hectares of excess vacant land which was expected to become available after the enactment of law only 14,589 hectares of surplus land is made available. So the Act has freezed the availability of land*, as a result real estate agents have pushed up the prices from 30 to 50 times in respect of some lands. Consequently, purchase of a piece of land anywhere in the urban area is beyond the means of a common man.

In case of a hotel project where 40 per cent of the total project cost is accounted for land cost, under such circumstances project becomes unviable, because the standard proportion of cost of land should be ideally 10 per cent. To reduce this gap or to bring down the land cost there should be some relaxation as to the height of building and area coverage, existing in present Urban Land Ceiling Act. In pursuance, Govt., of India, issued guidelines in 1990, to reduce distance from 500 ft to 200 ft for the construction of a resort/hotel at seashores.

The Government has fixed a target of 5 million foreign tourist arrivals by the turn of this century and as per its own estimation to accommodate these many number of tourists there should be 1,25,000 hotel rooms as compared to existing 67,000 available hotel rooms. This target would be seen quite ambitious unless government comes out with a massive dose to incentives and facilities to the industry especially by amending the existing Urban Land Ceiling Act in tune with growing demand of the industry.

2. Factories and Shops and Establishments Acts

Hotel industry in India faces a peculiar problem regarding the applicability of both these Acts. This peculiarity has emerged due to the argument of industry people that laundary, bakery and kitchen area of a hotel should be covered under Factories Act and the remaining areas should be covered by the Shops and Establishment Act. But important question which comes up is that how can two sets of different rules and regulations be made applicable to one industry? This kind of confusion leads to different legal verdicts and undue delays. Adding to this, further confusion occurs in its applicability due to the fact that in hotels, management of hotels own vehicles for pick up of their customers from port of entry and to send them off or to enrich customer services they have to employ transport workers and these operators come under Motor Vehicle Act. even though their main operation is not related to Motor Vehicles Act but they have to comply with it. In States like Uttar Pradesh and Madhya Pradesh there is a provision for certified standing order for hotel industry. In other States where such, standing orders donot exist, hotels have to frame their own service rules. Hence there should be one common law governing the applicability of Standing Orders and Service Rules throughout the nation.

As majority of Acts define hospitality services as an industry, it faces many peculiar legal problems. For example, Factories Act restricts the employment of women during night shifts in industries. Hotel industry provides services that are required throughout the year and round the clock. It is essential that both men and women are put on work on all shifts to fulfil the needs of the customers. Therefore, it comes as a violation of provisions of Factories Act.

Hotel industry has also the exception of being the only industry which is subject to all types of taxes imposed by the State Governments which includes sales tax, luxury tax, expenditure tax, license fees, excise duty, income tax, wealth tax, property tax, etc. When all these taxes are passed onto the guests, India comes out to be the most expensive destinations charging around 20 to 30 per cent taxes in comparison to 5 per cent in China and 7-10 per cent in other countries of S.E. Asian region.

SALES TAX AND LUXURY TAX

These taxes are the subjects of State Governments. That is why different rates on sale of food items and room tariff are formulated and imposed by different State Government. In the famous cases of Northern India Caterer, Supreme Court held that services by hotels can not be taxed as sale of goods.

And in case of Associated Hotels of India, Supreme Court went a step further and held that in the case of restaurants there is no sale of food because providing food is a part of overall activity to serve food in a proper atmosphere and so elements of services canot be taxed. Hence court commented that supply of food or drinks to guests did not imaort the character of sale of goods, thereby court recognises the distinction between hotel on one side and other industries on the other side. But this opinion of highest court of our land was shortlived because a change was initiated by Central Government through constitutional amendment which established that service of hoteliers are treated as sale of goods.

EXPENDITURE TAX

At present 10 per cent of expenditure tax is levied on all expenses incurred on all hotel services, if the expenditure exceeds Rs. 2000/- per person per day. But this tax is not applicable on foreign tourists who remit their expenses in yoreign currencies. Both hoteliers and hotel customers record their experiences regarding irrational levy of sales tax. The example of higher and unfair luxury and expenditure tax is available from Chennai where the rate of tax is 20 per cent while in Delhi no such tax is levied.

To put an end to all the problems the only possible solution would be to formulate a special and seperate Central Legal Code for hotel industry. Just by amending all concerned laws would not solve the purpose of targeting 5 millions foreign tourists arrival and of doubling the foreign exchange earning to 20,000 crores by 2000, will not be sufficient.

THE HOTEL RECEIPTS TAX ACT, 1980

Under this act the term 'Hotel' has been defined in Section 2(6) of the Act as to include a building or part of a building where residential accommodation is provided to the people in consideration of money earning and by way of business. At the same time under section 2(10) room charges means charges for a unit of residential accommodation in hotel which includes charges for furniture, air-conditioner, refrigerator, radio, music, telephone, television and for such other services as are normally included by a hotel in a room rent but does not include charges for food, drink, and any other services.

Hotel Receipt Tax means the tax chargeable under the provisions of this Act and 'assessee' means a person by whom the hotel receipt tax or any other sum of a money is payable and also includes every person in respect of whom any proceeding under this Act has been taken for the assessment of his chargeable receipt of the amount of refund due to him or of the chargeable receipts of any other person in respect of which he is assessable or of the amount of refund due to such other person.

Section 3 of the Act deals with the ambit and the scope of the Act and provides that the Act shall apply in relation to every hotel wherein the room charges for residential accommodation provided to any person at any time during the previous year and which is Rs. 75/- (seventy-five rupees) or more per day per individual.

The position has been further clarified under explanation to Section 3 that in case the room charges are payable otherwise than on daily basis or per individual, then the charges will be computed as for a day and per individual based on the period of occupation of the residential accommodation for which the charges are payable and the number of individuals ordinarily permitted to occupy, such accommodation according to the rules and customs of the hotel. Where a composite charge is payable in respect of residential accommodation, food, drink and other services or any of them, and the case is not covered by the provisions of this Section, this case is referred to the Income Tax Officer that the charges for residential accommodation, food, drink or other services are so arranged that the room charges are understated and the other charges are overstated. In such cases, the Income Tax Officer shall determine the room charges on such reasonable basis as he deems fit.

CHARGING OF HOTEL RECEIPTS TAX

Every person carrying on the business of a hotel covered within the purview of the Act shall be required to pay tax in respect of his chargeable receipts of the previous year at the rate of 15 per cent of such receipts as provided under Section 5 of the Act but in case chargeable receipts include any charges received in foreign exchange, then the tax payable by the assessee shall be reduced by an amount equal to 5 per cent of the charges or in other words the tax shall be required to be paid at the rate of 10 per cent of the charges in case it is paid in foreign currency. For the purpose of computing the charges, paid by the customer the amount payable by way of sales tax, entertainment tax and the tax on luxuries shall be excluded. It is further provided that the Hotel Receipt Tax shall also be charged from a person having close connection with the person carrying on the business of a hotel, in case any food, drink or other services are provided on the premises of that hotel by that person.

The person having close connection with the person carrying on the business or the hotel shall also be required to pay hotel receipts tax in respect of charges for food, drink or other services so provided by him as such charges are the chargeable receipts of the business of the hotel deemed to be carried on by him. For this purpose a person shall be deemed to be closely connected with the person carrying on the business of the hotel if in relation to the person carrying on such business of supplying food, drink or other services, the same are provided in the hotel or at any place appurtenant thereto and where the hotel is situated in a part of building, in any other part of the building.

RETURN OF THE CHARGEABLE RECEIPTS

Under Section 8 of the Act an obligation has been imposed on every person, who during the previous year, carried on the business of hotel in relation to which this Act applied or is assessable in respect of the chargeable receipts of any other person under this Act, to furnish a return of his chargeable receipts or the chargeable receipts of such other person of the previous year in the prescribed form and verified in the prescribed manner and setting forth such other particulars as may be prescribed, before the expiry of four months from the end of the previous year in respect of the business of the hotel or where there is more than one previous year in respect of such business, from the end of the previous year which expired last before the 30th day of June, of the assessment year, whichever, is later.

Under Section 9 of the Act there is provision for self assessment in cases where the Hotel Receipts Tax payable on the basis of the return exceeded the tax already paid under any other provisions of this Act. The assessee shall pay the Hotel Receipts Tax so payable before filing the return and enclose the proof of such payment along with such return. In case of failure on the part of the assessee to pay the Hotel Receipt Tax within the stipulated time period, he shall be liable to pay a penalty at the rate of 2 per cent per month as the tax payable on such assessement. But no penalty shall be imposed on the assessee unless he has given an opportunity of being heared as provided under

Section 17 of the Act. At the same time there is provision for filing appeal to the commissioner and further appeal to appellate tribunal as provided in Section 18 and 19, respectively of the Act. Under Section 21 of the Act it has been provided that notwithstanding anything contained in the Income Tax Act, in computing the income chargeable to income tax under the head 'profits and gains of business or profession' in the case of an assessee carrying on the business of hotel to which this Act applies, the hotel receipts tax payable by the assessee for any assessment year shall be deductable from the profits and gains of the business of the hotel assessable for that assessment year.

Under Section 29 of the Act it has been provided that if a person makes a false statement wilfully or renders a false account he is liable to be punished with an imprisonment ranging from 6 month to seven years or with a fine up to one lakh rupees.

CASES RELATED TO LAWS ON ACCOMMODATION SECTOR

Controversy of Radisson Hotel New Delhi

In New Delhi, there had been the storm over the park Royale Hotel clearance which has hardly been settled, but another similar controversy came up again. The hotel in question this time was Radisson, a five-star hotel near the Indira Gandhi International Airport. The hotel was about to open. The crucial question was—under, which bye-laws the hotel had to be constructed? Both the MCD and the DDA disowned the responsibility of doing anything with the project.

The hotel project had been constructed with the clearance from the Airports Authority of India (AAI). Senior officials said even if the AAI had given permission, the building had to be built under certain bye-laws. The rules can be either laid down by the MCD or the DDA. But neither of these bodies have made any such bye-laws. A senior official opined that the hotel seemed to be constructed without any rules. But the MCD officials maintained that it does not fall under our area. The land is in the Delhi

Development Area. So it should fall under the DDA's control. This statement was made by incharge of the MCD engineering wing.

The DDA officials denied having any role in the project and stated that the land belongs to the Airports Authority of India and so Airports Authority should take a decision on it.

Senior officials of AAI are surprised that the hotel is being constructed without any bye-laws. How can the Airports Authority of India make rules for the construction of a building.. It is the responsibility of the MCD or the DDA to frame rules. They said that the Airports Authority of India did not have the power to issue a completion certificate to a hotel. "The clearance has to be given by a municipal body," officials added.

Airports Authority of India chairman Rajan Chatterjee was not available for comment as he was out of town.

The 260-room Radisson Hotel was slated for a grand opening in February, 1998. Apart from two executive plaza floors with luxury rooms, there is a health club, executive club, business centre, banquet and conference hall facilities and a sports bar. The hotel had to be built at a whopping cost of Rs. 55.5 crore. But on completion, the cost went up to Rs. 70 crore.

In Delhi, the hotel is being promoted by the AB Hotels Ltd. It is a joint venture between the Unitech Ltd., and the A.L. Batra Group. The Unitech and Batra Group are each putting 25 per cent of the cost.

The Radisson brand is owned by the Radisson Hotels worldwide belonging to the Carlson Hospital Group. Situated on the National Highways No. 8, the hotel primarily caters to business travellers coming from the domestic and international airport. The Radisson Hotel happend to be the first five-star hotel to open in a decade. The Carlson Group is also slated to open a resort on the banks of Ganges near Haldia in Raicuk, 35 km. from Çalcutta. The hotel will be developed by the Ganapati Green fields, which is part of the Gujarat Ambuja Cement Group. The Radisson Land End Plaza Hotel had open in Mumbai in the end of 1997. The hotel have 536 rooms.

The Carlson Group also has property in several countries like the Maldives, Bhutan and Sri Lanka.

HOTEL ORDERED TO PAY 50 LAKHS IN DAMAGES

New Delhi, January 5, (1997) Ruling that the five-star hotel Oberoi Intercontinental's swimming pool was defective and the Delhi High Court ordered the management to pay Rs. 50 lakhs as damage to the family of a German pilot, who suffered head injuries during a splash in 1972, and subsequently died.

Justice R. C. Lahoti in his 72-page landmark judgement pronounced and also directed payment of six per cent interest per annum on the principal amount from September 27, 1985, after leading a paralytic's life following the accident in the hotel pool on Agugust 13, 1972. Holding that "if an injury hastens or accelerates the death, directly and not remotely, then in law the injury is one causing or resulting in death," Justice Lahoti ruled that the injuries sustained by the young pilot on August 13, 1972, caused his death on September 27, 1985. Further, the course of action services to the legal heirs under Section 306 of the Succession Act, and therefore the widow and daughter of the plaintiff, who died during the course of the trial suit filed in 1975, were entitled to prosecute the suit and also to a decree of damages Justice Lahoti added.

The judge said in his order that the plaintiff had proved that they were entitled to damages worth Rs. 1.03 crore under various heads like lost income and lost pension, treatment costs and general non-pecuniary damages relating to pain and suffering and loss of enjoyment in life. However, as the plaintiff had prayed for damages worth Rs. 50 lakh, the decree would remain confined to this amount only, he added.

Justice Lahoti decreed that the damages plus interest would be paid by East India Hotel Ltd., the owners of Hotel Oberoi Intercontinental, and by the hotel.

The Lufthansa Airlines pilot had checked into the Intercontinental while on a short break between flights and visited the hotel swimming pool on the afternoon of August 13, 1972. While diving, he met with an accident. He hit his head on the bottom of the pool and was then out bleeding from his right ear and appearing to be paralysed in the arms and the legs.

He was rushed to the Holy Family Hospital and remained there till August 21, 1972, on which date he was flown to Germany under medical escort. When he was discharged from a clinic in Heilelberg in March, 1973, his condition never improved. On August 11, 1975, he filed a suit against the hotel and its management for recovery of Rs. 50 lakhs by way of damages.

His counsel claimed that the accident was caused by the hotel's negligence in putting the diving board in such a way that suggested a proper depth of water. Having failed in ensuring the plaintiff's safety, the hotel was liable to compensate him for the consequences of the accident.

The hotel denied its liability and contended that the pilot had consumed wine at the time of the accident. Refuting any negligence on the part of the hotel, its counsel claimed that it was Mittlebachert who was negligent. It was claimed by the hotel that the pilot had stayed there on several earlier occasions and must have used the pool. Merely because he was involved in an accident in the pool on one occasion, the hotel could not be said to be guilty of negligence.

After examining some 13 witnesses on behalf of the plaintiff and 11 witnesses on behalf of the defendants, the court ruled that Mittlebachert did not consume wine at the time of the accident and was in no way negligent or careless.

After examining witnesses including architects and swimming pool designers and pursuing books on swimming pool designs, the court held that the Oberoi Hotel pool was structurally so designed as to achieve just the bare minimum depth at the plummet point, which was not enough.

"The swimming pool satisfied the bare minimum standards of safety and certainly not the standards which were to be preferred. Secondly, the standards relied on by the defendants by reference to the 1956 edition of the book (on swimming pools) was discarded by the year 1970.

Even if the defendants had chosen to go by the 1956 standards, in the year 1965, when the swimming pool was built, then in the year 1970, with the standards having been revised and updated, the defendants should have redesigned and renovated their swimming pool.

'A five-star hotel cannot be said to have discharged its

duty to care towards its guests by observing bare minimum standards of safety. It should have gone by preferred standards. A five-star hotel charging a high or fancy price from its guests owes a high degree of care to its guests as regards quality and safety of its structure and services it offers to make available. Any latent defect in its structure or services, which is hazardous to guests, would attract strict liability to compensation flowing from its breach of duty to take care.

"The five-star tag hanging on its service pack attracts and casts an obligation to pay exemplary damages if an occasion may arise for the purpose," Justice Lahoti added.

Source: *TOI- Jan. 6, 1997, New Delhi.*

DELHI COURT STAYS RE-ALLOTMENT OF MS SHOES' HOTEL SITE AT NEW DELHI

A Delhi court stayed the re-allotment of the five-star hotel site at Andrews Gunj in New Delhi which was earlier allotted to MS Shoes on October 31, 1994.

The Housing and Urban Development Corporation (HUDCO) had retendered the property after cancelling the earlier allotment to MS Shoes of Pawan Sachdeva and asked for fresh bids on the same property.

Mr. Sachdeva, who had challenged the cancellation order to the Delhi High Court, secured the order to maintain status quo in respect of the allotment of the site till the next date of hearing. It was feared by the promoter of MS Shoes that HUDCO might allot the property to fresh bidders in its board meeting on January 29, 1997.

Quoting the conditions of the allotment letter, the district and sessions court in its order noted that "the possession of the hotel site was to be handed over for raising construction upon the receipt of the first instalment of the premium." MS Shoes had paid the first instalment of around Rs. 25 crore on January 31, 1995.

The court further noted, "Admittedly, the plaintiff (MS Shoes Ltd.,) had paid the first instalment but neither the agreement of sub-lease has been made available nor the possession handed over for raising construction. Rather, for non-payment of second instalment, the allotment has been cancelled."

The retendering of the land property by HUDCO was also opposed by financial institutions who had advanced Rs. 202 crore to MS Shoes in good faith on the strength of the hotel projects proposed to be set up at the site allotted by HUDCO.

The court, in its order, observed that keeping in view the huge amount obtained by MS Shoes from financial institutions and the fact that Rs. 25 crore and above having been paid by MS Shoes to HUDCO by way of first instalment, it would not be contrary to equity if HUDCO was ordered to maintain stutus quo in respect of the allotment of the site.

PART-C : LAWS RELATING TO WILDLIFE PRESERVATION

A major factor responsible for the decline of wildlife all over the world is trade and commerce. International trade in wildlife and products thereof is added big business. In the late 1960s, and the early 1970s, the size of the trade grew to unprecedented proportions. This aroused such concern that an international treaty was signed in 1973, to protect wildlife against such over-exploitation and to prevent international trade from threatening species with extinction.

Known as CITES, the Convention on International Trade in Endangered Species of Wild Fauna and Flora came into force on 1st July, 1975, and now the treaty has 111 country members. In addition, EEC has also joined as a member to the Convention. The raising strength of the Convention is best stated in its preamble in the following words.

Recognising in addition, that international co-operation is essential for the protection of certain species of wild fauna and flora against over-exploitation through international trade.

Convinced of the urgency of taking appropriate measures to this end.... CITES covers both the wild animals and plants and the member countries act by banning commercial trade in an agreed list of currently endangered species paid by regulating and monitoring trade in others that might become endangered. In a sense, CITES is a protectionist treaty in as much as international trade in species threatened with extinction is severely restricted. It is also a trading treaty in the sense that specimens of species, whose survival is less threatened, can enter into international trade legally.

The provisions of CITES apply to species included in Appendix-I, Appendix-II or Appendix-III to the Convention, which need to be understood.

Appendix-I is expected to include 'all species threatened with extinction which are, or may be affected by trade. The criteria for adding species to Appendix-I, adopted by the parties, specify that if the status of the species is seriously declining it should be listed even if there is only a probability of trade.' In addition, whole general should be listed "if most of their species are threatened with extinction and if identification of individual species within the genus is difficult." The objective of this requirement is to control trade in species, even if they are widespread and common, which look alike and could be confused with a threatened species. So as not to endanger them further. No permits are issued for international trade in these species unless there are very exceptional circumstances.

Appendix-II is amended to regulate international trade in species which are not sufficiently endangered to warrant inclusion in Appendix-I, but which could become endangered unless trade in them is controlled. Its purpose is also to control trade in species which are similar in appearance to and could be confused with those listed in Appendix-I. International trade in these species is permitted with proper documentation issued by the Government of the exporting country.

Appendix-III is meant to provide a mechanism whereby a party which regulates trade in a species not listed in Appendix-I or it can seek international help in enforcing that regulation. Any party can list a species in Appendix-III for this purpose. For instance, India has invoked this provision of CITES for seeking international help in controlling smuggling of reptile skins by listing four species of snakes in Appendix-III.

In addition, CITES clearly stipulates that member states may enforce even strictly domestic controls than required by CITES, if they wish to give special protection to a listed species or may even ban trade in all their wildlife, as has been virtually done by India during last few years.

The enforcement of CITES is naturally the responsibility of the member states, who are required to establish Management and Scientific Authorities for the purpose. In most countries, enforcement of CITES regulations has been entrusted to customs officials. The member states are also required to submit regular reports, including trade date and statistics to the CITES Secretariat located in Switzerland to ensure effective enforcement, the Secretariat headed by a Secretary General who acts as a clearing house for the exchange of information and liaison between the member states and with other authorities and organization.

Perhaps the factor which has contributed most to India's image in the CITES network is its strong and consistent advocacy of conservation and as upholder of the basic philosophy of CITES founded on the bed-rock of deep concern and co-operation between the producing countries and the consuming countries of the world. This was best exemplified at the Gaborone (1983) and Buenos Aires (1985) and Ottawa (1987) meetings, where the Indian Delegation spoke out forcefully on these issues and championed, at times almost single handedly, the cause of conservation as opposed to consumption. It was in recognition of this role that, in a rather moving gesture, the representatives of more than 30 international and national non-government organisations signed and gave to the Indian Delegation at the Buenos Aires (1985) meeting, the following memorandum. To the Delegation of India attending the Fifth Conference of the Parties to CITES:

"We wish to express our deep gratitude and appreciation for the diligent efforts of India to uphold the letter and spirit of the convention, in spite of increasing efforts to weaken the treaty. Your Delegation's untiring work and eloquent spokesmanship in defence of the world's beleaguered fauna and flora are a credit to your country and an inspiration to the World."

There is no doubt that as far as CITES is concerned, a special role and responsibility has devolved on India on the world scene. At home, arising from this added responsibility and in recognition of the need for proper implementation and enforcement of the Convention within the country, there are some important issues which need to be addressed urgently. These are set out below:

CITES is an international agreement, which must be implemented and enforced both by national policy and law. India's present Export-Import Policy is well-attuned to the overall objectives of CITES. It is very important however that there should be regular periodic reviews of this policy to ensure that the objectives of CITES are not overlooked. The Ministry of Commerce and the Chief Controller of Import and Export have to be particularly sensitive to the need and the decision of parties to the Convention have always been implemented by India in letter and spirit. The recent ban on trade in African ivory under the Wildlife (Protection) Act is a glaring example.

The need for close co-operation and co-ordination between the Wildlife Organisation at the Centre and those in the States as well as the Customs and Revenue Intelligence is not necessary to be overemphasised. A complete understanding of rules and procedures on both sides and a spirit of mutual help and co-operation must be ensured, specially to check smuggling.

There should also be energetic and consistent efforts to educate the public regarding the objectives of CITES, and to enlist public support for its enforcement. To attain this objectives there can be nothing better than enlightened public opinion and co-operation. The non-governmental organisations can play a vital role in this regard and their help and co-operation should be taken.

Finally, the need for separate legislation to implement CITES in India also needs to be examined for obvious reasons.

On the global basis, it has to be recognised that CITES has been in force for just over a decade within which a considerable progress has been made. Most of the wildlife trading nations have become parties and many exporting countries are strengthening their ability to control exploitation of their natural resources. The quality of available date and statistics on international wildlife trade has improved considerably and the controls on such trade are being improved steadily to deal with gaps and inconsistencies revealed by the analysis of export and import records. Besides, efforts are being taken to strengthen regional co-operation to these ends. These are no meagre achievements for an international treaty with only a decade of existence behind it.

On the other side of the balance sheet there are some gaps in the geographical coverage; the lack of commitment even in financial terms on the part of some parties; the weaknesses arising from slack enforcement and implementation; and the complexity of procedures and appendices. However, the growing awareness amongst the Parties about their responsibilities and the very system established by the treaty, including the involvement of non-government organisations, holds promise for the future. CITES has come of age and can no longer be ignored.

While the Secretariat is responsible for the administration of CITES on oral basis, the real decision-making body on all matters related to CITES is Conference of the Parties, the official title given to a meeting of all the parts of the Convention. It meets regularly every two years and may hold extraordinary meeting on the written request of at least one-third of the Parties. Its task is to review the implementation of the Convention and to make such recommendations as it deems appropriate.

The scope of the Conference is wide indeed. The financing of the Convention and the budget of the Secretariat is its direct concern. At every biennial meeting of the Conference of the Parties, the budget for the next two years is prepared. It is also the direct responsibility of the Conference to make recommendations for improving the effectiveness of the Convention. For instance, the recommendation that the Parties should use standardised permits on security paper and stamps arose from the meeting of the conference held at New Delhi in 1981. The other major responsibility of the conference is to review and update the lists of species included in the Appendix-I, in fact, this has been a regular feature of every meeting and takes considerable time and attention in the agenda of each meeting.

In order to facilitate its task, the Conference of the Parties has established General Committee, the most important of which is, the Standing Committee. It is a permanent advisory committee with a voluntary membership of nine Parties. Some of whom are from different geographical regions and the other three are representatives of the Depository Government (Switzerland) and the Governments of the host countries of the previous and the next meetings of the conference. The Chief mandate of the Standing Committee is to act on behalf of the Parties in between meetings, in accordance with the guidelines or directions made by the Parties. The Standing Committee also oversees the execution of the Secretariat's budget, gives as 'bureau' at Conference meetings. It meets regularly about twice a year. Another committees include the Technical Committee, the Nomenclature Committee, Identification Manual Committee; the Ranching Committee and the Threatened Plants Committee which have specific roles and responsibilities and are expected to keep the Standing Committee informed of their work and activities from time to time as well as to report to the Conference when it meets biennially.

During this period, the number of Parties has risen steadily from 36 in 1976 to 111 in 1991, two-third of whom are from the developing world, the producer countries. This is a very important development, which clearly demonstrates the widespread appeal and acceptability of CITES.

India has been on the forefront of CITES almost since the beginning. The Government of India deposited the instrument of ratification on 20th July, 1976, and became Party to the Convention from 18th October, 1976. Thereafter, it has been actively involved in CITES and has played a significant role throughout. Apart from participating actively in each of the seven meetings of the Conference of the Parties held so far, India hosted the third meeting at New Delhi from 25th February to 8th March, 1981. This was described by the CITES Secretary-General as "the best attended as well as hosted Conference of the Parties." It is noteworthy that it was for this meeting that the CITES logo was designed in India. It was liked generally and was finally adopted by the Parties.

A major achievement from India's angle was the important role played by the Indian delegation throughout the third meeting. Apart from providing the Chairman for the plenary sessions, India chaired three important committees and played an active role in the meetings of the other committees set up by the Conference. At end of the meeting, India was elected as Chairman of the Standing Committee, the most prestigious body of the Convention. It was a unique honour to India that it was elected as Chairman of the Standing Committee for subsequent meetings held at Gaborone (Botswana) in 1983, Buenos Aires (Argentina) in 1985, and at Ottawa in 1987. This was an exceptional honour, signifying the confidence and trust enjoyed by India amongst the CITES Parties.

THE WILDLIFE PROTECTION ACT, 1972

It is an Act to provide for protection to wild animals and birds and for matters connected therewith or ancillary or incidental thereto.

Statement of Objects and Reasons

1. The rapid decline of India's wild animals and birds, one of the richest and most varied assets in the world has been a cause of grave concern. The wild birds' or animals' protection has become completely outmoded. The existing state legislations are not only outdated but provide punishment which are not commensurate with the offence and financial benefits which accrue from poaching and trade in wildlife produce that are prime reasons for taxidermy trade in wildlife and products derived.
2. Need for introducing a comprehensive legislation which would provide for the protection of wild-animals and birds in all other matters.
3. Parliament has no power to make law in this regard (entry 20 in State list in 7th Schedule) apart from Art. 249 and 250 unless the legislatures of two or more States pass a resolution in pursuance of Art. 252 empowering parliament to pass law on this subject. The legislatures of the States of

Andhra Pradesh, Gujarat, Haryana, Himachal Pradesh, Madhya Pradesh, Manipur, Rajasthan, Uttar Pradesh and West Bengal have passed such resolution.

4. The Bill seeks the following :
    - To constitute a Wildlife Advisory Board for each state.
    - To regulate hunting of wild animals and birds.
    - To regulate possession, acquisition and transfer of or trade in wild animals and trophies and taxidermy.
    - To provide penalties for contravention of this Act.

Chapter - I : (Preliminary)

This Chapter states title, extervient and commencement of this act (as given) and deals with the definitions of animal, animal article, big game. Board captive animal, taxidermy, collator, habital, huntry, etc., are defined.

Chapter - II: (Authorities to be appointed under the art.)

This Chapter deals with the following:

5. Appointment of the Director and other Officers—Central Government appoints and gives directions.
6. Appointment of the Chief Wildlife Warden and other Officers.
7. Power to delegate—of above Officers to Subordinates specified by them.
8. ***Constitution of Wildlife Advisory Board:*** The minister of forests in state or Chief Secretary, will be Chairman and two member of State or U.T (in case of U.T) legislature, Sec. to the State Government Chief Conservator of Forests *(ex-officio)*. Such other officials and non-officials not exceeding 15.
9. Procedures to be followed by Board are :
    (i) Board shall meet twice a year at place specified by State Government.
    (ii) Board shall regulate its own procedure.
    (iii) No Act or proceedings of Board will be invalid.
10. Duties of Wildlife Advisory Board is to advice the State Governments in the following matters:

- In selection of areas declared as sanctuaries, national parks, game reserves and closed areas, etc.
- In formulation of any policy of granting permits and licenses.
- Any matter related to amendment of Schedule.
- In any other matter connected to protection of wildlife, referred by State Government.

Chapter-III : (Hunting)

11. Hunting of Wild Animals of Schedule I is banned. Hunting licences can be obtained by application for a period for Schedule II, III and IV animals, subject to terms, restrictions and conditions. Rest of this Chapter deals with the following:
12. Maintenance of records of Wildlife killed or captured.
13. Hunting of Wild animals to be permitted in certain cases.
14. Grant of permit for special purposes—gene pool collection.
15. Suspension of licence.
16. Appeal against suspension of licence.
17. Hunting of female and young wild animals is strictly prohibited.
18. Declaration of closed time.
19. Restrictions on hunting.

Chapter-IV (Sanctuaries, National Parks, Game Reserves and Closed areas)

20. Declaration of Sanctuary: The State Governments by notification declare can any area to be a sanctuary if they consider that such area is of adequate ecological, faunal, floral, geomorphological, natural or zoological significance, for the purpose of protecting, propagating or developing wildlife or its environment. Up to Section 34 various laws in sanctuary are explained.
21. Articles 35 to 38 deals with declaration of National Park, Game Reserve, Closed area and Power of Centre to declare areas as sanctuaries or national parks.

Chapter- V: (Trade and Commerce in Wild Animals, Animal Articles and Trophies)

22. Wild animals, etc., are the Government's property. No person shall without written permission of Chief Wildlife Warden or the authorised officer can do the following:
    (a) Aquire or keep in his possessions, custody or control, or
    (b) Transfer to any person whether by way of gift, sale or otherwise, or
    (c) Destroy or damage the Government's property.

No person can keep captive animals for performance, etc., certificate of ownership can be taken from Chief Wildlife Warden for lawful possessions.

Prevention of purchase of animal, animal product other than licensee, cancellation of licence and appeal procedure are explained in the rest of Chapter.

Chapter - VI: (Prevention and Detection of Offences)

Director or any person authorised on behalf of Chief Wildlife Warden or Police Officer not below the rank of Sub-Inspector can entry, search arrest and detain on reasonable grounds for believing that a person has committed offence.

Penalty:

Any person guilty of an offence against this Act may be imprisoned for a term extended up to two years or fined up to Rs. 2,000 or both.

If this law is breached in case of Sanctuary or National Parks the 6 months term can be extended upto 6 years and fine not less than Rs. 500 with seizure of any related licenses, if he possesses. On presumption based search it will be the responsibility of accused to prove otherwise.

Chapter - VII : (Miscellaneous)

This Chapter states that officers are public servants and deal with the following:

- Protection of action taken in good faith.
- Power to alter entries in schedules.
- Declaration of certain Wildlife animals to be vermin.

- Power of Central and State Governments to make rules.
- Rights of Schedule Tribes to be protected (exceptional, Andaman and Nicobar), and
- Repeal or savings.

RECOMMENDATIONS OF SUBRAMANIAM COMMITTEE ON PREVENTION OF ILLEGAL TRADE IN WILDLIFE AND ITS PROTECTION

- Introduce dynamic management of protected areas using well-established wildlife management principles to reduce crop damage and cattle killing by wild animals.
- Recreate original grasslands and blanks to benefit wildlife in protected areas like Dudwa and Nagarhole by removing plantations like eucalyptus and teak.
- Make artificial islands and desilt wallows in protected areas like Kaziranga to improve habitat for rhino.
- Attach a wildlife biologist to each protected area like Kaziranga to improve habitat for rhino.
- Attach a wildlife biologist to each protected area to study habitat changes and advice management for action.
- Capture crop raiding elephants to reduce conflict with people and use them for park work.
- Use buffer zones to meet local needs through it for forest management and eco-development programmes.
- While resettling tribals and other communities take their socio-ethnic-magic needs into consideration.
- To recruit Kanjars and other hunting communities as wildlife guards, provide self-employment in Rodent Control Programmes and Snake Venom Production.

MEASURES TO PREVENT ILLEGAL IMPORT AND EXPORT OF WILDLIFE AND THEIR PRODUCTS

- Establish an institutionalised system to impart

comprehensive training to all custom's staff at various levels in the field.

- A comprehensive training capsule for custom's officials should be designed by Wildlife Institute of India in consultation with National Academy of Custom, Excise and Narcotics, New Delhi.
- The training capsule should be used on a monthly basis to train officers in Delhi.
- Codify and collect information and intelligence already available on gangs involved in wildlife trafficking with customs, police and wildlife wings on a continual basis and evolve systems for regular exchange of data.
- Prepare dossiers in a common format between wildlife, customs and revenue intelligence on offenders, their modus operandi, and associates, etc.
- Besides formal meetings among preventive agencies, encourage informal contacts to develop rapport between officers.
- Establish simple and immediately implementable incentive schemes of rewards to informats and staff who take initiative in apprehending offenders.
- Offenders should be booked under the Law/Act which provides maximum penalty.

A PETITION FOR PRESERVATION OF HABITAT

India, the flagbearer of preservation and propagation of biodiversity, has declared about, 1,48,850 sq. km. of its territory as the protected area either as tiger reserve, national park or a sanctuary. But, on the other hand, there is an acute pressure on the protected areas due to rise in population, rapid industrialization and imprudent capitalization of mineral and forest resources. The result is authorised or unauthorised destruction of such protected areas. This destruction to a large extent is attributable to commission on part of Government to take legal steps as provided under WPA. As of today, out of 521 WPA, in over 80 per cent of such areas, no step has been taken for settlement of rights of people, the government inaction has led to diversion of land for residential, commercial purposes leading to pollution, poaching and timber smuggling, etc.

WWF filed a petition with its legal arm, the centre for environment law, in Supreme Court, in that petition, WWF India has sought directions to all States and territories to implement provisions of WPA. The Supreme Court has admitted petition and directed government to reply as to why directions, as prayed for by WWF-India, shouldnot be issued. The petition is pending and is first of its kind as its scope covers about 4 per cent of India's total land mass with 30 States as respondents. Hopefully petition will be heard and decided within a stipulated time.

India has taken several steps in recent times to protect tiger and other species in trade through following actions:

- By setting up Subramaniam committee to look into issue of prevention of illegal trade in wildlife and wild products.
- By setting up J.J. Dutta committee to review management of tiger project and suggest the future course of action.
- Organising training of various enforcement agencies in wildlife institute of India for the cause of species preservation.
- Organising an enforcement training workshop in New Delhi with the help of the US Fish and Wildlife Service and CITIES for enforcement agencies as Customs, Revenue Intelligence, Indo-Tibetan Border Police, Coastguards, Border Security Force, State Police, Deputy Director of Wildlife Preservation and Scientific Organisations like Botanical Survey of India and Zoological Survey of India.
- Setting up a National Co-ordination Committee for control of poaching and illegal trade in wildlife with enforcement agencies mentioned above as well as army, the postal department, etc.
- The eco-development programme has been set up

around major protected areas for winning over support of fringe dwellers to cause wildlife preservation including tiger under national schemes.

- Initiating India Eco-development Project under GEF (Global Environment Facility) in eight protected areas which include seven prime tiger habitats (six tiger reserves).
- Launching a public awareness programme to involve NGOs and others for supporting the government in its efforts at tiger preservation.
- Supporting programme of some institution and NGOs in exploring tiger trade routes and developing a forensic identification reference manual for tiger parts and products.

Cases

If it is an offence for a person holding a licence to go about with a loaded gun in his possession.

The person is said to be either killed or attempted to kill one of the animals or birds mentioned in Schedules. But there is no evidence to show that he had actually fired at any bird or animal, much less at any mentioned in Schedules of Act. It is no offence for a person holding a licence to go about with loaded gun in his possession. Hence conviction could be quashed.

CONVICTION: WHEN COULD BE SET ASIDE

The accused was questioned and he was said to have made a statement admitting his guilt. This statement was reduced to writing. Then a complaint was filed in court of Additional Chief Metropolitan Magistrate. The complaint was proceeded with evidence of respondent and of one of *Panchas* came to be recorded. On the basis of this evidence, the learned Magistrate proceeded to frame a charge. On charge being framed, the accused pleaded "guilty". By his order and judgement dated 13th April, 1983, learned Magistrate convicted accused in various courts, and sentenced him. That in the evidence of prosecution witness there is no mention whatsoever the articles seized were made of such snakes and lizards, the species whereof have been enumerated in any one of the several Schedules.

The provisions of WPA 1972, have been designed to prevent discrimination and commercial exploitation of rare species of animals and reptiles, and prosecution needs to be undertaken and conducted in all seriousness. In this matter, however, right from complaint till completion of evidence the approach of the prosecution has been casual in nature in as much as the prosecution has failed to adduce any evidence that the articles seized were made of the skins of such lizards or snakes. At the end conviction and sentence set aside.

In the evening of May 8th, 1975, a tiger was shot dead by accused at about 5:30 p.m. at Changlai camp, while on sentry duty. The accused, prior to shooting, had informed the guard commander of presence of tiger and commander instructed that 2-3 rounds might be fired into air to scare it away, but while this was being done, tiger, instead of fleeing, charged at accused who fired two shots at it, one hitting left shoulder. The animal instead of fleeing away charged at accused seeing which accused fired two more shots at it which killed the tiger. The Deputy Commissioner, while convicting the accused under Section 51 (1), followed spirit of Act to protect wildlife but provisions of Section 11, were not brought to his notice.

NO FAULT CAN BE FOUND IN THE ACQUITAL WHERE EVIDENCE IS INSUFFICIENT

The respondents were charged with having allegedly killed two tigers on 21/22 March, 1978, by administering poison and skinned them, which was punishable under Section 51 of the Act. The prosecution case, in brief, was that appellant had mixed aldrin in water for drinking by animals, which resulted in the death of two tigers. Therefore, they took away these two tigers and skinned them, on receiving this information the Range Officer informed police authorities. Later on, the tiger skins, nails and meat were seized from some of the respondents. During trial the first witness for prosecution stated that police did not interrogate the respondents in his presence. He also denied that anything was seized in his presence. According to him he was called to police station where he saw tiger skins, nails and meat. He also denied memorandum having been made in his presence. The witness was therefore, declared hostile and was permitted for cross-examination. During the cross-examination he admitted his signatures on memo. He also admitted that respondents were his relatives and belonged to his village. The third witness did not support prosecution, as during cross-examination he was not able to say the sufficient quantity of aldrin to kill a tiger. According to him aldrin was an agricultural insecticide easily available in market. The aforesaid evidence, however, does not indicate that respondents had either mixed aldrin, or given any statement leading to recovery of articles at their instance. The evidence being insufficient, no fault can be found in the acquital of respondents.

PART-D: LAWS RELATING TO AIRLINE SECTOR

Air Craft Act, 1934: Salient Features

The Indian Aircraft Act, 1934, provides the basic constitutional law of aviation in India. It has been amended from time to time whenever needed.

The preamble of the Act states that it is "an Act to make better provision for the control of the manufacture, possession, use, operation, sale, import and export of aircraft".

The Act extends to whole of India and applies also:

(a) To citizens of India wherever they may be; and

(b) To aircraft and to the persons on aircraft registered in India wherever they may be.

Section 2 of the Act refers to a few definitions of aircraft, aerodrome, aerodrome reference point, import and export.

Section 3 is titled "power of Central Government to exempt certain aircrafts". Under this Section the Central Government may exempt any aircraft or person for the application of the Act.

Section 4 relates to "power of Central Government to make rules to implement to Convention of 1944".

It may be recalled that India is a member of the

Convention on International Civil Aviation made in 1944. This Section empowers the government to make rules for implementing this convention which includes the annexes to the convention which refer to international standards and recommended practices.

Section 5 (i) covers the "power of Central Government to make rules". This is an important provision whereby the Central Government makes rules for regulating manufacture, possession, use, operation, sale, import or export of aircraft, and for securing the safety of aircraft operations.

Under Sub-section 5 (ii) of Section 5 the rules may provide for authorities by which any of the powers under the Act may be exercised—the regulation of air transport services, the economic regulation of civil aviation, the inspection of aircraft, registration of aircraft, licensing of persons employed in operation, manufacture, repair and maintenance of aircraft, the air routes to be flown in the country. Section 5 is a significant provision which enables the Central Government to make necessary rules for the regulation of civil aviation in India.

Section 5A is a later addition to the Aircraft Act made in 1972. It has the "power to issue directions". By this enactment the Director-General of Civil Aviation or any other officers empowered by the Central Government may order or issue direction consistent with the provisions of the Act and rules made thereunder with respect to certain matters provided in sub-section (2) of Section 5. These matters include licensing of airlines, licensing of aerodromes, inspection of aircraft for maintenance, the conditions under which aircraft may be flown:

Section 6 provides for the "power of the Central Government to make rules in emergency."

Under Section 6 the Central Government may, in the interest of public safety or tranquility, issue orders to cancel or suspend a licence or certificate, prohibit flight of an aircraft, prohibit or regulate erection or maintenance of aerodrome, and to direct to disallow any aircraft, flying school.

Section 7 (1) refers to the "power of Central Government to make rules for investigation of accidents". This Section is yet another important part of the Act.

7(2) Under sub-section (2) of Section 7, Central Government has the power to make rules for accident in investigation which may also (a) require notice to be given of any accident, (b) apply any provision of law for accident investigation, (c) prohibit, pending investigation, access to or interference with an aircraft involved in an accident, (d) authorise cancellation or suspension of licences or certificates.

The "power to detain aircraft" is given under Section 8 of the Act. This is also a new addition, made in 1972. It empowers the Central Government or any authority authorised to detain an aircraft whose intended flight involves danger to the aircraft, or where such detention is necessary to secure compliance with the provisions of the Act or the rules made thereunder, or to implement an order from any court.

8(A)(B) : The powers to make rules for protecting the public health are provided under Sections 8A and 8B of the Act.

Under Section 9 of the Act the provisions of Merchant Shipping Act, 1958, relating to wreck and salvage shall apply to aircraft over the same as they apply to ships, and the owner of an aircraft is entitled to salvage services like the owner of a ship.

Regulation of building or structure around twenty kilometres is contained in Section 9A of the Act. It states that if the Central Government is of opinion that it is necessary or expedient so to do for the safety of aircraft operations it may be official notification.

The essential aspect of the power envisaged under Section 9A to ensure safety of aircraft operations.

Section 9A was incorporated in 1972. This provision is of much concern to the city municipalities where airports are situated. Town planning cannot ignore the limitations set by this Section upon the height of building within twenty kilometres from the centre of the airport.

However, under Section 9B the Central Government is required to pay of compensation, if in consequences of any direction contained in a notification issued under the section.

Section 10 provides for the penalties for contravention of rules made under the Aircraft Act.

Section 11 relates to the provision of penalty for flying so as to cause danger. Similarly penalty for failure to comply with direction issued under Section 5A is provided for in Section 11A. The penalty for contravention of directions issued under Section 9A is provided in Section 11B. Penalty for abetment of offences and attempted offences are given in Section 12 of the Act.

Section 14 provides that all rules made under the Act are to be published for three months before implementation. Under Section 14A all rules made hereunder the Act are to be laid before each house of Parliament while in session for a period of thirty days.

Section 17 states that no suit shall be brought in any civil court in respect of trespass or in respect of nuisance by any reason on the flight of an aircraft, over any property for the height because this would give an opportunity to Parliament to review the rules and if necessary reject them by a special resolution.

In Section 19 entitled "saving of application of Act". The Act or any other or rule made thereunder saves Section 8A or 8B relating to public health and does not apply to any aircraft belonging to or exclusively employed in the naval, military or air force of the Union, or to any person in any such forces employed in connection with such aircraft.

THE CARRIAGE BY AIR ACT, 1972

Object and Scope

An international agreement governing the liability of the air carrier in respect of international carriage was made between various members countries at Warsaw Convention of 1929, and India was also a signatory to that convention. It governed the liability of the air carrier in respect of international carriage of passengers' baggage and cargo by air. The said convention was amended by the Hague Protocol of 1955, and a provision had been made for applying rules contained in the convention in its original as well as amended form under Schedule II of the Act. Under Section 4 of the Act it had been provided that the rules contained in the second Schedule being the provisions of the amended convention relating to rights and liabilities of carriers, passengers, consigners, and other persons shall have force of law in relation to any carriage by air and to which the rules of the aircraft performing the carriage approved under Warsaw Convention for carriage of passengers and goods by air is still in force and to which India had been a party. The Carriage by Air Act, 1934, does not apply to internal air carriage in India. Section 5 of the Carriage by Air Act, 1972 provides that notwithstanding anything contained in the Fatal Accidents Act, 1855, the rules contained in first and the second Schedule shall determine the liability of the carrier in respect of death of a passenger.

The liability shall be enforceable for the benefit of such of the members of the passenger's sustained damage by reason of his death. The members of the family shall include wife or husband, parent, step parent, grand parent, brother, sister, half brother, half sister, child, step child and grand child as provided in explanation to Section 5 of the Act. An action to enforce liability could be brought by the personal representative of the passenger or any person for whose benefit the liability could be enforced as discussed above. It had been provided under Section 6 of the Act that the Central Government, may, by notification in the Official Gazette apply the rules contained in the second Schedule and any provisions of Section 4 or Section 5 or Section 6 to such carriage by air as defined in second Sechedule. Subject, however, to such exceptions adaptations and modifications, if any, as may be specified.

For the purpose of understanding the relevant provisions pertaining to carriage by air it becomes essential to take into account some basic rules contained in Schedule II and the Hague Protocol of 1955.

On your next flight, it is more than your seat belts you might have to hold on to because the wait by the conveyor belt may turn into a nightmare as you realise that the last suitcase on it, is also not yours.

Despite the use of state-of-the-art luggage monitoring and tracking systems, the problem of lost and damaged baggages continues to plague air travellers.

With an estimated 339.6 million international air passengers criss-crossing the globe last year and 100 million more expected to do so by 1998, the incidence of baggage loss is in all probability likely to get compound.

Though every airline is pulling out all the stops to ensure enhance customer service, both in the air and on the ground, none of them yet guarantees a safe passage for your baggage. And this, inspite of the use of state-of-the-art baggage handling and tracking systems.

Baggage loss and damage is not a new phenomenon and as many seasoned travellers would agree, the anxiety of loosing one's luggage is a part and parcel of the travel experience of most frequent travellers. According to, Mr. Mrinal Kumar Singh, Lufthansa's Public Relations Manager for South Asia, "No airline has been able to completely eliminate the problem despite the stringent procedures followed."

Bags get lost or onto the wrong flight when either the tags come off or when the loaders load the wrong bags on to the wrong flights, especially when the connecting time is at a premium or when two or three flights are taking off almost simultaneously.

With most airlines such as Lufthansa and Air France banking on the latest computerised baggage handling and tracking systems like, 'BAHAMAS', the problem of baggage misplacement is under control. Besides, with tags providing the clue to passenger's identity, airlines have hit upon an ingenuous way to narrow down the problem of wrong loading. Lufthansa has a special tag called 'Hot Connecting Tag' for luggage to be loaded on interconnecting flights while Thai Airways has 'Interline Tags' to identify such luggage. Tower Air had multi-coloured Tags, while Indian Airlines, which is currently flying on International routes as well has bilingual tags to assist loaders in identifying the destination of the baggage.

But complaints of lost, damage or pilfered baggage continue.

What recourse does a passenger have when faced with such a situation?

The passenger should immediately inform the duty officer and fill up the PIF (Property Irregularity Form) when it is an International Airline which is the offender or a Baggage Discrepency Report (BDR) if it is a domestic flight.

These forms specify the passengers' name, tag and flight number, sector flown and number and make the baggage missing, messages are immediately flashed to the airlines central unit and a computer search is conducted to track down the bag. If the bag is traced within 24 hours, it is forwarded to the passenger on the next available flight. If the search fails, the passenger is required to lodge a formal complaint by signing the 'contents form' and the tracking procedure continues. If the baggage remains untraced beyond the stipulated time period (it ranges from 6-8 days) the passenger is paid his due compensation. Further, a passenger who has left the terminal cannot return later to report the loss of baggage since there is every chance that it might have happened outside the terminal complex.

Besides the non-refundable interim relief which is paid immediately on a passenger reporting baggage loss. (Gulf Air pays $ 750 and Lufthansa between Rs. 1000/- to Rs. 1500/-), the compensation all international airlines pay for lost baggage is based on 1929. Warsaw Pact, fixed at $ 20 per kg., and excess for any additional weight declared, and domestic airlines pay only Rs. 300/- per kg for misplaced luggage.

Most airlines are of the view that since passengers are aware of the baggage loss terms and conditions, it is unjustified in asking for a higher one. Every year on the ticket, argues the airline and clearly stipulates that a passenger should not pack any valuables in the baggage which has to be checked-in. Valuable can be gold or jewellery even sets of designer clothes which the passenger might deem valuable. This advise of the airline, can be carried as cabin baggage or as declared baggage which is loaded on to the flight as a consignment. Otherwise the contents of such a bag should be insured. But the passengers, fearing custom check often go easy on either declaring the valuables or getting it insured. And when such a baggage is misplaced, airlines are expected to pay a compensation commensurating with a passenger's claims, when there is no proof to substantiate such claims.

An reputed firm of lawyers Bhasin and Bhasin Co, who has handled several cases regarding baggage loss and compensation criticises the compensation limits put by the airlines. According to them, "the airline is wholly responsible for the safety of the baggage it is carrying. Airline shakes off all responsibility by pledging adherence to the Warsaw Convention. But this convention was signed in 1929, and about 70 years have passed since then. With the present rate of inflation, can any airline deny the fact that the ticket price have risen since 1929? Why should the passenger pay so much to travel by an airline and then pay more money for getting his luggage insured."

CASES OF LOST AND DAMAGED BAGGAGE

Case I. Mrs. Ranjna Wahi Vs Indian Airlines

One piece baggage of Mrs. K.S. Wahi (Ranjna) was damaged at the conveyor belt at Delhi Airport on Oct. 3, 1995, while boarding the Del-CCU - IXZ flight of Indian Airlines.

A remark to this effect was made by the Duty Manager on the reverse of her boarding pass, however, the baggage could not be mended at the Delhi Airport when the damage was noticed. On arrival at CCU airport, a damaged baggage report (DBR) was issued by the baggage cell but no discrepancy in weight was reported or noted. On arrival at her destination (Portblair) the passenger submitted a claim for Rs 18,153/- which included the claim of Rs 3,250/- as the cost of damaged baggage and the rest Rs 14,903/- for the cost of damaged items.

The damaged baggage, a nylon zipper of medium size which the passenger left with the airport officials was forwarded to the concerned office.

The airlines approved the payment of Rs 5,250/- out of

which they admitted his claim of Rs. 3,250/- for the damaged baggage in full and sanctioned Rs. 2,000/- on *ex-gratia* basis as a special case considering his status and standing and with a view to maintain a better passenger relation. Furthermore, in order to expedite the payment the airlines arranged for cash payment of the compensation.

But the passenger did not accept the compensation. The statement of compensation of the passenger goes as follows:

1.	THE DAMAGE TO THE BAG	65 £	= Rs. 3250.00
2.	RAYBAN SUN GLASSES	180 £	= Rs. 9000.00
3.	A PAIR OF JEANS LEVI'S	42 £	= Rs. 2100.00
4.	CROCKERY		= Rs. 2400.00
5.	2 SHIRTS		= Rs. 900.00
6.	MISC. KITCHEN ITEMS		= Rs. 503.00
	@ ONE £ = RS 50/- TOTAL		= Rs. 18153.00

Judgement

The passenger did not report any loss of article at Delhi and at Calcutta also no weight difference was noticed and a DBR was issued recording damage of baggage only. Therefore, the Airlines was of the view that adequate compensation has been offered to him.

In terms of limited liability of Indian Airlines the maximum compensation payable to Mrs. Wahi, taking into account the total loss of her baggage works out to be Rs. 5400/- @ Rs. 300/- per kg for 18 kg.

Case II. Mrs. Maria D'souza Vs Air India

On Jan 2, 1996, Mrs. Maria D'souza flying with Air India from Bombay to New York lost one of her baggages that contained the lifetime research work. She had to present at the New York Conference.

Mrs. D'souza irked at the airlines' callousness filed a report asking for adequate compensation of $ 1 million. But according to Warsaw Convention 1929, the maximum compensation she was offered, was $ 220 @ $20 per kg for 11 kg.

No legal proceeding could have been undertaken because of the unquantifiable nature of the damaged item.

Case III. Mr. B.L. Kachru Vs Lufthansa

Source: *Economic Times*

Mr. B.L. Kachru, a resident of the South Delhi locality of Kalkaji, regrets the day in 1993, when he took the Lufthansa flight from Los Angeles to San Francisco.

On landing, after the 60 minutes flight, he discovered that the suitcase containing his wife's medical reports and expensive dresses were missing. Her treatment consequently received a setback and his claim for the $ 1100 compensation was rejected.

The Airlines offered only $ 623 which was calculated on the basis of the gross weight of the baggage lost as per the airlines rules (Warsaw Convention 1929).

Case IV. Station Manager, Indian Airlines and Ors. (Appellants) versus Dr. Jiteswarahir (Repondent)

Complainant alleges he boarded Airlines flight—when he occupied the seat he was told by the officials that his luggage was lying on the ground unidentified and he should disembark from the aircraft. He moved towards the door finding the step ladder, but before he could put his entire body on the staircase, the ladder was suddenly removed and he received injuries. State Commission awarded Rs. 5,01,000/- as compensation. Hence appeal whether the opposite were negligent? Whether the compensation awarded by State Commission is fair and reasonable?

We have heard the learned council for the parties and have gone through their cards. The finding of the State Commission was that there was negligence on the part of the appellant, leading to the fall of the complainant, is very seriously challenged. The complainant has caused his own accident and received consequent injuries as well as the ailment resulting from these injuries. Another affidavit Shri (Dr.) Babul Roy, who accompanied one complainant in the same flight IC-241 from Dumdum to Agartala stating the circumstances under which the complainant fell down from the aircraft is also on the record. The State Commission observed that the statement of the opposite parties that while the complainant was moving to the rear door he was shouted to by an Air-hostess not to proceed to rear door, has not been substantiated either by affidavit or by amination of the particular Air-hostess. The guard tape which is required to be put across their car door while is clearance to the ground supply department operator removing the step level from the rear door was not across. The door had not been guarded by the guard tape and therefore, there was no reason for the complainant to assume that the ladder was in the process of being removed. The step ladder remained attached to the door but was suddenly removed by the ground operator as soon as complainant could step on the stair before he could actually pass his entire body weight add step ladder resulting in the fall. We, therefore, uphold the finding of the State Commission there was negligence of the staff of the opposite parties resulting into the injuries caused to complainant.

The State Commission has assessed it at Rs. 4.00/- lakhs which assessment in our view is fair and reasonable considering the age of the complainant as 37 years at the time of accident and his having lost earning capacity. The State Commission rightly held that besides his mental suffering a agony as well as his feeling of inferiority in social relations, inability to move and work freely without any physical impediment, etc., have to be compensated and awarded a sum of Rs. 1.00/- lakh which we consider just and fair.

PART-E: LEGISLATIONS RELATED TO SURFACE TRANSPORT BUSINESS

Indian Railways are the principal mode of transportation for carrying freight and passengers. It connects people and places in the farthest corners of the country and brings them closer for the purpose of business, sight-seeing, pilgrimage, etc. The Indian Railways consisting of 9 Zonal Railways, now 6 new being added for administrative convenience. It has been a great integrating force and has grown into a vast network of 7043 Railway Stations spread over a route length of 62,486 kms., carrying on an average 3,915 million passengers per annum.

In order to meet the ever-increasing demand/ requirements of travelling passengers/rail users, the efficient scheme for the redressal of public grievances is available in Indian Railways. The public grievances redressal system envisages a three-tier set-up one each at the Railway Board, Zonal Railway and Divisional level, besides providing on the spot redressal of the grievances caused by the travelling commuters at the various stations by Senior Station Managers/Station Managers. At all these levels, senior officials are charged with the responsibility of redressal of public grievances.

This functioning of the Public Grievances Redressal Machinery is reviewed and scrutinised by the different governmental agencies. Users' Consultative Committees in the Railways are also playing a constructive role in this direction so as to bring about a customer-friendly service to our travelling public/rail users. Recently instructions have been issued at highest level asking frontline staff who come in contact with the passengers to be more polite and courteous to them. Staff is imparted regular training in courtesy and politeness so as to provide courteous service to our valued customers, giving little room for complaints.

AT RAILWAY BOARD LEVEL

At Railway Board's level, Executive Director (Public Grievances) is in-charge of the Public Grievances Redressal Machinery. Periodical meetings chaired by the Chairman, Railway Board are held with Additional General Managers of the Zonal Railways which are attended by all the members and the concerned Executive Directors of the Railway Board, to review the functioning of Public Grievances Redressal Machinery on Railways. In these meetings, detailed review of trend of public grievances, identification of areas of public grievances and time taken in their disposal is done with particular emphasis on removal of system deficiencies. The Executive Director (Public Grievances) co-ordinates the activities of Public Grievances Redressal Machinery on Railways.

There is a full fledged Public Grievance Cell functioning in the Railway Board for the redressal of grievances addressed directly to the Railway Board as wall as those received through other departments of the government. It is supervised by Joint Director, Public Grievances/Deputy Director Public Grievances.

AT ZONAL RAILWAYS LEVEL

At the Zonal Railway level, the Additional General Managers function as Directors of Public Grievances and co-ordinate the work of public grievances with the concerned heads of departments. They hold periodical meetings with Additional Divisional Railway Managers where the causes of public grievances are analysed and the major areas of public grievances are identified. Based on this analysis, policy decisions are made to see that public grievances are removed and minimised. Review of the time taken in finalisation of the public grievances is also done and a close watch is kept to see that no delay is taken place in this respect. At Zonal Railways, there is a separate branch dealing with public complaints under the charge of Assistant Secretary, Public Grievances/Deputy Secretary, Public Grievances who assist the Additional General Manager in the investigation of complaints and their redressal.

AT DIVISIONAL LEVEL

Similar arrangements exist and operate at divisional level where Additional Divisional Railway Managers are nominated as Public Grievances Officers. Additional Divisional Railway Managers hold periodical meetings with Divisional Branch Officers and Station Superintendents/ Station Masters.

At station level, Station Superintendents/Station Masters are personally responsible for public grievances. They hold periodical and daily meetings with senior Supervisors of other departments at their stations with a view to co-ordinate activities aimed at satisfactory service to the customers.

Suggestion Boxes/Public Grievances Booths are also provided at important stations.

Complaint Books are provided at all stations, with Guards of Trains, Refreshment Room, Goods Sheds, etc., where the complaints can be lodged by the public. These complaints are investigated and necessary follow up action is taken to remove grievances and to find solutions to problems faced by the public. In cases where in the spot redressal is not possible, remedial measures are undertaken thereafter.

Opportunities are provided to public to ventilate their grievances in person to Additional General Managers and Additional Divisional Railway Managers who set aside a specified time on nominated days for meeting them.

REDRESSAL MACHINERY IN RAILWAY BOARD

As regards the Public Grievances Cell of the Railway Board's Office is concerned, it receives grievances/representations from various channels such as :

1. President's Office
2. Prime Minister's Office
3. Cabinet Secretariat
4. Cabinet Ministers
5. Representation of MPs addressed to MR
6. Reference received from Department of Personnel
7. Department of Pensions and Pensioners' Welfare
8. Other VIP letters to MR
9. Suggestion called for by Subcommittee of Consultative Committee or MPs on Railways addressed to Executive Director/Public Grievances
10. Representation received through 'Helpline Zee TV.
11. Representation/grievances from actual Rail users (travelling public)
12. Representation of Retired Railway Employees
13. General Representations
14. Reports of the Subcommittees of the consultative, committee of M.P.s on Railways.

As a result of constant monitoring and chasing by the Public Grievances, Directorate of Railway Board with the Zonal Railways, complaints are redressed specially with regard to the complaints pertaining to unauthorised passengers in coaches, allotment of seats and berths, catering and vending services, booking and luggage parcels, refund of tickets, reservation, etc. There is close co-ordination between the various Directorates of the Railway Board's office which deal with the above-mentioned grievances of these representations, efforts are made to have the same solved and their complaints are redressed thereby giving prompt attention to the rail users. Meeting of high officials of Board's office is maintained so that a constant monitoring is done Inter-directorate within Board's office so as to provide instant relief and action taken on the complaints received from the travelling public. A close study of the comparative statement of cause-wise complaints for the financial years 1993-94, 1994-95, with that of 1995-96, will show that out of 21 headings which are closely monitored at Board's office, complaints with regard to the 09 headings have come down when compared to the figures of 1995-96, over that of previous year of 1994-95.

Railway Board gets regular feedback from the Zonal Railways, from the PCDO on Public Grievances Redressal Machinery which are consolidated month-wise and a consolidated statement of cause-wise complaints received from the public are compiled under 21 headings and the same are submitted to the Board. In this regard, after keeping constant watch and monitoring of the complaints received through the 21 headings, D.O. letters from Executive Director Public Grievances and Additional Member (Commercial) and Chairman, Railway Board are sent to General Managers of the Zonal Railways giving the observations of the Board's office and also giving other remedial measures so as to bring about an improvement in the working of the Railways with a view to bring down the number of complaints from the travelling public. In this regard, to review the working of the Public Grievances Redressal Machinery System on the Zonal Railways Additional General Managers of each Zonal Railway is nominated as Director, Public Grievances and all the cases which are received by the Public Grievances Directorate are addressed to Additional General Manager and regular meetings with the Additional General Managers and Railway headed by minister are held in Board's Office periodically and outcome of the minutes of such meeting giving guidelines to the Additional General Managers and also giving them a new thrust and impetus with regard to the working of the public grievances is given, where the special emphasis is imparted on staff training in courtesy and politeness so as to provide courteous service to our valued customers.

Apart from the above, the Passenger Amenity Committee nominated by the minister also sends in their suggestions with regard to the facilities to be provided to the travelling public and action has been taken to redress the same. The Ministry of Parlimentary Affairs under the orders of Minister for Railways has set up a Subcommittee of Consultative Committee of Members of Parliament attached to the Ministry of Railways with regard to the congestion on platform in the four metropolitan cities. The Committee has primarily been set up to examine the issue of congestion on the suburban railway stations of Bombay, Calcutta, Madras and Delhi and the need to restrict new allotment of tea/food stalls thereby providing more travelling space to the passengers on the railway platforms. The Committee has already undertaken a number of visits at the various metropolitan towns/stations and Executive Director, Public Grievances has been nominated as Secretary of the above Committee, and number of complaints are being received which are being scrutinised by the Public Grievances Directorate. The report has since been presented to Minister for Railways on 30.11.95.

The number of complaints by the travelling public which are received by the Railway Board, with regard to the theft of passenger and their belongings at the Railway Stations and if the running trains has brought a bad name to the Railways as RPF/RPSF an organisation of the Railways have no role to play in this regard. Law and order and protecting the life and property and the security of the railway passengers and their belongings are a state subject and the cases are registered by Civil Police, which is known as Government Railway Police and Railways has no part to play in this regard as we have no control over the GRP which is under the State Police Chief/Ministry of Home Affairs and number of Parliament Questions and other complaints have to be dealt with by close monitoring by the Security Directorate of the Railway Board' office with close liaison of the Ministry of Home Affairs. It is requested that Ministry of Home Affairs may prevail upon where State Governments to bring down the number of complaints being registered with GRPs.

Recently Standing Committee on Railways (both Lok Sabha and Rajya Sabha Members of Parliament) had taken up the issue of "Redressal of Public Grievances Machinery on Indian Railways" with the Ministry of Railways.

An oral evidence was held on 16-2-96 and 26-2-96, where the Hon'ble Members of Parliament had expressed the view the complaints received from the following :

(1) Standing of Committee of Parliament,

(2) Members of Parliament/Minister reference/VIP reference,

(3) Department of Cabinet Secretary (DPG),

(4) Department of Pensions and Pensioners' Welfare, Ministry of Personnel, and

(5) General public references registered their grievances on Zonal Railways be dealt with on priority basis and replies sent in target date or time.

While replying to the 'action taken note' on item No. 4 pertaining to Public Grievences Redressal Machinery was put up to Board (CRB) for approval who had issued specific directives regarding time limit for disposal of the above references as under:

(1)	Standing Committee reference	:	1.	10 days where information is available in Board's office.
			2.	30 days where information is to be collected from Railways.
(2)	VIP/MP reference	:		30 days.
(3)	Department of Cabinet (DPG)	:		45 days.
(4)	DOP and PW	:		90 days.
(5)	General public ref.	:	1.	90 days.
			2.	120 days where detailed enquiry is required.

Consequent upon the replies given to the Standing Committee, a D.O. letter from Additional Member (Commercial)/Executive Director, Public Grievances were sent to General Managers/Additional General Managers, Zonal Railways wherein time and again the need for speedy disposal of complaints/grievances received by Railways have been stressed to reiterate the standing instructions on dealing with complaints registered through Public Grievances Redressal Machinery.

ANNEXURE-VII

Statement Showing Cmparative Analysis of Public Complaints On Zonal Railways (During April '94 to December '94 vis-a-vis April'95 to December '94)

S. No.	Causes	April to Dec. '94	April to Dec. '95	Percentage of variation
1.	Improper Behaviour of other than Rly. Staff	152	115	(-) 24.34
2.	Thefts and Pilferages	159	131	(-) 17.61
3.	Unauthorised Passengers in Coaches	122	108	(-) 11.47
4.	Punctuality of Trains	2854	2558	(-) 10.37
5.	Booking and Carriage of Luggage Parcels	358	323	(-) 0.99
6.	Refund against Tickets	558	557	(-) 0.17
7.	Complaints Relating to Sleeper Class	472	474	(+) 0.4
8.	Reservation Issues	1366	1401	(+) 2.5
9.	Improper Behaviour of Commercial Staff	921	950	(+) 3.1
10.	Passenger Booking	1884	1998	(+) 6.1
11.	Improper Behaviour of Other than Commercial Staff	176	187	(+) 6.3
12.	Non-Availability of Water	404	430	(+) 6.4
13.	Bribery and Corruption	133	143	(+) 7.5
14.	Catering and Vending Services	597	646	(+) 8.2
15.	Mal-functioning of Electrical Equipments	570	636	(+) 11.6
16.	Working of Enquiry Offices	1083	1221	(+) 12.7
17.	Allotment of Seats / Berths by Train Staff	467	533	(+) 14.1
18.	Cleanliness at Stations	235	270	(+) 14.9
19.	Maintenance/Cleanliness of Coaches	422	491	(+) 16.4
20.	Non-availability of bedrolls	106	154	(+) 45.3
21.	Miscellaneous Causes	2862	2844	(-) 0.6
	Grand Total	15901	16170	(+) 1.69

Source : *Office of Directorate of Rail Board: Redressal Machinery*

Carriage by Land

The Carriage by land may be either by private carriers who act as ordinary bailees and for which there is no special enactment and are governed by the relevant provision of the Indian Contract Act. At the same time important legislation, namely, the Carriers Act, 1865, deals with common carriers of goods over land as well as inland navigation. The right and liabilities of common carriers are not governed by the Indian Contract Act rather basic principles of English Common Law in a modified manner have been incorporated under the Carriers Act, 1865, which regulate and decide disputes pertaining to common carriers. A common carrier in India is therefore, subjected to distinct clause of liability, one is in respect of losses for which the carrier is liable due to his obligation to carry goods safely. In other words, notwithstanding some general exceptions in the chapter of bailment, a common carrier's responsibility is not only confined within the limits of the Indian Contract Act of 1872. Therefore, the Indian Contract Act does not exclusively regulate the rights and liabilities of the common carrier through the Carriers Act allows the carrier to enter into some special contract for the carrying of goods but the obligation on the part of carrier is an obligation independent of the contract. Secondly under the Carriers Act of 1865, the Common Law liability of a carrier has been modified only to the extent that it can be limited by special contract as provided under Section 6 of the Act. So if there is no special contract between the common carrier and the owner of the goods the common carrier's liability will be according to common law of relevant provisions of Indian Contract Act. The liability of common carrier for the loss of goods if not covered within the description of various kinds of liabilities given in the Schedule of the Carriers Act 1865, could be limited by special contract signed by the owner excepting the cases where such loss might have arisen from the negligence or criminal act of the carrier or any agent or servant.

RIGHTS AND LIABILITIES OF A PRIVATE CARRIER

A common carrier is a person who carries goods for everybody and the carrier who is not a common carrier is called a private carrier. Such private carrier would own liability as bailee of the goods and the liability could be limited or excluded by virtue of the contract between the parties. On the other hand, with regard to common carrier the liability under similar circumstances is higher due to the fact that common carriers are considered to be in the position of insurers with regard to the goods entrusted to them except where it might be expressly stipulated between the parties that the carrier is not a common carrier and in such a case the carrier can not be made liable as common carrier. While in case of private carrier his liability is that of a bailee covered under Sections 151 and 152 of the Indian Contract Act, 1865, wherein it is possible for the parties to enter into a contract thereby reducing the liability of the private carrier.

DISTINCTION BETWEEN A PRIVATE CARRIER AND A COMMON CARRIER

If a person carries goods for some particular individual only, he is a private carrier, while the person carrying goods indiscriminately is a common carrier. Private carriers do not come under the purview of the Carriers Act and as such the legal liabilities and consequences are different. The private carriers are the ordinary bailees and not insurers and their responsibility is that of an ordinary bailee in the sense that they are required to take care and exercise due diligence like a prudent man taking care of his own goods. A bailee is not responsible for damage to the goods whilst in his custody unless loss or damage is due to his wilful act or negligence. In other words the ordinary bailee is bound to take reasonable care of goods of other person and in case the goods entrusted to him are destroyed or lost without any fault on his part he is not under any liability. The liability of a common carrier is an absolute one and will be imposed upon him even if he has taken reasonable care and precautions. So the liability of the common carrier is greater. The common carrier is as such liable for loss or damage due to rain, storm or curse of weather in any other forms. There are two excepted perils for which the common carrier, is not responsible, i.e., inherent vice or in-built defect of goods and consigner's own fault in one or other respect.

The decision whether the carrier is a common carrier or a private one is made by his professional conduct to the public. In case the carrier professed by their conduct even if not by public notice that would carry goods indiscriminately for all those who engage them from a place to various other places. In such cases they would be held liable for the loss of goods as common carrier *(Navigation Co. Ltd. Vs Shyam Sunder Tea Co. Ltd. (1961) 2 S.C. 295; (1961) 2 M.L.J. (S.C) 160.* The proprietor of the motor bus service or any other passenger transportation undertaking meant for carrying passenger and their goods can not be regarded as common carrier according to the Carriers Act. If a conductor of a bus belonging to such a service accepts the consignment of goods from a person other than a passenger travelling in his bus and takes payment for such transport, the conductor takes it as his own risk and the proprietor or the bus will not be liable for loss of such consignment. The liability of common carriers in respect of articles carried as passenger's luggage is that of carriers of goods as distinguished from that of carriers of passengers unless the passenger himself takes the personal charge of the luggage. In case of transport of goods for higher or in other words for stipulated payment to the Carrier the liability would arise within the scope of Carriers Act and in case of gratuitions carriage or carriage without any reward liability could not be imposed on a carrier as he could not be called a common carrier.

THE CARRIERS' LIABILITY IN RESPECT OF PROPERTY

The Carriers Act makes no distinction between personal luggage and goods or merchandise and merely speaks of property. It excludes from its ambit carriage of passengers but carriage of animals could not be excluded because carrier of passengers in not a common carrier according to this Common Carriers Act of 1865. But a carrier of animals would fall under the category of common carriers as provided in Section 73 of the Indian Railway Act.

Basic Features of a Common Carriers

According to Section 2 of the Carriers Act the main attributes of a common carrier are: (I) he must be a person including any association whether a body corporate or not, but excluding Government; (II) he must transport property and not passengers; (III) the transporting business be either by land or by inland navigation; carriage by air or carriage on high sea are excluded; (IV) he must be engaged in all the business of transport and the carriage must be for the business of transport as the carriage by a forwarding agent is thereby excluded because the forwarding agent does not carry for all the business of transport; (V) the transport must be for hire and it must be for some reward; and (VI) the business of transport must be carried without any discrimination.

CASES RELATED TO SURFACE TRANSPORT

Case I

India has one of the largest road networks in the world. The country's total road length was 19,98,500 km. in the year 1990-91. There are national highways, state highways and district rural roads that run all over the country.

The grievances and complaints regarding road transportation are filed with the Public Transport System's Office of that area or State. The States and Union Territories of India have their separate public transport systems that run all over the country or within that state. For example, the complaints of the travellers of DTC buses are filed at the office of Delhi Transport Corporation.

Can a public sector transport undertaking, operating a bus on hire, shift the liability of paying compensation to its owner; in case the bus is involved in a fatal road accident?

This important question of law, raised in three appeals in the case of *Rajasthan State Road Transport Corporation Vs. Kailash Nath Kothari and Others, etc.*, has been answered by the Supreme Court in a recent judgement.

The appeals were directed against a common judgement of the Rajasthan High Court dated January 22, 1991, upholding composite awards made by the Motor Accident Claims Tribunal on March 13, 1989.

Bus No. RSB 3945, besides some other buses were hired by the appellant-corporation from its owner, Mr. Sanjay Kumar, one of the respondents, to ply on the routes specified by it. An agreement was executed between both the parties containing the terms of hiring the bus.

The bus on the fateful day, July 17, 1981, being driven by Gopal, was plying on the route, Kekri to Jaipur, for which route, the corporation had the route had the route permit. At about 9.30 p.m. when the bus was near Renwal, it was noticed that water was flowing over the bridge on the river band, due to heavy rains in the catchment area. Despite requests from the passengers to the driver not to venture to cross the bridge in such a situation, he drove on the bus and as a result the bus was swept away, killing 23 passengers by drowning.

The legal representatives/heirs of the victim passengers, filed separate claim petitions under Section 110-A of the Motor Vehicles Act, 1939, claiming compensation from the corporation in its written statement denied its liability on the ground that though it had hired the bus in question from Shri Sanjay Kumar and the bus was plying on the route specified by it and the driver of the bus, Gopal, due to whose negligence and rashness. It was also pleaded that the liability to pay the compensation in case of an accident was that of the "owner" and of the hirer. Balance on this behalf was placed on condition No. 15 of the agreement to disown the liability.

The insurance company took the plea, in its reply to the claim petitions, that the bus at the time of the accident was under the control of the corporation, therefore, it was the liability of the corporation to pay the compensation and the insurance company was not liable. It was further pleaded that the liability of the insurance company, in any event, was limited and its liability could not exceed Rs. 75,000 in respect of all the claim petitions.

The owner of the bus, though a party to the claim petitions, did not file any reply.

A number of witnesses were examined by the parties and after considering both oral and documentary evidences the tribunal held that the accident took place due to rash and negligent driving by the driver. The tribunal held that in the light of the terms of the policy of insurance and the relevant provisions of the Act, the liability of the insurance company was limited in respect of the accident to a total amount of Rs. 75,000 only.

The tribunal noticed the condition No. 15 of the agreement between the corporation and the bus owner and opined that the same was against the "public policy" and, therefore, it could not discharge the corporation from its liability. It was noticed that the bus was plying on the route chosen by the corporation and the passengers had paid their fares to the conductor, who was admittedly an employee of the corporation and as such the corporation could not escape from its liability. The corporation was, therefore, held liable, to pay the compensation to the claimants. Different amounts were awarded in each of the claim petitions by a composite award while granting the relief sought for.

Aggrieved by the composite awards of the tribunal, the corporation filed appeals against each of the awards in the High Court. The High Court uphelp the composite awards. Thus, the corporation approached the Supreme Court.

The only issue, which left for consideration before the apex court was whether the corporation was liable to pay the compensation or not.

A division bench of the Supreme Court comprising Justice A. S. Anand and Justice K. Venkataswami in its judgement noted "the definition of "owner" under Section 2 (19) of the Act saying that it was not exhaustive. It has, therefore, to be construed in a wider sense in the facts and circumstances of a given case. The expression "owner" must include, in a given case, the person, who has the actual possession and control of the vehicle and under whose directions and commands the driver is obliged to operate. To confine the meaning of "owner" to the registered owner only would, in a case where the vehicle is in the actual possession and control of the hirer not be proper for the purpose of fastening of liability in case of an accident. The liability of the "owner" is vicarious for the tort committed by its employee during the course of his employment", the judges added.

The judges pointed out that in this case the registered owner could not ply the bus on the particular route for which he had no permit and he in fact not plying the bus on that route. The services of the driver had been transferred along with complete "control" to the corporation, under whose directions, instructions and commands, the driver was to ply or not to ply the ill-fated bus on the fateful day. The passengers were being carried, by the corporation on receiving fares from them. The corporation, therefore, had rightly been held liable to pay the compensation.

Source: *TOI- Sept. 21st, 1997, Legal Notes* by Awadh K. Singh.

RAILWAYS LIABLE TO PAY DAMAGES IN A MOTOR ACCIDENT

Case II

Do the Motor Accidents Claims Tribunal have the jurisdiction under Section 110 (1) of the Motor Vehicles Act 1939, read with Section 168 (1) of the Motor Vehicles Act, 1988, to adjudicate a claim against the Railways when a motor vehicle is hit by a train? Also can the tribunal make an award under Section 110 (B) of the Act against the Railways in addition to making an award against the owner of the vehicle, its driver and the insurer?

These questions of law, raised in a batch of appeals in the case *of Union of India Vs United India Insurance Co. Ltd., and Others,* have been settled by the apex court in a recent judgement.

An accident occurred on May 9, 1979, at an unmanned level-crossing in Akaparamao, near Kalady in Kerala, when a hired passenger bus was hit by the Jayanthi Janatha Express. Forty passengers in the bus and its driver were killed while some other passengers sustained injuries.

Two judgements of the Motor Accidents Claims Tribunal, Ernakulam, in regard to the accident had been brought by way of appeals before the apex court. In one batch of cases, filed by the dependents of the deceased and injured persons, the tribunal, by its judgement dated February 28, 1986, held that the driver of the bus was negligent and made awards against the owner of the bus and the insurance company, but dismissed the claim against the Railways on the ground that there was no negligence on the part of the driver of the train or the Railway

Administration. The liability of the insurance company was restricted to a maximum of Rs. 5,000 per passenger under statutory provisions then in force.

On appeals by the insurance company, cross-objections were preferred by the claimants in some cases. The appeals and cross-objections filed were partly allowed by the Kerala High Court, making the Railways also liable. In two other cases, which were decided in an earlier judgement dated September 27, 1984, the same tribunal had held that the railway administration was also liable on account of its negligence. However, in both the judgements it was held that under Sections 110 (1) and 110 (B) of the Motor Vehicles Act, 1939, an award could be made against the Railways also, which view was confirmed by the High Court.

Against all these judgements, the Union of India filed appeals before the apex court. A division bench of the Supreme Court, comprising Justice S.B. Majumdar and Justice M.J. Rao, in its judgement said that since the driver of the bus did not stop the vehicle at the unmanned crossing, it must be held that he was guilty of negligence even though there was no curve or obstruction at the point. "The tribunal and the High Court were, in our opinion, justified in finding negligence on the part of the driver," the judges added.

On the question whether the driver's negligence in any manner could vicariously be attached to the passengers of the bus, the court said that though there was a well-known principle in the law of tort called the' doctrine of identification or imputation', that principle was in a applicable to a passenger in the sense that the negligence of the driver of the vehicle could not be imputed to the passengers.

" A passenger is not treated as a backseat driver. It is, therefore, clear that even if the driver of a bus was negligent, the railways, if its negligence was otherwise proved, could not plead contributory negligence on the part of the passengers of the vehicle as in the present case. What is clear is that the passengers of the bus who were innocent, the driver and owner of the bus and, if proved, the Railways can all be joint tortfeasors," the Court observed.

Therefore, the Court held that the claimants could sue the railways concurrently for breach of the common law or statutory duties or for the breach of either of the duties as in this case there was not even a caution board at the unmanned level-crossing.

The Court also rejected the plea of the appellant that the tribunal had no jurisdiction to entertain any claims against the Railways and the appropriate forum for the purpose was a civil court.

It held that the claims for compensation were maintainable against other persons or agencies which were held to be guilty of composite negligence or were joint tort-feasors, and if arising out of use of a motor vehicle. "We hold that the tribunal and the high court were right in holding that an award could be passed against the railways if its negligence in relation to the accident was also proved," the Judges said while dismissing the appeals.

Source: *TOI- Sept. 9th, 1997, Legal Notes*
by Awadh K. Singh.

Case III: Bhanny Vs Shenoy, Karnataka SRTC (1991)

Details—A passenger who could not be conveyed to his destination owing to road obstruction was allowed to recover from the bus operator his ticket money to and fro.

Source: *Elements of Mercantile Law,*
by N.D. Kapoor

Case IV: Mr. Kata Suryanarayna Vs Dolphin Travels

Details—Mr. Suryanarayna booked two tickets from Bangalore to Ooty with Dolphin Travels but instead of promised videocoach he and his wife were made to sit in an uncomfortable cabin of a small bus and since his tickets were for to and fro journey, but the above said agency made no arrangement of return ticket as it was promised in right of passage. Mr. Suryanarayna and his wife had to pay Rs. 200 to buy return tickets for another bus. Mr. Suryanarayna then filed the case before district forum Bangalore which awarded a compensation of Rs 5000/-. But on an appeal from Dolphin travels in the state forum the claims of compensation was reduced to Rs. 2,000 on the ground that it would meet the end to justice.

Source: *E.L.R.A.T.B.- by S. Malik*
TOI-June 13, 1999

Case V: M. Meenakshi Sundaram Vs. The General Manager Southern Railway

The complainant purchase an A.C. chair car ticket and he was placed in the waiting list. The TTE allotted two seats to two VIPs who were holding non-A.C. tickets in preference to the complainant. It was held that the Railways were, responsible for the irresponsible conduct of their employee and the complainant was entitled to damages. It was further held that the Railways were not entitled to claim exemption from liability under Sec. 67 of the Railway Act or Rule 306 of the Railway Tariff Rules, which were meant for situations where seats are not available for the reasons beyond the control of the Railway Authorities. In this case the seats were available, but they were wrongly allotted to somebody else.

This case would be more explicit when we move on the details of Public Grieveances Redressal Machinery on the Railways.

Source: *Company Law* by Avtar Singh

Case VI: The Missing Coach

On July 23, 1993, S.S. Bansali reserved an A.C. two tier berth on the North East Express for his journey from Delhi to Jalpaiguri in September, relates *Consumer Confrontation*, a publication of the Consumer Education and Research Society in a recent news items titled *The Missing Coach*.

On the day of the journey, says the item, Bansali found that Coach No. AI, in which he was allotted a reserved berth, had not been attached to the train. There was neither information nor was there anyone to guide him. No alternative arrangements had been made for the passengers of the missing coach. Bansali somehow managed to get just enough sitting space in an overcrowded sleeper coach. But while he was trying to enter the compartment, his shirt tore and his spectacles broke. There was neither a light nor a fan in the compartment, as there was no power connection. The compartment was so crowded, he could not even get to the toilet. In the confusion, he even left a suitcase at the Delhi Railway Station, states the item.

Bansali did not receive a refund of the excess fare charged, either at Delhi or at Jalpaiguri Railway Station. At the end of the journey, he was in a shattered state and was unwell for 10 days. According to the item, he wrote several letters in October and November, 1993, for refund of the excess fare. In February, he sent the original certificate to the Chief Commercial Manager (Refund), New Delhi. At last on October 17, 1994, he received a cheque for Rs. 781 but, in spite of having given his Delhi address repeatedly, the cheque was made payable at Calcutta. He could deposit the cheque only on12th January, 1995.

A frustrated Bansali, continues the item, filed a case before the District Consumer Forum. The forum held that the coach must not have been attached because of compelling reasons and since the excess fare charged had been refunded, the complaint could not be allowed.

Bansali appealed against this order before the State Commission. It observed that the issue was not just the excess fare, but Bansali had been subjected to considerable harassment in spite of having made reservations two months in advance. There was not justification for the Railways not informing the passengers of the conditions. Further, there was inordinate delay in sending the refund cheque, and finally, it was sent to Calcutta. This, the commission held, was a clear case of deficiency in service. As the refund of the excess fare had been made, the commission directed the Railways to pay the complainant Rs. 3,000 as compensation, the item said.

Source: *Voyage; Jan. 1998, p. 8.*

PART-F: LEGISLATIONS RELATING TO FOREST PRESERVATION

Introduction

Existence of the green cover on the earth is the life sap of human society. It cannot be dispensed with at all, because each breath we take in is purified by the natural forests. Forests provide us fuel, fodder, timber and many other produces which are essential for our survival. Indiscriminate destruction of natural forests has brought an environmental crisis in our country. To prevent this the Government of India formulated the Forest Act.

Forest Act of 1927

The forest Act of 1927 is "An Act to consolidate the laws relating to forest, the transit of forest produce and duty liable on timber and other forest produces."

Scope of the Act

This Act deals with the rule of forest in 13 Chapters. The first Chapter deals with short title extent of Act and repetition of causes, the IInd Chapter deals with the law relating to reserved forest the word reserved forest has not been defined in the Act. The rest deal with topics such as cattle trespasing, power of forest off, etc.

This Act. extends to the whole of India except the territories which immediately before the Ist of Nov., 1956, were comprised of part B state (other than the Madhya Bharat and some region of the state of M.P.).

It applies to territories which immediately before the Ist of Nov., 1956, were comprised in the States of Bihar, Maharashtra, Delhi, Madhya Pradesh, Orissa, Punjab, Uttar Pradesh and West Bengal, but the Government of any state may by notification in the official gazette. Bring this Act in the force in the whole on any specified part of state to which this act extends and where it is not in force.

Now it also applies to the territories comprised of Madhya Bharat, Vindhya Pradesh, Bhopal and some regions of the State of M.P.

THE PRESERVED FOREST

The Indian Forest Act deals with reserved forests. The word "reserved" has not been defined in the Act. On the terminology employed by the Act "reserved forests" are those areas of forest land which are constituted as a "reserved forests" under Chapter second of the Act. This Chapter deals with reserved forests, power of the State Government to reserve forests, to issue notifications for the purpose, extinction of rights of private individuals subject to certain conditions, acquisition of land over which right is claimed by any person if found proper, etc. The full Bench of the

Allahabad High Court has stated about the scope of this Chapter that Section 3 of the Act gives power to the State Government to constitute any forest land or waste land which is the property of Government or over which the Government has the proprietary rights, or to the whole or any part of the forest produce of which the Government is entitled, a reserved forest in the manner prescribed in the succeeding Sections.

Section 4 provides that when it has been decided to constitute any land a reserved forest, the State Government shall issue a notification in Official Gazette declaring that it has been decided to constitute such land reserved forest, specifying as nearly as possible the situation and limits of such land, and appointing as officer to be known as the "Forest Settlement Officer" to inquire into and determine the existence, nature and extent of any rights alleged to exist in favour of any person in or over land comprised within such limits or in over any forest produce, and to deal with the same as provided in the Act.

Section 5 provides that after the issue of a notification under Section 4 no right shall be acquired in or over the land comprised to the notification except by succession or under a grant or contract in writing made or entered into by or on behalf of the Government or some person in whom such right was vested when the notification was issued. It also prohibits fresh cleanings for cultivation or for any other purpose except in accordance with such rules as may be made by the State Government in this behalf.

Section 6 provides that when a notification has been issued under Section 4, the Forest Settlement Officer shall publish in the local vernacular in every town and village in the neighbourhood of the land comprised therein, among other, this is a proclamation fixing a period of not less than three months from the date of such proclamation and requiring every person claiming any right mentioned in Section 4 or Section 5 within such period either to present to the Forest Settlement Officer a written notice specifying or to appear before him and state the nature of such right and the amount and particulars of the compensation, if any, claimed in respect thereof.

Section 7 provides for the Forest Settlement Officer to take down in writing all statements made under Section 6 and also to inquire into all claims duly preferred under that Section 4 or Section 5 and not claimed under Section 6 so far as the same may be ascertainable from the records of Government and the evidence of any persons likely to be acquainted with the same.

Section 8 gives to the Forest Settlement Officer the powers of a civil court in the trial of suits. It also authorises him either himself to enter upon any land and to survey, demarcate and make a map of the same or to authorise any officer to do so.

Section 9 provides that rights in respect of which no claim has been preferred under Section 6 and of the existence, of which no knowledge has been acquired by inquiry under Section 7 shall be extinguished. It, however, extends the period of making a claim up to the stage of publication of the notification under Section 20 in certain circumstances but not beyond that.

Section 10 deals with a claim relating to the practice of shifting cultivation in which case the Forest Settlement Officer is required to record a statement setting forth the particulars of the claim and any local rule or order under which the practice is allowed or regulated and submit the statement to the State Government together with his opinion as to whether the practice should be permitted or prohibited wholly or in part. If the practice is permitted wholly or in part the Forest Settlement Officer may arrange for its existence by altering the limits of the land under settlement so as to exclude land sufficient extent, of a suitable kind, and in a locality reasonably convenient for the purposes of the claimants, or by causing certain portions of the land under settlement to be separately demarcated and giving permission to the claim. Acts to practice shifting cultivation therein under such conditions as he may prescribe. All these arrangements are subject to previous sanction of the State Government. The practice of shifting cultivation shall in all cases, be deemed a privilege, subject to control, restriction and abolition by the State Government.

Section 11 provides that in the case of a claim to a right in or over any land, other than a right of way or right of pasture, or a right to forest produce or a watercourse, the same in whole or in part. If such a claim is admitted in whole or in part, the Forest Settlement Officer shall either exclude such land from the limits of the proposed forest, or come to an agreement with own or thereof for the surrender of his rights, or proceed to acquire such land in the manner provided by the Land Acquisition Act, 1894.

Under Section 12 in the case of a claim to right of pasture or to forest produce, the Forest Settlement Officer shall pass an order admitting or rejecting the same in whole or in part.

Section 13 provides as to whose record is to be prepared by the Forest Settlement Officer when passing an order under Section 12.

Section 14 provides that the Forest Settlement Officer, in case, admits in whole or in part any claim under Section 12, shall also record the extent to which the claim is so admitted, specifying the number and the description of the cattle which the claimant is entitled to graze in the forest the season during which such pasture is admitted and quantity of timber and other forest produce which he is from time to time authorised to take or receive, and such and other particulars as the case may require.

Section 15 provides that after making such record the Forest Settlement Officer shall, to the reserved forest in respect of which the claim is made pass such order so as to ensure the continued exercise of the rights admitted for this purpose. The Forest Settlement Officer may set out some other forest tract of sufficient extent and in a locality reasonably convenient for the purpose of such claimants, and record an order conferring upon them a right of pasture or to forest produce (as the case may be) to the extent so admitted, or so after the limits of the proposed forest as to exclude forest land of sufficient extent and in a locality reasonably convenient, for the purpose of the claimants or record an order continuing to such claimants a right of pasture or to forest produce as the case may be to extent so admitted at such seasons within such portions of the proposed forest and under such rules as may be made in this behalf by the State Government.

Section 16 provides that in case the Forest Settlement Officer finds it impossible having due regard to the maintenance of the reserved forest, to make such settlement under Section 15 as shall ensure the continued exercise of the said rights to the extent so admitted he shall subject to such rules as the State Government may make in this behalf commute such rights, by the grant of land or in such other manner as he thinks fit.

Section 17 provides that any person who has made a claim under the Act or any Forest Officer or other persons generally or specially empowered by the State Government in this behalf may within 3 months from the date of the order passed on such claim by Forest Settlement Officer under Sections 11, 12, 15, or Section 16. Section 18 then provides as to how an appeal shall be preferred and how it has to be heard.

Section 18 (4) provides that the order passed on appeal by such officer or court, or by the majority of the members of such court as the case may be shall subject only to revision by the State Government by final.

Section 19 provides that the State Government or any person who has made a claim under this Act may appoint any person to appear plead and act on its or his behalf before the Forest Settlement Officer, or the Appellate Officer or Court in the course of any inquiry or appeal under this Act.

Section 20 provides that when the period fixed under Section 6 for preferring a claim has elapsed and all claims if any made under that Section or Section 9 have been disposed of by the Forest Settlement Officer if any such claims have been made the period limited by Section 17 or appealing from the orders passed on such claims has elapsed and all appeals if any, presented within such period have been disposed of by the appellate office or court and all lands.

Section 21 provides that the Forest Settlement Officer shall, before the date fixed by the notification as referred in Section 20, cause a translation thereof into the local vernacular to be published in every town and village in neighbourhood of the forest.

Section 22 provides that the State Government may, within five years from the publication of any notification under Section 20, revise any arrangement made under Section 15 or Section 18 and may for this purpose recind or modify and order made under Section 15 or Section 18 and direct that any one of the proceedings specified in Section 15 be taken in lieu of any other proceeding or that the rights admitted under Section 12 be commuted under Section 16.

According to Section 23 no rights of any description shall be acquired over reserved forest except by succssion or under a grant or contract in writing made by or on behalf of the Government or some person in whom such right was vested when the notification under Section 20 was issued. And Section 23 imposes restrictions on the alienation of such right without the sanction of the State Government.

Section 25 deals with the powers of the Forest Settlement Officer to stop ways and watercourse in the reserved with the previous sanction of the State Government and also to provide substitute thereto.

Section 26, the last section of this Chapter, provides for prohibition of setting fire or any act done in contravention of any rules to damage the forest thus reserved, by any person including the forest clearing also as prohibited by Section 5 it also provides for prohibition of trespass.

APPEAL FROM ORDER PASSED UNDER SECTION 11, SECTION 12, SECTION 15 OR SECTION 16

Any person who has made a claim under this Act or any Forest Officer or other person generally or specially empowered by the State Government in this behalf, may within three months from the date of the order passed on such claim by the Forest Settlement Officer under Section 11, Section 12, Section 16 present an appeal from such order to such officer of the Revenue Department, of rank not lower than that of a Collector, as the State Government may, by notification in the Official Gazette, appoint to hear appeals from such orders.

Provided that the State Government may establish a Court (hereinafter called the Forest Court) composed of three persons to be appointed by the State Government, and when the Forest Court has been so established all such appeals shall be presented to it.

The Forest (Conservation) Act, 1980

An Act to provide for the conservation of forests and for matters connected therewith or ancillary or incidental thereto:

Be it enacted by Parliament in the thirty-first year of the Republic of India as follows :

(1) This Act may be called the Forest (Conservation) Act, 1980.

(2) It extends to the whole of India except the State of Jammu and Kashmir.

(3) It shall be deemed to have come into force on the 25th day of October, 1980.

With a view to checking further deforestation, The Forest (Conservation) Ordinance, 1980 has been promulgated on 25th October, 1980. The present Act has replaced the said ordinance and contains similar provisions. The Act extends to the whole of India except the State of Jammu and Kashmir and came into force on 25th October, 1980.

(2) Restriction on the de-reservation of forests or use of forest land for non-forest purpose, notwithstanding anything contained in any other law for the time being in force in a State, no State Government or other authority.

(i) That any reserved forest (within the meaning of the expression "reserved forest" in any law for the timebeing in force in that state) or any portion thereof, shall cease to be reserved;

(ii) That any forest land or any portion thereof may be used for any non-forest purposes.

(iii) That any forest land or any portion thereof may be assigned by way of lease or otherwise to any other organisation not owned, managed or controlled by Government;

(iv) That any forest land or any portion thereof may be cleared of trees which has grown naturally in the land or portion, for the purpose of using it for reafforestation.

(v) For the explanation, the following explanation shall be substituted, namely:

Explanation—For the purpose of this Section 'non-forest purpose' means the breaking up or clearing of any forest land or portion thereof for the following:

(a) The cultivation of tea, coffee, spices, rubber, palms, oil bearing plants, horticultural crops or medicinal plants;

(b) Any purpose other than reafforestation, but does not include any work relating or ancillary to conservation, development any management of forests and wildlife, namely the establishment of check-post, wireless communications and construction of fencing bridges and culverts, dams, waterholes, trench marks, boundary marks pipelines or other like purposes.)

Penalty for Contravention of the Provisions of Act

Whoever contravenes or abets the contravention of any of the provisions of Secion 2 shall be punishable with simple imprisonment for a period which may extend to fifteen days.

Offence by Authorities and Government Department

Where any offence under this Act has been committed:

(a) By any department of Government, the head of the department or;

(b) By any authority. Every person who at the time the offence was committed was directly in charge of and was responsible to the authority for the conduct of the business of the authority as well as the authority shall be deemed to be guilty of the offence and shall be liable to be proceeded against and punished accordingly; provided the nothing contained in the sub-section shall render the head of the department or any person referred to in clause (b) liable to any punishment if he proves that the offence was committed without his knowledge that he exercised all due diligence to prevent the commission of such offence.

THE FOREST (CONSERVATION RULES, 1981)

In exercise of the powers conferred by sub-section (i) of Section 4 of the Forest (Conservation) Act 1980 (69 of 1980) the Central Government hereby makes the following rules, namely:

(1) These rules may be called the Forest (Conservation) Rules, 1981.

(2) They shall extend to the whole of India except the State of Jammu and Kashmir.

(3) They shall come into force on the date of their Publication in the Official Gazette.

1. **Definitions** : In these rules unless the context otherwise requires:
   (a) 'Act' means the Forest (Conservation) Act, 1980 (69 of 1980);
   (b) Committee means the Committee consututed under Section 3;
   (c) 'Chairman' means the Chairman of the Committee;
   (d) 'Member' means a member of the Committee;
   (e) 'Section' means a Section of the Act.

2. 2-A: Composition of the Committee. The committee shall be composed of the following members:
   (i) Inspector-General of Forest, Ministry of Environment and Forest—Chairman
   (ii) Additional Inspector-General of Forests-Ministry of Environment and Forests—Member.
   (iii) Joint Commissioner (Soil Conservation) Ministry of Agriculture—Member
   (iv) Three Eminent Environment Scientists (no officials)—Members
   (v) Additional Inspector-General of Forests shall act as the Chairman in the absence of Inspector-General of Forests.

3. 2-B: Terms of appointment of non-official members shall be as follows:
   (i) A non-official member shall hold his office for a period of two years.

(ii) A non-official member shall cease to hold office if he dies, resigns, becomes of unsound mind becomes insolvent or is convicted by a court of law on a criminal offence involving moral turpitude.

(iii) Any vacancy in the membership caused by any reason mentioned in sub-rule (ii) shall be filled by the Government for the unexpired portion of 2 years, term.

(iv) Travelling and Daily Allowance shall be payable to the non-official members of the Committee at the highest rate admissible to the Government servants of Group A under the rules and orders made by the Central Government and, for the time being, in force;

Provided that the payment of Travelling Allowance and Daily Allowance to a member who is a member of the Parliament or a member of a State Legislature shall be regulated in accordance with the salary. Allowance and pension of Members of Parliament, Act 1954 or the respective provisions of law pertaining to the members of the concerned State Legislature.

PENALTIES FOR TRESPASS OR DAMAGE IN RESERVED FOREST ACTS AND PROHIBITED IN SUCH FOREST

Under Section 20 of the Andhra Pradesh Forest Act, 1967 the acts prohibited in reserved forests and penalties for the same have been provided under Section 21 of Act—

Penalties for Trespass, or Damage in Reserved Forest Acts and Prohibited in such Forest: Any person who—

(a) contravens the provisions of clause (b) of sub-section (1) of section 7;

(b) sets fire to a forest notified to be received under Section 4 or kindless in such forest any fire or leaves any fire burning in such a manner so as to endanger such forest;

(c) in a reserved forest—

(i) kindless, keeps or carries any fire except at such reason and subject to such conditions as the Divisional Forest Officer may from time to time, specify in this behalf;

(ii) trespasses pastures cattle or allows cattle to trespass;

(iii) causes any damage either wilfully or negligently in felling or cutting any tree or dragging any timber;

(iv) fell girdles, taps or burns any tree or strips off the bark of leaves from, or otherwise damages the same;

(v) quarries stones, burns lime or charcoal;

(vi) collects or subjects to any manufacturing process, any forest produce;

(vii) clears of breaks up or ploughs any land for cultivation or any other purpose;

(viii) hunts, shoots, fishes poisons water or sets traps or snares;

(ix) damages, alters or removes any wall, ditch, embankment, fence, hedge or railing; or

(x) removes any forest produce;

(d) abets any of the Acts specified in clauses (a), (b) and (c), shall in addition to such compensation for damages caused to the forest as the court may direct to be paid be punishable—

(i) in every case where any of the Acts, aforesaid relates to sandalwood or red sandalwood with imprisonment for a term which shall not be less than three months but which shall be exceeded one year and with fine which shall not exceed Rs. 10,000.

(ii) in any other case with imprisonment for a term which may extend to one year or with fine which may extend to Rs. 2,000 or with both.

CASE I: A Case of Appeal of Reserved Forest

Hon'ble Justice Sri O.P. Trivedi (Allahabad High Court) has observed in a recent case that finality does not attach to such order passed by the Forest Appellate Court which is passed in respect of the laid not covered by notification issued under Section 4 of the Indian Forest Act. Such order cannot act as res judicata in the case of declaration granted by the Revenue Court under Section 229-B, of the U.P. Zamindari Abolition and Land Reforms Act. The brief facts of the case are given as under :

A notification was issued under Section 4 of Indian Forest Act on 29th March 1954. The State Government proposing to constitute lands in village Baghauwa Pargana Balia Tahsil Nighasan, District Kheri as reserved forest. The petitioner's father Jagat Ram claimed to be a Sirdar of plots Nos. 21 and 15 comprising an area of 75.50 acres in the said village and he filed an objection under Section 6 of the Act on 3rd July 1954 claiming Sirdari rights over 75.50 acres of land in the said village. He challenged the validity of the land sought to be constituted as a reserved forest. It was stated that from the demarcation map prepared by the Forest Department it appears that about half of the objector's land was included in the notification on 4th April, 1956, the claim of the petitioner's father was accepted by the Forest Settlement Officer and he was held to be Sirdar of 75.50 acres of land. But Forest Settlement Officer did not enter into adjudication of the precise area of plots Nos. 21 and 15 which was covered by the notification against the order of the FSO. The Forest Department filed an appeal under Section 17 of the Act which was allowed by the Deputy Commissioner on 12th April, 1958 and the claim of the petitioner's father that he was Sirdar of plots Nos. 21 and 15 was rejected. The said appeal was decided behind the back of the petitioner's father was filed a suit under Section 229-B of the U.P. Zamindari Abolition and Land Reforms Act claiming a declaration that he continued to be a Sirdar of 40 acres of land out of plot No. 21 on the basis that so much area was not covered by notification issued under Section 4 of the Act to that suit the State Government and the *Gaon Samaj* were impleaded as defendants. This suit was not contested by the defendants and proceed exparte.

After considering the above noted facts the Hon'ble Judge observed that "no doubt there is a provision contained in Section 18 (40 of the Act) which confers finality on an order passed in appeal under Section 18 of the Act subject only to filed against the order of the Deputy Commissioner passed under Section 18 of the Act and therefore the order of the Deputy Commissioner passed in appeal became final. On account of the finality given to apellate orders under Section 18(4) of the Act having regard to Section 9 of the code of civil court but the finality to the orders passed in appeal under Section 18 of the act attached only to such orders as are passed in respect of matters over which the officer passing an order under Sections 11 and 18 has jurisdiction. It is clear that under Section 11 of the Act the Forest Settlement Officer has jurisdiction to pass an order on the claim of a person only in respect of such land as it covered by the notification issued under Section 4 of the Act and it is equally clear that the officer deciding the appeal under Section 18 of the Act also has jurisdiction only over such land as is covered by the said notification.

It is immaterial that Forest Department was not a party to the revenue suit because in asking for a declaratory from the revenue suit because in asking for a declaratory from the notification issued by the State Government under Section 4 of the Act and therefore, the State Government was the necessary party. The Forest Settlement Officer is bound by the decree passed by the revenue court because it is a department of the State Government.

CASE II

The Supreme Court of India civil original jurisdiction :- Write petition no. 202 (Civil).

The Case of T.N. Godavarman Thirumulkpad Versus Union of India and Ors

This Case was filed under Forest Conservation Act. The details of the case was not made available as how the case was argued and what were the grievances of the petitioner, what is of paramount importance is the outcome of the case. The Supreme Court, as a result of this case, had to revise and pass an order.

This is the latest case available till date. It was filled in 1995 and the final order was given in 1997.

ORDER

In view of the great significance of the points involved in these matters, relating to the protection and conservation of the forests throughout the country, it was considered necessary that the Central Government as well as the Governments of all the States are heard. Accordingly, notice was issued to all of them. On hearing the learned Attorney General for the Union of India, learned counsel appearing for the States and the parties/applicants and in addition, the learned *Amicus Curiae*, Shri H.N. Salve, assisted by Sarvashri U.U. Lalit, Mahender Das and P.K. Manohar who have rendered very valuable assistance to the court, was formed opinion that the matter require afurther indepth hearing to examine all the aspects relating to the National Forest Policy. For this purpose, several points which emerged during the course of the hearing require further study by the learned counsel and, therefore, they defer the continuation of this hearing for some time to enable the learned counsel to further study these points.

However, they were of the opinion that certain interim directions are necessary at this stage in respect of some aspects.

In has emerged at the hearing, that there is a misconception in certain quarters about the true scope of the Forest Conservation Act, 1980 (for short the 'Act') and the meaning of the word "forest" used therein. There is also a resulting misconception about the need of prior approval of the Central Government, as required by Section 2 of the Act. In respect of certain activities in the forest area which are more often of a commercial nature. It is necessary to clarify that position.

The Forest Conservation Act, 1980, was enacted with a view to check further deforestation which ultimately results in ecological imbalance; and therefore, the provisions made therein for the conservation of forests and for matters connected therewith, must apply to all forests irrespective of the nature of ownership or classification thereof. The word "forest" must be understood according to its dictionary meaning. This description covers all statutorily recognised forests, whether designated as reserved, protected or otherwise for the purpose of Section 2(i) of the Forest Conservation Act. The term "forest land", occurring in Section 2, will not only include "forest" as understood in the dictonary sense, but also any area recorded as forest in the Government record irrespective of the ownership. This is how it has to be understood for the purpose of Section 2 of the Act. The provisions enacted in the Forest Conservation Act, 1980 for the conservation of forests and the matters connected therewith must apply clearly to all forests so understood irrespective of the ownership or classification thereof. This aspect has been made abundantly clear in the decisions of this court in Ambica Quarry Works and Ors. versus State of Gujarat and Ors. (1987 (1) SCC 213), Rural Litigation and Entitlement Kendra versus State of U.P. (1989 Suppl. (1) SCC 504), and recently in the order dated 29th November, 1996 in W.P. (c) No. 749/95 (Supreme Court Monitoring Committee vs. Mussorie Dehradun Development Authority and Ors). The earlier decision of this court in State of Bihar vs. Banshiram Modi and Ors. (1985(3) SCC 643) has, therefore, to be understood in the light of these subsequent decisions. They considered it necessary to reiterate this settled position emerging from the decisions of this court to dispel the doubt, if any, in the perception of any State Government or authority. This has become necessary also because of the stand taken on behalf of the State of Rajasthan, even at this later stage, relating to permissions granted for mining in such area which is clearly contrary to the decisions of this court. It is reasonable to assume that any State Government which has failed to appreciate the correct position in law so far, will forthwith correct its stance and take the necessary remedial measures without any further delay.

It was also directed the following:

I. General

1. In view of the meaning of the word "forest" in the Act, it is obvious that prior approval of the Central Government is required for any non-forest activity within the area of any "forest". In accordance with Section 2 of the Act, all on-going activity within any forest in any State throughout the country,

without the prior approval of the Central Government, must cease forthwith. It is, therefore, clear that the running of saw mills of any kind including veneer of plywood mills, and mining of any mineral are non-forest purposes and are, therefore, not permissible without prior approval of the Central Government. Accordingly, any such activity is prima facie violation of the provisions of the Forest Conservation Act, 1980. Every State Government must promptly ensure total cessation of all such activities forthwith.

2. In addition to the above, in the tropical wet evergreen forests of Tirap and Changlang in the State of Arunachal Pradesh, there would be a complete ban on selling of any kind of trees therein because of their particular significance to maintain ecological balance needed to preserve bio-diversity. All saw mills, veneer mills and plywood mills in Tirap and Changlang in Arunachal Pradesh and within a distance of 100 kms from its border, in Assam, should also be closed immediately. The State Governments of Arunachal Pradesh and Assam must ensure compliance of this direction.

3. The felling of trees in all forests is to remain suspended except in accordance with the Working Plans of the State Governments, as approved by the Central Government. In the absence of any Working Plan in any particular State, such as Arunachal Pradesh, where the permit system exists, the felling under the permits can be done only by the Forest Department of the State Government or the State Forest Corporation.

4. There shall be a complete ban on the movement of cut trees and timber from any of the seven North-Eastern States to any other State of the country either by rail, road or waterways. The Indian Railways and the State Governments are directed to take all measures necessary to ensure strict compliance of this direction. This ban will not apply to the movement of certified timber required for defence or other purposes. This ban will also not affect felling in any private plantation comprising of trees planted in any area which is not a forest.

5. Each State Government should constitute within one month an Expert Committee for the following:
   - (i) To identify areas which are "forests", irrespective of whether they are so notified, recognised or classified under any law, and irrespective of the ownership of the land of such forest;
   - (ii) To identify areas which were earlier considered as forests but stand degraded, denuded or cleared; and
   - (iii) To identify areas covered by plantation trees belonging to the Government and those belonging to private persons.
6. Each State Government should within two months, file a report regarding the following:
   - (i) The number of saw mills, veneer and plywood mills actually operating within the State, with particulars of their real ownership;
   - (ii) The licensed and actual capacity of these mills for stock and sawing;
   - (iii) Their proximity to the nearest forest;
   - (iv) Their source of timber.
7. Each State Government should constitute within one month, an Expert Committee to assess the following:
   - (i) The sustainable capacity of the forests of the state qua saw mills and timber based industry;
   - (ii) The number of existing saw mills which can safely be sustained in the State;
   - (iii) The optimum distance from forest, qua that State, at which the saw mill should be located.
8. The Expert Committees so constituted should be requested to give its report within one month of being constituted.
9. Each State Government would constitute a Committee comprising of the Principal Chief Conservator of forests as another Senior Officer to oversee the compliance of this order and file status reports.

PART-G: CONSUMER PROTECTION ACT

According to the Preamble the purpose of the Act is to provide for the better protection of the interests of consumers and for that purpose to make provision for the establishment of consumer councils and other authorities for the settlement of consumers disputes and for matters connected therewith. So that the consumers can get cheaper and speedier justice. The Act provides for the setting up at the State level and also establishment of 'Consumer Disputes Redressal Agencies' for the purpose. Such Agencies are:

1. Consumer Disputes Redressal Forum to be known as "District Forum"
2. Consumer Disputes Redressal Commission to be known as "State Commission" and
3. National Consumer Disputes Redressal Commission.

Consumer

According to Section 2(d) "Consumer" means any person who buys any goods for a consideration which has been paid or promised or partly paid and partly promised, or under any system of deferred payment and includes any user of such goods other than the person who buys such goods for consideration paid or promised or partly paid or partly promised or under any system of deferred payment when such use is made with the approval of such person but does not include a person who obtains such goods for resale or for any commercial purpose, or hires any services for a consideration which has been paid or promised or partly paid and partly promised or under any system of deferred payment and includes any beneficially of such services other than the person who hires the services for consideration paid or promised or partly paid and partly promised, or under any system of deferred payment, when such services are valid with the approval of the first mentioned person. Thus, if any person either (i) buys any goods for a consideration or (ii) hires any service for a consideration, he is a consumer.

Hirer of services for a consideration

According to Section 2(d)(ii) any person who hires services for a consideration is a consumer. "Services" means service of any description which is made available to potential users and includes the provision of facilities in connection with, transport, banking and other information.

Service without Consideration

According to Section 2(d)(ii) the consumer must hire any services for a consideration. Section 2 (1) also stipulates that service does not include the rendering of any service at free of charge. When the services are rendered without consideration, the complaint cannot be entertained in a consumer forum. Thus, when the Housing Board of Naval Personnel is established to promote suitable services to its members free of charge, no member can bring an action as a consumer, for any deficiency in the apartment allotted to him.

Deficiency in Service

The term "Service" according to Section 2(1)(O) means service of any description which is made available to potential users and includes the provision of facilities in connection with banking, financing, insurance transport processing, supply of electrical or other energy board or does not include the rendering of any service at free of cost or under contract of personal service.

Deficiency, according to Sec. 2(1)(g) means any fault, imperfection, shortcoming or inadequacy in the quality, nature and manner of performance which is required to be maintained by or under any law for the timebeing in force or has been undertaken to be performed by a person in pursuance of contract or otherwise in relation to any service.

Consumerism in India is beginning to establish an identity of its own. Almost thirty consumer oriented legislations, impact of new professionals working in the media, the springing up of various active consumer association, have all contributed to changes.

It is CPA 1996, that provides the impetus and an extremely good opportunity for the aggrieved Indian Consumer. This Act incorporates provisions which ensure consumer with effective safeguards against unfair trade practices indulged in by both the manufacturer and public utility service.

Consumer Protection

The Consumer Protection Act, 1986 provides the consumers the following rights:

1. *Right to Safety:* It means right to be protected against marketing goods and services which are hazardous to life and property.
2. *Right to be Informed:* It means right to be informed about the quality, quantity, potency, standard and price of goods and services to protect the consumer against unfair trade practices.
3. *Right to Choose:* It means right to be assured, wherever possible, of access to a variety of goods and service at competitive prices.
4. *Right to be Heard:* It means that consumers' interests will receive due consideration at appropriate fora.
5. *Right to Seek Redressal:* It means right to seek redressal against unfair trade practices or unscrupulous exploitation of consumers.
6. *Right to Consumer Education:* It means right to acquire the knowledge and skill to be an informed consumer.

Consumers, you are not helpless as you think. Do not compromise with the quality of goods and services. Assert your rights and seek redressal in the consumer courts, whenever required.

Enactment and enforcement of the Consumer Protection Act, 1986 is to provide better protection to the interest of consumers:

- This Act applies to all goods and services, so long as the purchase is not for commercial/ resale purposes and covers all the sectors whether private, public or co-operative. The provisions of the Act are compensatory in nature.
- A three-tier consumer disputes redressal machinery (Consumer Courts) has been set up as per the Act at the National, State and District levels which provides inexpensive and speedy redressal to the consumer

disputes/complaints in respect of defective goods, deficient services, unfair trade and restrictive trade practices, excess price charged, etc.

- No court fee, no lawyer is required. Consumers can file complaints on plain paper for compensation including cost up to Rs. 5 lakhs in the District Forum, up to Rs. 20 lakhs in the State Commission and beyond Rs. 20 lakhs in the National Commission. Appear and argue yourself, when necessary.
- Since inception, 13057, 116805, and 915054 complaints have been filed in the National Commission, 32 State Commissions and 526 District Fora, respectively, out of which 7757, (58.6 per cent), 71353 (61 per cent) and 708049 (77.38 per cent) cases have been disposed of.

Amendment

On 21st June, 1993, the government issued an ordinance to amend CPA to make it more effective and people oriented which is very similar to the Consumer Protection (Amendment) Bill 1993. It provides:

- For enabling consumers and consumer organisations to file complaints in respect of goods whose use could be hazardous to life and safety like drugs and food products being sold after expiry dates.
- Against traders was adopt restrictive trade practices.
- On behalf of a group of consumers with a common interest.
- In respect of services relating to housing.
- Self employed persons could seek redressal in respect of the goods purchased by them to earn their living.
- For enlarging the scope of the Act, the redressal fora have also been conferred an additional powers to order withdrawal of goods likely to endanger life and safety.

- Removal of deficiency from services and to award costs.
- For a limited period of one year from filing complaints and empowers the State Government to constitute more than one forum in a district, wherever necessary.
- For constitution of Selection Committees at the State and National levels and to choose non-judicial members of redressal agencies.

Consumer Welfare Fund

A Consumer Welfare Fund was instituted on the Consumer Day, March 19,1994.

The announcement of the formation of the fund was made by Civil Supplies Minister, A.K. Antony while giving away the national awards for consumer protection in New Delhi.

The Consumer Welfare Fund consists of the amount of excess excise or customs duties which are not refundable to manufacturers or importers.

The money thus accruing to the fund would be used for promoting the welfare of consumers and the objectives of the fund was to strengthen the consumer movement in the country and to assist voluntary organisations in spreading consumer education.

Mr. A.K. Antony also formally invited applications from voluntary consumer organisations for availing assistance under the fund. The total quantum of assistance on an individual application should not exceed Rs. 5 lakh. However, larger assistance could be considered in very exceptional cases.

The applicant would be required to meet 10 per cent expenditure from his own resources. In exceptional cases this also could be relaxed. So far more than Rs. 46 crores have been credited to the fund and the assistance of about Rs. 263 lakhs have been sanctioned clearing 304 proposals.

RESPONSIBILITIES OF CONSUMERS

Only a responsible consumer can protect his rights. Some tips are as follow:

1. Purchase only when you need and do not purchase in a hurry.
2. Do not buy blindly. Demand full information before you buy.
3. Beware of false/misleading advertisements.
4. Do not compromise on the quality of goods and services. Purchase only quality products.
5. In case of electrical appliances, insist on buying goods with ISI mark. In case of food items, insist on Agmark products.
6. Do not forget to obtain proper receipt/cash memo. Always obtain the guarantee/warranty card duly stamped and signed by the shopkeeper, wherever necessary. These can be helpful in the Consumer Courts.
7. Always approach the appropriate authorities or the Consumer Courts in case of defective goods, deficient services and unfair and restrictive trade practices.

Case I: Air India Vs Yogendra Hiralal Parekh and Ors

Consumer Protection Act, 1986, Section 2(1) g. In this case Mr. Yogendra Hiralal Parekh purchased two-way confirmed air tickets from Air India agent. They were to leave India on 10.5.92 for Moscow and had to return on 16.5.92. After completing their business tour they requested the appellant on 16.5.92 at Moscow for seats. Airlines refused to accommodate them on the ground that as per rule they had to stay in Moscow for ten days and they can travel to India only on 19.5.92 though they were holding visas only upto 16.5.92. The main argument of each of the complaints was that the mistake has been committed by the agent of the Air India who issued the ticket for return on excursion fare basis when he must be knowing that 10 days stay was necessary in the foreign country before returning to India. Due to this action the party had to overstay in Moscow without valid visas and suffered mental pain and agony. They had to stay at a Hotel in Moscow and had to spend U.S.$ 300 per day and another U.S.$ 25 per day for transport from airport to hotel. The complainants alleged deficiency in service on the part of the opposite party, i.e., Air India and filed a complaint before the District Forum in Madras claiming Rs. 25,900/- spent in Moscow + Rs. 2,00,000 as a compensation for mental pain, agony and hardship.

The District Forum held that the tickets issued to the complainant was just like other ordinary tickets and no rule was printed on the ticket that the complainant had to stay for minimum period of 10 days in foreign country. Considering all the facts the District Forum was of the opinion that the complainant had to suffer a lot because of Air India therefore, District Forum directed Air India to pay Rs. 25,900/- to each of the complainant and Rs. 10,000/- were awarded to each of the complainant as compensation.

Both the parties then filed a separate appeals to the State Commissions. The State Commission dismissed the Appeal of Air India holding that there was gross deficiency in the service on part of the IATA agent and the compensation awarded to each of the complainant was fair and reasonable.

Air India has challenged the orders passed by the State Commission by way of these revision petitions filed by them before this commission.

(i) That the Moscow Manager offered to pay the difference in fare to convert their tickets into full fare economy class tickets. However, due to lack of funds the complainants did not pay the difference fare therefore, Air India did not allow the complainants to travel.

Air India has filed a letter issued by M/s Speeds Buds Pvt. Ltd., authorised travel agent wherein it has been clearly admitted that the tickets were issued by us and we do admit by oversight we failed to adhere to the minimum stay requirements in Moscow. Hence, the complainants can have the remedy against the travel agent.

In the light of the above observation they accept all the petitions and set aside the orders of the District Forum and the State Commission and dismiss the complaint filed against the revision petitioner Air India.

The complaints will, however, be at liberty to have their remedy, if advised, against the travel agent.

Source: *Supreme Court Library Through* Advocate Sharad Kumar Agarwal *(Supreme Court)* and Purnima Agarwal Adv. *(High Court)*

Case II: Geeta Arts Vs Modiluft and ANR

Complaint is lodged under Section 17/12 of CPA. In this case Geeta Arts availed of the Service of the Modiluft and ANR in the matter of travel and has purchased the travel pass advertised by them for sum of Rs. 2,00,000/-. He is therefore, a consumer with in Section 2(1)d(ii) of the Consumer Protection Act and the Complaint is maintainable. The opposite parties also offered to the buyers the travel passes on or before 31.2.93 and any of the following three prizes:

(i) Six nights/seven days all expenses paid holiday for two

(ii) A state of the art siva computer

(iii) A tread mill.

The complainant chose a tread mill and they were promised to deliver the tread mill to the complainant in Jan.1994. Till the filing of the complaint, the tread mill was not supplied. On 17.3.94 the opposite party refused to send a tread mill and offered compensation of Rs. 30,000/-. The complainant refused to accept the offer. He has therefore filed this complaint for compensation in the sum of Rs. 4,00,000/-. It is also alleged that the complainant has availed of the travel qualities only for a sum of Rs. 43,291 and has claimed the balance out of Rs. 1,56,709/- with interest of 240 per cent.

The diversion taken under this case is that no doubt there has been a default on the part of the opposite parties in a failure to supply the tread mill. But the facts remained that the tread mill could not be supplied due to import problems. The complainant is therefore entitled for compensation in a reasonable sum. The claim of Rs. 4,00,000/- as a compensation on this ground is arbitrary exercise and fanciful. There is no basis for such a claim, evidently taking advantage of the provisions of the Consumer Protection Act, the complainant has come to forward with the fabulous claim. We are inclined to raise the sum to Rs. 40,000/-.

The next compensation that he has availed of the travel qualities only to the tune of Rs. 43,291 and the balance is payable to the complainant. As there is no provision of the refund of the balance amount, the complainant is not entitled to claim any relief for refund. As a result, the complainant is entitled to cost of Rs. 1,000. The other claims by the complainant are disallowed.

The first party shall pay to the complainant Rs. 40,000 as compensation with interest there on at 18 per cent per annum from the date of complaint till payment.

Case III

In the case of Wg. Cdr. P.S. Sandhu and Ors vs Union of India, by awarding a compensation of Rs. 3 lakhs to Wg. Cdr Sandhu and Rs. 2.4 lakhs each to his two children for the death of Mrs. Sandhu in a boat tragedy, the National Commission made it clear that those who pay scant attention to safety will be held liable for any loss or suffering caused as a consequence of such negligence. In this case, the Court held the Army Authorities who ran the Boat Club at Barapani Lake near Shillong, guilty of negligence for not providing life jackets or any other safety measures.

Source: *TOI-March 15, 1998, N. Delhi.*

PART-H: LEGISLATIONS RELATING TO CONSTITUTIONAL REMEDIES

Passport Act, 1967

Title, extent and commencement

1. This act be known as Passport Act, 1967, and extends to whole of India.
2. This act was passed by Parliament and got the assent of President of India (thus commenced) on 26th June, 1967.

Definition of passport

3. *Passport:* A passport is an official document issued by a competent public authority to national or to alien residents (mostly stateless persons) of the issuing country. A passport establishes the bearers' identity and nationality and authorises passenger to travel abroad.
4. *Kinds of Passport:* There are three kinds of passports:

(i) Official passports or white colour passports issued to every person who is going abroad for Government of India job or a training on Government's finance.
(ii) Diplomatic passports or Red passports issued only to Secretary, Joint Secretaries, Deputy Secretaries and Ministers, etc.
(iii) Ordinary Passports (Blue coloured) issued to any Indian citizen going abroad jurisdiction wise.

5. Methods of getting passport to be issued:
A Regional Passport Office will issue a passport to any bonafide Indian nationals who can prove his stay or residence in India for atleast 2 years.
To obtain a passport a passenger must have to furnish the following formalities:
- Fill/sign one passport application.
- Produce 7 passport size photographs—two of which should be attested by a Gazetted Officer.
- Proof of Birth (SSLC certificate or LIC policy, etc.)
- Residential proof—Ration Card, Pass book, etc.
- Service certificate is required.
- For students a bona fide certificate.
- For unmarried ladies between the age 16 and 35 years—a certificate of no objection by the parents/guardian.
- If married—Marriage certificate.
- No Objection Certificate for Government employees.
- Degree Certificate.

All these documents along with passport an application has to be presented to the Regional Passport Office. A passport is valid for 10 years. After that, the passenger has to renew the validity of the existing passport.

At first, passports is to be valid for 5 years only. Now these are being renewed.

A Travel Agency is restricted to submit only 2 passport application a day for fresh passport.

The prescribed form IA(P), needs to be filled up which is available at the sales counter.

Before submission of application you must ensure that the following requirements are complied with full details.

(a) Specific and complete replies should be given against each column and no column should be left blank.

Photographs

Six or seven copies of passport size photographs 45/35 mm) properly attested on the reverse as true likeness of applicants name by SHO/Gazetted Officer of State of Central Government or Magistrate with their official rubber stamp and telephone number indicated.

Divorce Deed

In case of divorcee/divorced applicants the necessary school leaving certificates in support of date of birth. Illiterate persons should furnish an affidavit attested by a first class Magistrate/Notary Public indicating the place and date of birth along with supporting documents, such as the voters list/ration card, etc.

No Objection Certificate

No Objection Certificate in original if in Government service/public undertaking service/Statutory Body service.

Address

Correct and complete address both permanent and present.

Address for Last Two Years

If not resided at the present address for the last 2 years, the other addresses with duration and references, with addresses, who can vouch for you.

Educational Qualifications

Properly attested copies of certificates for educational qualifications both general and professional/technical.

Income Tax Payees

In case of Income Tax Payees/assessee, evidence for the preceding 3 years should be enclosed in the form of self assessment orders and challans.

Minor Children

Copies of birth certificate/school certificates in respect of children below 15 years to be included in mother's passport.

Previous Passport Details

Full details of the previous passports held if any and the same to be produced along with the application.

Case of Minor Applicants

In case of minors up to 18 years of age, the declaration to be signed either by the parents or legal guardian with legal guardianship affidavit duly executed on non-judicial stamp paper of Rs. 2/- before a Notary/Magistrate (proforma at Annexure "A").

Signatures

The specimen signatures and thumb impression duly filled.

Expanded Initials

All the entries should be legible and in capital letters and expansion of initials should be given.

Scrutiny of Application

Thorough scrutiny of the application before submission in the office.

Renewal of validity of existing passports/additional booklets/visa sheets when all the pages in the passports have been used up.

The prescribed form EA(P) 6 for the above service is available at this office.

Renewal

(a) A passport can be revalidated for a further period of 5 years from the date of its initial validity one year prior to the date of expiry of its initial validity.

(b) The passport can be revalidated at any time after the expiry of its existing validity but within its total life of ten years after which a fresh passport must be obtained.

7. Services on out of Jurisdiction case :
   (c) Out of jurisdiction such as passports issued by other passport offices can be serviced only on production of supporting documents such as ration card, bank pass book, etc., to prove the applicants stay in Delhi during the last two preceding years.
8. Additional Visa Sheets: If all the pages in the passports have been used up additional visa sheet not exceeding two are issued on visa sheet. A maximum of two visa sheets can be attached in a passport.
9. Additional Booklets: These are issued if all pages in the passports and the 2 visa sheets are completely used up. However, the validity of the additional booklet remains the same as that of the existing passport. Such request should be made on EA(P) 6 application form together with Rs. 50/- and 2 copies of passport size photographs duly attested.
10. Replacement Passports:
    (a) Replacement passports are issued if there is change in the appearance/specimen signature for which a sum of Rs. 50/- is chargeable. The application should be made in EA (P) 6 form alongwith 2 copies of passport size photographs duly attested on reverse by SHO/Gazetted Officer to State or Central Government or Magistrate.
    (b) Replacement passports are also issued in the case of female applicants holding passport in their maiden name and who wish to change their name after marriage (married name). In such cases the application is to be made in EA(P)6 form along 4 copies of passport size photographs duly attested on the reverse in the married name of the applicants together with the existing passport held in the maiden name and a sum of Rs. 60/- (Marriage Certificate or marriage invitation card together with a deed poll (specimen format at Annexure "B") duly executed on a Notary or First Class Magistrate are the pre-requisites in such cases.

Miscellaneous Services

Miscellaneous services on passports issued by this office are rendered on submission of prescribed application form in EA(P)8 a fee of Rs. 20/- for the following categories:

(i) Inclusion of child's name.

(ii) Deletion of child's name.

(iii) Police clearance certificates with the name of the country for which the same is required.

(iv) Change in Date of Birth.

(v) Change in profession.

(vi) Additional endorsement.

(vii) Other services such as correction of heights, colour of eyes and hair, visible distinguishing marks, etc.

In case of inclusion of child's name, the certified copies of birth certificates/schools certificates containing the name of child, place and date of birth, sex and relationship with the applicant should be submitted. Documentary evidence in support of change of profession change of address should be submitted.

12. Passports Containing Valid Visas : Special attention is paid to the safe-handling of passports containing visas for, the USA, the UK, etc., which are delivered within 48 hours after rendering the required service. However, all such cases are delivered only to the applicants and not on the basis of any authority letters.
13. Change of Name : For any change of name/ surname, etc., the prescribed application form EA(P)6 should be submitted together with 2 news paper clippings or gazette notification issued by the competent authority in support of change of name and an affidavit (deed poll) with 5 passport size photographs duly certified in the changed name.
14. Lost and Damaged passports : Duplicate passports are issued in lieu of lost/damaged passports on submission of prescribed application form in EA(P) 10 with the following requirements:

(a) The First Information Report (FIR) lodged with the police station in original in case of lost passport.

(b) Personal particulars form, in duplicate, duly completed with 5 copies of certified photographs.

(c) An affidavit on non-judicial stamp paper of Rs. 2/- denomination duly executed before a Notary or First Class Magistrate containing the following information;

(i) How the passport lost/damaged?

(ii) Whether travelled on the lost/damaged passport? If so, the last date of re-entry into India.

(iii) Whether there are any adverse remarks on the lost/damaged passports made by any authority/office.

(iv) Whether availed any of custom/ Repatriation/FTS concession?

If so, details thereof in the following manner:

(a) Date and place of availing of the concession.

(b) The amount of concession.

(c) Name of office from where the concession was obtained.

Non-Resident Indian are required to furnish the following additional information upon losing their passports:

(a) Address abroad.

(b) Exact date of loss of passport.

(c) Exact date from which the applicant has been residing abroad.

(d) Six additional personal particulars forms with six copies of photographs should be submitted.

15. "Emigration Clearance Not Required" Endorsement on Passport and the ECNR endorsement on passport is granted to the following category of persons who fulfil the criteria prescribed below:

(a) Persons going abroad in managerial capacity in Hotels, Restaurants, Tea-House or other places of public resort, etc., possessing specialised degrees in this fields.

(b) All Gazetted Government servants.

(c) All income tax payees (including Agriculture income tax payees) in respect of their individual capacity. Proof of assessment to income tax for last three years is required and not merely payment of advance tax.

(d) All professional degree holders, such as Doctors holding MBBS degrees or degrees in Ayurvedic or Homeopathy medicine, Accredited Journalists, Engineers, Chartered Accountants, Cost Accountants, Lecturers, Teachers, Scientists, Advocates, etc.

(e) Spouses and dependent children of category of persons listed from (a) to (d).

(f) All persons who have been staying abroad for more than 3 years. The period of 3 years could be either in stretch or broken.

(g) Seamen who are in possession of Continuous Discharge Certificate (CDC) and Sea cadets.

(h) All holders of Diplomatic/Official passports.

(i) Dependent children of parents whose passport is classified as E.C.N.R classification is restricted until the applicant attains 24 years of age.

(j) Persons holding Permanent Immigration Visas for the UK, the USA and Australia, etc.

(k) Persons holding graduate or higher degrees.

(l) Persons holding diplomas from recognised institutions like polytechnics.

(m) Nurses possessing qualifications recognised under the Indian Nursing Council Act, 1947. The application form for ECNR endorsement is supplied in the passport office at free of charge.

16. No Obligation to Return to India (NORI) Certificate: Countries like the USA, Canada require such certificates from Indian nationals who wish to settle in these country. All references in this matter

should be made to the consular section of the Ministry of External Affairs or the respective Indian Missions abroad. In case of applicants residing abroad they should approach the consular section of the Indian Missions with the prescribed application form together with an affidavit duly executed before a Notary Public of that country and with the prescribed fees leviably by the consular division of the Indian Mission. Such cases are referred to this "No Obligation to Return to India" Certificates if the applicant has not come to any adverse notice since the issue of passport and if there is nothing on our record to show that the applicant is under any obligation to return to India. The replies are sent to the Indian Missions concerned under intimation to the applicants abroad.

17. Applicants facing Court Cases: In such cases where an offence committed by the applicant is pending trial before any court of law and if the applicant desires to proceed abroad due to certain unavoidable reasons, the applicant should produce necessary Court's orders permitting the applicant to proceed abroad. Passport in such cases will be issued for the limited period specified under the Court's order in terms of Notification No. GSR-488(E) dated 16.8.79 issued by the Ministry of External Affairs.

18. General Regulations:
    - (i) No un-authorised travel agency/tours should be contacted for getting a passport.
    - (ii) The applicants should be present in person for submission of applications at the passport office so that any deficiencies pointed out while checking the applications could be rectified by the applicants on the spot.
    - (iii) Normally all passports are despatched to the applicants by registered post.
    - (iv) Passports ordered for delivery at the counters can only be collected by the applicants concerned except under extra-ordinary

circumstances where authority letters with the specimen signature of the authorised person duly attested by a Gazetted Officer only could be entertained.

19. Grounds for Refusal of Passport : Under Section 10 of the Passport Act the authority may refuse to issue a passport, then reasons for not issuing the passport has to be written and one copy has to be given to the applicant, but if the reasons are such that they are detrimental to the sovereignty and integrity of the country, security of the country or again the goodway of public then they may not give the copy to the person. The other reasons may be the following :
    (i) If the applicant is not a citizen of India.
    (ii) If the applicant, during 5 years preceding the date of submission of application has been convicted by a Court in India for any offences involving in moral turpitude, has been sentenced for not less than 2 years.
    (iii) If proceedings are pending in the Criminal Court.
    (iv) If the warrant or summon has been issued by the Court for not allowing the applicant to leave the country.
    (v) If the applicant has been repatriated and has not reimbursed the course of repatriation.

However the Section 10(30)(c) of Passport Act confers arbitrary power to passport authority and discussed in details the following leading case of Maneka Gandhi Vs. Union of India.

Verifications imparting or revocation of PP with the previous approval from Central Government passport authority aim vary the PP sent the notice to the person concerned to surrender the PP within the time as maintained offences and penalties.

A person is penalised if he:

(a) Wilfully furnishes the false information or
(b) Fails to produce the PP for inspection when called upon to do so

(c) Wilfully uses the PP of other person or give to other person.

20. Power to Arrest : Any Officer of Custom with power of Central Government or any Officer of police not below the rank of Sub-inspector can arrest any person without warrant against a reasonable suspicion exists that he has committed any offence.

21. Power to Search and Seize : The above written officers can search any place or seize any passport or T.D. from any person against or when reasonable suspicion exists that he has committed any punishable offence.

Previous sanction from Central Government—No prosecution shall be instituted against any person in respect of any offence under this Act without prior sanction of Central Government.

Passport or TD to be the property of Central Government. Passport or T.D. to be invalid to travel to certain countries like the following :

(a) A country which is assisting another country for external aggression or internal aggression against India.

(b) A country where armed hostility is in progress.

(c) Or where travel must be restricted in public interest.

22. Power to Make Rule : The Central Government may issue notification on the official bases making rules for carrying out the purpose of this Act.

CASES OF CONSTITUTIONAL REMEDIES BEFORE MANEKA V/S UNION OF INDIA

Case I: Gopalan View: Introduction to Constitution Remedies

Source: *Constitution of India*, D.D. Basu

Until 1978, i.e., decision in Maneka Gandhi case view which prevailed in Supreme Court was that there was no guarantee in our constitution against arbitrary legislation encroaching upon personal liberty. Hence, if a Competent

Legislature makes a law providing that a person may be deprived of his liberty in certain circumstances and in a certain manner, validity of law cannot be challenged in a court of law on the ground that the law is unreasonable, unfair or unjust.

Under the "Due process" clause of American Institution Court has assumed the powers of declaring unconstitutional any law which deprives a person of his liberty otherwise than in accordance with the court's notion of "due process", i.e., reasonableness and fairness.

Whereas in England, this is not possible because courts of law have no power to invalidate a law made by Parliament. As a result, person's liberty in England is a liberty confined and controlled by Law. It exists only so far as it is not taken away or limited by laws made by representatives of people.

(a) In Gopalan V/s State of Madras: Majority of our legal experts propounded the view that by adapting the expression "procedure established by law, Article 21 of constitution had embodied the English concept of personal liberty in preference to that of American "Due process". It was also held that there is no safeguard for personal liberty under our constitution, besides Article 21, such as natural law or common law. In the result, when personal liberty is taken away by a competent legislation, the person affected can have no remedy.

(b) Minority view in Gopalan Case : Result of majority's view was to throw most important fundamental rights to life and personal liberty at the mercy of legislative majorities' overturned majority in Maneka Gandhi case. Wherein 7 judges bench laid down the following proposition:

Articles 19 and 21 aren't water-tight compartments, expression of personal liberty in Article 21 is one of widest amplitude, covering a variety of rights some of which might have been included in Article 19. That is, there may be some overlapping, in the sense that Law coming under Article 21, must also satisfy the requirements of Article 19. In other words, a law made by state which seeks to deprive a person of his personal liberty must prescribe a procedure for which deprivation mustnot be arbitary, unfair or unreasonable.

(c) Once the test of reasonableness is imported to determine validity of a law depriving a person of his liberty, it follows that such law shall be invalid if it violates the principal of natural justice. For example, if it provides for the impounding of a passport without giving the person affected an opportunity to be heard or to make a representation against the order proposed.

Case II: Maneka Gandhi Versus Union of India

Petitioner's passport was impounded in public interest by an order dated July 2, 1977, and Government of India declined to furnish the reason for its decisions.

Thereupon she filed this writ petition under Article 32 of constitution to challenge the order. Challenge was founded on following grounds:

- To the extent at which Section 10(3)(c) of passports Act 1973 authorises the passport authority to impound a "passport" in interest of general public—it is violation of Article 14. Since it gives vague and unlimited powers of passport authority.
- Section 10(3)(c) is void as conferring an arbitrary power since it doesnot provide for a hearing of holder of passport before the passport is impounded.
- Section 10(3)(c) is violative of Article 21 of constitution since it doesnot provoke procedure (arbitrary and unreasonable).
- Section 10(3)(c) offends against Article 19(1)(a) and (g) since it permits restrictions to be imposed on the rights guarantee by those provisions even though restrictions arc such as cannot be imposed under Article 19 (2) or 6 freedoms originally seven—one to acquire, held and dispose property amended through an amendment (1978).

The reason later revealed by Government of India in a counter affidavit in answer to writ petition. It was stated that passport of petitioner was impounded because her presence was likely to be required in connection with a proceedings before a commission of Inquiry.

- It was held by Supreme Court that it was not good enough reason and petitioner had no opportunity of showing that for impounding it, either didnot exist or has no bearing on public interest.
- Section 10(3) (c) does not offend 16, 19 (1) (a) or (g) or Article 21 of constitution.
- The view of Supreme Court was that right to go abroad, in the circumstances of this case, wasnot a fundamental right.
- It is from here, that importance of this case established with reference to Article 21, 19, 14, for principal of equality about personal liberty V/s Right to go abroad.
- Expression as personal liberty in Article 21 is of widest amplitude and it covers a variety of rights which go to constitute the personal liberty of man and no person can be deprived of right to go abroad unless there is a State prescribing procedure for depriving strictly which cannot be arbitrary, unfair and unreasonable.

Source: *Constitution of India*
by D.D. Basu

Case 10, C

Union of India and Others (Appellants) Versus Smt. Charanjit Kaur Respondent.

Impounding of passport of wife of an extremist leader living abroad on ground of her links with the extremists in India and her activities detrimental to the security of India. Circumstances of her being wife of an extremist leader viewed in conjunction with other circumstances, relevant, though singly, by itself it may appear innocuous. Even if impounding order made two months after death of an Indian extremist leader with whom she had held meeting prior to his death, such event proximate and not stale or old. Her links with extremists in India cannot be said to have extinguished with the death of that leader. Held, impounding order based on relevant materials. Authorities entitled to review the order if so desired. Irrelevant and uncalled for remarks of High Court deprecated.

The Order of the Court had delivered by Chinnappa Reddy, J. The passport of Smt. Charanjit Kaur wife of Dr. Jagjit Singh Chauhan was impounded by the Regional Passport Office, Delhi by an order dated August 18, 1984. The reasons for the order were not furnished to her in view of the grave nature of her activities and serious implications in terms of sovereignty and integrity of India and the security of India, in terms of Section 10(5) of the Passports Act, 1967. The reasons are however, to be found in the note made by the Regional Passport Officer on the same day. Paragraphs 1 to 3 of the note are as follows:

1. Ref. Ministry of External Affairs, New Delhi letter No. V. 1/405/1/102/84 dated August 18, 1984 relating to the activities of Smt. Charanjit Kaur wife of Shri Jagjit Singh Chauhan. Smt. Chauhan is reported to have links with Sikh extremists and may engage in activities detrimental to the security of India. She is also planning to leave India shortly.
2. Reported activities detrimental to the security of India, attract the provision of Section 10(3) (c) of the Passports Act, 1967.
3. Due to the seriousness of the case and the likelihood of the subject trying to leave the country, in public interest, it is not considered necessary to issue a separate show cause notice. The same may, however, be incorporated in the impounding order. The right of the subject for appeal and the procedure in this regard may please also be explained in the impounding order, as per the Rules.

Case IV: Satwant Singh Sawhney V. Ramarathnam, Assistant Passport Officer, Government of India, New Delhi and Others

The petitioner carried on the business of import, export and the manufacture of automobile parts and in connection with his business it was necessary for him to travel abroad. For this purpose he was holding two valid passports when on August 31, 1966 and on September 24, 1966, the first and the second respondents, being the Assistant Passport Officer at New Delhi and the Regional Passport Officer at

Bombay, respectively wrote to the petitioner calling upon him to surrender the two passports as the Central Government had decided to withdraw the passport facilities extended to him. The petitioner filed the present petition under Art. 32 of the Constitution alleging that the respondent's action infringed his fundamental rights under Articles 21 and 14 of the constitution and prayed for a writ of mandamus directing the respondents to withdraw and cancel the decision contained in the two letters.

It was contended, *inter alia*, on behalf of the petitioner that the right to leave India and travel abroad and return to India is part of personal liberty guaranteed under Art. 21 of the Constitution. Refusal to give a passport of withdrawal of one given amounts to deprivation of personal liberty in as much as, (a) it is not practically possible for a citizen to leave India or travel abroad or to return to India without a passport; (b) instructions are issued to shipping and air travel companies by the Central Government not to take passengers on board without a passport; (c) under the Indian Passport Act, re-entering India without a passport is penalized. The deprivation of personal liberty in the refusal or impounding of a passport is not in accordance with any procedure established by law within the meaning of Art. 21, as admittedly there is no law placing any restrictions on the citizens of the country to travel abroad. Furthermore, the unfettered discretion given to the respondents to issue or not to issue a passport to a person offends Art. 14 of the Constitution.

Case V: State of Orissa Vs Dr. Binapani (AIR 1967 SC 1269)

If there is power to decide and determine to the prejudice of a person, duty to act judicially is implicit in the exercise of such power.

In recent years the concept of quasi-judicial power has been undergoing radical change. The dividing line between an administrative power and a quasi-judicial power is quite thin and is being gradually obliterated. For determining whether a power is an administrative power or a quasi-judicial power one has to look into the nature of the power conferred, the person or persons on whom it is conferred the framework of the law conferring that power, the consequences ensuring from the exercise of that power and the manner in which that power is expected to be exercised.

The net effect of these and other decisions was that the duty to act judicially need not be superadded, but it may be spelt out from the nature of the power conferred, the manner of exercising it and its impact on the rights of the person affected and where it found to exist the rules of natural justice would be attracted. In this court speaking through Hedge, J. in A.K. Karlapak's case AIR 1970 SC 150 quoted judgement of Lord Parke C.J. and proceeded to add.

The aim of the rules of natural justice is to secure justice or to put it negatively prevent miscarriage of Justice. These rules can operate only in areas not covered by any law validly made. In other words they do not supplant the law of the land but supplement it. Till very recently it was the opinion of the court that unless the authority concerned to act judicially, there was no room for the limitation, is now qestioned. The purpose of the rules of natural justice is to prevent miscarriage of justice. One fails to see why those rules should be made in applicable to administrative enquires, very often it is not easy to draw the line that demarcates administrative inquires from quasi-judicial enquires. Enquiries which were considered administrative at one time are now being considered as quasi-judicial in character, arriving at a just decision is the aim of both quasi-judicial as well as administrative enquiries. An unjust decision in administrative inquiry may have more far-reaching effect than a decision in a quasi-judicial enquiry. As observed by this Court in Suresh Koshy George Vs The University of Kerala. AIR 1969 Sec. 198 the rule of natural justice are not embodied rules. What particular rule of natural justice should apply to a given case must depend to a great extent on the facts and circumstances of that case, the framework of the law under which the enquiry is held and the constitution of the tribunal or body of persons appointed for the purpose. Whenever a complaint is made before a court, that some principle of natural justice had been contravened. The court has to decide whether the observance of that rule was necessary for a just decision on facts of the case. This view was reiterated in a subsequent decision of this court in D.F.O. Sauth Kheri Vs Ram Saneht Singh AIR 1973 Sec. 205. The law must therefore, now be taken as well settled that even in an administrative proceeding, which involves civil consequences, the doctrine of natural justice must be held to applicable.

In the instant case, a passport can be impugned by the Passport Authority only on certain specified grounds set out in Sub-sec (3) of Sec 10 and the Passport Authority would have to apply its mind to the facts and circumstances of the given case and decide whether any of the specified grounds exists which could justify impounding of the passport. The Passport Authority is also required by Sub-sec 50 of Sec 10 to record in writing a brief statement of the reasons for making on order impounding a passport and save in certain exceptional situation, the Passport Authority is obliged to furnish a copy of the statement of reasons to the holder of the passport, where the Passport Authority which has impounded a passport is other than the Central Government a right of appeal against the order impounding the passport is given by Sec 11 and in the appeal the validity of the reasons given by the Passport Authority for impounding the passport can be canvassed before the Appellate Authority. It is clear on a consideration of these circumstances that the test laid down in the decisions of this court for distinguishing between a quasi-judicial power and an administrative power is satisfied and the power conferred on the Passport Authority to impound a passport is quasi-judicial power. Even otherwise impoundment of the passport irrespective of the nature and character of function of the Government, involves civil consequences.

Therefore, rule of the "audi alteram partem" applies. The learned Attorney General, appearing, on behalf of the Union of India, fairly conceded that the "audi alteram partem" rule is highly effective tool devised by the courts to enable a statutory authority to arrive at a just decision and it is calculated to act as a healthy check on abuse or misuse of power and hence, its reach could not be narrowed and its applicability circumscribed.

He urged a very limited contention, namely that having regard to the nature of the action involved in the impounding of a passport the "audi alteram partem" rule must held to be excluded, because if notices were to be given to the holder of the passport and reasonable opportunity afforded to him to show cause why his passport should not be impounded, he might immediately, on the strength of the passport, make good his exist from the country and the object of impounding the passport would be frustrated. This argument was sought to be supported by reference to the statement of the law in A.S. De Smith, Judicial Review of Administrative Action, 2nd Edn, where the learned author says at page 174 that :

In administrative law a prima facie right prior to notice and opportunity to be heard may be held to be excluded by implication where an obligation to give notice and opportunity to be heard would obstruct the taking of prompt action, espepcially action of a preventive or remedial nature. There are certain well recognised exceptions to the "audi alteram partem" rule established by judicial decision and they are summarised as under:

If we analyse these exceptions a little closely, it will be apparent that they do not in any way violative of the principle which requires fair play in administrative action. The word 'exception' is really a misnomer because in these exclusionary cases, the "audi alteram partem" rule is held inapplicable, not by way of any exception to fair play in action, but because nothing unfair can be inferred by not affording an opportunity to present or meet a case. The "audi alteram partem" rule is intended to inject justice into the law and it cannot be applied to defect the ends of justice or to make law lifeless, absurd stultifying, self-defeating or plainly contrary, to the common sense of the situation. Since the life of the law is not logic but experience and every legal proposition must be in the ultimate analysis, be tested on the touch stone of pragmatic realism, the "audi alteram partem" rule would by the experimental test, be excluded, if importing the right to be hard has the effect of paralysing the administrative process or the need for promptitude or the urgency of the situation so demands. But at the same time it must be remembered that this is a rule of vital importance in the field of administrative law and it must not be jettisoned in very exceptional circumstances where compulsive necessity so demands. It is a wholesome rule designed to secure the rule of law and the court should not be too ready to eschew it in its application to a given case. True is that in its application to a given case. True is that in questions of this bind a fanatical or doctrinaire approach should be avoided but that does not mean that merely because the traditional methodology of a formalised hearing may have the effect of stultifying the exercise of the statutory power, the "audi alteram partem" rule should be wholly excluded. The court must make every effort to salvage this cardinal rule to the maximum extent permissible in a given case. It must not be forgotten that natural justice is pragmatically flexible and is amendable to capsulation under the compulsive pressure of circumstances.

The findings are based on no evidence at all.

Source: *AIR 1967, SC 1269.*

Case VI: Ramana Dayram Shetty V/s the International Airport Authority of India AIR 1979, S.C. 1629

Facts:

The International Airport Authority of India invited tenders for running a second class restaurant and two snack bars at the Bombay Airport through a notification on the terms and conditions mentioned in it, which includes *inter alia*: (a) for second class restaurant, person with atleast 5 years experience and registered second class Hoteliers, and (b) for snack bar 3 years experience under paragraph (8) of the notification it was made clear that the acceptance of the tender will rest with the Airport Director who does not bind himself the right to reject all or any of the tenders received without assigning any reasons thereof.

The appellant was a person in the business hotelier but did not satisfy the condition mentioned in the notification so he did not apply for tender. On opening of tender, all tenders except one that of Resp No. 4 was incomplete due to one reason or the other. The Resp. No. 4 also did not have experience of five years as regd. second class Hotelier for he has experience of running canteens, etc. Only which the appellant also possesses. The tender was allotted in favour of Resp No. 4 but the site could not be handed over due to the fact that it was in occupation of the previous contract holder Mr. A.S. Irani, who refused to vacate the premises and consequently, the suit for eviction against him was filed by the authority. But we are not concerned with this suit.

In the case before us, the appellant contended that the tender was allotted in favour of the Resp. No. 4 who did not fulfil all the conditions mentioned in the notification. Had he known this fact that the Authority will relax the conditions and allot the tender even to person not fulfilling the terms and conditions of the notification, he would have applied the Action of the Authority in accepting the tender of the Resp No. 4 had, therefore, the effect of denying him equality or opportunity in the matter of consideration for award of contract and hence violative of the equality clause and should be declared unconstitutional.

Meanwhile the Resp No. 4 spent much amount of funds to start the restaurant and purchased many items which were necessary for running the restaurant.

The argument on behalf of Resp No. 1 the authority and the Resp No. 4 are follows:

(a) That the Authority has reserved and right to reject all tenders without assigning any reasons and that it was competent to accept the tender of Resp. No. 4.

(b) The terms and conditions of the notification do not have any statutory force, and so authority was not bound by the standard laid down in the notification.

(c) The appellant is not really interested in the restaurant and nominee of Mr. A.S. Irani and was guilty of laches.

Issue Before the Court

Whether by accepting the tender of Resp No.1 the authority acted arbitrarily and hit by Art. 14 of the Constitution or not?

Decision

The S.C. observed that nowhere a corporation is an instrument or agency of Govt, it would, in exercise of its power or discretion be subject to the same constitutional or public law limitations as Government. The rule inhibiting arbitrary action by Government must apply equally where such a corp., dealing with the public, whether by way of giving job, or entering into control of otherwise, and it cannot act arbitrary and enter into relationship with any person it likes at its sweet will, but its action must be in conformity with some principle which meets the test of reason and relevance.

This rule also flows directly from the doctrine of equality embodied in Art. 14.

The court observed that it is now well-settled. This rule also flows directly from the doctrine of equality emboided in Art. 14. It is not well-settled as a result of the decisions of this court in E.P. Rayappa Vs State of Tamil Nadu AIR 1974 SC 555 that Article 14 strikes as arbitrariness in state action and ensures fairness and equality of treatment. It requires that state action must not arbitrary but be based on some rational and relevant principle which is non-discriminatory. It must not be guided by any extraneous or irrelevant consideration because that would be denial of equality. The principal of reasonableness and rationality which is legally as well as philosophically an essential element of equality or non-arbitrariness is protected by Art. 14 and it must characterise every state action, whether it be under authority of law or exercise of executive power without making of law. The State cannot, therefore act arbitrarily in entering into relationship, contractual or otherwise with a third party but its action must conform to some standard or norm which is rational and non-discriminatory.

It is therefore, obvious that both having regard to the constitutional mandate of Article 14 as also the judicially evolved rule of administrative law the Ist respondent was not entitled to act arbitrarily in accepting the tender of the 4th respondents, but was bound to conform to the standard or norms laid down in paragraph 1 of the notice inviting tenders which required that only a person running a registered second class hotel or restaurant and having atleast five years experience as such should be eligible to tender. It was not the connection of the appellant that this standard or norm prescribed by the first respondent was discriminatory having no just or reasonable relation to the object of inviting tender's namely to award the contract to a sufficiently experienced person who would be able to run efficiently a second class restaurant at the airport. Admittedly the standard or norm was reasonable and non-discriminatory and once such a standard or norm for running of second class restaurant should be awarded was laid down, the first respondent was not entitled to depart from it and to award the contract to the 4th respondent who did not satisfy the condition of eligibility prescribed by the standard or norm. If there was no acceptable tender from a person who satisfied the condition of eligibility the Ist respondent could have rejected the tenders and invited fresh tenders on the basis of a less stringent standard or norm prescribed by it and arbitrarily accept the tender of the 4th respondents even though they did not have 5 years experience of running a second class restaurant or hotel, it denied equality of opportunity to others similarly situate in the matter of tendering for the contract. There might have been many other persons, in fact the appellant himself claimed to be one such a person who did not have five years experience of running a second class restaurant, but who were otherwise competent to run such a restaurnat and they might also have completed with the 4th respondent for obtaining the contract but they were precluded from doing so by the condition of eligibility requiring five years experience. The action on the Ist respondent in accepting the tender of the 4th respondents, even though they did not satisfy the prescribed condition of eligibility was clearly discriminatory, since it excluded other persons similarly situate from tendering for the contract and it was also arbitrary and without reason. The acceptance of the tender of the 4th respondents was, in the circumstances invalid as being violative of the equality clause of the constitution as also of the rule of administrative law inhibiting arbitrary action.

Therefore, the Supreeme Court quashed the order of Govt. accepting the tender.

Source: *AIR 1979, S.C. 1629*

Case VII: K.S. Abdulla (Appellant) Versus Asstt. Director of Enforcement Directorate, Calicut (Respondent)

Appellant permitted to go abroad subject to conditions laid down in the order of Constitution of India, Article 136.

1. Special leave granted: We have heard Mr. P.H. learned counsel for the appellant and Mr. G. Ramaswamy, Additional Solicitor General for the respondent.
2. The appellant is permitted to go abroad subject to the following conditions:
   (1) The appellant will furnish a bank guarantee of Rs. 10 lakhs (Rs. Ten Lakh) of a nationalised bank in favour of the Astt. Director of Enforcement, Calicut, within 4 weeks from today after which the passport will be released.
   (2) The appellant is permitted to leave India to visit any of the countries in the Middle East, including Saudi Arabia for a period of two months from the time the appellant leaves India.
   (3) The appellant will furnish the itinerary of his tour programme to the Assistant Director of Enforcement, Calicut, before leaving India.
   (4) The appellant's wife, Mrs. Beepathumma, aged 41 years and his children, namely:
      (a) Mariyam (daughter) aged 22 years, married.
      (b) Hajara (daughter) aged 20 years, married.
      (c) Hannefabi (daughter) aged 18 years, married.
      (d) Misiriya (daughter) aged 14 years, unmarried.
      (e) Abdul Rehman (son) aged 7 years.
      (f) Mohamad Sadat (son) aged 5 years.
      (g) Kairunnisha (daughter) aged 4 years. All of them will not leave India without the permission of the Magistrate, till the appellant returns to India.

(5) The appellant will not dispose of and/or alienate any of his immovable properties, except for the purpose of raising bank guarantee of Rs. 10 lakh till he returns from abroad.

(6) On his return from the foreign tour within a period of two months the appellant will surrender his

passport to the Assistant Director of Enforcement, Calicut. On the appellant returning to India and handing over the passport to the Assistant Director of Enforcement, the bank guarantee will be returned to the appellant. If the appellant does not return within two months Rs. 10 lakh will be forefeited.

(7) On his return from abroad, the appellant will join in the investigations, as and when required.

(8) In case the appellant desires to go abroad in future after his return he shall have to take prior approval of the Chief Judicial Magistrate.

(9) The present order is passed without prejudice to the rights and obligations of both the parties.

Case VIII: High Court Stays Collection of Levy from Passengers at Calicut Airport

The Kerala High Court stayed from November I, the levy of Rs. 500 by the Airport Authority of India (AAI) from passengers going abroad from Calicut Airport.

When a petition by the Calicut Airport Users 'Forum and two others challenging the collection of the levy-users development additional fee' came up before Justice P.K. Balasubramanyan, he said the levy was prima facie not authorised.

The petitioners contended that the fee was being collected only from Calicut Airport. The Malabar International Airport Development Service (MIADS) had come forward to advance about Rs. 6 crore without interest to AAI to take up expansion work and raise it to international standards.

However, MIADS could collect only Rs 3.28 crore from Indians in the Middle East, following which it took a Rs. 60 crore loan from HUDCO and lent it to AAI without interest.

The petitioners submitted that despite AAI having no liability to pay interest, it was collecting Rs. 500 from passengers which would go towards the interest paid by MIADS to HUDCO.

The judge accepted the petitioners' contention that if at all anyone had to pay towards any liability for payment of interest, it should not be collected from the passengers, but from the operators of the airlines.

The judge held that prime facie it was not for AAI to meet the interest obligation of MIADS, nor could it be passed on to the embarking passengers.

Source: *TOI-March, 1998.*

PART-I: ANTIQUITIES AND ART TREASURE ACT, 1972

An Act to regulate the export trade in Antiquities and Art Treasures, to provide for the prevention of smuggling of and translucent dealings in, antiquities, to provide for the certain other matters connected therewith or incidental or ancillary thereto.

[9th September, 1972]

Short Title: Extent and Commencement

(1) This Act may be called the Antiquities and Art Treasures Act, 1972.

(2) It extends to the whole of India.

(3) It shall come into force on such date as the Central Government may, by notification in the Official Gazette, appoint and different dates may be appointed for different provision of this Act and for different states and any reference in any such provision to the commencement of this Act shall be construed as a reference to the coming into force of that provision.

Definitions

(1) In this Act, unless the context otherwise requires

(A) " Antiquities" includes—

(i) Any coin, sculpture, painting, epigraph or any other work of art or craftsmanship;

(ii) Any article, object or thing detached from a building or cave;

(iii) Any article, object or thing illustrative of science, art, crafts, literature, religion, customs, morals or politics in bygone ages;

(iv) Any article, object or thing of historical importance;

(v) Any article, object or thing declared by the Central Government, by notification in the Official Gazette, to be an antiquity for the purposes of this Act, which has been in existence for not less than one hundred years.

(B) (a) Any manuscript, record or other document which is of scientific, historical, literary or aesthetic value and which has been in existence for not less than seventy-five years;

(b) "Art treasure" means any human work of art, not being an antiquity, declared by the Central Government by notification in the Official Gazette, to be an art treasure for the purposes of this Act having regard to its artistic value.

(c) "Export" means taking out of India to a place outside India.

(d) "Licensing Officer" means an officer appointed as such under Sec 15.

(e) "Registering Officer" means an officer appointed as such under Sec 15.

(f) "Prescribed" means prescribed by rules made under this Act.

(2) Any reference in this Act to any law which is not in force in any area shall, relation to that area, be construed as a reference to the correspondig law, if any, in force that area.

Regulation of Export Trade in Antiquities and Art Treasures

(1) On and from the commencement of this Act, it shall not be lawful for any person, other than the Central Government or any authority or agency authorized by the Central Government in this behalf to export any antiquity or art treasure.

(2) Whenever the Central Government or any authority or agency referred to in sub-section (v) intends to export any antiquity or art treasure such export shall be made only under and in accordance with the terms and conditions of a permit issued for this purpose by such authority as may be prescribed.

Antiquities to be Sold Only under a Licence

As from the date of expiry of a period of six months

from the commencement of this Act no person shall, himself or by any other person on his behalf carries on the business of selling or offering to sell any antiquity except under and in accordance with the terms and conditions of a licence granted under Section 8.

Appointment of Licensing Officers

The Central Government may, by notification:

(a) appoint such persons, being Gazetted Officers of Government as it thinks fit to be licensing officer for the purposes of this Act.

(b) define the limits of the area within which a Licensing Officer shall exercise the powers conferred on licensing officers by or under this Act.

Application for Licence

(1) Any person desiring to carry on, himself or by any other person on his behalf, the business of selling or offering to sell antiquities may make an application for the grant of a licence to the licensing officer having jurisdiction.

(2) Every application under sub-section (1) shall be made in such form and shall contain such particular as may be prescribed.

Grant of Licence

(1) On receipt of an application for the grant of a licence under Sec 7, the licensing officer may, after holding such inquiry as he deems fit, grant a licence to the applicant having regard to the following factors, namely:

(a) The experience of the applicant with respect to trade in antiquities;

(b) The village, town or city where the applicant intends to carry on business;

(c) The number of persons already engaged in the business of selling, or offering for sale of antiquities in the said village, town or city;

(d) Such other factors as may be prescribed;

Provided that no licence shall be granted to the applicant if he is convicted under the Antiquities (Export Coutior) Act

(31 if 1947), unless a period of ten years has elapsed since the date of the conviction.

(2) Every licence granted under this section shall be on payment of such less as may be prescribed.

(3) Every licence granted under this section shall be for such period, subject to such conditions and in such for us and shall contain such particulars, as may be prescribed.

(4) No application for the grant of a licence made under Section 7 shall be rejected unless the applicant has been given a reasonable opportunity of being heard in the matter.

Registration of Antiquities

(1) The Central Government may, from time to time by notification of the Official Gazette, specify those antiquities which shall be registered under this Act.

(2) In specifying the antiquities under sub-section (1), the Central Government shall have regard to the following factors; namely:

(i) The necessity for conserving the object of act;

(ii) The need to preserve such objects within India for the better appreciation of the cultural heritage of India.

(iii) Such other factors are also likely to, contribute to the safeguarding of the cultural heritage of India.

(3) Every person who owns, controls or is in possession of any antiquity specified in the notification issued under sub-section (1) shall register such antiquity before the Registering Officer—

(a) In the case of any person who owns, controls of possession of such antiquity on the date of issue of such notification, with us three months of such date; and

(b) In the case of any other person within fifteen days of the date of which he comes into ownership, control or possession of such antiquity, and obtain a certificate in token of such registration.

Transfer of Ownership, etc., of Antiquities to be Intimated to the Registering Officer

Whenever any person transfers the ownership, control or possession of any antiquity specified in any notification issued under sub-section (1) of Sec 14, such person shall intimate, with in such period and in such form as may be prescribed, the fact of such transfer to the Registering Officer.

Note: Since Indian tourism is still largely cultural tourism main motivation for top of total tourist arrival is only the cultural attraction of our country. If we continue to spoil or destroy the beauty and grace of our cultural heritage, the day would be at our doorstep to signal the downfall of tourism in India. Since historical monuments and archaeological sites are expanded as important asset for tourism. It becomes imperative to study saws made to protect the monuments and archaeological sites and remains of national importance.

Part-J : LAWS RELATING TO PRESERVATION OF CULTURAL HERITAGE

Since Indian tourism is still largely cultural tourism. Main motivation for 70 per cent of total tourist arrival is only the cultural attraction of our country. If we continue to spoil or destroy the beauty and grace of our cultural heritage, the day would be at our doorstep to signal the downfall of tourism in India. Since historical monuments and archaeological sites are regarded as important assets for tourism. It becomes imperative to study laws made to protect the monument and archaeological sites and remains of national importance.

THE ANCIENT MONUMENTS AND ARCHAEOLOGICAL SITES AND REMAINS ACT, 1958.

Object of reasons and scope

Main objective of this Act is to provide for the preservation of ancient and historical monuments and archaeological sites and remains of national importance, for the regulation of archaeological excavations, for protection of sculptures, carvings and other likewise objects. The Act extends to whole of India.

Act defines

Ancient monument as antiquity which means any structure, erection or place of internment or any cave, rock sculpture, inscription or monolith which is of historical, archaeological or of artistic importance and which has been in existence for not less than 100 years.

Term Antiquity Includes under this Act:

1. Any coin, sculpture, epigraph or other work of art or of craftmanship.
2. Any article, object or thing detached from a building or cave.
3. Any article, object or thing illustrative of science, art, craft, literature, religion, customs or of politics in bygone ages.
4. Any article, object or thing of historical importance.
5. Any article, object or thing declared by the Central Government by notification in the Official Gazette, to be an Antiquity for the purposes of this Act.

Under this Act Archaeological Sites and Remains— means any area which contains or is reasonably believed to contain remains or relics of historical or archaeological importance which have been in existence for not less than 100 years.

Central Government is Empowered and Declare— a monument, archaeological site or remains as a national monument when it is certain that the monument, etc., is deemed to be of national importance it is eligible for declaration as monument of national importance.

Section 6 confers power to the collector when directed by Central Govt. to acquire the protected monument or to propose owner of a protected monument to enter in an agreement with Central Government within a specified period for protection of monument.

Section 7 provide the way, if the owner of the protected monument is unable to enter into agreement for the reason of infancing or other disability to act for himself the person legally competent to act on his behalf may exercise the powers conferred upon an owner and if any owner competent to enter into an agreement under Section 6 for the maintenance of protected monuments or fails to enter into such an agreement the Central Government may institute a suit in the Court of the Distt. Judge.

Section 10 confers power to Director General to make orders prohibiting contravention of agreement under Section 6.

Section 11 provides for the enforcement of agreement under Section 6. The Director General may authorise any person for the maintenance of monument and owner shall be liable to pay the expenses of doing any such act or such portion of the expenses as the owner may be liable to pay under the agreement.

Section 13 empowers the Central Government to acquire the protected monument under the Land Acquisition Act, 1894 if the protected monument is in danger.

Under Section 15 Director General may receive voluntary contributions towards the cost of maintaining a protected monument.

Section 16 is for protection of place of worship from misuse, pollution or desecration.

Protected Area according to this Act would mean any archaeological site or remain which is declared to be of national importance by or under this Act.

Section 19 it is discussed in that no person including the owner shall construct any building within the protected area without the permission of Central Government

Section 24 deals with Archaeological Execensivation relations according to which no State Government shall undertake or authorize any person to undertake any excavation for archeological purpose in any area which is protected area except with the previous approval of Central Government

Section 25 empowers the Central Government to control movement of any antiquity.

Central Government realises that any antiquity is in danger of being destroyed then the Central Government may order for compulsory purchase of such antiquity at its market value [Section 26].

Principles of compensation is discussed under Section 27 which says that owner who has sustained any loss by reason of any excavation on his land shall be paid compensation by Central Govt.

Section 29 confers power to such officers or authorities subordinate to Central Govt. or to such State Govt. or such officer or authority subordinate to the State Govt. besides the Central Govt.

It is under Section 30 that clause of penality is discussed for whoever is found causing harm of protected monuments.

Note: Significance of foreign tourist arrivals has always been over-emphasized by government of both developed and developing countries and India is not the exception but regulations and legislations have to be provided to prescribe and control the conduct of these foreigners when they enter in stay, and depart from our country. Although it is not an easy job to control the conduct of approximately 2.2 million foreign tourists who come to India but need for such a legislation was felt in 1946, when Foreigner's Act was enacted.

ANNEXURE-VIII

AUTHORITIES FOR ANTIQUITIES ACT

New Delhi	Director General, Archaeological Survey of India, Janpath, New Delhi-110 011 (Tel: 3019451, 3018848 Telex: 031-66242 ASI-IN)
Bombay	Superintending Archaeologist, Antiquities, Archaeological Survey of India, Sion Fort, Sion Bombay - 400 022 (Tel: 4071102)
Madras	Superintending Archaeologist, Archaeological Survey of India, Madras Circle, Fort St. George, Madras-600 009 (Tel: 560396/7, Telex: 041-6837 ASSC IN)
Calcutta	Superintending Archaeologist, Archaeological Survey of India, Calcutta Circle, 27 Biplabi Trailokya Maharaj Sarani, Narayani Building, Calcutta-700 001 (Tel: 261933, Telex: 021-5340 ASCC IN)
Bangalore	Superintending Archaeologist, Archaeological Survey of India, Bangalore Circle, No. 364, 13th Main, 4th T. Block, Jayanagar, Bangalore-560041 (Tel: 655901, Telex: 0845-8845 ARCH IN)
Bhubaneswar	Superintending Archaeologist, Archaeological Survey of India, Bhubaneswar Circle, Old Town, Bhubaneswar - 750 002 (Tel: 56575 Telex : 0675 - 393 ODRA IN)
Srinagar	Superintending Archaeologist, Archaeological Survey of India, Srinagar Circle, Mintoo Building, Raj Bagh, Srinagar (Tel : 32758 Telex: 0375-349 ASOI IN)
Note :	Addresses and telephone numbers given in the Appendices are based on January, 1994, information.

INDEX

Accomodation, Regulation Regarding, 93
Acquital where evidence is insufficient, 173
Adam Smith, Scottish Professor, 13
Additional Divisional Railway Manager, 186
Agent
  Capacity to Appoint Agent and to become, 128
  Contracts for a named Principal, 137, 139
  Contracts for an unnamed Principal, 139
  Kinds of, 133
  Meaning of the Term, 126
  of Necessity, Wife as an, 132
  Personal Liability of the, 142
  Substituted, 136
Agency
  by estoppel, 129
  by Necessity, 131
  by ratification, 130
  Creation of, 128
  Distinguishes, 127
  Irrevocable, 144
  Law of, 126
  Termination of, 143
  Test of, 126
Airline sector, Law relating to, 174
Allied Chemical, 40
American Management Association, 37
Andaman and Lakshadweep Islands, 79
Antiquities Act, Authorities for, 261
Appeals from Order Passed Under Section 11, 12, 15, 16, 208
Applicant, Particulars of, 64
Application, 88
Approval
  from Department of Tourism, 54
  of Hotel Projects, 90
Archie B. Croll, 41
Associate
  Industry, 66
  Industry Members, 63
Asta Member's, 45, 46

Baggage
  Insurance, Personal Effects and, 86
  Liability Limitations, 118
  Rule, 1995, 84
Baltic Shipping Co. Vs Dhillon the 'Mikhail Lermantov, 51
Bangladesh, 20
Bingham, L.J. in Watts Vs. Morrow (1991), 52
Boric Norman, 42
Burkart, 1981, 15
Business Ethics, 38
  in Tourism, 35, 41
Business in India, Incorporation of, 23

Canada, Regulations and Legislations in, 122
Canadian Transport Commission, 123
Cargo
  Rate, 102
  Rates and Charges, 101
  Regulations, 100
Carriage by
  Air Act, 1972, 177
  Land, 192
Carriers' Liability in respect of Property, 194

Cases Related to Legislations on Travel Agency
  Sector in India, 145
Changing Values, 37
Chargeable Receipts, Return of the, 153
Charges
  Minimum, 101
  Other, 103
CITES, 159-164
Class Cargo, 102
Clients, Responsibility to the, 43
Committee for Economic Development, 37
Common Law
  Duties in General, 87
  Liability standards, 115
Companies, Various Kinds of, 29
Comparative Analysis of Public Complaints, 191
Condition of ratification, 130
Conference Area, 56
Constitutional
  Remedies before Maneka Vs. Union of India, 238
  Remedies, Legislation Relating to, 228
Consumer
  Protection Act, 220
  Responsibilities of, 224
Continuum of social Responsibility, 35
Contract,
  Condition of, 116
  made by Third Parties, Effect of Agency on, 137
  Vs Tort Law, 110
Conviction: when could be set aside, 172
Co-operative society, 23
Criminal Vs Civil Law, 110
Critical
  Analysis, 40
  Approach, 38
Cultural Heritage Laws Relating to Preservation of, 257
Custom and Migration, 83

Definition and Meaning, 33
Delegation of Authority, 13
Departing traveller, 17
Department of Tourism, 55
Depository Government (Switzerland), 164
Deregulation Act, 1978, 113
Derck Box, 40
Dhillon, Mrs., 51
Differences Amongst Three Forms of Organization, 31
Divisional level, 186
Down to Earth Approach, 37

Effluent treatment Plants, 38
Emigration Clearance not required, 234
Employees, Responsibility of, 44
Environments: Human, socio-cultural Physical, 17
Escorts Heart Research Centre of Escorts Group, 37
Ethical
  Conducts, Principles of, 44
  Standards, Factors that raise, 40
  Theories, 39
Executive Director (Public Grievances), 185
Expenditure Tax, 151

Facilities, 94
Factories and shops and Establishments Act, 149
Federal
  Highway Administration, 108
  Tourism Legislation Covering, 107
Federation Tourism Related Legislations, 107
FERA, 85
Financing of Partnership Firm, 26
First point of view includes Companies to be incorporated, 29
Five Star Catagory, 93
Foreign
  Exchange Regulations, 85
  Origin, Tourist of, 83
Forest
  (Conservation Rules, 1981), 211
  Preservation, Legislation Relating to, 202
Fo mation of Partnership, 25

Form of Organisation in Travel Trade, 30
Four Star Catagory, 95
Fourth point of view includes Companies like, 30
Francies. Ms. Cannie, 121

General Electric, 40
Girikand Travels Vs. A.N. Pujari, 147
Government/Carrier, 66

Hague Protocol of 1955, 178
Harvard Business School, 40
Health Certificate Regulations, 82
Helbert, 1978, 16
Heritage Hotel's, 99
Heuristic Definition, 14
Hotel
  becomes functional, Conditions to be fulfilled, 91
  Member, 66
  Receipt Tax, 153
Receipt Tax, Charging of, 152
HRACC, Department of Tourism, 100

IATA, 56
  Approval, Application for, 58
  Approval of, 54
  Regulations for Recognition of, 55
Identification Manual Committee, 164
Implications, 37
Impliedly (Sec. 187), 129
Income Tax Act, 154
Incorporation, 28
Indian
  Missions and FRRO'S, 72
  Partnership Act, 24, 26
  Tourism, 19
Industry, 66
Institutionalising Ethics, 40
Insurance
  Air passenger, 86
  Regulation Regarding, 85
  Trip Cancellation, 86
International
  Passengers Limitation of Liability, 118
  Sales Statement of, 59
  Tourist Traffic to India, 20
Internet Business Machines, 40
Interstate Commerce Commission, 108
Iron Exchange Enviro Farms Ltd. Environmentally conscious, 38

Jafari (1989), 14
James Webes, 40
Joint stock company, 23, 28

Kaiser, 16
Kaul, 1981, 16
Kaul, 1985, 15

Laws on Accommodation sector, Cases Related to, 154
Legal Moral Regulations, Governments', 42
Legislation Regarding Hotel Industry, 148
Leiper (1979), 16, 17
Location, 57
Lost and Damaged Baggage, 181

Major Documentation Areas Like, 67
MEA Approval of, 54
Members, Responsibilities of All, 46
Middleton, 49
Mill and Morrison, 1985, 15
Month-wise Variations in Tourist Arrivals in India, 22
Motar Accidents Claims Tribunals, 198
MS Shoes' Hotel site, 158

National Highway Traffic Safety Administration, 108
Neighbouring Countries Visa Offices for, 79
New South Wales Court of Appeal, 52
Nomenclature Committee, 164

Oberoi Intercontinental, 150
Obligations
  to Government, 36
  to Individuals, 36
  to Other Organizations, 36
  to Society in General, 36
One Star Category, 98

Operator, 66
Order, 216
Organization
  of a medium sized agency, 32
  of a small agency, 32
  of a large size agency, 32

Package tour, 13
Pakistan, 20
Partnership, 23
  Act, 27
  Form of Organization, 24
Passport,
  How to oblain a, 68
  Kinds of, 68
  Renewed, How to Get, 69
  Replacement of, 69
PATA
  for membership, 62
  India Chapter, 65
  India Chapter Dues Structure, 66
  India Chapter Secretariat, 63, 64
  International Membership Dues, 66
  Membership Formalities For, 63
Penalties for Trespass or Damage in Reserved Forest Acts, 212
Popular Notion, 14
Preamble, 45
Preservation of Habitat, 170
Preserved Forest, 203
Private
  and Public Companies, Distinction between, 30
  Carrier and a Common Carrier, 193
Professional Conduct and Ethics, 45
Promotion, 28
Public Vs Private Law, 109

Radisson Hotel, New Delhi, 154
Railway
  Board Level, 185
  liable to pay Damages in a Motar Accident, 198
Rate, General Cargo, 102
Redressal Machinery in Railway Board, 187
Registrar
  of Companies, 54
  of Joint stock Companies, 28
Registration of a Firm, 27
Regulation
  for Membership, 61
  Regarding Documentation, 67
Regulatory Laws for Accommodation Sector, 86
Rejected application can be, 70
Related Regulation, Special Paper's, 79
Requirements, 88
  Miscellaneous, 69
Reserve Bank of India's approval, 55
Restricted/Protected Areas, Places open in, 80
Rights
  and Liabilities of a Private Carrier, 192
  Theory, 39

Sales Tax and Luxury Tax, 150
Second point of view includes Companies like, 29
Services, 94
Setting up a Travel Agency, 54
Social
  Obligation, 33
  Reaction, 34
  Responsibility, 33-35, 37
  Responsiveness, 35
Sole Proprietorship, 23
Specific Commodity Rate, 102
Standing Orders and Service Rules, 150
Stone, Christopher, 42
Subramaniam Committee on Prevention of Illegal Trade in Wild life and its Protection, 169
Substantive Vs Procedural Laws, 109
Surface Transport
  Business, Legislation Related to, 184
  Cases Related to, 195

TATA Cancer Research Centre, 38
Technical
  Committee, 164
  Definition, 14
Theodore Purcell, 40

Theory of Justice, 37
Third point of view includes Companies with, 29
Threatened Plant Committee, 164
Three Star Catagory, 96
Top Ten Markets Generating Arrivals to India, 21
Tamas, 13
Tourism
  Business in India, Regulatory Laws, 53
  Concepts and Forms, 13
  Industry, 16
  Laws and Regulations, 49
  Legislations, Taxonomy of, 125
  Markets, 15
  Sectors, 53
  System, 16
Tourist
  Card, 71
  Destination, 17
Transit Routes, 17
Transport Sectors, 106
Travel
  Agencies in India Regulations for, 53
  agency, 30, 41
  Agency, Business, Legislation Related to, 126
  and Tourism Industry, 18
  Generating Region, 17
  trade, 106
  Trade Association, 66
Two Star Catagory, 98

United Nations Conference on International Travel and Tourism at Rome, 54
Universal Federation of Travel Agents Association, 61
U.S.
  and Canada Tourism Regulations in the, 105
  Laws on Accomodation, 120
  Laws on Transportation, 110
Utilitarian Theory, 39

Vaccination, 82
Vendors, Responsibility to, 44
Visas, 71

Warsaw Convention, 1929, 116
W.H.O., 82
Wildlife
  Preservation, Law Relating to, 159
  Protection Act, 1972, 165

Zonal Railways Level, 186